AF778324

Origins and Components of Behaviorology

Photo by Stephen F. Ledoux

Burrhus Frederic Skinner

The original behaviorological scientist (1904–1990)
(Shown here in conversation at the 1982 ABA convention.)

Origins and Components of Behaviorology

Stephen F. Ledoux

Published by ABCs of Canton, NY, USA.

Copyright © 1997 by Stephen F. Ledoux & Lawrence E. Fraley
& David R. Feeney & Glenn I. Latham

Origins and Components of Behaviorology

Stephen F. Ledoux, Ph.D.

First published by ABCs of Canton, NY, USA, in 1997 (for US$50 retail per copy).

ISBN 1-882508-07-6 (Hardcover) **First Edition** (with jacket)

Printed in the United States of America.

***Prospective* cataloging–in–publication data** (prospective call number based on the Library of Congress classification of the 1992 edition of this book whose LCCCN was 92–97400):

Ledoux, Stephen F., 1950–.
Origins and components of behaviorology / by Stephen F. Ledoux, with contributions by Lawrence E. Fraley and David R. Feeney and Glenn I. Latham.
xxxii, 336 p. ill. 26 cm.
Includes bibliographical references, full–outline contents, annotated bibliography, and index.
1. Behaviorism. 2. Human behavior. 3. Operant behavior. 4. Behavior modification. 5. Verbal behavior. 6. Behaviorology [Future primary subject heading?].
I. Title. II. Fraley, Lawrence E., 1936–. III. Feeney, David R., 1966–. IV. Latham, Glenn I., 1931–.
ISBN 1-882508-07-6 (acid–free paper)
BF199.L4 1997 96–84449

Library of Congress Catalog Card Number: 96-84449

This edition is printed on acid–free paper to comply with the permanent paper Z39.48 standard of the American National Standards Institute.

Printing: 1 2 3 4 5 6 7 8 9 10 11 12 13 14 15 16 >16
In (next nearest year): 2000 05 10 15 20 25 30 35 40 45 50 >2050

Copyright Notice/Warning:

Copyright © 1997 by Stephen F. Ledoux and Lawrence E. Fraley and David R. Feeney and Glenn I. Latham, as per paper authorship. All rights reserved. This book and its contents are protected by the Federal Copyright Laws of the United States of America. Reproduction or copying of these materials, by *any* means whatsoever, in whole or in part, without the express, hard–copy, written permission of the copyright holder(s) is prohibited and may subject the violator(s) to civil sanctions, criminal penalties, or both. Permission to reprint individual papers for worthy purposes is easy to obtain by writing ABCs care of the author.

Contents

Summary Contents

Full–Outline Contents

Dedication

This book is

dedicated to my children

Miles & Susannah

who

experienced a little parental deprivation while this book
was in preparation so that they and the rest of their
generation and their offspring would be closer
to taking behaviorology for granted, relying
on it along with other natural sciences
as we today rely on biology.

May we and they all soon experience the benefits
of behaviorologically informed cultures. *SFL*

Acknowledgments

The author expresses appreciation to *Behaviorology* for permission to include the paper "Behaviorology Curricula in Higher Education" in this book of readings. This paper is quite similar to a paper previously peer–reviewed and accepted by that journal under the title "Behaviorology Curricula in Post–Secondary Education." *Behaviorology* subsequently transferred this paper to the incipient Journal *The International Behaviorologist* due to the evolving nature of the types of articles each of these journals was to publish. The author also expresses appreciation for the copyright policy of the journal *Behaviorological Commentaries* (later renamed *The International Behaviorologist*). After peer–reviewing and accepting papers for publication, this journal leaves article copyrights with the authors. This has eased the republication process for many of the papers in this collection.

Dr. Jerome Ulman especially deserves appreciation for providing access to, and use of, the significant 1989 exchange of letters between himself and B.F. Skinner.

Furthermore, the author expresses appreciation to **Anne Marsh** for invaluable assistance on library–related tasks, as well as to the staff of *Commercial Press* of Canton, NY, to the staff of *BookCrafters* of Chelsea, MI, to **Joanne Thornhill,** and also to **Scott Beach**, for their informative and cooperative advice and assistance which helped to clarify and smooth the publication process at several points.

Last but certainly not least, the author expresses special appreciation to his spouse, musicologist **Dr. Nelly Maude Case,** not only for the understanding and support that enable a project like this book to come to completion, but also for valuable comments on the whole manuscript.

Note: In the Winter 1990 issue of *TIBA Newsletter* (Volume 2, Number 3, p. 16), the By–laws of The International behaviorology Association (TIBA) contain a relatively common organizational provision that states (Section 9–C): "The name of the organization may not be used by any member in a way that implies an official endorsement by the organization unless such an endorsement has been extended by TIBA and the member is acting in accordance with the provisions of that endorsement." Subsequently, at the Executive Board meeting of 2 January 1992 (see "Minutes" in the Fall 1993 issue of the TIBA newsletter, *Selections*, Volume 5, Number 2, p. 9) TIBA passed a further motion requiring that: "...any activities of any TIBA member which mention TIBA ... include a specific statement disavowing any connection with or endorsement by TIBA." In agreement and compliance with these stated policies, the authors (as members of TIBA) hereby specify that this book is published as an addition to the scientific understanding and improvement of human behavior relations; in publishing this material the authors have appropriately neither sought nor received either official connection of the book to TIBA or endorsement of the book from TIBA.

Preface to the 1997 Edition

This book is addressed to behaviorologists, historians, scholars of science, and any who either would sharpen their discrimination among behavior–related disciplines or would care to apply such disciplines to benefit humanity.

The accidents of history (such as birthdate, birthplace, and life span) have allowed some people to experience personally the events and contingencies surrounding the emergence of behaviorology. These same accidents have prevented others from doing so. This book is especially addressed to the latter so that they may be informed about what those in the behaviorology movement did and went through as behaviorology emerged, and as these and other behaviorological scientists strove to apply this discipline for humanity's benefit.

This report is based mostly on the contingencies that are and have been extent in North America. But the implications of the reported events, concerning increasing effectiveness in improving cultural practices, extend beyond those borders and around the world. The lessons that can be drawn from the accounts presented here may make easier for others the task of elsewhere advancing behavior science and its benefits.

The 1992 edition of this book was titled *Origins, Status, and Mission: The Emergence of the Discipline of Behaviorology.* That edition has gone out of print. In the intervening years, the value of certain improvements and extensions has become apparent. The present book addresses these concerns. However, the general description of the book presented in the preface to the 1992 edition is still accurate (and that preface is included in the present volume). That preface states:

> Through this volume, the history of the emergence of behaviorology is available both for the first time and comprehensively. As current today as when originally written, this book is unique because it is also the only analyzed historical treatment of the emergence of an independent natural science of behavior written during the early years of that emergence by participant–observers of that emergence.

Yet the present volume differs from the 1992 edition in an important way. As its title states, the present volume encompasses not only the emergence of behaviorology but also includes some coverage of the various disciplinary components of behaviorology. After an introductory paper, each of the remaining papers addresses, either directly or by an example, one or another disciplinary component. Here is the title of each paper following the component each paper addresses (in their order in this book, which both partly reflects the interrelationships existing among the papers and partly reflects the sequence in which the papers were originally written):

- *Introduction:* An Introduction to the Origins, Status, and Mission of Behaviorology: An Established Science with Developed Applications and a New Name.
- *Philosophical component:* An Introduction to the Philosophy Called Radical Behaviorism.
- *Historical component* (co–authored with Lawrence E. Fraley): Origins, Status, and Mission of Behaviorology.

- *Developmental component:* Behaviorology Curricula in Higher Education.
- *Analytical / interpretative component* (example): Behaviorology in China: A Status Report.
- *Conceptual component* (example): Increasing Tact Control and Student Comprehension through such New Postcedent Terms as Added and Subtracted Reinforcers and Punishers. (This paper is new to the 1997 edition.)
- *Experimental component* (example): Multiple Selectors in the Control of Simultaneously Emittable Responses. (This paper is new to the 1997 edition.)
- *Applied component* (example): Successful Smoking Control as an Example of a Comprehensive Behaviorological Therapy. (This paper is new to the 1997 edition.)
- *Technological component* (example by David R. Feeney): Creative Life–style Management Through On–line and Real–time Application of the Behaviorological Education Practices of Precision Teaching. (This paper is new to the 1997 edition.)
- *Social action component* (example by Glenn I. Latham): China Through the Eyes of a Behaviorologist. (This paper is new to the 1997 edition.)

The Papers

The first five papers of this volume formed the 1992 edition of this work. A brief description of each of these papers appears in the preface to the 1992 edition (minor editorial changes were made to that preface before including it in this edition). The other papers joined the collection in the 1997 edition; here is a brief description of each paper that is new in this edition (author initials appear in parentheses after each title):

Increasing Tact Control and Student Comprehension through such New Postcedent Terms as Added and Subtracted Reinforcers and Punishers (S.F.L.)

This paper reports efforts to improve behaviorological terminology. The efforts focus on terms which concern events in the third term of the three–term contingency. The result is an integration of various old and new terms into a systematically related set of terms. The terms in this set are *postcedents, selectors, consequences, accidental selectors* and the opposites of these terms. In addition, the terms positive and negative, with respect to reinforcers and punishers, are replaced by the terms *added* and *subtracted,* and the reasons for doing so are discussed. This set of terms reduces the terminological confusion that students in the past experienced on their initial contact with behaviorological science. Researchers in the science may also find their tacting to be more accurate, and their effectiveness enhanced, through use of this set of terms.

Multiple Selectors in the Control of Simultaneously Emittable Responses (S.F.L.)

This paper reports an experiment and describes a research program that extends this experiment. Analyzing contingencies of extinction and continuous reinforcement, the experiment addresses a procedure for studying multiple operants. These are operants that (a) can occur simultaneously, and (b) can have separate (i.e., independent) selectors (e.g., reinforcers) also occurring simultaneously. This complexity of operants is a part of the behavior of animals, especially humans, and so deserves the attention of behaviorological researchers. A research program that extends this experiment is designed to study, catalog, and characterize an ever widening series of contingencies involving these multiple–behavior/multiple–selector operants. The conceptual level of the basic program is such that the program can stimulate and allow the interest and participation not only of more advanced students and researchers but also of undergraduate students. The latter's participation would let them experience both the patience required in research and the thrill of discovery when they ask and answer basic research questions in a relatively short period. They might also gain a further measure of satisfaction should they apply those answers to concerns in the world at large.

Successful Smoking Control as an Example of a Comprehensive Behaviorological Therapy (S.F.L.)

This paper derives from the author's and, especially, others' research. It originated as lecture and discussion material using smoking–control therapy as an example to convey two points to students: The material (a) details how a therapy can and should focus *comprehensively* on the problems, such as smoking, presented for therapeutic intervention, and (b) describes how explicitly *analyzing and addressing* the variables directly responsible for those problems appears to be substantially responsible for the success of some therapies. The substantial clinical success rate of a particular smoking–control therapy shows it to be a valuable example of how this general approach—behaviorologically analyzing and addressing explicit functionally controlling variables—can benefit clients with smoking problems. Extension of this approach to many other kinds of problems, large and small, will likely enable people with those problems to attain similar success rates.

Creative Life–style Management Through On–line and Real–time Application of the Behaviorological Education Practices of Precision Teaching (D.R.F.)

This paper reports efforts to expand delivery methods for behaviorological interventions. Pilot research combining problems from life–style management with solutions from precision teaching are discussed. The interventions are delivered on–line and occasionally in real time using personal computer technologies. Precision teaching practices are applied to life–style management problems regarding decreases in smoking and weight, and increases in college study through creative computer–based interactions between the client and the educator.

China Through the Eyes of a Behaviorologist (*G.I.L.*)

This paper is essentially a well–stated and well–justified "call to action" issued to all behaviorological scientists. They are called to help develop and extend the whole behaviorology discipline to any place in the world where its benefits are as yet unavailable. Here the focus is on extending behaviorology to the People's Republic of China where one quarter of the world's population resides. Many concerns, particularly involving child–rearing and education, crystallized for the author during his second professional speaking visit to that country in the fall of 1996. This paper originates partly as a brief report of that trip. More importantly, it originates as a brief description of some actions—especially the hosting of visiting scholars who are determined to become expert in this science—that behaviorological scientists can take as part of fulfilling those responsibilities of scientists which pertain to assuring the comprehensive dissemination of their science as widely as possible in the service of others. As such, this paper nicely rounds out this collection of components of behaviorology by providing readers with a continuously timely reminder that the continuation of any science owes as much to reaching out to others, through dissemination, as to conceptualization, experimentation, application, and organization.

Appendices (*S.F.L.*)

The appendices provide some additional material while also tying up some loose ends. Included among the appendices are a short paper *(Adventitious Control),* some excerpts from the title paper in the 1992 edition of the book, and several short items supplying information—extending some of the other papers in the book—on behaviorology curricular concerns, TIBA conventions, and the formal organizations of the independent behaviorology discipline. The latter is particularly relevant to the ongoing historical development of behaviorology. It is discussed in the last appendix, encouraging readers to take part in one way or another in that development.

Authorship

In the 1992 edition of this book, Lawrence E. Fraley was the first author of the title paper which filled half of the book. I was second author on that paper, and sole author of the remaining papers. As a result Dr. Fraley was listed as co–author of that edition. That substantial, dual–author paper, on the origins of behaviorology, is the core of the present edition as well. However, this edition of the book appears under only one author's name. Our reasons for this are two: (a) Dr. Fraley's editorial and authorship responsibilities continue to pertain only to our joint paper (though he has provided collegial reviews of the other papers), and (b) the addition of more papers to this edition makes our joint paper less than half of the volume.

Reference Note

Most of B.F. Skinner's papers have been republished in books of readings such as *Cumulative Record.* References to Skinner's papers here in *Origins and Components of Be-*

haviorology often cite the original publication dates. However, readers may find easier access to these papers through the collections. Most of the collections are listed in the bibliography at the end of the book (i.e., Skinner, 1968, 1969, 1972, 1978, 1987, & 1989); see the "Books: Directly Related Issues..." section of the bibliography.

Conclusion

Books of readings sometimes entail repetitions; this book is no exception. Readers will occasionally come across paragraphs in one paper that are very similar to paragraphs in a previous paper. This is because, out of respect for the integral place of these paragraphs in their respective papers, no editing occurred to eliminate the repetition.

The present volume encompasses both *comprehensive* coverage of the historical emergence of the discipline of behaviorology, as the one disciplinary component receiving such treatment, and *some* coverage of most other disciplinary components. The history of behaviorology continues to accumulate. But the historical paper in this volume does not extend coverage of that history beyond 1993 (other than to supply a few, more accessible sources officially presented or published a year or three later). Other authors are sure to supply the history since 1993 in due time. The range of other disciplinary components covered in this volume is more extensive than in the 1992 edition. I extended this range because all of these disciplinary components work together to help people understand and deal with their own behavior and that of others.

I believe that important abilities and wisdom accrue from the study of behaviorology. These are likely to prove crucial to the successful resolution of many, perhaps all, of the large, subtle, and sometimes new threats to human security or survival, such as global warming, that people must faced in our common future. I hope that study of this volume will encourage readers to develop further knowledge and skills in the natural science of behavior relations, behaviorology. May doing so help them improve their sorely needed contributions to humanity.

Stephen F. Ledoux

Canton, NY, USA ***December 1996***

On This Book, Typography, and Interests / Orders / Other ABCs Books

The author designed and executed the layout of this book on an early Apple Power Macintosh computer with a QMS PS–410 printer, using the Microsoft Word 4.0, Aldus SuperPaint 3.5, and Adobe PageMaker 5.0 programs. The book is set in the Adobe Garamond, Adobe Garamond Expert, and Tekton collections of typefaces. (The publisher and author request that readers finding errata send corrections to the author for inclusion in a future printing.) Address correspondence regarding this book to the author at the State University of New York—College of Technology, Canton NY 13617–1096 USA.

In addition, a valuable basis for the typographic decisions followed in this work (for which the author and publisher take full responsibility) deserves acknowledgment. As much as possible, this book follows the practices described in two highly recommended little volumes by Ms. Robin Williams (both published in Berkeley, CA, USA, by Peachpit Press). One is the 1990 edition of *The Mac is not a Typewriter.* The other is the 1996 edition of *Beyond the Mac is not a Typewriter.* (For example, on page 16 of the 1990 book, Williams specifies practices regarding the placement of punctuation used with quotation marks, an area in which some ambiguity has existed over what is "proper.")

If readers cannot obtain desired copies of this book through bookstores, or if they are interested in the discount available for direct orders on any ABCs books, or if they wish to be kept informed of the publication of new behaviorology titles from ABCs, then they should contact one of these people for information on how to fulfill their desires:

Stephen Ledoux
SUNY—CTC
Canton NY 13617–1096 USA
Phone/FAX: (315) 386–2684/386–7961
E–mail: ledoux@scanva.canton.edu

David Feeney (c/o Onlearn Co.)
183 Pinehurst Avenue / Suite 54
New York NY 10033 USA
Phone: (212) 928–4099
E–mail: drfeeney@onlearn.com

Lawrence Fraley
West Virginia University
Morgantown WV 26506–6122 USA
Phone: (304) 864–3443

Glenn Latham
Mountain Plains Regional Resource Ctr.
1780 N. Research Parkway / Suite 112
Logan UT 84341 USA
Phone/FAX: (801) 752–0238/753–9750
E–mail: latham@cc.usu.edu

Send name, address, and phone number, along with a description of interests or desires, to ABCs, care of one of those ABCs authors. Here are some other ABCs titles:

- *Grandpa Fred's Baby Tender or Why and How We Built Our Aircribs* (by S.F. Ledoux & C.D. Cheney; includes the article "The first baby tender" by B.F. Skinner), and

- *The Panda and Monkey King Christmas—A Family's Year in China* (by N.M. Case & S.F. Ledoux; concerns experiences that can help others to prepare for a visit to China, or at least to understand conditions there better).

Foreword to the 1992 Edition

Through this text, Drs. Ledoux and Fraley provide the reader a unique opportunity to develop an understanding and appreciation for a current scientific movement of historic dimension. Labelled "Behaviorology" by its proponents, this discipline of research and practice can show humanity how to solve our most pressing problems; how to progress toward our fondest ends. Glimpses of this phenomenal promise can sometimes be seen directly in the authors' words and at other times it can be developed by reflection on the part of the reader. While the aim of the authors is modest, that is, to document "an analyzed history" of Behaviorology, the more sweeping value of this text also deserves direct recognition.

First I will comment on the directly presented content of this important text. In the thoughtfully developed Preface and papers/chapters that follow, the authors provide us with fundamental information, conceptions, and encouragement regarding the science and practice of Behaviorology. The early papers describe the discipline of behaviorology and differentiate it from apparently similar paradigms of science. Later chapters inform us more about the contributions and promise of the "behaviorological movement."

Students of behavioral science are well served by the authors' careful development of the philosophical, historical, and rational underpinnings of the discipline they advocate. The internal consistency of their analysis is admirable and effective. These qualities equip the reader to witness the shortcomings of other approaches and to recognize why they might select to be proponents of Behaviorology.

In the second half of the text we are treated with papers that indicate the wide scope of study and application that behaviorologists can enjoy. In these pages we are introduced to how major aspects of human affairs, for example, educational systems and cultural sciences, can benefit by being developed in a "behaviorological" manner.

Throughout the text the authors are careful not to stray from empirical fact or legitimate extension from the established principles of behavioral science. Their objectivity is well taken. Certainly, to build an appreciative audience or attract adherents for this currently little–known discipline, it is important to establish a firm basis of understanding. With this they succeed while avoiding temptation to proselytize their descriptions of the great values of Behaviorology for its students and for humanity.

Those of us who are not so constrained can immediately suggest some of the outstanding virtues associated with the practice of Behaviorology. Uppermost for the individual practitioner might be the enormous stimulation, and the functional utility, offered by this unitary, comprehensive system called Behaviorology. By being equipped with an encompassing approach, the behaviorological scientist is generally able to interpret, predict, and support constructive alterations in the behavior of people.

This generative capability brings with it an ease for appreciating the deliberations and applications of all sorts of disciplines and endeavors. That is, all manner of scientific and applied activities are open to constructive analysis and contribution by behaviorologists. To realize this great potential of behaviorology requires sophisticated use of interprofessional skills, which should be given more direct attention in the literature.

While the positive motives for adopting the authors' view are attractive, the reasons that behaviorological science must be widely applied are becoming more pressing each day. Namely, for the well being of all inhabitants of the earth, we have to develop and apply systems that support adaptive behaviors, an assignment for which Behaviorology is more suited than any other discipline. Pollution, conservation, education, and all forms of interaction are legitimate areas of concern that should benefit from the promise and power of behaviorological productivity.

Drs. Ledoux and Fraley offer us a fine text and succeed with sharing information about a substantial approach to the study of humanity. This text is easy to appreciate for what it delivers so effectively. Appreciable, also, are the vistas that the authors begin to open for us. We can hope that this is only one in a collection of publications by these authors and similarly inclined others from which we can benefit.

Robert E. Crow, Ph.D.
Human Development Center (Director)
School of Allied Health Professions
Louisiana State University Medical Center
New Orleans, 1992

Preface to the 1992 Edition

Through this volume, the history of the emergence of behaviorology is available both for the first time and comprehensively. As current today as when originally written, this book is unique because it is also the only analyzed historical treatment of the emergence of an independent natural science of behavior written during the early years of that emergence by participant–observers of that emergence.

This book is thus persistently timely for both the uniqueness of the authors' perspective and because it can provide generations of readers with insights into new and recurring lessons about the origins and developments of natural sciences in general and of a natural science of behavior in particular.

As a natural science discipline on the life science continuum, behaviorology is the science and technology of behavior relations. First, it discovers the variables that are in "causal" relationships with the behavior of individuals during their lifetime. Then it designs and implements changes to these accessible variables bringing beneficial change and expansion to the individual's behavior repertoire.

These behavioral engineering applications contribute to all human endeavors, including child and health care, education, rehabilitation, environment policy, international relations, industrial management, and even science itself. In such areas, behaviorology as a natural science addresses what no social science has been able to address effectively, namely the ancient question: "Why do people do what they do?" Furthermore, behaviorology effectively addresses the extension of that ancient question, namely: "And what can be done about it?"

This book reviews, in historical context, the incompatible paradigms and philosophical developments among disciplines addressing the behavior of individuals. In familiarizing the reader with the history of behaviorology's emergence, this book also makes further comprehension and application of behaviorology's science and technology easier and more effective and beneficial. (An extensive bibliography is provided to enable further pursuit of behaviorology.)

The 1992 edition proceeded to press under the title: *Origins, Status, and Mission: The Emergence of the Discipline of Behaviorology* and listed Lawrence E. Fraley as co–author. It contained five papers plus a bibliography and an index.

The Papers

The overall theme of this book, especially the title paper, is to provide an analyzed history both of the emergence of the discipline of behaviorology and of the behaviorology movement. Each of the included papers elaborates on one or another aspect of this theme, as a brief (relative to length) description of each paper shows (author initials appear in parentheses after each title; regarding authorship of this book as a whole, Dr. Fraley's author and editorial responsibilities pertain to that half of the book which is comprised of the co–authored title paper for which he is first author):

An Introduction to the Origins, Status, and Mission of Behaviorology: An Established Science with Developed Applications and a New Name (S.F.L.)

This opening paper summarizes the general themes of the book. Here are the questions that this paper briefly addresses: What is behaviorology? Where does it come from? How does it differ from other disciplines and fields that evince some interest in why people do what they do? How is it related to other disciplines? What are its contributions? Why should anyone learn anything about behaviorology? Questions such as these typically arise when people, especially students, first come across behaviorology. This first paper presents some initial answers to these questions by surveying an analyzed history of the origins, status, and mission of behaviorology (the title paper provides extensive elaboration).

An Introduction to the Philosophy Called Radical Behaviorism (S.F.L.)

This paper addresses some major characteristics of the philosophy of science that informs behaviorology and thereby implies how this philosophy differs with the underlying philosophies of other disciplines. Such information helps set the record straight regarding some basic premises for a natural science of behavior, especially since the other papers appropriately provide little detail on those premises. This paper discusses four basic components of the radical behaviorist philosophy of science, components which have value beyond the boundaries of behaviorology itself: (a) Radical behaviorists respect behavior as a *natural* phenomenon as part of respecting the continuity of events in space and time which, in natural sciences, accumulates as a natural history. (b) Radical behaviorists emphasize experimental control over dependent variables and the application of that control in culturally beneficial ways. (c) Radical behaviorists recognize private events, such as thinking or emotions, as covert behaviors involved in the same lawful relationships that involve overt behavior. (d) Radical behaviorists acknowledge that scientists are also behaving organisms whose behavior, scientific or not, is affected by the same variables that affect other behavior, and that those variables include scientists' philosophy of science.

Origins, Status, and Mission of Behaviorology (L.E.F. & S.F.L.)

This is the *title paper* of the book [in the 1992 edition]. This work especially addresses *future* behaviorologists, scholars of science, and other interested persons. It describes in detail the origins of the behaviorology movement and of behaviorology as a concept and as a verbal community organized around this discipline. Included are (a) a history of the concept of behaviorology as a separate discipline—from earlier formulations under other names through early appearances of the term "behaviorology" and forward to the present recognition of a comprehensive philosophy, science, and related set of applied technologies under that label, (b) reasons for the independence of behaviorology, (c) a detailed analysis of the relation of behaviorology to other behavior–related disciplines, principally psychology, (d) an analysis of the interrelations among contemporary professional organizations of behaviorally trained persons, (e) the formal organization of the independent behaviorology discipline through formation of The International Behaviorology Association (TIBA), (f) a review of issues related to training in behaviorology, (g) the place of this discipline among related natural science disciplines, and (h) the cultural implications of an independent discipline of behaviorology. This paper is divided into seven chapters, with the middle five chapters (Two through Six) comprising the main parts.

Chapter 1: Introduction. Chapter One introduces the content and topic order of the rest of the chapters. This chapter also reports the context in which this paper was written, and clarifies the purposes and non–purposes, and the audience, for which the paper was written. It also addresses chronology issues and writing policies.

Chapter 2: The Evolution of the Concept of Behaviorology. Chapter Two reviews the evolution of the concept of an independent behaviorology including the paradigmatic and historical differences between behaviorology and other disciplines and fields. This chapter also introduces the difference between the *discipline* of behaviorology and the behaviorology *movement.* With any relatively new discipline the nature and origins of its conceptualization become prime questions of interest. Before concrete actions were taken to launch an organized discipline, the concept of that discipline had to be shaped to maturity in the verbal repertoires of many people. Chapter Two describes how that concept arose, what variables shaped people's responses to it, and the impact of its nature and origins on its increasing ill fit within organized psychology.

Chapter 3: Issues Driving the Independence Movement. Chapter Three addresses the analytical differences between behaviorology and other disciplines and fields and considers the contingencies supporting individual commitments to a disciplinary independence movement. This chapter reports the increasing strength, in five different classes of contingencies, to incur the high costs of organizing an independent discipline. This involves reviewing the accumulating and intensifying reasons for the actions of the early behaviorologists. Chapter Three analyzes these different classes of contingencies, each affecting individuals to varying degrees, that controlled personal commitments to the behaviorology movement. Among the kinds of contingencies participants most frequently identified as having been important in individual cases were these five: (a) paradigmatic incompatibility (mainly with psychology), (b) control of arrangements to train future behaviorologists, (c) better professional position in relation to job markets, (d) improvements in one's capacity to make scientific contributions to the culture, and (e) control over the disciplinary infrastructure.

Chapter 4: The Transition Period: Organizing the Discipline and Developing its Infrastructure. Chapter Four presents a comprehensive overview of the activities to establish the organized discipline of behaviorology. This chapter discusses the cultural engineering by which the new discipline was formalized, rendered operational, and debuted in the natural science community. To do this, the chapter describes (a) the relevance of other professional organizations, and (b) the rise of TIBA, the scientific professional organization of behaviorology, including its statement of purpose.

Chapter 5: The Continuing Debate: Reactions from the Behavioral Community at Large. This chapter (a) explores the prevailing cultural milieu, reviewing the support for the growing behaviorology movement, and the opposition to it, as the community at large witnessed its coalescence on the scientific professional scene; and (b) describes the self–management problems facing those who were taking the lead in formalizing the new discipline. While the behaviorologists moved steadily ahead to refine the concept of their discipline and organize the scientific verbal community that would exercise intellectual proprietorship over it, the general behavioral community continued an increasingly moot debate on the concepts of a behaviorology discipline and movement.

Chapter 6: Interdisciplinary Context: A Cultural Role for the New Discipline. Chapter Six considers the relationship of the behaviorology discipline to other disciplines and fields, and also discusses "culturology." This chapter extends the account of the emergence of the discipline of behaviorology to an examination of the prevailing views of the early behaviorologists on where their discipline fit both among the community of natural science disciplines extant in the culture and in the cultural marketplace. Chapter Six also lists the range of areas affected by behaviorology's contributions, and some of the unique, culture–level aspects of those contributions.

Chapter 7: Conclusion. Chapter Seven concludes this paper by briefly reaffirming behaviorologists' concerns for continued, even enhanced, cultural survival, including concerns for the increased risks to that survival that continue when the balancing effects of a natural science of behavior relations are unavailable. As the last sentence of this chapter points out, "The early behaviorologists believed, of course, that that was what was at stake, or they would not have organized the behaviorology movement, incurring the costs of doing so."

Authorship history. To reduce confusion in the historical record, an account of this paper's authorship is in order. I began this *emergence of behaviorology* paper early in 1987. Within the year, due to the importance and extent of the topic, I had invited Professor Fraley, whose repertoire in this topic was extensive, to collaborate. He accepted. During the next five years, *many* drafts followed. Each of us continually revised and extended each other's work with additions and improvements as we passed the material back and forth with enthusiasm. We presented versions at different annual professional meetings, and we appropriately listed me as first author for these occasions and for other early published versions. Then, as the paper neared general publication, Professor Fraley's growing contributions became the greater. So, since then, we have appropriately listed him as first author.

Behaviorology Curricula in Higher Education (*S.F.L.*)

This paper contains details typical of behaviorology training programs, reflecting the depth and range of basic behavior science training unavailable elsewhere. The question "How do behaviorologists arrange behaviorology training time when we are entirely responsible for it?" forms the basis for describing these curricula. The paper discusses several possible academic behaviorology programs, especially in terms of different audiences to be served including potential behaviorological professionals, professionals in other human–service and human–development disciplines and fields, and the general population. The discussions include course descriptions, course sequences within programs, and issues common to all the programs. The paper also addresses some implications for the future of the discipline of early consensus on these questions.

Behaviorology in China: A Status Report (*S.F.L.*)

This last paper [in the 1992 edition] provides a concrete example of some effects that can occur when a natural science of behavior relations is unavailable. The paper focuses on the status of behaviorology in relation to the situation in psychology in the People's Republic of China. Chinese behavior science professionals in Xi'an, Shaanxi, provided the author with commentary on that situation while he was there teaching courses on Verbal Behavior, and Behaviorology and Education, during the 1990–1991 academic year.

The discussions uncovered several points of interest to both Chinese and Western behavior scientists. In the 1950s, the Chinese lost contact with Western developments. They spent the 1980s trying to update, and thought the update complete. But they were disturbed by what they saw as very few advances in principles and practices, in those missing years, relevant to solving practical, behavior–related problems. In beginning to look elsewhere for solutions, they were discovering that their update was not complete. It involved little beyond the traditional Western psychology sources (literature, texts, personnel) and these contained little of the substantial behavioral advances from those years. The Chinese were discovering that they had overlooked virtually all the advances in principles and practices in the behaviorological science originally founded by B.F. Skinner. This occurred because at about the same time that the Chinese lost contact, the greatest proportion of those advances began to be, and have since been, increasingly reported and supported *outside* psychology. The Chinese are considering the possible reasons for this situation, including the incommensurable paradigm differences indicating and validating separate disciplines.

Beyond the paper's specific attention to those points, other topics also receive attention. These include (a) some historical and philosophical aspects of Chinese behavior science, (b) some circumstances that may interfere with improvements, especially in relation to certain aspects of Chinese culture and the Chinese higher education system, and (c) some steps that non–Chinese behavior scientists can take to contribute to Chinese efforts to modernize behavior science in China.

Design and Benefits

This book was produced on user–friendly Macintosh computer equipment (rather than on what my colleague Carl Cheney often called his "user–surly" equipment). This preface was written for all versions of the 1992 edition. These included a *Student Manual* version, which you may be reading, that I designed to address better the educational needs of students. They would benefit from a design that could increase response density since that could improve retention. The design of the student version could do that by increasing response opportunities. This was achieved by incorporating "Notes and Quotes" boxes on each page. The presence of these boxed areas would provide the reader with clear space to respond in writing to the material. Many of the boxes also contain quotations of particularly important material for rereading and emphasis, and many of these quotations contain fill–in blanks for more student responses. Also, the comb binding on this version would more easily allow the open pages to lie flat. Readers would then be more able to relate quotes in the "Notes and Quotes" boxes to their original locations, and hence contexts, on the appropriate open page.

Summary

Again, the overall concern of this book, especially the title paper, is an analyzed history of the emergence of the discipline of behaviorology, and the behaviorology movement.

Thus the book is not a comprehensive review of the natural laws describing the relations between behavior and independent variables as discovered and applied by behaviorology. Nor is it a review of behaviorology's philosophy of science, interpretations, or analyses (although elements of these are covered). Nor is it a comprehensive review of behaviorology's past, current, and potential cultural contributions, however important these may be. Those kinds of coverage would take several more books. Many such books and a multitude of articles are already available on these topics (see the selected bibliography for an initial list).

I hope that by providing these analyses, the reader will be more likely, and better prepared, to acquire an even larger knowledge and skill repertoire in the natural science of behavior relations, behaviorology.

Stephen F. Ledoux

Canton, NY, USA ***Summer 1992 (Revised: Summer 1996)***

Origins and Components of Behaviorology

A review of the history of this independent natural science that supports international cultural evolution, and effective human endeavors, plus samples of the disciplinary components of this comprehensive science.

BIOLOGY
BEHAVIOROLOGY
B.F.SKINNER
Culturology

An Introduction to the Origins, Status, and Mission of Behaviorology: An Established Science with Developed Applications and a New Name

Stephen F. Ledoux

Behaviorology? What's that? Where does it come from? How does it differ from other disciplines and fields that evince some interest in why people do what they do? How is it related to other disciplines and fields? How much is encompassed by behaviorology, such as its contributions? Why should anyone learn anything about behaviorology? Questions such as these typically arise when people first come across the term *behaviorology.* This paper presents some initial answers to these questions by surveying an analyzed history of the origins of the discipline of behaviorology and the behaviorology movement. The survey includes some corroborative evidence from the status of behaviorological science in China. (For elaboration of the points introduced in this paper, see Fraley & Ledoux, 1997, and Ledoux, 1997a, b, c.)

What is Behaviorology?

Put too simply, behaviorology is the science and technology of behavior relations. This may appear similar to the way some other disciplines define themselves. A more elaborate definition, an expansion of the definition written for the By–laws of TIBA, The International Behaviorology Association (an expansion undertaken when experience indicated some lingering confusion over the discipline's range and depth of coverage), should help discriminate between behaviorology and those other disciplines:

> Behaviorology, a comprehensive discipline with philosophical, experimental, analytical, and technological components, is the natural, life science, emphasizing the causal mechanism of selection, that discovers, interprets, and applies the simple and multiple variables that are in functional relations with the simple and complex, overt and covert behaviors of individual organisms (especially people) during their lifetime (and beyond, with respect to cultural practices), and that takes into ac-

---

This paper was originally part of an invited address to faculty and graduate students of the School of Management, Xi'an Jiaotong University, Xi'an, Shaanxi, People's Republic of China, 20 March 1991, as well as to other Chinese audiences. It was prepared for those and other audiences, including students, who wanted a brief introduction to the concept of a discipline of behaviorology separate from psychology. As indicated by its title, it also serves as the introduction to a larger work (i.e., Fraley & Ledoux, 1997).

count socio–cultural and physical variables from the environment as well as variables from the biological history of the species.

Here is a simpler way to present that thorough definition:

The discipline of behaviorology,

- being a comprehensive discipline with philosophical, experimental, analytical, and technological components,
- is a natural, life science;
- emphasizes the causal mechanism of selection;
- discovers, interprets, and applies the simple and multiple variables that are in functional relations with the simple and complex, overt and covert behaviors of individual organisms (especially people) during their lifetime (and beyond, with respect to cultural practices); and
- takes into account socio–cultural and physical variables from the environment as well as variables from the biological history of the species.

Where Does Behaviorology Come From?

As a current *discipline*, behaviorology comes from the interaction of the previously developed behaviorological science and technology with the current behaviorology *movement*. The conditions under which the original behaviorological science and technology developed gave rise to the current behaviorology movement, and that movement has enabled recognition of the current disciplinary status of behaviorology.

Science and Technology Origins

The science, and the technology originally developed from the science, began about sixty years ago, early in the career of B.F. Skinner. Paradigmatically, Skinner never really was a psychologist in the sense of accepting the *transformation* paradigm of psychology. Sometime during his work in the 1930s, he began using the life–science *selection* paradigm, typical of the natural science of biology, in the task of developing a natural science of behavior, especially the behavior of people. Skinner was operating within a department of psychology, a social science, at Harvard University. However, he did much of his pre–graduation work under W.J. Crozier, the head of the physiology branch of Harvard's biology department (Skinner, 1979, p. 16). Crozier had been a student of the biologist Jacques Loeb, and both Crozier and Loeb had emphasized the causal mechanism of selection in their natural science work. Skinner, perhaps without initially realizing he was doing so, transferred the concept of selection from biology to behavior relations. He thereby brought a particular, natural science paradigm to bear on the questions of a scientific study of behavior.

With respect to behavior, selection refers to the lasting effects, on a person's or other organism's behavior, of the consequences of that kind of behavior. For example, a child who must ask loudly and repeatedly for a cookie (the response) before receiving one (the consequence) is a changed person. He or she is changed physically and thus behaviorologically by the occurrence of the consequence. The consequence alters the bodily structure in a manner that can be observed at the physiological level and at the behaviorological level. At the physiological level the alteration can be seen as nervous system changes the specifics of which physiologists are making better known. At the behaviorological level it can be seen as a changed behavior repertoire in that, in the future, asking–for–cookie responses will be even louder and more persistent. These inseparable effects occur because receiving that past cookie selected for loud and persistent asking. Selection causes physical changes now that are seen as altered behavior later.

Behaviorologists address those altered behaviors by referring to the probability of behavior and changes in that probability occasioned through selection by consequences; consequences select behavior to occur more often or to occur less often. In selection causality on the behaviorological level, a response A is followed by (and usually has actually produced) a consequence B. The occurrence of B leads to responses of *class* A being more, or less, likely to occur again in the future. That is, in the selection causal mode, B *affects (class)* A. Selection is thus a type of causal mode different from the more familiar mechanical causal mode where A *leads to* B. In the mechanical mode, for example, too high a temperature in cooking (A) burns the food (B), or, in reflexes, an increase in light (a stimulus, A) elicits a decrease in pupil size (a response, B). With selection causality, at the level of the behavior of organisms during their lifetime, behavior is selected *by its consequences* to occur again or not; from this arises the more common term, *selection by consequences* (see Ledoux, 1997d, for more detailed terms).

The specifics of selection causality operate differently at other levels of life science (while the shared use of selection causality attests to the interrelationships of the disciplines at all levels of life science). On the biological level selection causality affects species through natural selection. On the level of cultures, selection causality involves selection of cultural practices. (Among natural sciences, a mechanical causal mode is emphasized in physical sciences while the causal mode of selection is emphasized in life sciences.) Behavior is functionally related to many other variables as well, but the selection mechanism is usually a necessary component of those relations (e.g., stimulus control variables). The relationships found in nature between all these variables and behavior are described by, and often as a group referred to as, the natural laws, or nature's laws, of behavior.

In conjunction with the philosophy of science called radical behaviorism, decades of research by Skinner and those trained in this new approach followed Skinner's use of the paradigm of selection by consequences as the fundamental component of studying behavior. (See Ledoux, 1997a, for an introduction to some basic elements of radical behaviorist philosophy; the selection paradigm is not included as one of those elements even though, for behaviorologists, this philosophy and paradigm may have become inseparable.) The efforts of Skinner and those other researchers produced discoveries of the elementary natural laws involving the behavior of organisms. By the 1950s, those researchers were developing technologies to change accessible environmental variables and so produce behavior change. Further, they were applying these technologies to improve various aspects of the human condition. These applications help people to do more, act better, and behave more effectively in all facets of life (for example, in child care, health care, education, daily living, work, leisure, art, entertainment, academic pursuits, and even science itself).

Ever since those early discoveries and applications, new generations of researchers have continued to make further advances, discovering more complex principles and interactions and developing more complex technologies. The application of these technologies extends into ever wider areas, continually improving personal and cultural practices. The term *behavioral engineering* provides a general description of these applications for it suggests both the technical process of changing the relevant environmental variables and the resulting changes in behavior. (This name, behavioral engineering, supersedes an earlier name, behavior modification, partly because the older name is misleading. The older name implies that behaviorological practitioners directly manipulate behavior whereas they actually arrange—engineer—changes of the particular environmental variables related to the behavior of concern, with the result that the behavior changes.)

Movement Origins

The behaviorology movement encompasses the efforts of behaviorologists in developing professional organizations and academic homes to preserve and extend the behaviorology discipline and its contributions to humanity. This movement arose from the conditions under which the original behaviorological science and technology developed. Those conditions involved incommensurable differences between a discipline of behaviorology and the discipline of psychology, especially concerning their respective paradigms. Incommensurable differences are differences that are incompatible, and that cannot be compared like those between apples and ghosts.

Lett (1987) explains paradigmatic incommensurability as "the question of whether rival theories can be compared and evaluated according to a standard measure" (p. 35). Lett also points out that alternative paradigms need not be incommensurable:

> If two paradigms agree about the nature of the problem to be solved and about the appropriate means of solving that problem, they are commensurable. Furthermore, paradigmatic commensurability is a relative matter. Two paradigms may agree about the problems to be investigated but disagree as to the means of solution. Scientific evolution and "scientific creationism," for example, are both concerned with the origins of the human species, but the two paradigms have radically different epistemological principles. If one paradigm chooses to rely upon experience as its epistemological foundation, it can make no impact upon a paradigm that appeals ultimately to revelation (pp. 35–36).

So, "if the participants in such a debate restrict themselves to the terms and assumptions of their own paradigm, they can have nothing to say to one another" (Lett, 1987, p. 36). They are incommensurable (see Ulman, 1992, for elaboration).

Behaviorological science had arisen and existed for some decades, mainly within the realm of psychology, before the accumulating effects of incommensurable differences required independence-oriented actions. During this time, behaviorological professionals had become accustomed to trying (and failing) to change psychology fully into a natural science of behavior. By the 1960s the differences between the two became more openly incommensurable. Events in later decades showed more and more why the earlier strategy of trying to remake psychology was inappropriate (see Fraley & Ledoux, 1997). But the momentum of decades of that strategy was hard to break. Behaviorological professionals found considering other strategies difficult. Some of them finally did so however, and thereby initiated the behaviorology movement.

Effects of incommensurability. By the 1970s, behaviorological professionals were experiencing the *effects* of the incommensurability of their science and psychology. (By this time they were called behavior analysts, the name still used by, among others, some professionals trying to engage in behaviorological science, with its selection paradigm and radical behaviorist philosophy of natural science, within the social science of psychology.) The effects of incommensurability are varied. Some concern the extent to which behaviorology can make its contributions to the culture. Others concern employment opportunities and the control of disciplinary infrastructures. And still others exist also (Fraley & Ledoux, 1997).

One effect of incommensurability was that within psychology the science of behavior was increasingly underrepresented, underfunded, de–emphasized in most departments, and simply dropped in others. As a result, students were less and less able to receive training in the science of behavior. (Ledoux, 1997b, provides a description of some behaviorology curricula in higher education. The contents of these curricula reflect the depth and range of the behavior science training unavailable in psychology.) Students covered few courses related to the science of behavior in their degree programs because few were offered by psychology departments. More likely, the student's required exposure to the laws of behavior involved a single chapter, or part of a chapter, from the twenty or so included in standard introductory psychology textbooks. And those chapters not only typically misrepresented behavior science (e.g., the usual confusion between negative reinforcement and punishment) but also they were increasingly out–of–date; researchers were reporting advances in behaviorological work mostly in journals *outside* those of the usual psychology literature perused by textbook authors.

With so little exposure, substantial interest in the science developed in fewer students. Those who did become interested usually did so due to studying under a behaviorologically oriented faculty member. But the opportunities to do that were also decreasing. After reducing the number of behavior science courses, programs reduced the number of behavior science faculty. So even interested students could not easily be fully trained in the science of behavior and its applications; not enough courses or teachers were accessible. But these students still had to take plenty of courses covering unparsimonious, non–natural science in their programs. As a consequence these fewer, newer natural scientists of behavior were less trained in the available behaviorological science than they might have been (and perhaps less trained than the earlier generations of faculty and personnel whom they replaced). So they were likely to be less effective than they could have been as scientists, as teachers, and as behavioral engineers, and so were *their* students, and so on.

If those effects of incommensurability were the only ones, and no effective actions occurred to change that trend, the long term result could have been the practical disappearance of an effective and advancing scientific and systematic approach to people's behavior and how to change and improve it. Fortunately, positive effects of incommensurability were also detectable, along with appropriate and supportive actions to consolidate and further advance the science. For instance, personnel in various cultural agencies were increasingly looking specifically toward behaviorological science as the provider of effective behavioral engineering, relevant to their concerns. To mention but a few, these personnel included (a) educators looking beyond the typical resources of their field, (b) workers and managers in business and industry looking for ways to increase productivity and job satisfaction, etc., and (c) government units, especially at state level, responsible for services to citizens with disabilities. (For example, in the 1970s some California state officials wanted to spot whether or not applicants for certain jobs had specific training in behavior management. To make this easier to do, Joseph Morrow, a behaviorological scientist at California State University, Sacramento, arranged for students to receive a "Certificate in Behavior Modification"—using the designation common at the time—if their studies included a particular pattern of courses that specifically expanded their skills in the area of behavioral engineering.)

Early independence actions then the behaviorology movement. From the 1960s through the 1980s, both positive and negative effects of incommensurability prodded some initial actions, early moves towards independence. Behavior analysts founded numerous behavioral journals and their own professional organizations. Most of these were separate from psychology's literature and organizations. None of them, however, openly espoused the disciplinary status implied by the incommensurable differences with psychology. Some behavior analysts and behaviorological professionals also founded academic programs (especially at the graduate training level). Many of these programs were also organizationally independent of psychology through their association with academic departments representing various applied behavioral *fields* which could be informed by various disciplines, including behaviorological science (e.g., special education). A few programs functioned with the status and structure of a separate *discipline* by forming a natural science training alternative in a distinct department separate from their respective university's psychology department. These departments, typically describing themselves with the term *behavior analysis* (the term *behaviorology* not yet being in use at their founding), did begin to reflect the independent disciplinary status implied by the incommensurable differences with psychology.

The effects and implications of incommensurability made the need for separation into independent disciplines increasingly clear. Some behaviorological professionals finally began to take the necessary actions. They contributed to the academic debates (which began in earnest in 1984) in the behavior–analytic literature about an appropriate name and directions for the comprehensive natural science discipline concerned with behavior relations. In 1987 they (a) formally recognized the separate and independent status of that discipline, (b) accepted *behaviorology* as the name denoting that discipline, and (c) founded the scientific organization now called The International Behaviorology Association. By the end of 1992, their organizational efforts were reflected in (a) a continuing series of annual conventions with, as a sample, the second in Mexico at the Los Horcones community in January 1990, and the fourth in New Orleans, USA in January 1992, (b) a newsletter, originally called the *TIBA Newsletter,* and now called *Selections,* in its fourth volume, (c) a carefully planned, comprehensively peer–reviewed disciplinary journal to appear in 1993, called *Behaviorology,* (d) a non–copyright–retaining journal, with short–process peer reviewing, in its third serial, called *Behaviorological Commentaries* (which was later to be renamed *The International Behaviorologist*) for articles that fall between the respective domains of the newsletter, *Selections,* and the journal, *Behaviorology,* and (e) the allocation of one–fourth of all dues explicitly for the support of behaviorological research.

How Does Behaviorology Differ From Other Disciplines and Fields?

The original question was longer: "How does behaviorology differ from other disciplines and fields that evince some interest in why people do what they do?" An initial response is that behaviorology is interested in more than this. It is also interested in *what can be done* about what people do. Encompassing this difference, and substantiated by other differences (in philosophy of science, subject matter, methodology, etc.), is the fundamental and incommensurable difference in paradigms between behaviorology and these other disciplines and fields. So most of this answer focuses on the paradigm difference. (See Vargas, 1991, whose names for the paradigms are used here; also see Fraley & Ledoux, 1997, for additional details, including consideration of the other differences as well.)

Of Paradigms and Eclecticism

The two paradigms are the *selection* paradigm Skinner had adopted from biology and the *transformation* paradigm of psychology and some other disciplines. Psychological subscribers to the transformation paradigm are most interested in positing (with emphasis on a hypothetical–deductive model) the causes of behavior chiefly in the transformations that they believe occur inside the person. These are the transformations that external variables (inputs, to use current cognitive terminology) seem to undergo before becoming apparent as behavior (outputs) in a basically mechanical causal mode. Since this paradigm does not support much interest in the inputs or outputs for their own sake, the possibility of, and consequently concern for, effective control is diminished. In contrast, behaviorological subscribers to the selection paradigm are most interested in discovering (with emphasis on an inductive model) the causes of behavior chiefly in the genetically affected, potentially manipulable behavior–environment interactions, with selection by consequences as the fundamental causal mode. Since this paradigm explicitly supports interest both in behavior for its own sake and in the variables of which behavior is a function, the possibility of, and consequently concern for, effective control is enhanced.

Psychology's transformation paradigm has played a particular role regarding eclecticism. Psychologists have generally considered their discipline as an eclectic aggregate. Their eclecticism seemed originally pragmatic. It allowed them to search along multiple paths for an effective approach to the general question of "Why do people do what they do?" But could it allow them to find such an approach? They were convinced that multiple, eclectic paths constituted the best course for them to follow. However, their eclecticism had no built–in need for resolution. They could continue working under eclecticism indefinitely (and have been doing so). Eclecticism actually *does not require* either ultimately adopting, or even looking for, an effective approach. Indeed, the notion of an effective approach, as in a single, substantive, systematic, comprehensive approach, seems to be anti–eclectic by definition. In addition, as psychologists were to discover, they already *shared* a paradigm, the transformation paradigm, that allowed them their eclectic differences. So the availability of a more effective approach, especially one with a different and incommensurable paradigm, evoked little interest. Psychologists' paradigm and eclecticism remain thoroughly intertwined.

The fact that different schools and approaches divided psychology merely masked its otherwise characteristic transformational paradigmatic unity. Psychologists' stress on eclecticism focused on differences in emphases and particulars of the various schools and approaches. Consequently they have only gradually apprehended their common transformation paradigm. Outside psychology critics often complained about the apparent lack of a unifying paradigm in psychology, thereby casting doubts on the disciplinary status of that aggregate. The critics also seemed influenced by the differences in emphases in the various psychological approaches. So they too were distracted from apprehending the basic paradigm. In defending against these criticisms, psychologists stressed their eclecticism since they had not yet clearly recognized their paradigmatic unity. They stressed it to the point that the previously pragmatic eclecticism became an inherent aspect of their self–description (as passed on by countless repetitions throughout a psychology student's training).

Conveniently, however, the transformation paradigm not only encompasses the similarities of psychologists' perspectives but also allows them their eclectic, even contradictory differences. Most psychologists, regardless of eclecticism or perspective, seem little interested in behavior or the variables of which it is a function. They are little interested in inputs (the variables) and outputs (the behavior). They try to relate these mainly for other reasons. They try to relate these as a social science adapting an older (and changing; see Chiesa, 1994) natural science *x leads to y* (or *x is followed by y*) type of mechanical causality. But psychologists cannot easily relate a given input to a given output as cause. So psychologists presume something must happen to the inputs before outputs occur. Somewhere and somehow the inputs must be changed, *transformed,* into outputs. Those changes, as they do not seem apparent elsewhere, must be happening inside the organism, possibly because of something the organism can be seen as doing. Psychologists try to relate the inputs and outputs to learn something about what they presume is behind them. Psychologists then undertake to tell the world, from their various perspectives, all the things they assume are happening inside the organism, perhaps because of the organism. In placing their interests inside the organism, they keep to their familiar mechanical causality. Now, however, this causality takes the form of *x leads to* o *leads to y.* Here, o (for organism) represents the various *transformations* different psychologists believe occur inside the organism as inputs are then said to *become* outputs. However, the transformation paradigm does not address the makeup of transformations; it addresses only their position between the inputs and outputs. Psychologists' various perspectives theorize numerous types of transformations and these can be contradictory and even mutually exclusive. The result is the interplay between the transformation paradigm and eclecticism. The paradigm supports transformations in general, whether agreeable or contradictory, while under eclecticism the latter are automatically tolerated.

Even though the many, specific psychological approaches differ among themselves, they all adhere to the transformation paradigm. Giving them a label like "school" does not change this characteristic. None of them adheres to the selection paradigm. At this level of analysis, only the science of behavior founded by Skinner adheres to that paradigm (but see Ulman, 1991, also). And the selection paradigm is as different from the transformation paradigm as evolution is from creationism.

The Skinnerian Alternative

Skinner was doing research in the 1930s using the selection paradigm; but he was operating *within a unit of organized psychology.* The location of this research may simply be a product of what evolutionary biologists call historical contingency (see Gould, 1989) since Skinner could, and under Crozier's influence almost did, pursue his work officially from within a unit of organized biology. Yet the venue of this research constitutes the beginning of an historical trunk, shared by both behaviorology and psychology. This trunk lasted only for about three decades and has since divided, forming two distinct branches, each with its own continuing disciplinary history.

The roots of this trunk are also as different as the two paradigms and disciplines that shared the trunk before diverging. The history of these roots traces back, in Western culture, to various early Greeks and their philosophies and approaches, and the ideologies of those and other times. As Lerner (1991) reports, the early Western versions of "The empirical and the deductive methods...both arose around 500 B.C. They emerged from a fierce social conflict to determine what sort of society would succeed Bronze Age civilization—a society of free labor or one of slave labor" (p. 62).

The characteristics of the selection paradigm and behaviorology have their Western roots in the preferences of the Ionian Greeks (e.g., Thales, circa 550 B.C.E., and Anaxagoras, circa 450 B.C.E.). With navigation and other needs prompting developments in science and technology, the Ionians preferred the empirical method, its associated philosophical approach known as materialism (which takes matter, nature, as primary, that is, reality exists whether or not people are around to think about it), and the inductive (observation– and measurement– and action–based) approach to knowing. These Ionian roots are found to be ascendant or prevalent in societies during periods of increasing social progress, for example, during the time of the Ionian trading cities when "new societies of traders, craftsmen, and freeholding peasants—the first limited attempts at democracies and republics" (Lerner, 1991, p. 63) were forming, as well as during the Renaissance and the nineteenth century (Lerner, 1991, p. 419) and to some extent the present (e.g., in Japan around the 1980s).

In contrast, the characteristics of the transformation paradigm and psychology have their Western roots in the preferences of the dualist Greeks (e.g., Plato, circa 350 B.C.E., and Aristotle, circa 325 B.C.E.). The dualist Greeks preferred the deductive method, its associated philosophical approach known as idealism (which takes ideas, thoughts, as primary, that is, reality does not exist apart from what people think exists), and the hypothetical–deductive (pure reason and little observation) approach to knowing. These dualist roots are found to be ascendant or prevalent in societies during periods of decreasing social progress, for example, during Greek slave–holding society, during the Western middle ages, and in many ways during much of the 1900s (see Sagan, 1995).

Both these roots and their differences have some impact on most disciplines. The branching of the psychology–behaviorology shared historical trunk is not an isolated instance in academic history. It may be part of an ongoing scientific revolution. For example, in his 1991 book *The Big Bang Never Happened*, Eric Lerner argues compellingly that these very differences are the basis of the current competition between big bang cosmology and plasma cosmology. Big bang proponents continue in the Plato–Aristotle tradition. However, observational evidence seems to show their position to be less parsimonious than their competitor's position. Meanwhile, plasma proponents continue in the Ionian tradition, and their position seems to be more consistent with observations. Parallels with psychology and behaviorology, and their paradigm clash, are evident. (See Lerner, 1991, for details on the supporting historical, social, and physical analyses. Even so, whether or not a Big Bang happened is still unresolved.)

Sometimes in paradigm clashes, one position ultimately eclipses or subsumes the other, as when quantum mechanics superseded Newtonian mechanics in physics. The positions co–exist for a time as one develops and advances while the other declines. With other paradigm clashes, such as the one between behaviorology and psychology, the positions co–exist for a time, sharing their history. Then they branch off, going their separate disciplinary ways.

Figure 1 illustrates the shared history, its roots, and its later branching for behaviorology and psychology:

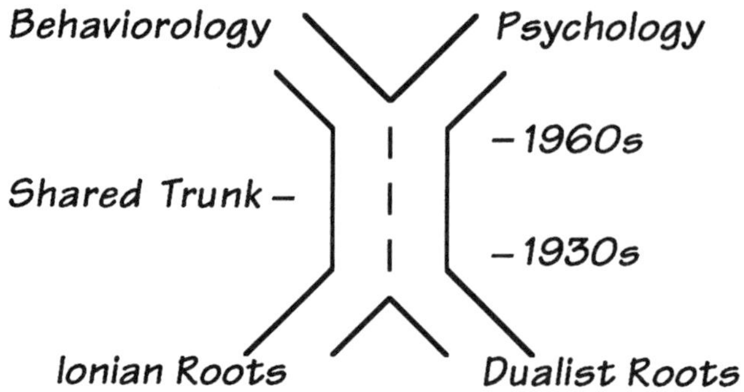

Figure 1. Branching disciplinary tree and philosophical roots.

Different kinds of reasons bring about those different paradigm–clash scenarios. Regarding behaviorology and psychology, how could the shared historical trunk come about? How was Skinner's beginning behaviorological science from within psychology possible, given the incommensurable differences between the paradigms?

Skinner's doing such work from within psychology was possible because the psychology of the time was much more sensitive to differences at the level of schools and approaches than to differences between paradigms. Various schools of thought were already contending within psychology. All these shared the transformation paradigm. But no school was able to demonstrate itself to be better than the other schools nor could they show that other schools were inadequate. So they all had to tolerate each other and co–exist, which they did under the rationale of eclecticism. When Skinner originated the operant approach, it also could not be shown to be inadequate and so it also was tolerated. The fact that the operant approach did not share the transformation paradigm with the psychological schools but was based in the selection paradigm did not originally occasion much comment.

By the 1960s, however, circumstances had changed. Those who continued to advance the science and technology Skinner had originated had come to be known first as operant behaviorists and then as behavior analysts or *radical behaviorists.* (The latter was more concise since usage of the other names had become blurred over time; now, *behaviorologists* is the best descriptor, at least for those who are part of the behaviorology movement.) By using the criterion of *effectiveness in action regarding subject matter,* radical behaviorists were demonstrating the value of their science. That same evidence was also showing the various psychological approaches to be less effective and unparsimonious. Yet parsimony receives scant attention in psychology, and *effective action regarding subject matter* was then—and still among psychological approaches today is—but a minor criterion for adopting explanations (see Fraley & Ledoux, 1997, Ch. 5). As a result, the stage was set for various substantial changes in the positions of both psychologists and radical behaviorists. The effects of incommensurable paradigms were driving both the overt paradigmatic differentiation and the subsequent historical separation into officially independent disciplines.

The Reaction for a Non–Natural Science Tradition

Also during the 1960s, psychology was undergoing the "cognitive revolution" (or, depending on one's perspective, "cognitive counterrevolution"). One aspect of that development was psychologists' increased acceptance that they had little interest in behavior for its own sake or in demonstrations of effective control. So they could not convince themselves of much need to heed the concerns of radical behaviorists. But they were not unmoved by those concerns. They were paying more and more attention to the paradigmatic similarity among the various psychological approaches and less attention to their eclectic differences. They began to apprehend the role of their paradigm in emphasizing their similarities without threatening their differences. As a consequence they began to disassociate from any group that did not share their transformation paradigm. This especially meant disassociation with *radical* behaviorism since several other forms of behaviorism do operate under the transformation paradigm (including interbehaviorism, methodological behaviorism, paradigmatic behaviorism, and Watson's original behaviorism).

Radical behaviorists, after decades of a history shared with psychology, experienced the disassociation as the effects of the incommensurability of the respective paradigms. Before the cognitive movement, psychology had tolerated and benefited from radical behaviorism. However, since the cognitive movement began, psychologists have labeled and treated as dead any non–transformational positions regardless of the facts (see Wyatt, Hawkins, & Davis, 1986). Radical behaviorism was a common target of such unjustifiable slurs because its paradigm was fully incommensurable. Consequently the demonstrated quality and quantity of its research and applications were given less and less consideration. Accumulated scientific evidence for its more parsimonious and practical accounts of behavior no longer received the attention their effectiveness had earned. Instead, political and economic concerns prevailed, with programmatic emphases, funds, and other resources being more emphatically directed towards hypothetical cognitive transformations. The result of these developments was the objective, though not necessarily immediately recognized, differentiation of the transformation and selection paradigms. And this differentiation provided the foundation for the separation of the independent disciplines of psychology and behaviorology.

Also, psychology is not entirely consistent in these matters. It continues to claim *that behaviorism is dead.* However, this is only true within psychology and only in the sense that psychology all but ignores transformational behaviorisms while the work of radical behaviorists is no longer advancing in psychology (although this work does continue to advance in behaviorology and in the efforts of behaviorological scientists who remain employed in units of organized psychology). Yet psychology also claims *that behaviorism still is part of psychology.* This also is only partly true in that various transformational *behaviorisms* continue to exist within psychology. Also, the principles and practices of the first few decades of radical behaviorist research did occur mostly in units of organized psychology and so are a part of that historical time shared with psychology. Introductory psychology textbooks still faithfully report, usually as part of the chapter on learning, this outdated material, and little beyond it. While over thirty years out of date, that material is presented as though it were the latest material available, which it generally is—*in psychology.* However, the years of advances since the paradigm differentiation of the 1960s are arguably not part of psychology and are rarely covered in those textbooks. (As an exception the text by Poling, Schlinger, Starin, and Blakely, 1990, is somewhat more up to date.) Again, the advances were generally reported in journals (beginning, for example, with the *Journal of the Experimental Analysis of Behavior*) that, being independent of psychology's principal disciplinary literature, are seldom perused by most psychology textbook authors. The benefits from those advances accrue mostly according to the extent to which one has acquired and maintains a verbal and skill repertoire in behaviorology or, at least, in behaviorological science.

The experience in China. The situation of behavior science in the People's Republic of China provides corroborative evidence for the separateness and independence of behaviorology and psychology. Chinese behavior science professionals in Xi'an, Shaanxi, provided commentary on the situation in China to the author while he was there, as part of a faculty exchange, teaching courses on Verbal Behavior, and Behaviorology and Education, during the 1990–1991 academic year.

The discussions uncovered several points of mutual interest. The Chinese use a word they translate as *psychology* to encompass the three sources they currently see for their discipline: traditional Chinese views on why people do what they do, the views adopted from the discipline in the Soviet Union (especially the work originating with Pavlov on reflex/emotional, that is, respondent, behavior), and Western perspectives. The Chinese have included three parts in the Western component of their discipline: psychoanalytic (i.e., Freud), cognitive/mentalistic (e.g., Maslow and Piaget), and behavioral (i.e., the science of behavior originated by Skinner).

The Chinese report a special preference for the Pavlovian and Skinnerian work based on the natural science approach and experimental methods these two share. In part, this preference for Pavlov and Skinner may be due to a particular aspect of Chinese history. The Chinese culture has been less burdened than Western culture has been by philosophically idealist dualism, a dualism that pervades Western culture. So Chinese culture has suffered less from the unscientific separation of phenomena into the different realms of mental and physical (soul/body, spiritual/material, mind/reality) that results from philosophical dualism. Western psychology traditionally prefers the non–physical aspect. (The Chinese language, while it has a rich variety of terms for most of the Western usages of the term *mind,* actually lacks a direct translation of mind as Western psychologists use that term—as a dualistic, uncaused metaphysical cause. Instead, for that usage, Chinese professionals generally use a word that, less appropriately, translates back into English better as "brain.")

However, in the 1950s, Chinese behavior science professionals lost contact with Western developments. They spent the decade of the 1980s trying to update, and thought the update complete. But they were disturbed by what they saw as very few advances in principles and practices, from those missing years, relevant to solving practical, behavior–related problems.

In beginning to look elsewhere for solutions, they are discovering that their update is not complete. It involved little beyond the traditional Western psychology sources (literature, texts, personnel) and these contain little of the substantial behaviorological–science advances from those years. The Chinese are discovering that they have overlooked virtually all the post-1950s advances in principles and practices in the science originally founded by B.F. Skinner. This occurred because at about the same time that the Chinese lost contact, the greatest proportion of those advances began to be, and have since been, increasingly reported and supported *outside* psychology, greatly reducing access to them from within psychology. The Chinese are also considering the possible reasons for this situation, including the incommensurable paradigm differences indicating and validating separate disciplines. (See Ledoux, 1997c, for a more complete discussion of behaviorology in China.)

Transformations and eclecticism revisited. Are hypothesized, internal transformations a reasonable alternative to behavior–environment interactions? The variety of psychology's transformations may indeed be more initially captivating than the patient discovery and tested application of complex behavioral laws. Transformations seem smoothly consistent with the philosophically dualist cultural history that pervades the milieu of Western society. Are these a rationale for the many people attracted to psychological theorizing? This attraction occurs in spite of the much greater difficulty in later making use of theorized transformations to help solve society's various general and personal problems, compared to the more technological applications of behavioral laws to such concerns. Is this another example of being affected more by short–term variables (e.g., the fun of discussing competing transformational accounts) than by delayed variables (e.g., the later, improved effectiveness, in helping situations, after having studied behavior–environment interactions)?

In any case, some of these transformations are simply mentalistic inventions that violate a basic premise of the natural sciences, namely respect for the continuity of events in space and time that accumulates, link by related link, in a researchable natural history. Hence the scientific status of those transformations is questionable and unparsimonious. The transformation paradigm allows and invites such untestable, metaphysical inventions to enter the chain of space–time events, breaking and thereby disrespecting the continuity of those events. Such transformations, their related paradigm, and disciplines or parts of disciplines supporting that paradigm have thus removed themselves from consideration as part of any *natural science* discipline or field.

Many other transformations are not transformations at all but rather are the physiological bases of behavior, an appropriate subject matter for a natural science such as physiology. For example, neurons firing (in the central or peripheral nervous systems), in ways often but not necessarily connected to muscles contracting or glands secreting, etc., are physiological aspects of the same fact whose behaviorological aspects observers might witness as, say, salivating or the movements of a hand or of the vocal cords under particular conditions and with particular consequences.

Sometimes the physiological and behaviorological aspects cannot be separated, such as when the behavior is covert. Muscles or glands may not even be involved. For example, due to having learned to observe and verbally report the occurrence of private responses (Skinner, 1953, Ch. 17), people may observe and report themselves seeing something, regardless of whether the thing seen is present to be seen or not; yet all that the properly instrumented physiologist observes about this *seeing* is neurons firing at the back of the brain. These neurons firing (physiological level) and the behavior of seeing (behaviorological level) are inseparable aspects of the same fact, the same phenomenon. Neither overt nor covert behavior can occur without nervous system activity; but the nervous system activity aspect may sometimes occur only along with a covert behavior aspect. Exactly what is happening physiologically when behavior (overt or covert) occurs and when related variables occur (the particular conditions and particular consequences) are important questions to which the natural science discipline of *physiology* can provide answers.

Is psychology's crossover to physiology an appropriate one? Psychologists who take this route show some preference for natural science, physiology in this case. However, psychologists may be the only ones viewing the crossover as a reasonable disciplinary activity. For the crossover interrupts physiology's mission and further compromises the status of psychologists' own discipline by shifting their subject matter into areas legitimately claimed already by a different discipline. Psychologists may find academic turf battles with physiology far more common than with behaviorology.

As for eclecticism, observers can already note a decrease in its importance even in psychology. The shift in emphasis under the cognitive movement to stressing similarities (e.g., the transformation paradigm) seems to have prompted the decrease in eclecticism which is evident in the relative coverage of the psychological perspectives. Perusal of various psychology film series (e.g., the *Discovering Psychology* series) and any number of introductory psychology textbooks shows the cognitive perspective to be filling the stage. Next in coverage is information derived from another discipline, physiology. Other perspectives (e.g., psychoanalytic, humanistic, or gestalt) often receive little more than lip service. Unfortunately, this waning of eclecticism has not paralleled any commitment for changing toward an effective science concerned with why people do what they do and what can be done about it. (The Poling, *et al.*, 1990, text is one exception in that it provides some natural science standards with which to compare and evaluate the several alternative perspectives it includes at appropriate points.)

The Historical Division

Psychology's increasing stress on similarities like the transformation paradigm had contributed substantially to the differentiation of the established disciplinary paradigms. That *differentiation,* in the 1960s, objectively created two separate and independent disciplines out of the previous shared history. The historical trunk divided into separate branches. These disciplines differ not only in paradigms but also, in associated ways, in subject matters, philosophies, methodologies, etc. Not until the 1980s, though, did the resulting changes in contingencies (the effects of incommensurability) begin affecting people enough for them to emit behavior consistent with the fact of different disciplines. Not until the 1980s did they begin to name and reorganize behaviorology.

How is Behaviorology Related to Other Disciplines and Fields?

The distinction between *social science* and *natural science* is relevant because the interest behaviorologists have in people is taken by some professionals as placing behaviorology in the social science arena. However, social sciences not only derive from an interest in people (an interest shared by many natural sciences), but from another commonly acknowledged characteristic as well; social scientists easily reach contradictory conclusions after following the same scientific procedures. This is partly because social scientists allow metaphysical events to enter their explanatory accounts. In contrast, natural scientists more easily reach consistent conclusions after following the same scientific procedures. This is partly because natural scientists disallow the inclusion of metaphysical events in their explanatory accounts, for such events are untestable. Unlike social sciences, natural sciences respect the continuity of events in space and time that accumulate in a researchable natural history. These are major defining characteristics of natural science. Behaviorology shares these and other defining characteristics with other natural sciences.

Among the natural sciences, behaviorology is one of the foundation life sciences (along with biology) rather than one of the foundation physical sciences (such as physics or chemistry). Figure 2 illustrates behaviorology's position along a life science continuum (see Fraley & Ledoux, 1997, about the term *culturology*).

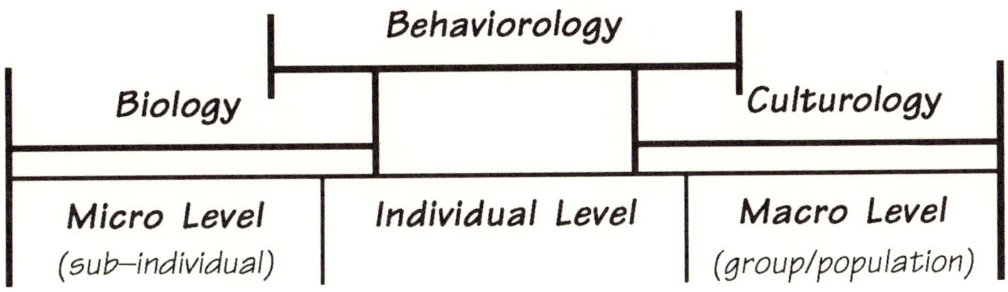

Figure 2. Disciplinary coverage for the three main levels of analysis in the life sciences.

(The study of ecosystems, species evolution, and the behavior of animals in groups by some animal biologists implies that a disciplinary overlap also exists between biology and culturology. So Figure 2 might be redrawn as a triangle with extended sides that cross each other. Each side would represent one of these domains and its associated discipline. The areas where the lines cross would then represent the overlap in the interests of the intersecting disciplines.)

As a basic science, behaviorology provides the foundations that inform the considerations and technologies of various applied behavioral fields (e.g., organizational behavior management) as they seek to fulfill their respective cultural missions (a *field* is where one applies a foundation science *discipline*). Such fields range from advertising to zoology, with many currently in a scientific limbo without an appropriate basic science informing their efforts. Fraley (1987), in a paper addressing the cultural mission of behaviorology, stresses the role of behaviorology as the appropriate science to inform these areas (also see Fraley & Ledoux, 1997).

How Much is Encompassed by Behaviorology, Such as its Contributions?

Plenty, but thorough coverage goes beyond the bounds of this paper. The point of this paper was to introduce an analyzed history of the emergence of the discipline of behaviorology through the behaviorology movement. In the process the status and mission of behaviorology were introduced as well. One must still address the basic and advanced natural laws involving behavior as discovered by behaviorological scientists as well as behaviorology's philosophy of science, interpretations, and analyses, plus its technologies and applications. All of these constitute parts of behaviorology's past, current, and potential cultural contributions.

For instance, here are some basic components of the radical behaviorist philosophy of science; these components have value beyond the boundaries of behaviorology itself, and some have been mentioned already: (a) Radical behaviorists respect behavior as a *natural* phenomenon as part of respecting the continuity of events in space and time which accumulates as a natural history. (b) Radical behaviorists emphasize experimental control over dependent variables and the application of that control in culturally beneficial ways. (c) Radical behaviorists recognize private events, such as thinking or emotions, as covert behaviors involved in the same lawful relationships that involve overt behavior. (d) Radical behaviorists acknowledge that scientists are also behaving organisms whose behavior, scientific or not, is affected by the same variables that affect other behavior, and that those variables include scientists' philosophy of science. (See Ledoux, 1997a, for some elaboration; see Chiesa, 1994, for extensive discussion.)

The laws involving behavior essentially reflect the functional relations between behavior and the variables inherent in an organism's (a) species history, (b) personal history, (c) current situation and, for people, (d) cultural setting. These contain the variables a behaviorologist addresses when trying to analyze, understand, predict, control, and interpret the behavior of organisms. A peek at some of the advances in researching and applying these laws (advances arising since the paradigm differentiation in the 1960s) would involve describing numerous topics: (a) the distinction between event–shaped and verbally–mediated behavior (Vargas, 1988), (b) the analysis of verbal behavior (Skinner, 1957), (c) the recombination of repertoires (Epstein, 1981), (d) establishing operations (Michael, 1982), (e) multi–term (n–term) contingencies (Sidman, 1986a, 1986b), (f) the function–altering effects of contingency–specifying stimuli (Schlinger & Blakely, 1987), (g) stimulus equivalence relations (Sidman, 1994; Stromer, 1991), (h) the general level of reinforcement (Cautela, 1994), and (i) behavioral engineering and cultural design (Skinner, 1971; Ulman, 1991; West & Hamerlynck, 1992). These topics highlight some of the state–of–the–art aspects, in the 1990s, of the scientific comprehension and handling of complex human behavioral relations.

Other cultural contributions involve continuously developing and extensively tested behavioral engineering technologies applicable to all facets of life, with particular value in resolving both personal and cultural concerns. These range from preventative measures in child–rearing practices, to making education effective (e.g., Johnson & Layng, 1992) including the critique of developmentalism, to enhancing business, industrial, and organizational management, to the design and redesign of cultures and cultural practices including those related to rescuing the planetary environment and so helping restore the mutually beneficial balance between the Earth and its inhabitants (see Gore, 1993; see the bibliography at the end of Ledoux, 1997e, for references to other examples, as well as to works covering more of the depth and range of the behaviorology discipline and its cultural utility.) Either a general–behaviorology textbook (e.g., Fraley, 1996) or issues of the *Journal of Applied Behavior Analysis* can provide a starting point for reviewing the research on many of these applications.

Why Should Anyone Learn Anything About Behaviorology?

The laws of behavior (that is, the relations described by those laws) do not always produce benefits; at least as often as not, they may produce problems. For instance, many families fall victim to the accidental, unplanned conditioning of various undesired behaviors. Without contact with behaviorological science, parents may never realize that yelling at or even spanking a child may actually strengthen the behavior they are trying to weaken, especially if that is the only or main kind of attention the child receives. Parents may never realize that the general rule to provide appropriate kinds of attention more when children are behaving in the ways parents desire (i.e., to "catch your children being good") is both more effective than just ignoring them, and more effective than just catching and punishing them when they are bad. "Catching them being good" is more effective in increasing desired behavior and thereby reducing the occasions for undesired behavior. (See Christophersen, 1988, for details on this and other behaviorologically based, prevention oriented child–rearing practices.)

As that example shows, the accidental or unplanned operation of behavioral laws having undesirable effects on behavior becomes a tyrant affecting people's lives. Until after behaviorological research began in the 1930s, few could do much to stop that tyranny for those laws were little understood. Today, through behaviorology, people can increasingly replace that tyranny by designing and redesigning the world in which they live. They can take the responsibility to use the ongoing discoveries about those laws to improve the human condition (and even to evaluate scientifically what words like "improve" mean; see Krapfl & Vargas, 1977; Vargas, 1975, 1982). These actions are possible because one of the behaviors generated and maintained by the operation of these laws is the behavior of people in general taking control of themselves, and the environmental variables that affect them, in informed ways (which also enables them to countercontrol for potential misuses of this science). The greatest initial significance of behaviorology may not be in the management of day–to–day individual affairs nor, perhaps, even in providing solutions to large social problems (e.g., the crisis in American education). Instead the greatest significance may be in providing some critically needed tools to help understand and deal with the world–wide environmental and outer space concerns and crises facing the generations of today and tomorrow.

The basic reason to study behaviorology, then, is to reduce the risks and derive more than the minimal, automatic benefits from the way nature's laws govern behavior. Studying behaviorology expands your repertoire of behavior with respect to those laws and their applications. The more extensive your training in behaviorology is, the greater can be your effectiveness, your success, with its applications to human concerns.

How much behaviorological knowledge and skills is right for you? Everyone should be as familiar with the basics of behaviorology as they are with the basics of biology and physics and other standard natural sciences covered through primary and secondary education. Beyond the basics, "How much is right?" depends on the complexity of the applications appropriate to your areas of concern. The more complex the applications are in a particular area, the greater is the amount of behaviorology study needed if you are to be effective in that area. For instance, look at some of the areas involving children, for these are typical of the complexity levels of most areas of human concern. While a lack of study leaves anyone's potential for success to accident or chance, parents can, by design, attain a quite reasonable level of informed effectiveness in child–rearing practices with only a basic amount of behaviorology study (the equivalent of one or two courses in behaviorology; see Ledoux, 1997b). Educators, on the other hand, find that teaching effectively requires substantially more study. And working with autistic children requires even more. In each of the two latter cases, the complexity of both the applications and the relevant controlling variables increases (while gaining access to those variables is often more difficult as well). Such circumstances demand a more professional level of training (starting with a Bachelor's degree in behaviorology) if practitioners are to be as effective as possible in areas such as these.

A Matter of Epistemology Also

The "Why study behaviorology?" question need not be answered only with respect to complexity and effectiveness. Consider also this answer: "We should study behaviorology because we are affected by nature's laws anyway; perhaps the more we know concerning these laws, the better off we will be." But what does "know" mean? Let us take a little trek into a scientific *epistemology* (the question of what *knowing* is) to help understand this answer better, including how it relates to the complexity and effectiveness answer.

Nature's laws, the laws of the universe, affect us at different *levels of knowledge.* They affect us (a) whether we like it this way or not, (b) whether we have used those laws or not, (c) whether we "know *about*" those laws or not (as in "can use the laws effectively," that is, whether our use–skills have come effectively under the control of those laws or not), and (d) whether we "know" those laws or not (as in "can state and use them," that is, whether our talk, or better, our talk and our use–skills, have both come effectively and explicitly under the control of *statements* of the relationships inherent in those laws or not). In these levels, *knowledge* refers to the range and depth of our behavior repertoires. To illustrate these levels of knowledge (repertoire), consider an example from the teaching profession.

Persons untrained in chemistry but trained in English literature (and even trained in teaching literature as well) would be quite out of place conducting a chemistry class. They do not know the names or properties of the chemicals under discussion in that class (i.e., their behavior repertoire does not include responses appropriate to the pertinent variables, such as the discriminative stimuli and consequences, present in that situation). Yet if they mix some of the chemicals before them, they will produce the same chemical reactions that their trained chemistry colleagues would have produced had those colleagues mixed those same chemicals. The laws of chemistry are in force whether they like it or not, *and* whether they use them (by mixing some of the chemicals before them) or not.

What about the trained chemistry colleagues? Are they trained only in chemistry or are they also trained in teaching, and does that make any difference, especially to teaching? After accumulating, usually over years, certain kinds of experiences (which typically occur by accident or chance), the chemistry teachers who are trained only in chemistry come to *know about* teaching. At least, you would say they do so to the extent that they come to be effective in teaching, that is, in expanding the chemistry–related repertoires of their students. Their teaching–related use–skills have come effectively under the control of the laws involved in successful teaching. Yet even after decades of teaching, they are unlikely to be able to describe, in terms of nature's complex laws relating to the expansion of repertoires (i.e., the scientific foundations of teaching and learning), the reasons for their effectiveness. They cannot tell another *chemistry–trained* person how to *teach* chemistry effectively. (They can, of course, make up theories about their successes; but that is a different matter entirely, and something to be avoided if teaching in general is to become effective.) While they can effectively teach chemistry, and can model doing so, they cannot effectively *teach* teaching, even of chemistry. They do not *know* teaching as they know chemistry.

Effectively expanding the repertoires of students through knowing teaching (an instructional design repertoire), and effectively handling chemicals (a subject–matter repertoire), are very different behavior repertoires. The latter is informed by chemistry while the former is informed by behaviorology. If the would–be teachers of chemistry or any subject matter want to become effective teachers, want to know teaching, want a comprehensive repertoire of teaching skills, and want it by design in a shorter time rather than by chance over a longer time, then they must study the discipline that informs teaching. To the extent that they learn both to teach a particular subject matter (i.e., to expand their students' repertoires in that subject matter) and to accurately and scientifically explain what it is that they are doing which results in that expansion of repertoires, to that extent you would say not only that they *know* their subject matter but also that they *know* teaching as well. Their talk and use–skills have both come effectively and explicitly under the control of *statements* of the relationships described by the laws of behavior relevant to teaching. (You might even say they *know* teaching even if only their *talk* has clearly come under that control.) And teaching is but one example of the many human endeavors where levels of knowledge/repertoire relate to effectiveness.

Vargas and Fraley (1976; also see Vargas, 1996) discuss some benefits of separating these two major repertoires in education, the repertoires of subject–matter expertise and instructional design expertise. These repertoires might be too complex to expect most individuals to expend the effort to master both thoroughly. However, two experts, each with mastery of one of these repertoires, can combine their efforts and thereby achieve greater overall educational effectiveness. Indeed, one design expert can combine efforts with a dozen or more content experts to achieve such improvements. The subject–matter experts can concentrate on the subject–matter content of the courses or programs of study while the instructional design expert concentrates on the instructional arrangements to teach those contents with scientifically sound methods.

The point Vargas and Fraley make is significant because the usual emphasis on subject–matter expertise generally leads to ignoring the complementary need for instructional design expertise. People presume, incorrectly, that someone who is a subject–matter expert automatically has a thorough enough repertoire appropriate for *teaching* that subject. Yet usually the teaching repertoire is minimal. That is especially common in post–secondary education. However, as our example with teaching chemistry showed, *early* and long–sustained effectiveness requires training in both expert repertoires. Vargas and Fraley refocus attention on the need for employing a scientifically based instructional design repertoire if educational effectiveness is to improve. The question is, will effectiveness arise by chance in the slow, lucky accumulation of the necessary experiences, or will it accrue by design through training and practice, especially in the so–far neglected arena of instructional design? Vargas and Vargas (1992) extend the discussion to current instructional materials and programming.

Our trek into epistemology helps put into perspective the differences between *just being affected* by nature's laws (whether we like them or not, *or* use them or not), *knowing about* them, and *knowing* them, as these relate to increasing complexity requiring more comprehensive study for effectiveness. This applies especially to behaviorology, as the science of behavior relations, since so many areas of interest involve human behavior. The more extensive your training in behaviorology, the more effective you can be in dealing with behavior in the contexts of concern to you. (For reasons of this sort, TIBA included among its purposes support for a basic "behavior literacy" graduation requirement of appropriate content and depth at all levels of education; at the college level, that would likely involve a couple of courses. See Fraley & Ledoux, 1997, and Ledoux, 1997b.)

A Matter of Hygiene Also

Yet another answer to the "Why study behaviorology?" question is available. With so many human problems (and potential threats to survival itself), the importance of learning and applying behaviorology today is akin to the importance of learning and applying the then new discoveries of biological science about 150 years ago. The discovery of the relation between micro–organisms and disease formed the basis, in the first half of the 1800s, of today's standards for biological hygiene. (Biological hygiene is that vital ounce–of–prevention whose success, in reducing the frequency of disease, we take for granted today, so many years after the discovery of the relevant scientific facts.)

Learning and applying behaviorology could be called a matter of *behavioral hygiene,* the next step, especially in problem prevention, after having successfully developed and adopted biological hygiene. We would not consider risking hepatitis by eating without first cleaning our hands after using the toilet. Why should we then continue to risk, for example, low success rates (relative to potential) in education when we can, *if appropriately trained,* bring about consistently demonstrated high success rates in both deportment/emotional and academic/intellectual areas? (See Johnson & Layng, 1992; Latham, 1996; Skinner, 1968; and West & Hamerlynck, 1992.) Why should we take those risks when we can, instead, clean up our *actions* by applying some behavioral hygiene? How many years will pass before we achieve *today's* potential successes and take behavioral hygiene for granted? The sooner we become more informed by this science, throughout society, the less time it will take.

Let us take the responsibility to learn and apply behaviorology's discoveries about the laws of behavior at least for the sake of behavioral hygiene. Let us do so to improve the human condition, to take control of our interactions with our environments, and to master control of ourselves.

Endnotes

From the original address prepared for Chinese and other audiences, this paper was revised for publication (1992) in *Behaviorological Commentaries, Serial No. 3*, pp. 11–31. Subsequently, it was the first—and principal—part of a presentation at the second Behavior Analysis Around the World Conference, held in 1992 at Keio University in Tokyo, Japan (the other part of that presentation coming from Ledoux, 1997c). Before receiving further minor revisions for inclusion in *Origins and Components of Behaviorology*

(Ledoux, 1997e) it received minor revisions for inclusion in the 1992 edition of this book of readings. In any case this paper presents only a starting point for further, more in–depth examinations of behaviorology to be found in other behaviorological–science resources (such as Fraley & Ledoux, 1997).

The author thanks those Chinese and Western colleagues, especially Shi Ming de, Guy Bruce, John Eshleman, and Lawrence Fraley, who provided many helpful comments on various drafts of this material. Address correspondence regarding this paper to the author at SUNY–CTC, Canton NY 13617–1096 USA.

References

Cautela, J.R. (1994). General level of reinforcement II: Further elaborations. *Behaviorology, 2* (1), 1–16.

Chiesa, M. (1994). *Radical Behaviorism: The Philosophy and the Science.* Boston, MA: Authors cooperative.

Christophersen, E.R. (1988). *Little People, (Third Edition).* Kansas City, MO: Westport Publishers.

Epstein, R. (1981). Of pigeons and people: A preliminary look at the Columban simulation project. *The Behavior Analyst, 4,* 43–55.

Fraley, L.E. (1987). The cultural mission of behaviorology. *The Behavior Analyst, 10,* 123–128.

Fraley, L.E. (1996). *General Behaviorology* (fall edition). Morgantown, WV: Lawrence E. Fraley (609–C Allen Hall, WVU, Morgantown WV 26506–6122 USA).

Fraley, L.E. & Ledoux, S.F. (1997). Origins, status, and mission of behaviorology. In S.F. Ledoux. *Origins and Components of Behaviorology.* Canton, NY: ABCs.

Gore, A. (1993). *Earth in the Balance.* New York: Plume.

Gould, S.J. (1989). *Wonderful Life.* New York: W.W. Norton.

Johnson, K.R. & Layng, T.V.J. (1992). Breaking the structuralist barrier: Literacy and numeracy with fluency. *American Psychologist, 47* (11), 1475–1490.

Krapfl, J.E. & Vargas, E.A. (Eds.). (1977). *Behaviorism and Ethics.* Kalamazoo, MI: Behaviordelia.

Latham, G.I. (1997). *Behind the Schoolhouse Door: Eight Skills Every Teacher Should Have.* Logan, UT: Mountain Plains Regional Resource Center.

Ledoux, S.F. (1997a). An introduction to the philosophy called radical behaviorism. In S.F. Ledoux. *Origins and Components of Behaviorology.* Canton, NY: ABCs. Reprinted with revisions from (1992) *Behaviorological Commentaries, Serial No. 4,* 3–10.

Ledoux, S.F. (1997b). Behaviorology curricula in higher education. In S.F. Ledoux. *Origins and Components of Behaviorology.* Canton, NY: ABCs. Reprinted with revisions from (in press) *The International Behaviorologist, 1.*

Ledoux, S.F. (1997c). Behaviorology in China: A status report. In S.F. Ledoux. *Origins and Components of Behaviorology.* Canton, NY: ABCs. Reprinted with revisions from (1992) *Behaviorological Commentaries, Serial No. 4,* 24–36.

Ledoux, S.F. (1997d). Increasing tact control and student comprehension through such new postcedent terms as added and subtracted reinforcers and punishers. In S.F. Ledoux. *Origins and Components of Behaviorology.* Canton, NY: ABCs. Reprinted with revisions from (in press) *The International Behaviorologist, 2.*

Ledoux, S.F. (1997e). *Origins and Components of Behaviorology.* Canton, NY: ABCs.

Lerner, E.J. (1991). *The Big Bang Never Happened.* New York: Times Books.

Lett, J. (1987). *The Human Enterprise: A Critical Introduction to Anthropological Theory.* Boulder, CO: Westview Press.

Michael, J.L. (1982). Distinguishing between discriminative and motivational functions of stimuli. *Journal of the Experimental Analysis of Behavior, 37,* 149–155.

Poling, A., Schlinger, H., Starin, S., & Blakely, E. (1990). *Psychology: A Behavioral Overview.* New York: Plenum.

Schlinger, H. & Blakely, E. (1987). Function–altering effects of contingency–specifying stimuli. *The Behavior Analyst, 10,* 41–45.

Sidman, M. (1986a). Functional analysis of emergent verbal classes. In T. Thompson & M. Zeiler (Eds.). *Analysis and Integration of Behavioral Units* (pp. 213–245). Hillsdale, NJ: Erlbaum.

Sidman, M. (1986b). The measurement of behavioral development. In N.A. Krasnegor, D.B. Gray, & T. Thompson (Eds.). *Developmental Behavioral Pharmacology* (pp. 43–52). Hillsdale, NJ: Erlbaum.

Sidman, M. (1994). *Equivalence Relations and Behavior: A Research Story.* Boston, MA: Authors Cooperative.

Skinner, B.F. (1953). *Science and Human Behavior.* New York: Macmillan.

Skinner, B.F. (1957). *Verbal Behavior.* New York: Appleton–Century–Crofts. Reprinted, 1992, Cambridge, MA: The B.F. Skinner Foundation.

Skinner, B.F. (1971). *Beyond Freedom and Dignity.* New York: Knopf.

Skinner, B.F. (1968). *The Technology of Teaching.* New York: Appleton–Century–Crofts.

Skinner, B.F. (1979). *The Shaping of a Behaviorist.* New York: Knopf.

Stromer, R. (1991). Stimulus equivalence: Implications for teaching. In W. Ishaq (Ed.). *Human Behavior in Today's World* (pp. 109–122). New York: Praeger.

Ulman, J.D. (1991). Toward a synthesis of Marx and Skinner. *Behavior and Social Issues, 1* (1), 57–70.

Ulman, J.D. (1992). Behaviorology and psychology are incommensurable paradigms: a rejoinder to Staats. *Behaviorological Commentaries, Serial No. 2,* 23–28.

Vargas, E.A. (1975). Rights: A behavioristic analysis. *Behaviorism, 3* (2), 120–128.

Vargas, E.A. (1982). Hume's "ought" and "is" statement: A radical behaviorist's perspective. *Behaviorism, 10* (1), 1–23.

Vargas, E.A. (1988). Verbally–governed and event–governed behavior. *The Analysis of Verbal Behavior, 6,* 11–22.

Vargas, E.A. (1991). Behaviorology: Its paradigm. In W. Ishaq (Ed.). *Human Behavior in Today's World* (pp. 139–147). New York: Praeger.

Vargas, E.A. (1996). A university for the twenty–first century. In J.R. Cautela & W. Ishaq (Eds.). *Contemporary Issues in Behavior Therapy: Improving the Human Condition* (pp. 159–188). New York: Plenum.

Vargas, E.A. & Fraley, L.E. (1976). Progress and structure: Reorganizing the university for instructional technology. *Instructional Science, 5,* 303–324.

Vargas, E.A. & Vargas, J.S. (1992). Programmed instruction and teaching machines. In R.P. West & L.A. Hamerlynck (Eds.). *Designs for Excellence in Education: The Legacy of B.F. Skinner* (pp. 33–69). Longmont, CO: Sopris West.

West, R.P. & Hamerlynck, L.A. (Eds.). (1992). *Designs for Excellence in Education: The Legacy of B.F. Skinner (Limited Edition).* Longmont, CO: Sopris West.

Wyatt, W.J., Hawkins, R.P., & Davis, P. (1986). Behaviorism: Are reports of its death exaggerated? *The Behavior Analyst, 9,* 101–105.

An Introduction to the Philosophy Called Radical Behaviorism

Stephen F. Ledoux

The work of B.F. Skinner simply did not follow the majority views of his time. In this he was not the first. He stood, as the saying goes, on the shoulders of giants. He advanced another major step in a trend whose continuity in the West began nearly 500 years ago. That trend is one of replacing what could be characterized as humanity's self–centeredness with an increasingly more effective natural science perspective about people's place in the order of things. This trend got a big push when Copernicus reiterated what Aristarchus of Samos and the ancient Ionian Greeks had discovered much earlier but which had been lost in the intervening centuries: the Earth, and thus humanity, were not the center of everything. Later, Darwin showed that our bodies (our physical forms, structures, and functions) are also products of the same natural laws that apply to all other living and non–living things. Then Skinner, through the behaviorology discipline arising from his work, demonstrated that our very being, our consciousness, our conduct, our behavior, is also necessarily and properly within the reach of natural science. From that demonstration, and its associated applied technologies, arises an increased opportunity for humanity to solve its problems: from day–to–day personal difficulties, through challenges such as the crisis in education, to the global problems threatening survival itself. To benefit from that opportunity, people must expand their behavior repertoires with respect to behaviorology, the discipline responsible for the relevant science and technology. An appropriate starting point is the *philosophy of science* that informs that discipline. This paper introduces that philosophy.

Skinner gave the name *radical behaviorism* to the philosophy of science under which he operated. That philosophy now informs the behaviorology discipline, a continuing extension of Skinner's work. The term, *radical,* in radical behaviorism, means thoroughgoing or fundamental (Ulman, 1991). Radical behaviorists use this term to distinguish this form of behaviorism from other forms of behaviorism such as Watson's original behaviorism (Watson, 1913), methodological behaviorism, interbehaviorism, or paradigmatic behaviorism (Ulman, 1992a). The distinction is necessary because the criticisms commonly leveled at behaviorism are not applicable to all forms. Those criticisms have become appropriate only for the other forms of behaviorism because radical behaviorism developed partly as a corrective response to some legitimate concerns raised in the criticisms. Skinner provides a comprehensive discussion of these issues in his 1974 book *About Behaviorism.*

This paper was originally prepared as a basis for discussions in a graduate *Behaviorology and Education* class at the Xi'an Foreign Languages University, China.

Simply as a name originating in an historical context, the name radical behaviorism has little problem itself as an acceptable name for the philosophical position informing the behavior science Skinner started, at least to practitioners of that science. However, some authors have expressed legitimate concerns over misunderstandings caused outside that science and historical context by the terms used in this name. Schneider and Morris (1987) try to reduce the misunderstandings by providing a thorough history of the use and evolution of the terms radical and behaviorism. Meanwhile Vargas (1990) argues for avoiding the misunderstandings by using a different term, such as *selectionism,* to replace the older terms in naming this philosophy of science. Ulman (1992b), while not insisting that a change was unnecessary, questioned selectionism as a good choice for an appropriate name. He pointed out a particular problem with selectionism: one can be a selectionist without holding to a radical behaviorist philosophy (for example, Hegel or Tielhard de Chardin). Since no alternative name is as yet generally accepted, this paper continues to use the name radical behaviorism.

This philosophy of science, radical behaviorism, has many components. These components are at the core of the science and movement that became the natural science behaviorology discipline (several applicable components are shared by other natural sciences). As radical behaviorists and natural scientists, behaviorologists respect these components. Four of these components arise regularly in discussions of radical behaviorism and were especially important in the emergence of behaviorology. Rather than saying "radical behaviorism does this or that," certain behaviors of radical behaviorists represent these components: (a) Radical behaviorists respect behavior as a *natural* phenomenon as part of respecting the continuity of events in space and time which, in natural sciences, accumulates as a natural history. (b) Radical behaviorists emphasize experimental control over dependent variables and the application of that control in culturally beneficial ways. (c) Radical behaviorists recognize private events, such as thinking or emotions, as covert behaviors involved in the same lawful relationships that involve overt behavior. (d) Radical behaviorists acknowledge that scientists are also behaving organisms whose behavior, scientific or not, is affected by the same variables that affect other people's behavior, and that those variables include scientists' philosophy of science. Other concerns are inseparably intertwined with these components of radical behaviorism. Some of these concerns include the preference for single–subject experimental designs rather than group statistical designs, the refusal to allow metaphysical events to enter explanatory accounts, and the question of parsimony in accounts of human behavior (see Chiesa, 1994).

Any and all of these components might be covered in discussions of radical behaviorism. Some authors take (a) and (b) for granted and mainly cover (c) and (d) in descriptions of this philosophy (e.g., Hake, 1982). Similarly, this brief introduction concentrates on (c) and (d), only mentioning (a) and (b) in passing. But this is partly because (a) and (b), and their implications, are extensively covered in a paper by Fraley and Ledoux (1997; also, see Ledoux, 1997a).

Private Events: Covert Behaviors

Radical behaviorism has been misunderstood and misrepresented concerning private events, their evaluation, and their place in a science of behavior (e.g., Mahoney, 1989).

Radical behaviorists do not deny that such events occur inside the skin. They ungrudgingly accept the reality of the physiological events occurring within the body, some as behavior. They take private events into account. But in so doing, they also insist that, in any serious scientific endeavor, private events be considered in ways respectful of the natural science continuity of events that accumulates as a natural history. That is, they insist that private events be considered without appeal to metaphysical causality or metaphysical implications. Since this precludes mentalistic and cognitive explanations, those who court such explanations resist radical behaviorism. Skinner (1974) addressed this issue in *About Behaviorism:*

> But if a behavioristic interpretation...is not all we should like to have, it must be remembered that mental or cognitive explanations are not explanations at all. (p. 106)

Adherents of radical behaviorism assume that the same natural laws prevail on both sides of the skin. This, of course, does not change the nature of either the person, the events inside the skin, the events' effects, or the events' independent variables. The skin is not any special sort of boundary to the laws of the universe. Furthermore, radical behaviorists recognize that a person may at times be the *only* observer in a position to detect or discriminate the occurrence of certain events within his or her skin (words like "detect" and "discriminate" need not imply agency; see Baum, 1995). So radical behaviorists invest scientific consideration also in events detectable by only one person. They do not restrict scientific consideration to events detectable only by more than one person. And they are willing to work with the resulting increase in technology required to manage the greater inaccessibility of such events.

Radical behaviorists find that the most effective way to handle private events is to recognize them as covert behaviors under the same laws affecting overt, public behaviors. Private events are lawful in the same way that one would regard public events. Radical behaviorists cannot grant scientific status to private events invented to be causes of behavior. Nor do they use real private events as primary causes of behavior. They do not need to, because they analytically pursue any causal chain to other, outside events. They do this for the sake of control in their subject matter. They do not treat private behavioral events as indicators of internal hypothetical constructs conjured up, or conveniently given just the right characteristics, to explain those events.

Instead, radical behaviorists see behavior, on the overt level, as neurologically based actions of the glands and muscles (both smooth and striped). They see private events as covert behaviors, under the same laws as overt behaviors. These covert behaviors are usually less accessible than overt behaviors, often being observable and reportable only by a public–of–one (see Ledoux, 1973). And sometimes these covert behaviors involve only the neurological–level events; the behavior of "seeing in the absence of the thing seen" is one example (see Ledoux, 1997a; also see Skinner, 1953, Ch. 17).

The Behavior and Philosophy of Scientists

When considering the behavior and philosophy of scientists, perhaps radical behaviorism has been more overlooked than misunderstood, as well as confused with other behaviorisms. That is unfortunate, because the practice of science itself, and philosophy of science, are both effectively addressed by the principles of radical behaviorism.

The Behavior of Scientists

The work of scientists is twofold. It is (a) to be exposed to precise and controlled contingencies that are unlikely to have affected others in this controlled way. It is also (b) to pass along descriptions and applications of those contingencies to others.

Scientific work is initially the behavior of the scientist under direct control of the contingency relations (that is, under the direct control of the complex of multiple stimuli, behaviors, and consequences) experienced in research. This is the point of science. After extensive study and preparation, scientists are exposed to the contingencies of the unknowns in their disciplines. Due to their study and preparation, they derive the maximum benefit from that exposure. And that is what doing science is all about.

The rare and precise arrangement of contingencies experienced in research generally limits the availability of these particular contingencies to scientific contexts. Hence only people operating in those contexts have their behaviors effectively shaped by those contingencies. The subsequent steps a scientist takes are largely determined by the consequences of the previous steps. The result is a unique, contingency–shaped expansion of the scientist's scientific behavior repertoire. Due to this expansion, scientists can behave more effectively with respect to the subject under their study than others who lack that exposure to those contingencies.

The disciplinary behaviors of scientists also include the behavior repertoires of summarizing, reporting, and applying their expanded scientific repertoires. These disciplinary repertoires involve verbal stimuli. And these verbal stimuli provide *rules.* The rules are statements of the contingencies the scientists have experienced. These rules affect the behaviors of others. Colleagues, disciplines, fields, and the public benefit from using these rules because when their behavior is affected by these rules (that is, when their behavior comes to be rule–governed—i.e., verbally mediated) their behavior often becomes more effective than it would be without the rules. As a result the rules become responsible for much of the behavior of these groups. In essence, such benefits accrue by expanding the repertoires of those people without each of them having to await the unlikely experience of the research contingencies themselves. In this way they benefit from scientists' work. While much of scientists' scientific behavior is contingency–shaped in vital ways, the behaviors of these other groups is to a large extent rule–governed (see Skinner, 1969, about this distinction).

Vargas (1988) has recently recast the distinction between contingency–shaped and rule–governed behavior as the distinction between event–governed and verbally–governed (or mediated) behavior. This distinction and its implications, and several other advances, provide the current state of the art for the scientific comprehension and handling of complex human behaviors. Some of the other advances include (a) the analysis of verbal behavior (Skinner, 1957), (b) recombined repertoires (Epstein, 1981), (c) establishing operations (Michael, 1982), (d) multi–term (n–term) contingencies (Sidman, 1986a, 1986b), (e) the function–altering effects of contingency–specifying stimuli (Schlinger & Blakely, 1987),.(f) stimulus equivalence relations (Sidman, 1994; Sidman, Wynne, Maguire, & Barnes, 1989; Stromer, 1991), (g) the general level of reinforcement (Cautela, 1994), and (h) behavioral engineering and cultural design (Skinner, 1971; Ulman, 1991; West & Hamerlynck, 1992). Indeed, the radical behaviorist and behaviorological perspectives encompass a far wider domain than that denoted traditionally as "respondent and operant conditioning in the learning of new behavior."

The Philosophy of Scientists

Scientists, like everyone else (including radical behaviorists), are behaving organisms whose behaviors, scientific or not, are affected by the same laws that affect other behaviors. Those laws essentially reflect the functional relations between behavior and the variables inherent in an organism's (a) species history (e.g., genetics), (b) personal history, (c) current situation and, for people, (d) cultural setting. These contain the variables which a behaviorologist addresses when trying to analyze, understand, predict, control, and interpret the behavior of organisms.

A scientist's philosophy of science is itself among the variables affecting his or her work. The philosophical repertoire derives partly from the history and setting variables. This repertoire later affects the scientist's work as a part of those variables. The philosophical repertoire includes various underlying assumptions. Comprised mostly of verbal behaviors, a discipline's philosophy of science is usually learned at advanced stages in disciplinary training, although precursors are present long before that (parts of the personal history variables). This repertoire is behavior, and as such continues to be subject to the laws of behavior. But, through the scientist's colleagues and discipline which share it, the philosophy itself becomes one of the variables affecting the scientist's subsequent work (part of the cultural setting variables).

A scientist's philosophy of science affects her or his work in several ways. One way involves the philosophy evoking investigations of certain variables and not others. Cooper, Heron, and Heward (1987, p. 12) provide some examples:

> ...the philosophical decisions to ignore all private events or to use explanatory fictions as the causes of behavior may both produce a similar effect on research and practice. Both positions restrict practice and research even though for different reasons. Methodological behaviorism is restrictive because it ignores areas of major importance for an understanding of behavior. Mentalistic positions are also restrictive, for as noted by Skinner (1974), "Mentalistic explanations allay curiosity and bring inquiry to a stop. It is so easy to observe feelings and states of mind at a time and in a place which make them seem like causes that we are not inclined to inquire further." (p. 12)

A philosophy of science can also affect a scientist's work by playing a role in the conditioning of a scientist to be reinforced by certain classes of events and not others. Hake (1982, p. 24) provides some examples:

> The issue here is what the radical behaviorist believes the reinforcement contingencies for the scientist should be. The most common view and that of the methodological behaviorist is that inclusion of a finding in the body of knowledge or theory is based on acceptability to the scientific community in the terms of (1) the research procedures used (e.g., agreement among observers, replicable individual data, precise measurement and control) and (2) the relation of the content to the existing theory (e.g., related to a productive content area but an extension of it). The radical behaviorist would not believe those contingencies alone to be totally desirable, because they include insufficient reinforcement for innovative content and procedures, and thereby delimit the growth of science... The radical behaviorist would suggest workability, stimulation, and contribution to society as additional worthwhile contingencies that would encourage innovation of content and method. The

major contention is that scientists should recognize that all aspects of their scientific behavior are shaped by the reinforcers of some scientific community and that this control of their behavior affects the science.

Conclusion

The philosophy of science called radical behaviorism played a fundamental role in B.F. Skinner's determination that our very being, consciousness, conduct, and behavior is necessarily and properly within the reach of natural science. (Regarding these concerns radical behaviorists have addressed relevant aspects as far–afield as ethics and religion; see Krapfl & Vargas, 1977; Schoenfeld, 1993; and Vargas, 1975, 1982.) The result has been increased opportunities for humanity to solve its problems through the science informed by that philosophy, namely, behaviorology.

A question that often arises in discussions of philosophy of science concerns how the radical behaviorist philosophy differs with the philosophies of science in other disciplines, most notably psychology. That question was not covered in this introductory paper. Extensive coverage can be found, for example, at appropriate points in a paper by Fraley and Ledoux (1997) which weaves its comprehensive way through the origins, status, and mission of behaviorology. However, comprehensive coverage of the radical behaviorist philosophy of science is beyond the scope of either that paper or this one. (For comprehensive coverage, see Skinner, 1953, 1974. For more recent comprehensive coverage, see Chiesa, 1994.) ☙

Endnotes

The author thanks the members of the graduate *Behaviorology and Education* class in Xi'an, China (see Ledoux, 1997b), for whom this paper was originally prepared, for their discussions which provided a good foundation for subsequent improvements. The author uses this material to help students and colleagues begin to understand the philosophical basis of behaviorology in a way that encourages them to seek details from more extensive sources (e.g., Skinner, 1953, 1974; Chiesa, 1994). The paper was revised for publication (1992) in *Behaviorological Commentaries, Serial No. 4,* pp. 3–10. Then, before receiving further minor revisions for inclusion in *Origins and Components of Behaviorology* (Ledoux, S.F. [1997]. Canton, NY: ABCs.), it received minor revisions for inclusion in the 1992 edition of this book of readings.

The author also thanks John Eshleman, Lawrence Fraley, and Jerome Ulman for providing helpful comments on various drafts of this material. Address correspondence regarding this paper to the author at SUNY–CTC, Canton NY 13617–1096 USA.

References

Baum, W.M. (1995). Radical behaviorism and the concept of agency. *Behaviorology, 3* (1), 93–106.

Cautela, J.R. (1994). General level of reinforcement II: Further elaborations. *Behaviorology, 2* (1), 1–16.
Chiesa, M. (1994). *Radical Behaviorism: The Philosophy and the Science.* Boston, MA: Authors cooperative.
Cooper, J.O., Heron, T.E., & Heward, W.I. (1987). *Applied Behavior Analysis.* New York: Macmillan.
Epstein, R. (1981). Of pigeons and people: A preliminary look at the Columban simulation project. *The Behavior Analyst, 4,* 43–55.
Fraley, L.E. & Ledoux, S.F. (1997). Origins, status, and mission of behaviorology. In S.F. Ledoux. *Origins and Components of Behaviorology.* Canton, NY: ABCs.
Hake, D.F. (1982). The basic–applied continuum and the possible evolution of human operant social and verbal research. *The Behavior Analyst, 5,* 21–28.
Krapfl, J.E. & Vargas, E.A. (Eds.). (1977). *Behaviorism and Ethics.* Kalamazoo, MI: Behaviordelia.
Ledoux, S.F. (1973). *The Experimental Analysis of Coverants.* M.A. thesis, California State University, Sacramento.
Ledoux, S.F. (1997a). An introduction to the origins, status, and mission of behaviorology: An established science with developed applications and a new name. In S.F. Ledoux. *Origins and Components of Behaviorology.* Canton, NY: ABCs. Reprinted with revisions from (1992) *Behaviorological Commentaries, Serial No. 3,* 11–31.
Ledoux, S.F. (1997b). Behaviorology in China: A status report. In S.F. Ledoux. *Origins and Components of Behaviorology.* Canton, NY: ABCs. Reprinted with revisions from (1992) *Behaviorological Commentaries, Serial No. 4,* 24–36.
Mahoney, M.J. (1989). Scientific psychology and radical behaviorism. *American Psychologist, 44* (11), 1372–1377.
Michael, J.L. (1982). Distinguishing between discriminative and motivational functions of stimuli. *Journal of the Experimental Analysis of Behavior, 37,* 149–155.
Schlinger, H. & Blakely, E. (1987). Function–altering effects of contingency–specifying stimuli. *The Behavior Analyst, 10,* 41–45.
Schneider, S.M. & Morris, E.K. (1987). A history of the term *radical behaviorism:* From Watson to Skinner. *The Behavior Analyst, 10,* 27–39.
Schoenfeld, W.N. (1993). *Religion and Human Behavior.* Boston, MA: Authors Cooperative.
Sidman, M. (1986a). Functional analysis of emergent verbal classes. In T. Thompson & M. Zeiler (Eds.). *Analysis and Integration of Behavioral Units* (pp. 213–245). Hillsdale, NJ: Erlbaum.
Sidman, M. (1986b). The measurement of behavioral development. In N.A. Krasnegor, D.B. Gray, & T. Thompson (Eds.). *Developmental Behavioral Pharmacology* (pp. 43–52). Hillsdale, NJ: Erlbaum.
Sidman, M. (1994). *Equivalence Relations and Behavior: A Research Story.* Boston, MA: Authors Cooperative.
Sidman, M., Wynne, C.K., Maguire, R.W., & Barnes, T. (1989). Functional classes and equivalence relations. *Journal of the Experimental Analysis of Behavior, 52,* 261–274.
Skinner, B.F. (1953). *Science and Human Behavior.* New York: Macmillan.
Skinner, B.F. (1957). *Verbal Behavior.* New York: Appleton–Century–Crofts. Reprinted, 1992, Cambridge, MA: The B.F. Skinner Foundation.
Skinner, B.F. (1969). *Contingencies of Reinforcement: A Theoretical Analysis.* New York: Appleton–Century–Crofts.

Skinner, B.F. (1971). *Beyond Freedom and Dignity.* New York: Knopf.
Skinner, B.F. (1974). *About Behaviorism.* New York: Knopf.
Stromer, R. (1991). Stimulus equivalence: Implications for teaching. In W. Ishaq (Ed.). *Human Behavior in Today's World* (pp. 109–122). New York: Praeger.
Ulman, J.D. (1991). Toward a synthesis of Marx and Skinner. *Behavior and Social Issues, 1* (1), 57–70.
Ulman, J.D. (1992a). Behaviorology and psychology are incommensurable paradigms: A rejoinder to Staats. *Behaviorological Commentaries, Serial No. 2,* 23–28.
Ulman, J.D. (1992b, January). On the philosophical origins of behaviorology. Paper presented at the fourth annual convention of The International behaviorology Association, New Orleans, LA.
Vargas, E.A. (1975). Rights: A behavioristic analysis. *Behaviorism, 3* (2), 120–128.
Vargas, E.A. (1982). Hume's "ought" and "is" statement: A radical behaviorist's perspective. *Behaviorism, 10* (1), 1–23.
Vargas, E.A. (1988). Verbally–governed and event–governed behavior. *The Analysis of Verbal Behavior, 6,* 11–22.
Vargas, E.A. (1990). A name for our philosophy. *TIBA Newsletter, 2* (3), 11–12.
Watson, J.B. (1913). Psychology as the behaviorist views it. *Psychological Review, 20,* 158–177. Reprinted in T. Shipley (Ed.). (1961). *Classics in Psychology.* New York: Philosophical Library.
West, R.P. & Hamerlynck, L.A. (Eds.). (1992). *Designs for Excellence in Education: The Legacy of B.F. Skinner (Limited Edition).* Longmont, CO: Sopris West.

Origins, Status, and Mission of Behaviorology

Lawrence E. Fraley **Stephen F. Ledoux**

§

...either psychology must change its viewpoint so as to take in the facts of behavior...or else behavior must stand alone as a wholly separate and independent science. (John B. Watson, 1913)

...I think I am beginning to see the scope of a behavioral—or behavioristic—analysis. It does talk about the important things; it does point to conditions which can be changed; it does show what is wrong with other ways of talking about things. (B.F. Skinner, 1983a, p. 347, from a note written about 1972)

...[I've] been slow in throwing off the notion that a science of behavior is the future of psychology.... Now I think this is a world of our own. (B.F. Skinner, 1989, *declaring the disciplinary independence of the science he founded; from a transcript of his major address to close the convention of the Association for Behavior Analysis*)

§

Chapter 1:

Introduction

This record is especially intended to facilitate analyses and interpretations by those who study the origins and emergence of the discipline of behaviorology. The manifestation of any new discipline evokes questions: What is the nature of the new discipline

---

Ledoux began this paper in early 1987 to analyze the variables leading to the independent development of behaviorological science. As the necessity of the behaviorology movement, and the significance of behaviorology's contributions to the culture, became more apparent, Ledoux invited Fraley to collaborate. Over five years of countless exchanges produced this paper, with each exchange extending and improving the work, and with Fraley's contribution becoming the greater—hence his listing as primary author.

in terms of both subject matter and organization? What has been the course of its evolution both as a concept and as a formally organized verbal community? And why, along that course, did organizational independence become necessary? How does both the subject matter addressed by the new discipline and the organization of its people relate to those of other disciplines, especially to those with which it might share a common history? How should one prepare oneself to work within this discipline? And, importantly, what is the cultural mission of this organized discipline—what is it supposed to accomplish, and how does its mission relate to those of peripheral disciplines or fields?

In addressing these questions, this work describes the historical facts of the emergence. Additionally, beyond a description of the "facts" that answer such questions, a principal objective has been to describe contingencies under which the founders of this discipline operated when producing those facts. To that end, from this behaviorological perspective, this paper reports particular circumstances in which those leaders found themselves. This work includes some behavioral events not because the positions they reflect are likely to be of lasting import, but rather to sketch the behavioral milieu in which the founders operated at the time. Quotations appear from letters and other informal communication sources to reveal the nature of the verbal community in which the early leaders were enmeshed. *This paper thus takes the form of a behaviorologically analyzed record.* The authors hope that this report will have adequately described the functions of these many critical variables so that the subsequent course of this movement can be related to the behaviors of those working for or against it during the period described in this account.

The authors did not edit this work for conformance to current political strategies. Reviewers occasionally objected to what they saw as publicity for persons whose views on certain matters they disrespected or deemed unworthy. Editing on that basis has been resisted. The roles of such persons in the behaviorology movement, acting both for and against its interests, have been included in this account on the basis of the effects of their actions on the history of behaviorology. Nor have the authors tried to cast this work as a recruiting instrument for the gentle persuasion of uncommitted potential converts to a movement. Articles of that type frequently appear as authors, in support of their respective causes, strive to appeal convincingly to various elements in the at–large professional community. But in contrast, this article, presenting an analyzed description of the movement recorded near the time of the reported events, simply answers the kinds of questions that naturally arise through the study of any newly emerging discipline. (Except to add a few, more accessible sources officially presented or published a year or three later, writing this work occurred from early 1987 to 1993.)

This work is divided into five parts plus short introductory and concluding chapters. Among them some normal chronology is evident. Within parts, where appropriate, a chronological order has also been followed. However, in places, a strict historical chronology would have failed to capture the more episodic and thematic nature of the contingencies that affected the leaders and participants of movements. People become involved in important episodes, and each episode preoccupies them for a time while the currents of other events continue to swirl around them. Their behaviors are better understood in light of historical treatments that, while not losing contact with the calendar, nevertheless preserve and deal with that episodic and thematic integrity, even though doing so departs in places from a strictly chronological record.

The five main parts of this paper are Chapters Two through Six. Chapter Two (**The Evolution of the Concept of Behaviorology**) examines the nature and origins of the behaviorology concept worldwide—and its increasing ill fit within organized psychology where the incipient stages of its organizational coalescence occurred. Chapter Three (**Issues Driving the Independence Movement**) explores the increasing strength, in five different classes of contingencies, to incur the high costs of organizing a separate and independent discipline. Chapter Four (**The Transition Period: Organizing the Discipline and Developing its Infrastructure**) presents a comprehensive review of the subsequent activities to organize the behaviorology discipline and considers the cultural engineering by which the newly named discipline was formalized, rendered operational, and installed in the scientific community. Chapter Five (**The Continuing Debate: Reactions from the Behavioral Community at Large**) reviews the prevailing cultural milieu and analyzes the support for, and the opposition to, the behaviorology movement, as well as some self–management problems facing those who were taking the lead in formalizing the behaviorology discipline. Chapter Six (**Interdisciplinary Context: A Cultural Role for the New Discipline**) emphasizes the prevailing views of the early behaviorologists on where their discipline fit both among the community of natural science disciplines extant in the culture and in the cultural marketplace. It also comparatively explores the different levels of analysis characteristic of the existing behavior–related natural science disciplines, and examines the cultural basis of resistance to behaviorology. (Partially to facilitate possible serial publication of the paper's parts, each chapter starts with a review of previous material and finishes with a preview of the next chapter. In serial publication, with each installment perhaps including its own references, the introductory Chapter One would appear with Chapter Two while Chapter Six would appear with the conclusion Chapter Seven and the endnotes and complete references.)

Chapter 2:

The Evolution of the Concept of Behaviorology

Before concrete actions were taken to launch a newly organized discipline, the concept of that discipline had to be shaped to maturity in the verbal repertoires of many people. This chapter, Chapter Two of this account of the emergence of behaviorology, examines the nature and origins of the behaviorology concept worldwide—and its increasing ill fit within organized psychology where the incipient stages of its organizational coalescence occurred.

Behaviorology, broadly construed, is a comprehensive discipline including philosophical, analytical, experimental, and technological components. "Behaviorology" in a more limited context denotes *the science featured within that discipline*—a natural, life science of functional relations yielding change in the behavior of individuals, with emphasis on the causal mechanism of selection. Behaviorology takes into account determinants from the environment, both socio–cultural and physical, as well as determinants from the biological history of the species. While many behaviorologists focus on human behavior, the science is relevant to the behavior of all organisms. From such components, comprehensive definitions of behaviorology arose after its formal organization in the late 1980s. (For example, see Ledoux, 1997a, for two versions of a comprehensive definition.) These defining components of behaviorology owe their cogency to the evolution of the *concept* of behaviorology. The first section of this chapter qualifies the nature of some of these defining components.

The Concept of Behaviorology

Behaviorologists have provided natural science answers to perplexing questions that have endured since antiquity: Why do people do what they do? What, exactly, *is* behavior? What is sentience? What are such things as *knowing, feeling,* and a *sense of importance*? What are the causes of behavior? How can knowing those causes help us to do more, act better, and behave effectively in all facets of life (for example, in child care, health care, education, daily living, work, leisure, art, entertainment, academic pursuits, and even science itself)? Can accurate descriptions of behavioral processes lead to practical behavioral technologies, especially ones conducive to cultural survival? To such questions behaviorology provides a kind of answer that is satisfying to scientists and professionals as well as engineers because it enables effective action.

Behaviorology emerged in the last quarter of the twentieth century from other disciplines through which its origins can be traced. This account compares and contrasts behaviorology with its disciplinary predecessors—explaining how it differs and why its people departed from those organized disciplines. It describes how the founders justified the existence of a separate discipline apart from others also focused, in their own ways, on behavior. E.A. Vargas (1988) wrote:

> ...our discipline is simply the verbal community that results from a scientific effort pursued in common. No [other] science covers the same subject mat-

> ter, though many of the efforts of other science communities overlap with ours. (p. 2)

Different basic disciplines begin with different basic assumptions, ask different questions, and generate different methods and technologies. To a substantial degree behaviorologists do not use the same methods nor measure the same things as do practitioners based either in other disciplines or in applied fields informed by those disciplines—even those that are behavior-related. Nor do behaviorologists share the same philosophies of science and analytical paradigms prevailing in most of those disciplines.

On the Nature of the Disunity

The natural science *discipline* of behaviorology and the behaviorology *movement* are different concepts. The *emergence* of an independently organized verbal community of behaviorology was an early product of an independence movement. That movement, while acknowledging the shared, early history with psychology (Ledoux, 1997a), took this scientific discipline from under the organizational umbrella of psychology where behaviorological science and philosophy could not be made to fit. The behaviorology movement resolved an issue of intellectual property rights.

A study of any separatist movement logically begins with the question of why people would have borne the substantial costs of the undertaking. Two domains of variables suggest themselves: (a) the aversive reactions to one another among proximal groups as their differences become extreme, and (b) the contrasting natures and implications of their respective paradigms. The former domain is predictable and can be expected to emerge in whatever forms circumstances facilitate. Early behaviorologists, most of whom were formally affiliated in some way with psychology, represented a tiny minority there. Limited in their capacities for countercontrol as is typical with minorities, they faced pervasive difficulties from which they could escape only by taking their discipline elsewhere. But reiterations of specific wrongs done to individuals as revealed in examination of the former domain, although necessary to make the point and while perhaps therapeutic for those individuals, are less important than examining the latter domain, the *nature* of the disciplinary differences and the implications of those differences for the culture. That is where secessionists seek and find more fundamental and broadly relevant justifications. This work now turns to those issues.

The Early History of Behaviorology

The discipline *now* called behaviorology traces back over three quarters of a century before this writing, having evolved continuously at least over that period. Moments such as its formal organization and naming are simply steps in that longer history. Tracing the branch that became behaviorology takes us back in time along limbs, and down an historical trunk, through periods shared with other contemporary movements.

Those shared evolutionary paths are pieces of the history of each discipline involved. Many observers of that history mark Watson's conception of behaviorism, in the early 1900s, as a starting point for behaviorology (Watson, 1913; also see Drash & Freeman, 1973, for a detailed historical account). While Thorndike's (1911) emphasis on the consequences of behavior and Watson's emphasis on behavior as the proper subject matter for a science of behavior both preceded B.F. Skinner's research, other observers, including the authors, mark the beginning of behaviorology with Skinner's early experimental work and the publication of his book *The Behavior of Organisms* in 1938.

The focus on behavior by both Thorndike and Watson represented one evolutionary trend in traditional psychology—a minority movement that focused more on behavior itself as the phenomenon of primary concern though still approached with many traditional psychological assumptions and perspectives. But behavior remained a minority interest in traditional psychology. Later, when B.F. Skinner came on the psychology scene in the early 1930s, many saw his work as a continuation of that minority interest based in psychology. But Skinner, as we will review in more detail, had been trained primarily in biology–based natural science. When historical accidents pertaining to early training opportunities diverted Skinner into organized psychology, he came not only as a natural scientist (and stayed that way) but also with a repertoire of scientific principles derived from biology, some of which had been neglected in psychology and, Skinner's efforts notwithstanding, would remain largely unappreciated there.

The history of behaviorology tracks only temporarily through the historical turf of psychology—an historical thread inserted from the natural sciences, especially biology, into the psychology domain by way of Skinner (and the accident of his being in psychology)—and subsequently departing psychology by way of the newly organized and independent behaviorology discipline (for example, see E.A. Vargas, 1993).

Skinner's conceptual contrast with traditional psychology, first saliently posited in *The Behavior of Organisms,* relied strongly on the causal mode of selection in analyzing the production of behavior, and set forth the radical behaviorist perspective. (Selection, which addresses the postcedent effects of behavior and thus focuses analyses on its consequences, differs from the more purely methodological behaviorism of the early behaviorists who pursued studies of behavior in the stimulus–response [S–R] mechanical causal mode). Skinner extended the selectionist causal mode from biological phenomena to behavioral events. That selectionist causal mode, along with the radical behaviorist natural science philosophy, differentiated behaviorology, the science of behavior relations, from other approaches to behavior. (For an introduction to the philosophy of radical behaviorism, see Ledoux, 1997b.)

Skinner wrote *The Behavior of Organisms* long before his ultimate ambivalence about considering himself to be any kind of psychologist. Yet in it he noted that his extensive experimental work had contributed little to reducing psychology to physiology, a trend in some approaches to studying behavior to which he explicitly objected. He recognized very early that, while he had adapted biology–based selectionist concepts to behavior, the analysis of behavior that that adaptation afforded represented its own unique level of analysis—a discipline of its own apart from both biology and psychology. Skinner stated (1938) that:

> ...there are two independent subject matters (behavior and the nervous system) which must have their own techniques and methods and yield their own respective data....
>
> I am asserting, then, not only that a science of behavior is independent of neurology, but that it must be established as a separate discipline... (p. 423)

As behaviorologists now construe the origins of the discipline, scientific problems to be solved and subject matter issues to be addressed came from pre–1930 psychology. But the philosophy of modern behaviorological science stemmed from the natural sciences. And biology, in particular, supplied the essential selectionist causal modalities that behaviorological scientists adopted for application to the new level of analysis required for the study of behavior.

The philosophical and scientific foundations of behaviorology were well established by the time Skinner published *Science and Human Behavior* (1953). That book detailed the discoveries of the science up to that time, delineated its philosophy of science, and extrapolated its applications to broad sectors of the culture. Of *Science and Human Behavior* Skinner wrote, "It is still, I think, the best introduction to my position" (letter to Ledoux, 14 April 1987). But through all of those years two things had been missing—a discrete disciplinary identity for the separate discipline to which Skinner referred and an appropriate name to connote emphatically its independent status.

Skinner's Philosophy of Science and the Behaviorology Movement

The philosophical foundation that informs behaviorological science is the philosophy of science that Skinner called radical behaviorism. This philosophy is also at the core of the movement that brought forth the organized behaviorology discipline. Four of the components of radical behaviorism were especially important in the emergence of behaviorology (and receive due attention in relevant contexts in this work). These four are: (a) Radical behaviorists respect behavior as a *natural* phenomenon as part of respecting, along with all other natural scientists, the continuities of events in space and time which, in natural sciences, accumulate as a researchable natural history. (b) Radical behaviorists emphasize experimental control over behavioral variables and the application of that control in culturally beneficial ways. (c) Radical behaviorists recognize private events, such as thinking or emotions, as covert behaviors involved in the same laws discovered to involve overt behavior. (d) Radical behaviorists acknowledge that scientists are also behaving organisms whose behavior, scientific or not, is affected by the same variables that affect other behavior, and that those variables include scientists' philosophy of science (see Hake, 1982; Ledoux, 1997b; also see Skinner, 1953 or 1974, or Chiesa, 1994, for more thorough treatment).

Radical Behaviorism plus the Causal Mode of Selection

Long before the behaviorology movement became organized (and even afterward) ambivalence about disciplinary identity plagued many of those who operated under Skinner's radical behaviorism. That philosophy, together with its experimental analysis of behavior and the resultant practical technologies, connotes a comprehensive natural scientific discipline that some have thought more aligned with biology than with any previously established discipline (Ator, 1986; Logue, 1988; Michael, 1985; Skinner, 1953, 1974). Skinner was the first to describe many of the basic principles of behaviorological science. However, although earning his doctorate through the psychology department at Harvard University, he conducted much of his pre–graduation work under W.J. Crozier, head of the physiology branch of Harvard's biology department (Skinner, 1979, p. 16). Crozier had been a student of biologist Jacques Loeb, and both Crozier and Loeb emphasized studying the behavior of an organism as a whole as well as the causal mechanism of natural selection. Skinner, while also emphasizing the behavior of an organism as a whole, transferred the concept of natural selection from genetics to behavior, a context in which *selection* refers to the lasting effects of the consequences of an individual's behavior. Behaviorologists retain that departure and it serves as a *major* point of difference with psychologists. It also puts behaviorology on the life science continuum near biology, although the abstract selectionist concept that they share supports a relation only at the level of analogy—leaving behaviorology as an independent discipline.

Psychologists of the 1930s construed Skinner's adaptation of biological selection to behavior as just another small conceptual step on the broad scientific frontier of psychology. Its implications for a separate discipline passed unnoticed. Among those psychologists, selection represented an unfamiliar and subtle concept not readily incorporated into traditional repertoires. Nor were its implications obvious. Skinner began researching the implications of his conceptual breakthrough and developed a small school of operant behaviorists within psychology. But, increasingly, to understand and appreciate his movement required particular scientific training that only his students were getting. Over time his work impressed the psychology community, which toyed with behaviorism especially in the 1940s, 1950s, and into the 1960s. But the philosophical and scientific divergence was never eliminated or even significantly reduced.

The occasionally reported *dominance* of behaviorism in psychology through the 1940s and 1950s has been disputed by Lovie (1987) who argued that it was an exaggerated propagandistic myth. Furthermore, by the 1950s, many psychologists were beginning to sense the profoundness of the departure of the behavioral movement, especially the operant school, from the original assumptions underlying the psychological paradigm. The shift in psychology during the 1960s toward the information processing and computer simulation models of cognitive psychology was perhaps partly a counter reaction because it preserved a role for the internal agent while probing continued for the mental mechanisms by which that agent affected behavior. Lovie (1987) suggested that cognitive psychologists had, in fact, over–implied the earlier influence of behaviorism to create a straw man over which their so–called "cognitive revolution" could be seen to have triumphed.

As Skinner forged ahead, he pursued a consequence–driven mode of inquiry rather than the theory/method–biased investigations prevailing in psychology (Skinner, 1956). The expanding implications, of what he subsequently discovered to have been his novel adaptation of a *selectionist* paradigm, opened paths to solving fundamental problems traditionally definitive of psychology as a field. Across the widening scientific gulf created by his movement, Skinner's experimental analysis of behavior solved old problems in psychology in ways that ran counter to psychology's dominant internal *transformation* paradigm. Furthermore, in disposing of the mystery in problems that had always intrigued psychologists, the new analytical approach destroyed a kind of allure to which some have always appeared particularly responsive. But Skinner's solutions were resisted and ignored by most psychologists, partly because they were little trained in the science and philosophy upon which Skinner's perspective was based (see Ledoux, 1997c).

E.A. Vargas (1991a) compared the paradigms of disciplines concerned with behavior. He examined and named both the selection paradigm of behaviorology and the transformation paradigm of the other behavior–related disciplines, most notably psychology. E.A. Vargas (1991a) described the transformation paradigm as follows:

> An event occurs, described in any number of ways. The meaning of that event inheres in the action of the organism. The organism perceives, interprets, assesses, integrates, and processes its perceptions and cognitions, and then stores the results of its own actions. It then (or later) engages in a performance with respect to that event—or, rather, the transformed nature of that event. In psychology's paradigm, some aspect of the world incites the organism to take action; but before that action occurs, the organism engages in a series of operations, typically called mental or cognitive, that determines the significance

> of the event and thus determines the nature of the action. In the transformation paradigm, the organism itself, through structures and processes inherent in it, is the agency of its action. (p. 141)

Psychology as a whole has always left open the question of whether the internal cognitive operations and transformations required the guidance of an implicitly metaphysical self, a characteristic of the mentalistic tradition that has always flourished within psychology. Implicit reliance on some kind of an internal agent–manager can be seen in most general psychology–related textbooks (e.g., the currently popular Biehler & Snowman, 1990, p. 389). Skinner's detailed exploration of this issue in Chapter One of *Beyond Freedom and Dignity* (Skinner, 1971) included Karl Popper's illustrative question, posed in the mid 1960s: "What we want is to understand how such nonphysical things as *purposes, deliberations, plans, decisions, theories, tensions,* and *values* can play a part in bringing about physical changes in the physical world" (p. 8). Seeing no physical bases for such events, and with concepts of those events that leave their definitions vague, many psychologists have been content to accept them as non–physical.

In the selection paradigm of behaviorology, behavior is not forced out of the organism by transformed events, nor does an internal creative agent originate or manage such events. The body simply behaves in the natural and functional way determined both by its immediate structural condition and the environmental milieu in which it exists. The body is then altered by the consequences of its behavior so that the changed body that confronts future occasions behaves more in accordance with the implications of those past consequences. The consequences of the past behaviors are said to have *selected* the behaviors that now occur, and the selection paradigm takes its name from that interpretation. But in each instance of behavior, the body is assumed to behave *in the only way that it can behave* under the existing circumstances—an assumption that respects the deterministic natural science philosophy that informs behaviorology. No explanatory appeal is made to a redundant psychological self that would decide or choose the behavior to be exhibited by the body. E.A. Vargas (1991a) continues:

> The essential characteristic of behavior is that it affects its immediate milieu. The results of these effects determine the degree to which that milieu shapes adaptive and maladaptive behavior. Whether the organism eats or runs, for example, is determined by the consequences of its prior actions, or the consequences of prior actions of the biological and cultural communities to which it belongs. What follows behavior selects the future forms it will have and that will be maintained. Changes that occur do so through the "agency" of the particular properties of the environment as these interact with the specific characteristics of the organism operating upon that environment. (p. 142)

The paradigm difference between behaviorology and psychology provided a theoretical and philosophical basis for acknowledging the existence of different, separate and independent disciplines.

Organized psychology resisted the implications of both the selection mechanism and the deterministic natural science philosophy ever since Skinner's scientific departure based upon them. Catania (1987), reviewing Bowler's (1983) *The Eclipse of Darwinism,* suggested a parallel between (a) opposition to selection as a principle of behavior, and (b) opposition to selection as the mechanism of Darwinian evolution. Darwinism in biology survived its opponents. Similarly, having answered the criticisms leveled at earlier forms (Skinner, 1974), and having survived premature claims of its demise, radical behaviorism has survived and continues to expand and evolve, even amidst widespread resistance (see Wyatt, Hawkins, & Davis, 1986, for more detail; see Thyer, 1991, for data; and see Catania, 1991, p. 62, for additional references).

The David Krantz Assessment

The behavioral movement, arising historically in a confluence of intellectual traditions from biology and psychology, enjoyed the innocence of its youth from Watson, through Skinner's *The Behavior of Organisms* (1938), and into the 1940s. During that interval the psychology community debated behaviorism on merit, generally regarded it as interesting, and mostly remained oblivious to many of its implications. When, in the late 1940s, bands of enthusiastic advocates began to develop programmatic emphases around operant behaviorist studies, the contingencies driving the debates began shifting from the scientific to the political (e.g., see Keller, 1986).

The issues around which mentalistic psychologists focused their attacks on the behaviorists, and which seemed safe to debate in public, increasingly dealt not with the scientific evidence but with the nature and quality of organized scientific disciplines. A typical suggestion held that the behavioral movement, in spite of obvious scientific successes and benefits, ultimately portended adverse effects on scientific progress. Questions were raised: How should people who thought themselves in possession of powerful new principles and practices conduct themselves as citizens of the long established disciplinary community in which their careers had developed but in which their work did not fit? How should the remainder of the community behave toward them? Does an emerging philosophical and scientific faction within a field of study help or hinder the ultimate effectiveness of that field?

Within psychology a local eruption of the broader philosophical clash of social science and natural science was occurring, though few protagonists of those times appear to have viewed their squabbles in that way. Calling behaviorology a natural science raises questions about other types of science. Since the coverage of behaviorology includes, even emphasizes, human behavior, is it, for instance, a social science? The answer involves the distinction between natural science and social science. Social sciences not only have an interest in people but also easily reach contradictory conclusions after following the same scientific procedures. This is partly because social sciences allow untestable and metaphysical events to enter their explanatory accounts (also, see Skrtic, 1991). Natural sciences like behaviorology often have an interest in people also. More importantly, however, natural sciences, including behaviorology, more easily reach consistent conclusions after following the same scientific procedures. This is partly because natural sciences disallow the inclusion of untestable or metaphysical events in their explanatory accounts (see Ledoux, 1997a).

A *separate* discipline of behaviorology was not yet in view. The movement was evident within the psychology community only as certain facets of today's more comprehensively defined behaviorology. A manifestation called "operant psychology" had been identified as the salient aspect upon which attention focused. A dichotomy between operant and non–operant psychology was increasingly mentioned in the literature. Perhaps the most influential treatment of that split appeared in 1971 when David Krantz published "The Separate Worlds of Operant and Non–Operant Psychology," a special featured article in the *Journal of Applied Behavior Analysis,* a publication normally devoted to applied experimental work, but which made an exception for that article.

Krantz's treatment was scholarly and sophisticated. Though not thoroughly trained in operant psychology, Krantz had familiarized himself with critical elements of its science and philosophy so that he might address the rift as an informed historian and philosopher of science. His main data base for that article consisted of tape recorded interviews with 35 "key researchers" prominent in "operant" circles, at least a few of whom were critical of the operant movement. Krantz referred to "encapsulated schools of thought," or "movements," occurring *in* established sciences. Thus his perspective subtended a divergence between factions only *within* a discipline; the emergence of a separate discipline entered his considerations only as a somewhat remote implication.

Krantz first documented the extent of the mutual isolation by using data obtained from journals. The paucity of cross–referencing between operant and non–operant journals offered convincing evidence of the increasing differentiation of the operant school from others within psychology. Next addressing the "incommensurability" question, Krantz acknowledged that if operant and non–operant psychologists were really measuring and talking about different things, the mutual failure to cite would be justified. Two disciplines would exist, not one. But Krantz let stand a quoted phrase from one of his interviewees that described this as an "extreme" view. He did, however, elaborate on it descriptively so that readers might better understand the nature of what some operant psychologists argued *was* a fundamental disciplinary difference between operant and cognitive/mentalist views of behavior. Krantz referred to Sidman (1960) for the central point: As Krantz phrased Sidman's view,

> ...between–groups designs *[favored in traditional psychology]* assume that variability is intrinsic to the organism, thus the need for its statistical control; the within–groups design *[favored by the behavioral people]* assumes an imposed variability, thus the need for experimental, not statistical, control. (p. 63)

Underlying this difference is a major philosophical assumption that Krantz did not pursue: The operant people in general have always assumed that behavior is a *natural* phenomenon, and that behavior of any kind therefore occurs only in *total* functional relation with the controlling environmental milieu (including genes). However, among those in the non–operant majority, acceptance of intrinsic variability in many cases meant more than variability stemming merely from natural but unknown events occurring within the behaving organism. The *operant* analytical scheme easily accommodated those cases because, in the operant paradigm, part of the total controlling environment pervades the body. Therefore, independent variables of a valid and functional nature can exist on *either* side of the skin, although many of them—especially those inside the skin—resist accurate detection and analysis, and remain beyond the practical reach of intervention technologies. But for many non–operant researchers, the unexplained variation due to internal causes left operating room not only for thus–far unexplained natural causes but for *non–natural* internal causal events as well. For those scholars the internal variations could still be due to spiritual or mystical entities of non–natural origin (e.g., see Scoresby & Price, 1991). The way remained open for intervention by deities, spiritual selves, or similar non–natural entities, a belief in which is strongly shaped by various traditional cultural agencies. Unexplained internal variation also preserved the domain of mystery important to some scholars whose reinforcers are attached to an unending pursuit of the unattainable (one of academia's most venerated facades from behind which misdirected scholars have attacked the views of others as well as protected their own through the ages).

Krantz (1971) pursued the question of whether the operant/non–operant division represented a true disciplinary divergence or merely differences in procedures, terminology, and concepts inhering in the pursuit of investigations that could, and perhaps should, be conducted more in common. Could the differences between the factions be products of their isolation, or are those differences the fundamental reasons for the isolation in the first place? The *majority* of the operant researchers interviewed by Krantz made clear that they preferred the latter interpretation as well as the benefits of continued exclusiveness. They saw little reason to modify the direction and nature of their work to mesh more closely with traditional psychology.

Then, in a section on "conceptual imperialism" (a phrase which Krantz credited to Don Baer), Krantz (1971, pp. 66–67) described the confident attitude exhibited by many operant psychologists who insisted "the operant strategy can deal successfully not only with its own domain of problems but handle, as well, if not better, many diverse issues in psychology" (p. 66). Krantz described as "brusque" those operant researchers who, in providing what they deemed better approaches, did not cite or give much credit to the more traditional strategies that the putatively more effective science and technology was displacing. Krantz chided such "imperialists" for their failure to accommodate, and assimilate with, the traditionalists whom he assumed *had to be persuaded.* This was in spite of the fact that, in the history of most fields including psychology, as a matter of economy, disciplinary traditionalists have often been circumvented and left behind rather than confronted and changed. To the behavioral researchers who thought it pointless to cite or dwell upon ineffective approaches when in possession of a more powerful one, Krantz (1971) wrote:

> To maintain militantly such a position is to make the philosophically naive and inter–personally insensitive assumption that one can change the science without the consent of the scientists. To act in contradiction to this truism, that scientific ideas are produced, evaluated, and changed by scientists, is to invite conflict, lack of success and very likely, rejection and other's isolation of the imperialist's position. (p. 66)

But science is *supposed* to change in response to demonstrations of greater effectiveness. So perhaps Krantz here alluded to additional non–scientific controls on the behavior of scientists. Most such controls remain unaffected by improvements in science. They also retard the change that those improvements should produce. Also, the implicit consensus of the behavioral subcommunity was that Krantz was wrong: Science, if not scientists, *could* be changed without the consent of the scientists. It would simply be done by *other* scientists. Insofar as science is merely behavior in the first place, to change it is only to start behaving differently; the operant behaviorists had already been doing that for some time. They did not see progress in their own scientific discipline as requiring the persuasion of those in another discipline—especially a discipline with a paradigm so antithetical to their own. And they thought that their neglect of that questionable task should not be charged against them as a breach of propriety.

To exemplify the kind of attacks that the offended traditionalists might mount, Krantz referred in detail to Wendt's (1949) criticism of the pure operant program developed by Fred Keller (Keller & Schoenfeld, 1949) at Columbia University. Wendt had argued that although the Columbia program successfully attracted students from engineering and other natural sciences and was enthusiastically received by students, the program was academically unhealthy because its rejection of eclecticism promoted a "behavioral cult," a kind of isolationist movement that no good academic discipline can afford. Obviously, Wendt did not view those events as the loyalty and enthusiasm that students in most natural sciences give their disciplines. He ignored the effectiveness of the behavioral science taught in the program as the basis of its success. Instead Wendt attributed the popularity of the Columbia program to a supposedly *propagandistic* tactic of introducing implicitly invalid simplification into what was justifiable confusion. He implied that an allegedly more balanced, long term search for truth would eventually reveal the purported inadequacies in any such narrow approach that a small enthusiastic band might develop and impose on an institution. (Keller, 1986, reported that he "ignored Professor Wendt's assault," [p. 144] and that, upon reflection, so had Skinner. See Ledoux, 1997a, on the role of eclecticism in these debates.)

Krantz also quoted an anonymous critic of the behavioral isolationists who spoke of the operant psychologists' "self–maintenance of true conceptual imperialism, at the expense of actually succeeding in practical imperialism or conceptual assimilation by others." Again, neither Krantz, Wendt, nor the anonymous critic construed that a separate discipline was gaining prominence. Thus they did not consider applicable the principle that scholars of one discipline need not expend themselves, to the detriment of their contributions, by trying to win over, or to resolve their differences with, scholars of another. The unnamed critic was also wrong. The operant people *were* succeeding at the practical level. They tacted (Skinner, 1957, Ch. 5) carefully, having acquired that skill through its important consequences. They strived for accurate descriptions of relevant behavioral and environmental events. The resulting scientific principles reliably related environmental and behavioral events—yielding in the process the power of prediction. When subsequently they altered independent variables to produce prescribed behavioral outcomes (i.e., control), they were so effective that a new discipline, though not inferred by many, was nevertheless implied. The operant people had done nothing less than discover the conceptual key or approach to practical behavior technology, and they were beginning to appreciate the vast enabling power inhering in that discovery.

Krantz (1971) was apparently unprepared to describe effectively the concept and function of scientific (event–shaped) verbal communities. But he appeared alert to some implications of isolating both verbal and nonverbal event–shaped communities when he provided the following cognitive approximation:

> Graduate education can be viewed as the main socializing force in communicating the norms of being a scientist and in training for particular orientations and strategies within a scientific field. ...the learning of a scientific approach occurs not only through a verbalizable, didactic strategy but also through ostension via relevant "doing." Such resultant knowledge is tacit, implicit, and not immediately accessible to awareness. The failure to teach other systematic options, or the consistent devaluation of other approaches, coupled with ostension experience in only one systematic option, can lead to a non–critical acquisition of a scientific approach and perpetuation of a modeled style of conceptual and practical imperialism in evaluating others' research strategies. (p. 67)

Krantz did not appear equally bothered by a *cognitive* imperialism. He ended his discussion of "imperialism" by suggesting that behaviorists either can be "rude" and aggressive or can opt for a "softer sell" aimed both at converting cognitivists to the behavioral view and at assimilating the two schools, again as if that were necessary. He said nothing about whether time exists for the slow progress characteristic of the latter approach. Nor did he appear to take seriously that criteria for separate disciplines were relevant in this case, though his article did mention these criteria.

In his discussion section Krantz said some typically erroneous things about the operant position: He spoke of establishing validity on the basis of correctness of prediction, but it is to the more rigorous level of *control*, not merely prediction, that radical behaviorists carry that test. He stated, from a modest analytical perspective, that inferences or statements about consciousness are not valuable to operant people in a science of psychology. But that idea was entertained only by the methodological behaviorists. Even before Krantz wrote his article, the radical behaviorists, operating at a more complex level of analysis, had already developed a useful science of private (singly observed) events including those behaviors of the kind known as "consciousness" or "awareness" (e.g., see Skinner, 1953, Ch. 17; 1957; also, see Ledoux, 1973).

Nevertheless, Krantz's basic conclusions, though endowed with shortcomings for other reasons, were little damaged by such inaccuracies. He reiterated his warnings about allowing truth to be defined by fiat as one school politically displaces another. Ironically, much of what he seemed to fear along those lines has occurred because of a suppression of the behavioral minority, that is, because of a cognitive imperialism, not a behavioral one. Krantz did not, however, explicitly reject the argument that "operant psychology" represented "revolutionary" differences yielding "incommensurability" between the conflicting systems. At one point he referred to the settlement of that fundamental issue as "unclear." Many readers, however, reacting to the overall tone and style of Krantz's article, inferred that the rift might *not* be justified on the basis of incommensurability. As Coleman and Mehlman (1992) noted:

> ...Krantz's investigation—and the widely held interpretation of its findings, to the effect EAB [Experimental Analysis of Behavior] is in an unhealthy state—came out of an historically situated 'ideology' regarding scientific progress in general and the progress of psychology in particular. (p. 48)

Coleman and Mehlman (1992, p. 48) attributed that ideology, and its influence on Krantz, mainly to the reports published in the 1960s by the American Psychological Association's *Project on Scientific Information Exchange in Psychology.*

The Krantz article was well reasoned and rather sophisticated in the development of its arguments (though not without its own propagandistic slant). As an exceptionally featured piece in a highly respected journal, it undoubtedly had a moderating effect on the operant separatist movement within psychology. Krantz's article exerted pressure on operant psychologists to move back toward the path of reconciliation and gentle persuasion, a path which, in the view of behaviorologists, has since proven costly to the integrity of the science as well as strategically ineffective. Unfortunately, at a practical level, for many behaviorists that togetherness amounted to little more than compromising their philosophical probity. They found themselves continually acquiescing and maintaining pretenses that eclecticism connotes respect for some academic procedural ideal instead of merely lack of resolution on the question of how best, scientifically, to proceed (see Ledoux, 1997a).

Krantz's (1971) article appeared in the middle of the eight years of discussions that ultimately led to the founding of the Midwestern Association of Behavior Analysis (MABA, later known as the Association for Behavior Analysis [ABA]). The extended time required to establish an independent MABA, and the very gradual recognition of the significance of the revolution represented by that movement, may both be due in part to

Krantz's article. Even as this is written, in 1991, 20 years after Krantz's article, some who might otherwise join readily with the behaviorology movement, linger hesitantly and plead for yet another inquiry into Krantzian wisdom on the merits of togetherness as opposed to separation.

Like many who reviewed the rift, Krantz implicitly framed his research question to test the hypothesis that the "operant movement" represented just one of any number of "sciences" or "perspectives" in an eclectic social science mix denoted by the psychology label. But increasingly, the followers of Skinner's movement were reacting to the rift as if it were fundamentally of a more simple *dualistic* nature: On one side was natural science, represented in this instance by themselves, and featuring a predominantly selectionist mode of causality. On the other side was social science, represented by traditional psychology, and featuring a theory–based paradigm, laced with metaphysically inspired assumptions and dwelling on presumed transformations of experience into behavior by way of cognitive mental mediations.

Krantz (1971) both described and contributed to the attitudes prevailing during a critical period of discontent that preceded the formal emergence of behaviorology. His assessments have been reviewed here because, as an influential and respected analyst of science history, Krantz seemed to lend scientific validation to then–prevailing biases and arguments favoring abandonment of the "behavioral" revolution.

Recent History: Disciplinary Identity, Name, and Support

In the 1970s radical behaviorists in psychology established a professional organization (discussed later in detail) outside of the American Psychological Association (APA). It became the Association for Behavior Analysis (ABA). It evolved, however, more as a scientific and professional interest group than as the anchor point for an independent discipline. Most ABA members who began as psychologists continued to give themselves that disciplinary identification. By also calling themselves "behavior analysts" they implicitly classified behavior analysts as psychologists. Since the 1980s, with the emergence of an independent behaviorology discipline, some behavior analysts, anxious to preserve organizational ties with a well–entrenched and endowed organized psychology, have grown more explicit, as will be seen, in proclaiming behavior analysis to be a kind of psychology.

ABA has continued to focus, not on establishing an independently organized discipline, but on how most effectively to endow psychology with a more worthwhile science. Along these lines the ABA leadership has remained consistently critical of the science pursued in mainline psychology. For instance, Philip Hineline, who would later serve as president of ABA, noted that psychology is pursued with verbal repertoires based on often inconsistent terminology adopted with few restrictions from everyday language (Hineline, 1984). In his 1990 ABA presidential address, and again in a later article (Hineline, 1991), he thematically reiterated that view and counseled renewed efforts to change psychology. But by then the behaviorologists had abandoned that strategy and organized an independent discipline.

The separation debate. The years between 1984 and 1987 were a time of extensive debate about disciplinary status as numerous authors discussed, pro and con, the disciplinary separation from psychology of what is now called behaviorology (see Ator, 1986; Barry, 1986; Comunidad Los Horcones, 1986; Deitz, 1986; Epstein, 1984, 1985,

1987a, 1987b; Fraley, 1987; Fraley & Vargas, 1986; Gaydos, 1986; Lee, 1987a; Leigland, 1985; Malagodi & Branch, 1985; Staats, 1986; and E.A. Vargas, 1987).

Epstein (1984) began this debate with a proposal for a new discipline under the name "praxics." Leigland (1985) and Malagodi and Branch (1985) disagreed both with some of Epstein's arguments (though not with the possibility of separation) and with his proposed name; Epstein (1985) rejoined. Fraley and Vargas (1986) summarized the issues, disagreed with Epstein's disregard for the philosophy of the science, and spoke for separation under the name "behaviorology." Barry (1986) subsequently objected to both "praxics" and "behaviorology," preferring "anthroponomy," a name proposed much earlier by Hunter (1925). Gaydos (1986) objected only to the name "praxics." Comunidad Los Horcones (1986) supported "behaviorology."

Staats (1986) objected to separation from psychology, arguing instead for unification under a philosophy called *paradigmatic behaviorism* which "characterizes psychology as a disunified science" (p. 232) and which tolerates that disunity. Many contemporary psychologists welcomed such attempts to make a virtue of the paradigmatic differences within psychology (e.g., Hishinuma, 1989). The troublesome problem of how incompatible philosophies and sciences can all represent a single discipline was made to vanish by redefining "discipline."

Catania (1973) had earlier taken a different approach. He insisted "psychology is not in the midst of a paradigm clash" because points of contact cannot be found. By that he meant that the "different schools of psychology, ...have been concerned with different problems" (p. 442). But if they *did* ask different questions, in what way were they different? Was it merely interest in different aspects of the complex problems being addressed by psychologists (subject matter differences), or would the different schools not find each other's questions valid because those questions arose out of analytical paradigms too different to garner respect across those schools? Or, to cast the issue in another light, if those schools were to trade problems for awhile, would the paradigmatic treatments of those problems remain unchanged? That is, did cognitive and behavioral psychologies represent only *problem*–imposed differences in work informed by a *common* paradigm? Or, in contrast, are different kinds of problems, arising out of different subject matters, addressed with fundamentally *different* paradigmatic approaches? If so, different disciplines are implied. In the prevailing view among behaviorologists, when common problems had been addressed by the different schools in psychology, real Kuhnian paradigm clashes (Kuhn, 1970) did appear. Those differences manifested in very different technological implications. A typical example was described in the article "Cognitive Analysis of Language and Verbal Behavior: Two Separate Fields" (J. Vargas, 1990).

Epstein returned to the debate with an appeal targeted mainly to students (1987a). He argued again for the emergence of *"an independent, multi–disciplinary, biologically–based science of behavior."* He criticized the fragmentation of behavior–related studies across a broad spectrum of separate disciplines and called for their unification:

> A true science of behavior must be *multi–disciplinary,* ...because behavior is a complex subject matter that requires the *joint efforts* of individuals in many specialities, both to advance our understanding and to devise effective treatments. Behavior is affected profoundly by nutrition, physiology, sleep deprivation, ...sexual deprivation and trauma, chemical interventions, social phenomena, surgical interventions, physical trauma, anatomical variables, or-

> ganic disease, hormonal cycles, air temperature, humidity, illumination, airborne chemicals, radiation, electrical stimulation, genes—and, of course, learning history. It is not folly to think that individuals with different specialities can be brought together to build a new science; it is folly to think that a handful of scientists who now study behavior in almost complete isolation from each other in a dozen different disciplines can advance our understanding significantly. (p. 128).

Epstein reminded us that no comprehensive behavioral science can afford to treat the behaving body as a constant while focusing exclusively on contingencies of reinforcement. And behaviorologists, while emphasizing the importance of contingency relations, do respect a far broader range of concerns and principles than those implicit in an overly simplistic understanding of the phrase "contingencies of reinforcement," as did Skinner.

But Epstein continued to insist that the work of a collection of scientists with diverse behavior-related specialties can be coordinated under control of natural contingencies without their sharing a common supplementary verbal repertoire of the kind known as a philosophy of science. He envisioned praxics as a "pure science, driving real and promised applications, and uncluttered by an irrelevant and unattractive credo..." (p. 128). (Also see Epstein, 1987b.) Behaviorologists, among others, disagreed with Epstein. One's philosophy of science *does* share in the control of one's scientific responses to data—a general principle recognized far beyond the bounds of behaviorology (e.g., see Hake, 1982). And, importantly, people doing scientific work inevitably bring *some* philosophy to that work. That philosophy shares in controlling the person's behavior regardless of the intensity of the *natural* consequences of the work upon which Epstein seemed to be counting for a rather exclusive control.

For other authors, the issue of an independent and comprehensive scientific discipline of behavior arises implicitly and without expressed concern about its name or organizational status. For instance, Lee (1987b) stated that:

> ...behavior analysis is outside the mainstream of psychology, and its foundation in assumptions that depart markedly from those of the mainstream let most psychologists ignore it with impunity. (p. 145)

But on another occasion, and apparently concerned about reversals in progress toward a distinct identity, Lee (1987a) asked in a published book review if we should "expect a commitment to radical behaviorism in a book on behavior analysis" (p. 95), observing that:

> ...the less-than-full commitment of many of us is apparent in the conceptual poverty of applied behavior analysis, in the infiltration of cognitive terminology, in the re-appearance of traditional group designs, and in the reduced interest in behavioral control techniques, among other things. (p. 95)

Fraley (1987) described the difficulties with unification, the reasons for separation, and the cultural mission of the independent discipline of behaviorology, especially as it affects many other fields that deal with human behavior. Concurrently, E.A. Vargas (1987) linked the survival of effective behavioral science to disciplinary independence. He argued that departure from psychology can be supported not only on the basis of differing subject matters, but also on the basis of the sociological considerations relevant in the development and governing of professional disciplines. Vargas noted that psychologists whose actions suppress behaviorology within organized psychology act rationally in defense of their own self–interests.

Then, on 17 October 1987 in a general session for all in attendance, the annual meeting of the Southeastern Association for Behavior Analysis concluded with a formal debate chaired by Fred Keller. Lawrence Fraley and Ernest Vargas (pro) debated Mark Branch and Peter Harzem (con) on the establishment of behaviorology as a separate discipline. (The debated issues are addressed throughout this paper.)

Debate, however, was rapidly being rendered moot by independent actions establishing behaviorology as a comprehensive natural science of the behavior of organisms. In the name of behaviorology, its adherents were pursuing applications to, and interpretations of, a broad range of human affairs (Barry, 1986; Fraley & Vargas, 1986). For example, in May 1988 Guy Steven Bruce produced the first master's thesis to reflect its behaviorological content in its title (NTSU, 1988), "Problem Solving: A Behaviorological Analysis with Implications for Instruction." His thesis committee at North Texas State University, chaired by Sigrid Glenn, included Ernest Vargas, of West Virginia University, under whom Bruce subsequently earned his doctorate.

Debate continues anyway. Some behaviorists who were opting to remain within organized psychology continued publicly to draw distinctions between mainline psychology and the behavioral science and philosophy that they believed should supplant it. These distinctions paralleled the points raised by behaviorologists. The presidential address of Steven Hayes (1988a) to the behaviorally oriented Division 25 of the APA, is one example. The distinctions to which Hayes and others pointed were often the same ones to which behaviorologists were pointing. Philosophically and scientifically, the discipline advocated by Hayes and others is fundamentally different from mainline psychology. The residual issue pertained only to how best to act upon this difference.

Burns (1988) reiterated Staats's attempt to link together the verbal subcommunities within psychology by ascribing to each its own level of analysis (i.e., its own approach to theory construction) and arranging them hierarchically from "basic" to "less basic." The whole assemblage is then said to be the unified "discipline" of psychology. Jerome Ulman (1990a) rejected that concept, referring to it as "hierarchically schematicized eclecticism." Burns also accused radical behaviorists of "rejectionism" which, he argued, "does not foster harmony" within psychology. On the latter point, Burns was correct. Behaviorologists saw no long–range cultural benefit from elaborate reinterpretations intended to make psychology seem like a coherent discipline. Nor were behaviorologists, as natural scientists, sanguine about the political, social, and economic negotiations that inevitably replace scientific persuasion in academic alliances that, scientifically, are too disparate to bind in that way. Harmony in psychology was simply not the goal of the behaviorologists.

Psychology, in the broadest concept, had not evolved as a single discipline. Even authors of articles in publications sponsored by the APA had occasionally reiterated this point. For example, Nessel (1982), in an article on the state of psychology, had referred to "the *various disciplines* of psychology" (emphasis added). The disunity of psychology was also evident in the other competing and often mutually contradictory perspectives that long comprised the area—others besides the behaviorological/psychological rift. Evidence for this could be seen in Nessel's article (1982). The majority of psychologists had long agreed on a broadly encompassing paradigm respecting internal transformations as the essence of behavior. Yet, as Nessel's article revealed, in spite of that paradigmatic commonality, eleven distinguished psychologists showed little agreement in their perceptions even about the most important developments in psychology over the preceding fifteen years.

In her book *Beyond Behaviorism* (1988), Vicki Lee presented a comprehensive analysis of both the recent and historical differences characterizing the disciplinary fragmentation in psychology. Lee's book offers a compelling argument for psychologists to "make over" their field by bringing themselves less under control of economic and political contingencies and more under control of scientific ones. But over the decades attempts to do that have fallen short. Organized psychology does not seem amenable to overhaul merely by demonstrations of better science. The frustration of those who have proffered a more effective science only to have it ignored as if irrelevant can be seen in Lee's (Lee, 1989) quote of Murray Sidman (1986b, p. 44), that:

> ...the reluctance of some psychologists to use the body of knowledge that has accumulated in behavior analysis suggests 'a kind of scientific malpractice.' (p. 86)

In September 1990 Lee herself would send an open letter to her behavioral colleagues worldwide describing and lamenting the scientific isolation she experiences as a behaviorist within her Australian psychology verbal community:

> I have given up talking about radical behaviorism and behavior analysis unless "invited" to do so in a conversation with an interested listener. It is simply hopeless to do so otherwise. Even if the misconceptions can be cut through in the presence of an audience, ...there is the impossibility of getting over the hurdle that requires the listener to see the insanity of much that passes as psychological research and theory.

The name. The *science and philosophy* of behaviorology can be traced at least to the early decades of the twentieth century along certain historical paths, and even further back to early recognition in biology of the selection mechanism. But the *name* "behaviorology" followed different historical routes from multiple origins. A December 1986 computer database search for references to behaviorology (or behaviourology, the British spelling) revealed only two references. But that search, of Dialindex's Biosci and Socsci databases, proved not to be exhaustive for it did not reveal some known cross–references to, or uses of, the term.

The earliest discovered author using the name behaviorology *consistent with the present usage* was Makram Samaan (1973). Samaan's description of behaviorology focused on the behavior modification technologies of the 1970s and did not dwell on radical behaviorist philosophy. Others had used the term before him, though differently. In a one paragraph article, Vitulli (1969) suggested changing the name of psychology to behaviorology because people rely more on behavior than on the psyche. Even *Time* magazine, he noted, had begun a "Behavior" section in 1969. But Vitulli's usage implied no change in mainstream psychology other than its name, and nothing came of his suggestion.

On the other hand, Samaan's (1973) opening statement, from his university–published book (English was not his native language) advocated a more sweeping change:

> With the discovery of the functional relations of human behavior and its contingencies, and the successful technology of behavior for effecting behavior change, a call for the independence of behaviorology from psychology which was conceived as a study of the "self," "mind," and "soul," is in order....

> It is time now for the scientific analysis of behavior to call for its own scientific discipline. It is contradictory to its function, objective, methods and content to stay within the realm of psychology. The discipline of "Psychology" is originally derived from the Greek term "psyche," which means "soul," "mind," or "self." ...psychology was conceived as the science of the soul, mind, or self. ...behavior was assumed a function of the "mind," the "psyche," or the "self." (p. 5)

Samaan noted that in 75 years of searching, psychologists had not found the autonomous behavior–controlling mind. But scientists of the kind who were to become behaviorologists *had* discovered the basic controlling relations between environment and organism that account for behavior. Samaan continues:

> It is a contradiction to carry a name of a so–called science of inner process, souls, and minds for a discipline of operationally defined behavior. ...independence of Behaviorology is a necessary and significant step to abolish the confusion of incongruence between the name of the discipline and its methodology and subject matter. (pp. 5–6)

Samaan is historically important for his early explicit call for an independent discipline of behaviorology. However, he contrasted behaviorology with only one concept of psychology, which might be classified as non–natural science wherein mind is viewed as the locus of a behavior–controlling ethereal essence.

In the years since Samaan, others, acting independently, coined or adopted the name behaviorology to tact the same discipline, although with radical behaviorist philosophy more clearly included. In 1974, cultural engineers within the Los Horcones Community in Mexico coined the name behaviorology. They defined it as "the natural science that studies the behavior of organisms" (Comunidad Los Horcones, 1986). To them behaviorology encompassed "basic research, applied research, and a philosophy" (p. 227). While teaching in Australia, Stephen Ledoux (1977) coined and similarly used the term to describe the position of radical behaviorists who would separate from mainstream psychology. Like others, he was unaware of Samaan. After Joseph Morrow, at California State University, Sacramento, mentioned Samaan's work (letter to Ledoux, August 1977), Samaan was discovered to have been writing his 1973 book in a different department at that same university where Ledoux was then studying. Although Ledoux had commented in his paper that his usage would likely be unrelated to any previous appearances of the term, Samaan and others were later discovered to have used the term in much the same way.

Communications with colleague and library searches revealed two examples of the use of "behaviorology" by mainline psychologists. Dr. A. Ph. Paschalis, a behaviorally oriented counseling psychologist in Greece, reported to Jerome Ulman (letter to Ulman, 6 July 1989) that cognitivists and social learning theorists in Greece had used that name "a number of years back" to distance themselves from those reflecting a radical behavioristic approach to which these theorists were opposed. However, such counter–use of the name did not spread among members of the world–wide cognitive verbal community. Much earlier, David Sherbowsky, in his apparently self–published book *An Outline of Behaviorology—The Psychology* (Sherbowsky, 1935) used "behaviorology" as the name for what he viewed as his correction of Watson's behaviorism. Preferring to call Watson's behaviorism "Watsonism," he stated "Behaviorology is not Behaviorism (Watsonism)" (p. 3). This usage also did not spread.

After E.A. Vargas's coining of the term anew, Fraley and Vargas (1986) gave their reasons why behaviorology should be the name of a discipline (including its experimental, applied, and philosophical aspects) that would be independent of other behavior–related disciplines. Comunidad Los Horcones (1986), based on their own longer history with the name, endorsed the attendant philosophy and offered this support:

> First, [the name behaviorology] is etymologically appropriate. The word "behaviorology" is a combination of the English word "behavior" and the Greek word "logos."
>
> Second, "behaviorology" does not eliminate the experimental analysis of behavior, applied behavior analysis, or behaviorism. Instead, this new term includes them as sub–fields of the same science. It is an integrative name.
>
> Third, "behaviorology"...does not imply that behavior analysis pertains only to experimental analysis. Once, perhaps, the inclusion of "experimental" in the name of the science was necessary in order to emphasize its empirical basis, but...no longer....
>
> Fourth, by using the term "behaviorology," the length of the name for the science is shortened considerably [from "The Experimental Analysis of Behavior"], which is an obvious advantage when talking and writing. (p. 227)

The repeated coining of the term *behaviorology* to name this discipline presumably occurred because of similarities in the contingencies under which its professionals operated. But some behaviorists remaining within organized psychology were not similarly affected. Lamal (1988) objected that behaviorology is "unfelicitous." Hayes (1988a) also criticized the term, saying "...'Behavior' is too readily viewed as the act separated from the context," adding "this is one reason that the call by some for a field of 'behaviorology' is misguided" (p. 14). But behaviorologists, like other scientists, take for granted that they must study their subject matter in its functional context. On appropriate occasions behaviorologists explain that theirs is the science of behavior *relations*, not behavior in isolation. This distinguishes them from those said by Skinner (1972) to endow behavior with a curious ontological status, to explain it with "appeals to events taking place somewhere else, at some other level of observation, described in different terms, and measured, if at all, in different dimensions" (p. 69).

Different names will serve a movement in different ways, each affording some gain from one perspective while costing with respect to others. Before deciding on a name, it is important to determine precisely which problem the name is to help solve. Followers of a discipline quickly adapt to whatever name is used. But how the general population responds to the name is more important for a discipline that would contribute scientific underpinnings to inform all behavior–related fields. The founders of the behaviorology movement wanted a term that worked in the culture at large. The multiple coinages of "behaviorology" suggested that they had found it.

Such an intuitively obvious name was deemed more important than a less useful though etymologically pure term based on ancient languages. Skinner, during a 1987 ABA symposium, expressed displeasure with the name "behaviorology" for its polyglot etymology featuring English, French, and Greek derivatives. But Skinner's objection to the ancient history of the term seemed irrelevant to many of those who appreciated its appropriate functional control over the behavior of most contemporary listeners, lay as well as professional. At that same symposium, Robert Epstein was also critical of the name "behaviorology." He had earlier, and without documentation, speculated in print that the term had probably been considered and rejected by others half a century ago (1987a, p. 129). But he had not said why such a history, even if documented, should reduce interest in the current usage.

As the behaviorologists pondered the question of whether members of the general public would respond appropriately to the stimulus "behaviorology," historian Daniel Bjork (letter to Fraley, 14 February 1989) offered a historian's perspective: Bjork speculated that many lay people associate "psychology" with "intellectual"—which might imply arrogance or elitism plus an impractical science. Because "behaviorology" has a more practical ring, it sounds more useful, and certainly less mysterious. People might be more comfortable associating with its practitioners. The founders, guessing that that name would tact the activities of behaviorologists without inducing confusion, began informal testing of the term with a variety of people. Confirming reports came trickling back. Most were of this kind: When Ernest Vargas (personal communication, 28 December 1987) responded "I'm a behaviorologist" to his dental hygienist's query about his occupation, she paused very briefly and then said, "Oh, that's different from psychology; you study behavior." Similar responses came from his barber and from his cat's veterinarian. Through many such simple probes, the founders gained confidence in their choice of "behaviorology"—an informal mode of confirmation that has continued with virtually unchanged results.

European support. The behaviorology movement was not exclusively of American origin. Support arose in different parts of the world. European activity was easy to document, and early reports about it bolstered the importance of organizing the movement internationally.

After a conference in West Germany in 1986, Julie S. Vargas reported having encountered a Belgian, Werner Matthijs, who had told her that the Dutch equivalent of "behaviorology" was sometimes used in his country. This suggested the possibility of a European movement toward separate disciplines. Lawrence Fraley accepted the task of directing inquiries to some Europeans who might be involved.

Claus Thiermann of the German Behavior Academy in Stuttgart, West Germany, responded (25 September 1987) that he and his colleagues had started their work in 1976 "on the straight behaviorology line you are favoring." He described the Academy as a private institution existing to "distribute the application of Behavior Analysis and nothing else." He reported that his group had given training to about 500 people in the past ten years; he said about 50 had become recognizable as "behavior analysts."

Thiermann provided a brief history of the movement in Germany: A German translation of Skinner's *Science and Human Behavior* (1953) had appeared in the late 1960s. But the translation had been poor and its philosophy seemed unconventional to continental Europeans. So few read it and even fewer understood it. In 1971 Holland and Skinner's *The Analysis of Behavior* (1961) was published in German. It was easier to read, and a few thousand people apparently did so. According to Thiermann, that book spawned a short-lived German behavior therapy movement in the early 1970s. But he called that movement "superficial"—practiced mainly by persons who did not comprehend the underlying science and philosophy. Thiermann concluded his historical report as follows:

> Behavior therapy soon gained a very bad reputation. Some who did it got punished, and, though reinforced by therapeutic success, had their behavior suppressed and emitted avoidance behavior by developing cognitive behavior

> therapy, following Mahoney. By the end of the 1970s pure and clean behavior modification/behavior therapy was out. A combination of cognitive methods and behavior therapy is fashionable today. Hard core evaluation methods, of course, have no chance under those circumstances. (Thiermann to Fraley, 25 September 1987)

As among Americans, some European behavioral practitioners doubted the efficacy of a separatist movement, preferring instead continued operations within organized psychology. As the European psychologist Marc Richelle wrote (letter to Fraley, 22 October 1987), they feared that "leaving psychology to opposite trends, essentially cognitivism, ...might give them [the cognitivists] an easy victory on an abandoned territory." Richelle reported that he thought he detected a reaction against the most extreme forms of cognitivism, and that he looked forward to a better future for behaviorists in European psychology "within a few years."

Werner Matthijs, the Dutch speaking behaviorist in Belgium, answered a further inquiry with two more letters to Fraley (8 & 29 July 1987) In these he described his own commitment to behaviorology and his efforts to promote a separate discipline.

Matthijs reported that almost all European psychologists were mentalists who regard behavior only as a symptom of important events in the mind. He also mentioned some interest in cognitive behavior modification among European psychologists. But he regarded this trend as a further indulgence in mentalism.

Matthijs described his own antithetical reaction to all of this as follows:

> The more psychological theories about the "psyche" that I had to absorb during my graduate studies, the more carefully I began to read Skinner's work, and the more obstinate and uncompromising I became in my verbal resistance to the full–fledged mentalism to which I was daily exposed. This, in turn, only served to increase the opposition I experienced, even up to the point that one of my professors, whom I had criticized because of his constant misrepresentations of Skinner's views, no longer allowed me to take his courses on psycholinguistics.

The contrast between his own behavior–focused science and the mainstream psychology featured in his formal training led Matthijs to seek a better disciplinary name:

> Finding such a term was especially reinforcing.... The Dutch translation of "behavior" is "gedrag"; *gedragsologie* is a term which in the most direct way refers to the study of "gedrag." "Gedrag–sologie" is thus the Dutch equivalent of behaviorology. For people whose verbal behavior has been shaped by a Dutch speaking verbal community, gedragsologie is easier to pronounce than psychologie (the Dutch term for psychology). For those of us whose verbal behavior has...been shaped by the behaviorological community, the term gedragsologie has not the aversive connotations associated with the term psychology. In fact, reading, hearing, and speaking about gedragsologie is...automatically reinforcing.

Matthijs reported first using the term *gedragsologie* in print when in 1980 he surveyed reactions to that name by colleagues. He said that he found increasing comfort with the term as people used and encountered it more frequently.

Matthijs also added this anecdote to the history of the "behaviorology" name:

> By the time R. Epstein published his praxics article [Epstein, 1984], I and a few colleagues of mine had already grown accustomed to the term

> gedragsologie. In our own teaching and seminars we found it quite natural to speak about "gedragsologie." I wrote a letter to Epstein asking him whether he had...considered using "behaviorology" as a new term for our science. I also explained to him that I would greatly appreciate knowing whether he had other objections to the term behaviorology besides, perhaps, stylistic ones. In a very short letter, he said that the term behaviorology is "a bit silly" and that in English, the term wouldn't have "any chance to be accepted." I believed him and gave up the idea of writing a short article (for the "On Terms" section of *The Behavior Analyst)* in which I would have proposed behaviorology....

Matthijs also disagreed with Epstein's argument that the study of behavior should be separated from radical behaviorism, writing that:

> ...without radical behaviorism, you can only pay lip service to the study of behavior. That seems to be an extreme and intolerant view, but one function of radical behaviorism is precisely to be intolerant...of mentalism.... The problem is not that we are radical behaviorists, but that we are not radical behavioristic enough....

Echoing a sentiment also expressed by E.A. Vargas, Matthijs observed that:

> ...psychologists are right when they do not allow us in their mentalistic departments (just as behaviorologists would be right not to allow psychologists in their future behavioristic departments). I...was...pleased with Epstein proposing to separate from psychology, but I don't see how you can successfully separate from psychology without also radically separating from mentalism, which has always dominated each kind of psychology.

Contact with China. The behaviorology movement also discovered supporting information on the other side of the world from Europe. During the 1990–1991 academic year, Stephen Ledoux taught behaviorology courses in the People's Republic of China as an exchange professor at the Xi'an Foreign Languages University in Xi'an, Shaanxi. While there he held discussions about behaviorology with locally based senior members of the behavior science disciplines (see Ledoux, 1997d, for details).

Ledoux found that the Chinese define psychology to encompass more than what the term implies in English. In Chinese, "psychology" connotes a broad discipline drawing upon three sources. The first features traditional Chinese perspectives. The second stems from the discipline as pursued in the Soviet Union (especially the work originating with Pavlov on respondent behavior). The third is a mix of Western perspectives. The Chinese have included three parts in the Western component: (a) psychoanalysis (i.e., Freud), (b) traditional cognitive/mentalistic psychology (e.g., Maslow and Piaget), and (c) a behavioral approach based largely on Skinner's science.

The Chinese, strongly oriented toward practical results, reportedly liked the natural science approach and experimental methods in the work of Pavlov and Skinner. And unlike Western philosophical thought, the Chinese seemed to have avoided much of the Western extremes in separating phenomena into mental and physical realms (soul/body, spiritual/material, mind/reality). The Chinese language, while it has a rich variety of terms for most of the varied Western usages of the term *mind,* actually lacks a direct translation of "mind" as Western psychologists use that term, with "mind" implying a metaphysical locus from which mysterious variables exert controls over behavior. Instead, for that usage, Chinese professionals generally use a word that better retranslates back into English as "brain."

Interestingly, the term Chinese professionals use for their "behavioral" component is *Xingwei Xue.* This term translates accurately, if generally, as behaviorology, behavior analysis, behavior science, or science of behavior. But they have no current specific term with *organizational* connotations to which they respond as we respond to the term behaviorology in the sense of a separate and independently organized discipline.

However, the Chinese were out of date, having lost contact with Western developments since the mid 1950s. They had been operating with a behavioral component that was 30 years old. Certain dissatisfactions with the behavioral approach stemmed from the antiquity and superficiality of the version that they knew. It often seemed inadequate to account for the complexities of human behavior. Ledoux found that the Chinese had spent the decade of the 1980s trying to update their 30 year gap in knowledge of Western developments. But accidently their update had pertained only to the psychoanalytic and traditional cognitive approaches. They had not realized that the mainstream psychology sources for their update lacked information on the continuing disciplinary evolution and developments of the behavioral component. From their studies of recent cognitive/mentalistic literature, the Chinese professionals had learned little about the advances in behavior science or about the movement that culminated in establishing behaviorology as an independent discipline.

In addition, Chinese professionals had noted that their update of traditional Western psychology yielded little of practical use in dealing with the cultural, social, or personal problems to be addressed. But some Chinese scholars subsequently discovered that reports of more practical and wide ranging research and applications do exist in *behavioral* journals like the *Journal of the Experimental Analysis of Behavior* and the *Journal of Applied Behavior Analysis.* That discovery prepared them to attend more closely to the behaviorology that Ledoux had been invited to teach.

Establishing behaviorology in China, however, presents its own set of challenges. The higher education system of China is small relative to the size of the population. The American concept of general education is not widely known. Most Chinese higher education institutions feature a targeted curriculum. Before an academic discipline receives institutional attention, it must meet a requirement for demonstrated applicability. Furthermore, some of China's senior education leaders have long held outmoded opinions about behavior science in general, and some of these opinions are now thoroughly incorporated into the system. For example, everyone in China who is involved in language training knows Chomsky's theories. But since applying them effectively in language training is not feasible, few people show much interest in them; they are just something that everyone is expected to know. Unfortunately, the urgent preoccupation with immediately applicable techniques, and the concomitant reluctance to invest in basic science training, leaves the Chinese with little maneuvering room in which to get themselves well trained in the kind of basic behaviorological science that *can* readily spawn the practical and workable behavioral technologies that they seek.

Historical summary. Behaviorological science and its philosophy originated earlier than the formally organized discipline that coalesced during the 1980s to accommodate them (see Ledoux, 1997a). E.A. Vargas set priorities, which were included in Fraley and Vargas (1986): "…developing an academic home to reproduce our scientific culture is the larger problem. The middle–sized problem is the organization to foster our radical behaviorism. ...The smaller problem is what we call ourselves" (p. 54). The smaller problem was solved, and a long term solution for the middle–sized problem was established—steps that will facilitate solving the larger problem.

As the decade of the 1990s began, the culture was still in the grip of psychology (whose mainstream advocates are devoted to understanding a mysterious *internal* locus of behavioral determinants) and theology (whose disciples are devoted to understanding a mysterious *external* locus of behavioral determinants). But an organized behaviorology movement was present as well, a movement providing a natural science alternative based largely on the selection paradigm. Here was a discipline that treated behavior as a *naturally* occurring phenomenon. Behavior occurs as dependent variables in functional relations featuring environmental properties as independent variables. Behaviorologists define behavior to include not only mechanical movements of body parts, but also all emotional reactions, and all verbal behaviors (the latter being a large class that incorporates speaking, thinking, awareness, consciousness, knowing about, and similar phenomena). Behaviorologists view all of these as kinds of behaviors, each occurring in accordance with well understood basic principles that often recombine in ways accommodating greater complexity. This brings behavioral outcomes (including the behaviors of affect and intellect) within reach of an appropriate behavioral technology for any applied field. The discipline of behaviorology could provide scientific support for a behavioral engineer addressing behavior–related problems in *any* applied area.

Summary of Chapter Two

Before concrete actions were taken to launch a newly organized discipline, the concept of that discipline had to be shaped to maturity in the verbal repertoires of many people. Chapter Two described both how that concept arose and the variables that shaped people's responses to it. This chapter also discussed the nature and origins of the behaviorology concept, and its increasingly ill fit within organized psychology, even though much of its origin can be traced in the history shared with that discipline. Disunity in psychology stimulated reconsideration of the place of the *behavioral* science that had begun early in the century—in part with the work of Watson and Thorndike, and subsequently with Skinner's definitive biology–inspired departure from both a strict stimulus–response (S–R) psychology and its attendant preoccupations with the nervous system.

Skinner's paradigmatic revolution brought to the study of behavior a line of biology–based scientific thought for dealing with behavior–related subject matter. It emphasized selection causality and produced an increasingly isolated behavioral scientific community within organized psychology. A continuing question was whether or not psychology would change by adopting that behavior–focused paradigm and its attendant natural science philosophy. The rift eventually attracted the attention of scholars of science including David Krantz who, while apparently somewhat offended by the behaviorists' adamant defense of their scientific integrity, discovered substantial evidence for that integrity. Nevertheless, Krantz's prominent article (1971) emphasized what he implied were rebellious social improprieties. The chided behaviorists were perhaps slowed in their turn away from psychology, and many might have been influenced toward accommodations with traditional psychologists—a trend that certainly became evident.

In the two decades that followed, the behavioral psychologists and semi–independent behavior analysts toyed with the concept of a separate discipline. By the late 1980s this issue was under intense debate, especially within ABA. When a name (behaviorology) was proposed for a separate discipline, an historical search revealed several different origins for it and for some earlier flirtations with concepts of disciplinary independence. Reviews of the status of behavior science around the world revealed that significant potential for an organized behaviorology movement existed, especially among a subset of the radical behaviorists on the North American continent.

The next chapter, Chapter Three ("Issues Driving the Independence Movement") will review and analyze five kinds of reasons to incur the high costs of organizing a separate and independent discipline. ❧

Chapter 3:

Issues Driving the Independence Movement

After the introductory Chapter One, Chapter Two of this account of the emergence of behaviorology examined the nature and origins of the behaviorology concept and its emergence worldwide. An idea like behaviorology can rise to the level of a mature concept, but subsequently to do something concrete about such a concept requires strength in the reasons for bothering. This chapter, Chapter Three, explores the increasing strength, in five different classes of contingencies, to incur the high costs of organizing a separate and independent discipline. It reviews the accumulating and intensifying reasons why the early behaviorologists would be led to take the actions that will be described in Chapter Four.

Disciplinary independence movements are costly and not undertaken lightly. Few of the potential early supporters of such movements actually become involved. Various contingencies must operate in some combination: The punishers from which people are escaping must have grown strong. Access to critical reinforcers must have come under serious threat. And participation in a new movement must hold promise of important outcomes, though some might be deferred.

The rarity and difficulty of such personal commitments evoke a special scrutiny with respect to why those commitments occurred. The early behaviorologists were individually affected by different sets of causal factors. This chapter turns from *what* was happening to *why* it was happening, and discusses several of the reasons which, in some combination, might explain the commitment of any given individual to the behaviorology movement. Each of the five following sections explores a different class of motivating variables. The first, concerning *the scientific rift,* addresses, in several subsections, various components of this perhaps most critical of those classes.

(1) The Essential Scientific Rift

By the latter part of the 1980s, the decade in which an independent behaviorology emerged, some behaviorists had developed in applied fields without ever having been affiliated with organized psychology. The many behaviorists of all kinds, who did operate within organized psychology, still represented a minority in psychology of only a few percent. For example, a 1990 list of regular members in the American Psychological Association (APA) Division 25, the behaviorist's division, contained only about 1200 people including student and affiliate members (Division 25, 1990). In contrast, in 1987, APA had nearly 65,000 members (Hayes, 1987b, p. 41). By that time the rift between behaviorist and cognitivist/mentalist camps had become a salient problem for many persons concerned with the disciplinary future of psychology. Many argued that the differences did *not* or *need* not conflict. Some even invented new concepts of "discipline" more tolerant of disparity (Staats, 1986). But others emphasized seemingly irreconcilable differences and distrusted the implications of disciplinary integration.

Having thoroughly criticized cognitive psychology in 1977 (Skinner, 1977), Skinner a decade later (1987b) asked rhetorically why "the experimental analysis of behavior as a function of environmental variables and the use of that analysis in the interpretation and modification of behavior in the world at large" have not *become* psychology (p. 782). He offered some reasons in the form of obstacles that he identified as humanistic psychology, psychotherapy, and cognitive psychology. Having described the essential effects of those obstacles, he concluded that:

> ...by their very nature, the anti–science stance of humanistic psychology, the practical exigencies of the helping professions, and the cognitive restoration of the royal House of Mind have worked against the definition of psychology as the science of behavior. (p. 784)

Skinner, until as recently as May 1989, had always hoped to change psychology into a useful science of behavior. He had presented a lifelong analysis of why it is not. Concurrently he was providing the natural science and philosophy that psychology would have to adopt to fulfill its cultural mission. Yet it remained for the vast majority of psychologists to adopt that science and philosophy.

Some argued that the prolonged dominance of less effective or impractical science in psychology was largely a result of politically defended access to a variety of reinforcers, some extraneous, within that organized discipline. Resistance to behaviorism on the scientific and technical front where Skinner had fought his battles (e.g., see Baer, 1987) was of lesser importance. Others might have been reluctant to turn away from the familiar implications of mentalism. Either way, some therefore saw a *political* rather than a purely scientific solution as appropriate and increasingly necessary. They saw recognizing a behaviorology discipline, separate both in subject matter and organization, as that kind of step.

The scientific rift hinged on two major classes of difference: paradigmatic and thematic—or, roughly, *how* to think, and the subject matter *about which* to think. The following four parts of this section examine significant components of these aspects of the scientific rift.

Mentalism versus behavior–behavior relations. Historically the internal agent has been difficult even to locate much less analyze. In more ancient times false starts had seemed to lead to the lungs or heart. But many contemporary psychologists, following the quest of these predecessors going back to the time of the ancient Greeks and Romans, now seek the elusive agent in the brain. An organ (the brain), rather than an organism, is said to behave. Presumably, the brain acts like another person within. It processes this, recognizes that, perceives something else. Those who accept the premise of internal autonomous causal agency are limited in their scientific approach to searching out some physical reality presumed either to be the heretofore ill–described agent or to be symptomatic of its ethereal presence. In either case the agent is circularly inferred from the same behavior to be explained (Michael, 1989, Ch. 6; Skinner, 1953, Chs. 1–3). From a natural science perspective, laboratory methodologies are wasted to investigate what is not really there, while legions of students are trained to replace the professionals expended on the crusade. (An enlightening exposition appears in *Beyond Freedom and Dignity* [Skinner, 1971, Ch. 1].)

Behavior analysts Hayes and Brownstein (1986), in their article "Mentalism, Behavior–Behavior Relations, and a Behavior–Analytic View of the Purposes of Science," argued that the majority of psychologists are mentalists because their philosophies and sciences provide no analytical means to avoid mentalism. They noted that treating thinking as a "mental" event treats it as a hypothetical "non–spatiotemporal" activity—that is, as non–natural.

In contrast, radical behaviorists have long regarded thinking as *behavior,* mostly verbal and controlled, as is all behavior, by variables in the natural environment. Thinking is apparently all, or nearly all, behavior of the operant kind. Though usually covert, thought has the same properties as more overt behavior (also see Moore, 1981, 1984). Construing thought to be natural, radical behaviorists transform the troublesome question of how metaphysical mental events can control physical events, like behavior, into the more rational and answerable question of how covert behavior can control overt behavior. Hayes and Brownstein referred to that class of relations as "behavior–behavior relations" wherein the second behavior (an observable overt kind) occurs under the antecedent control of a preceding behavior (such as a thought). These sequential relations, though at times obscure, are not mystical. They merely involve two kinds of behaviors—a covert one serving an antecedent stimulus function for the next. And, especially when contemplating intervention, behaviorologists are quick to go back a link in any causal chain and search in the accessible environment for the functional public antecedents of that covert event. By tracing the functional relations back to events in an *accessible* part of the environment, they locate potentially manipulatable variables. This affords control over the subsequent internal and otherwise inaccessible parts of the sequence as well as over the external parts. The previously insoluble problem, recast in this way, becomes routinely manageable. (Also see Hayes & Brownstein, 1985.)

The mentalistic account of thinking, prominent in psychology, does not even reach the point of behavior–behavior relations, in part because the controlling antecedent variables, called thoughts, are seldom if ever regarded as behavior. The psychological analysis of an observable overt *behavior* that has been "stimulated" by an antecedent covert behavior usually stops at the interface between the exterior and interior domains. The behavior is regarded merely as the final emitted stage of some changing entity that undergoes a transformational sequence—usually entering the body as information and emerging as behavior. Thus, transformations from some preceding state in the internal domain are thought to yield the observed behavioral manifestations. That internal domain is, by some accounts, possessed of mysterious properties, and metaphysical events thus supplement the processes. In other accounts, information is accepted as something real, and therefore real mental processors have to be hypothesized to deal with it. Without the kind of science necessary to carry analyses of multi–term contingencies back through the functional chain—and tending to attach little importance to such an effort anyhow—mentalists are ill–prepared to avoid what behaviorologists construe to be the fallacy of original internal causation (Sidman, 1986a; Skinner, 1969).

Conversely, behaviorologists regard "mental" events as covert behavior, mostly (if not all) verbal. An understanding of these events can support *prediction* of the overt behavior that they may share in controlling. However, behaviorologists do not regard analyses to be complete until not only prediction but also *control* is attainable. That usually requires tracing any causal chain further back ...back to locations—generally outside the body, in the external environment—where controlling variables are *accessible.* Behaviorologists describe these analytical moves to the exterior in terms of "four–term contingencies of reinforcement" (see E.A. Vargas, 1991b). Unless that move to accessible variables is accomplished, effective behavioral technologies, which depend on manipulating accessible independent variables, cannot be developed by design and must emerge, if at all, as intuitive or scientifically unsupplemented practice.

Engineering versus inquiry. Cognitivists sometimes *do* attain control adventitiously in direct response to practical contingencies. But too often when that happened, the radical behaviorists were left to contend with invalid claims of credit made by the cognitivists on behalf of the prevailing cognitive science.

Mentalists sometimes disavow control as their goal, because their approach does not readily facilitate analyses that backtrack through the chain of functionally related variables to the "environment." (Radical behaviorists define "environment" as that domain, part of which might be inside the skin, in which independent variables *can be manipulated in behavior–controlling relations.*) Instead of stressing control, mentalists emphasize "understanding." Their practical work is often confined to predicting behavior from other behavior—as when behavior on a specific occasion is predicted from a putative causal trait induced from behavior on previous occasions. For example, educational psychology courses in the measurement of behavior typically ignore direct measurements of the properties of behavior (as delineated, for example, by Johnston and Pennypacker [1980, Ch. 7]) and instead feature textbooks devoted to identifying and measuring the intensity of what are assumed to be behavior causing traits.

The quest to gain control of behavior is sometimes criticized as an allegiance to superficiality. However, as Hayes and Brownstein (1986) wrote, control

> ...is a required element for the successful functioning of the [behavioristic] perspective. Thus, mental causality is a form of theorizing rejected because its pursuit threatens the successful operation of science as viewed from the standpoint of behavior analysis. [p. 187] ...an emphasis on prediction and control is not arbitrary in behavior analysis because it is a necessary part of successful forms of the philosophy [of radical behaviorism] that underlies behavior–analytic theorizing. (p. 175)

Failure to include control as a planned final step condemns a science to immaturity (see Skinner, 1953, Ch. 2). As a practical matter, those who would not attain control in their subject matter can only *interpret* life in various ways. And mere *interpretations* evoke little threat to the acceptance either of the science that informs them or of the persons who offer them. But most important scientists echo Gould's (1987) notion about life—that "the point ...is to change it" (p. 154). Those whose science carries to the level of effective control must confront a world well organized to defend established modes of access to long and strongly conditioned reinforcers. Those who resisted the behaviorologists did so in ways never wasted on others who merely teased with counter interpretations but who lacked the technologies to affect actual changes.

Among persons working under the rubric of psychology, those pursuing the developing behavioral paradigm increasingly gained more of a capacity to control behavior than did the cognitive/mentalistic remainder. Reinforced for their successes in the domain of practical behavior engineering, the behavioral people increasing concentrated on exploiting *that* aspect of their science. This widened the scientific rift, because the cognitive/mentalistic psychologists, lacking that opportunity, focused their efforts on understanding, in their own way, the inner workings of what they construed to be a behavior–controlling mind.

Quality of science issues. Since the concept of mind had been induced entirely on the basis of behavioral evidence in the first place, efforts to explain behavior through appeals to the features and functions of the mind were logically circular. This offended the scientific sensibilities of many behavioral people, whose analytical paradigm paralleled the non–circular logic common to the well–established natural sciences. When, across the last half of the twentieth century, the cognitive/mentalistic psychologists turned increasingly to physiologically based brain science for independent corroborations of their theories of mind, the future behaviorologists again took umbrage, because old theory was being carted to new evidence in *theory–biased searches* for fits and matches. These were inevitably "successful" because something physiological is always occurring internally. No matter how fanciful or far–fetched the theory, some physiological activity is always present to be correlated with the behavioral events said to be external representations of whatever internal functions the theory hypothesizes—an approach prone to fallacies and low on the quality scale in scientific practice. Some future behaviorologists, especially those more sensitive to quality of science issues, were embarrassed before the at–large community of natural scientists by the psychology community to which many of them were nominally attached. And, becoming more so as time passed, they increasingly recognized the need to regroup separately; they wanted out.

Irrelevant subject matter. The physiological alternative to non–natural mentalism pursued by many psychologists focuses on a subject matter somewhat irrelevant to behaviorology. Behaviorologists distinguish between (a) the valid natural science of physiological linkages between behavior and environment (a field of study in which they have had limited though valid scientific interest) and (b) the science (or pseudo–science) of mentalism which they construe to be an indulgence in metaphysics unworthy of status in the scientific community at large. Unfortunately, those two scholarly traditions have remained so intertwined within psychology that they can be difficult to discriminate there.

Those scholars of mind who eschew a metaphysical mentalism and assume thinking to be a purely natural physiological activity nevertheless also depend on cognitive science. But that approach does not bring thoughts and feelings unequivocally into the realm of behavior in accordance with the kind of scientific principles recognized by behaviorologists. Those cognitive psychologists probe for independent, non–behavioral variables in the nervous system, a line of inquiry going back to when people first noticed that from nerves come the behavior–initiating impulses that stimulate muscles. But because the activity within nerves only mediates the functional relations between a controlling environment and exhibited behaviors, that effort can be somewhat like searching myopically through the mechanical steering linkages of an automobile in an effort to discover the driver who remains external to that system and cannot be found within it. From the behaviorological perspective, the behavior–mediating neural events that might be discovered there, though necessary if real, are little relevant to the practical operations that constitute behaviorological technologies. The classic argument was set forth by Skinner (1938) in his often–quoted chapter 12 (entitled "Behavior and the Nervous System") of *The Behavior of Organisms.* There Skinner defended his assertions

> ...not only that a science of behavior is independent of neurology but that it must be established as a separate discipline whether or not a rapprochement with neurology is ever attempted. (pp. 423–424)

E.A. Vargas put it this way (1990; also see E.A. Vargas, 1991a):

> The fact that cellular action underlies every muscle action that underlies every limb movement that underlies the behavior of two teams playing foot-

ball does not explain why the game is played as it is or why those teams play *that* game.

The extensive physiologizing by cognitive psychologists also shifted their subject matter into disciplinary territory claimed by physiology. However, whether those internal events are real events or not, the independent variables that are relevant to practical concerns always remain in the behavior–controlling environment or milieu. The inter–nerve variables that play a mediating roll between independent variables and behavioral manifestations do not lend themselves to feasible intervention even if one could possibly determine, on given occasions, what changes within those nerves might be worthwhile. Thus psychologists cannot attain the capacity for control over behavior through analyses focused on nerve functions.

Increasingly, the behaviorists within psychology exploited their growing capacity to develop effective behavioral technologies based on the manipulation of external variables. They were becoming behavioral engineers, and discovering largely untapped markets for those skills in all facets of the culture. Internal physiological linkages, though necessary, played little or no role in the practical interventions undertaken to produce behavior change and remained of little concern to the behaviorists. Most others who called themselves psychologists—a vast majority—continued to focus on those internal events. The subject matter difference was becoming ever greater.

Summary of the scientific rift. Most early behaviorologists saw themselves organizing a new disciplinary support structure—a scientific verbal community—apart from the organized discipline of psychology. They viewed psychology as a discipline focused, with an unreliable mix of natural and non–natural science, on subject matters largely irrelevant to behaviorological concerns.

Behaviorologists, in separating from psychology, would be leaving the enormous problem of purging that discipline of non–natural mentalism to the psychologists. Should the psychologists eventually succeed in doing that, the residual natural science of internal events will still pertain to a field largely apart from behaviorology. A demystified psychology could leave its natural scientists in far more territorial conflict with the discipline of physiology than with behaviorology. As Skinner (1974, Ch. 13; 1983b, 1987b) has noted, the discipline of physiology relates internal physiological events to observable behaviors as an aspect of *its* mission, and it is far better prepared to do so than is psychology.

The work of behaviorologist Carl Cheney (1988, 1991, 1992) later exemplified the *appropriate* natural science bond between behaviorology and physiology. In his work Cheney completes accounts of some behaviors by treating the body as a set of independent variables in environment/behavior relations. That differs from attempting to exploit the findings from physiological studies to validate what most behaviorologists construe to be ill–conceived mentalistic theorizing.

(2) Behaviorological Training Issues

The problems in training behaviorologists are largely those of training scientists in any discipline that provides complex scientific alternatives to common wisdom and traditional assumptions. But in the 1980s those who would soon acknowledge themselves as behaviorologists faced increasing difficulty training their students within their respective nominal disciplines, especially organized psychology and its satellite fields. The repertoires of behaviorology—its philosophy, science, technologies, and vocabulary—are as extensive, and as difficult and demanding to acquire, as those of any other scientific discipline. The verbal community of behaviorology, like those of other natural sciences, must therefore claim access to the controls on all of the discipline–related behavior of its trainees. This monopoly on control over training in behaviorology is further necessitated by a particular characteristic of the task: The substantial lore about behavior that pervades the general culture will have informed the prior training of behaviorology students in nearly all subject matters. The training must eliminate that legacy from their technical repertoires as it shapes their new verbal skills (just as it must for students of other natural sciences so that, for instance, astronomy students learn not to refer to "the sun rising" in technical contexts).

Where behaviorologists and psychologists have been compelled to share the same training program and compete with each other for sufficient student contact to get students properly trained, both sides have tended to regard as extreme any efforts of the other to monopolize the training. But to master behaviorology, like any other complex natural science, requires a substantial commitment on the part of behaviorological aspirants. However, "commitment" merely describes the strength of certain controls over the trainees' behaviors that their verbal and social communities have managed to arrange. A trainee's aspirations are also products of the community's behavior–controlling practices. Their aspirations are functions of the reinforcers to which the trainees are conditioned and of the schedules of reinforcement (Ferster & Skinner, 1957) by which trainees are afforded access to those reinforcers. Given (a) the degree of control that must be established between subject matter variables and trainee behavior, (b) the extensive new verbal repertoire that must be acquired, (c) the traditional repertoire that must undergo extinction (at least in technical contexts), and (d) the new and different reinforcers that the trainee must behave to contact (i.e., the new perspective of the trainee in approaching the subject matter), the necessary interaction between trainee and the behaviorological community is too great for the trainee's time to be shared with the verbal community of another discipline.

To the extent that they dilute the training curricula, compromises with any other discipline reduce students' opportunities not only to acquire skills in their own discipline but also to acquire the supportive emotional behaviors as well (see Branch & Malagodi, 1980). Also, the trainees' reliance on the science of their discipline diminishes. For example, Mahoney (1989) reported a longitudinal attitude survey conducted on 42 "influential representatives" of cognitive and behavioral psychology using a "lengthy questionnaire" on "beliefs about scientific method, the nature of learning, and so on." Having discerned three subsets among his *psychologist* subjects—(a) extreme behaviorists, (b) cognitive–behaviorists, and (c) extreme cognitivists—Mahoney reported that all three groups had become more cognitive, though behaviorists changed least. The extreme cognitivists found even less merit in behavioral ideas than what little they previously conceded, while the cognitive–behavioral psychologists had shifted the balance in their views significantly toward the cognitive perspective. Mahoney noted that:

> ...both cognitive–behavioral and extreme behavioral respondents showed signs of shifts in the direction of personal agency as an important counterbalance to exclusive environmental determinism. Cognitivists appeared to be going even further in this direction, exhibiting a clear trend toward acknowledging the influence of unconscious processes. (p. 1375)

Mahoney found that behaviorists *in psychology* were increasingly variable in their "meanings and models of behaviorism" which in his view were "in the throes of dramatic revision"—away from what he characterized as the extremism of radical behaviorism. Extremism in this context, though, mainly reflects characteristics that imply a different discipline whose practitioners resist training compromises that degrade the scientific repertoires of their students.

Furthermore when students, whose skills and enthusiasm for behaviorological science are reduced by mixed training, eventually succeed the behavioral faculty members in the programs of research, practice, and training, they tend to enter into those positions as less competent behavioral experts than the former mentors whom they replace. This reduction in the behaviorological competence of each succeeding generation of faculty decreases the capacity of the science to contribute to the culture. (For an early warning, see Michael, 1980, p. 16; for an analysis of the implications when one operates concurrently in incompatible verbal communities—a probable circumstance for behavioral psychologists—see Fraley, 1984; for tactics to nurture behavioral repertoires within non–supportive environments, see Morse & Bruns, 1983.)

Many training problems in behaviorology stem from delaying the study of behaviorology until a student enters higher education—in many cases, graduate school. Unlike other basic sciences, which are introduced to students in primary and secondary schools, behaviorological science *under any label* has been generally unavailable to students until they have become adults. In contrast, mentalistic and cognitive psychology courses are occasionally offered in high schools. Perhaps worse, most kindergarten–through–twelfth grade curricular materials on other subjects are heavily laced with inaccurate references to behavior that are based on the mentalistic assumptions prevailing throughout the culture. Behaviorologists support replacing that cognitive/mentalistic psychology with appropriate, practical behaviorology in those curricula (e.g., Ledoux, 1987a). A strictly natural science, behaviorology provides young learners with *explicit* principles by which to deal more effectively with behavior in *practical* contexts.

Some behaviorologists have deemed as acceptable the practice of providing behavior–related training for lay persons and beginners *in lay language,* believing that students would then more readily understand behaviorology. But lay language is implicitly cognitive and mentalistic—a legacy of Western cultural history (Ledoux, 1997a; based on Lerner, 1991). That language legacy maintains a counter–implication to the very concepts that the teachers would be seeking to establish. The rather widely understood realities of the *physical* world, which are contrary to ancient and mistaken wisdom, are appreciated by lay persons to the extent that the technical language of physics has become part of the ordinary citizen's language. *That* circumstance is the legacy of two or three centuries of science teaching in the schools. Other behaviorologists have therefore counter–argued that the most educationally sound approach to teaching the science of behaviorology is to get people to talk and think in behaviorological language—and to do so as part of their everyday mode of expression.

On a more practical level, some behaviorologists who were attempting to train students in university units controlled by other disciplines found themselves without behavior laboratory facilities. Administrators representing the interests of other disciplines do not tend to divert resources to the laboratory space and equipment that behaviorologists deem important. In 1993 Ernest Vargas, after years of unsuccessful efforts to secure behavior laboratory space at the College of Human Resources and Education

(West Virginia University), opened a laboratory in the basement of his home. With assistance from Carl Cheney, he and graduate student David Feeney began to conduct behavior research. This represented the first experimental laboratory facility opened under the general umbrella of organized behaviorology. A small research support grant to Carl Cheney from The International Behaviorology Association—the first such grant made by that organization—defrayed some of the costs.

Summary of training issues. Some behaviorologists came to the movement in part out of a conviction that their discipline could only continue and advance through relief from the constrained and limited training opportunities available, especially within the psychology community. However, behaviorologists must still solve the curricular and tactical problems intrinsic to instruction in any basic natural science. Creative interim measures have included private ventures to fill gaps in research and training opportunities within university units controlled by advocates of other disciplines.

(3) Employment Opportunities

The modern psychology establishment, for its part, has already arranged a kind of separation based on hiring. "Behavioral" psychologists are, in general, no longer hired in psychology. For example, the September 1989 issue of the *APS Observer* (The coherence, 1989) advertised over 85 employment opportunities for psychologists organized by categories, including 15 under "Cognitive Psychology Positions." No corresponding category for behavioral psychologists was present. Most of the remaining ads specified or implied a cognitive orientation among desired applicant characteristics, while no ad was equally explicit about a behavioral orientation. Earlier, Epstein (1987a) had reported finding a similar pattern in the *APA Monitor.* For some years he had been tabulating the Monitor's job listings and considered those for 1985 as "typical for nearly a decade." He called them "good indicators of the composition of future psychology departments." He found no entry–level, tenure–track positions for "animal learning, behavior analysis, or any related area" (p. 127).

The rare advertisement for a "behavioral" psychologist is the exception that proves the rule: Mainline psychology continues to provide no niche for behavioral people. One can infer that psychologists do not construe the behavioral approach to represent their field. Behaviorologists agree. Since behavioral types did not seem likely to get hired as psychologists, the behaviorology movement became attractive in part because it would afford access to the job market under an independent disciplinary label. Applicants also hoped that their entrance into the job market as disciplinary independents would facilitate appealing to an even broader spectrum of potential employers than those traditionally seeking to hire psychologists.

Summary of employment opportunities. The appeal of the behaviorology movement was increased in part due to few positions being available for behavioral people within job markets controlled by organized psychology. The appeal also increased in part because a broader job market seemed accessible through training provided by an independently identified behaviorology discipline.

(4) Capacity for Contributions to the Culture

Whether behaviorists could fully provide their potential contributions to the culture (Fraley, 1987) without an independently organized discipline had, by the mid–1980s, become an urgent question for many of them. Increasingly they saw important long–term implications in that issue. The contributions of behaviorology, both actual and potential, were being ignored and often stifled by the traditional bond to organized psychology. Behaviorologists encountered impediments in the areas of training and funding—and, in the perception of many of them, behaviorologists were denied appropriate recognition, respect, and other common consequences of successful and meaningful scientific and academic endeavors (see Fraley & Vargas, 1986).

Psychologists of many varieties continue to denounce behaviorism and behavioral approaches while enthusiastically describing the latest cognitive and mentalistic models. In some cases those psychological constructs depend on reiterations, in imprecise cognitive language, of well established, purloined, behaviorological principles that have found their laundered way into the cognitive literature. In one example Kauffman, describing conceptual models in the fourth edition of his *Characteristics of Behavior Disorders of Children and Youth* (1989, p. 85), regarded contributions from behavioral research as inadequate and touted the putatively more complete "social cognitive theory" said to represent the "natural–science perspective." That model has two main features. One deals with behavior in its relations with a controlling environment. Although Kauffman gave no hint of it, those relations constitute a basic *behaviorological* concept (attributed in part to Bandura, although Skinner had been the one who had earlier spent years experimentally probing those functional relations and authoring several books developing that concept). The second main feature of social cognitive theory is a reliance on "personal agency." This is a remnant of theological epistemology to which many cognitivists cling in outright antithetical rejection of natural science. "Personal agency" requires that one either be ignorant of the science of verbal behavior or fail to appreciate it. (For another example, see Fraley & Vargas, 1986, pp. 49–51.)

Vicki Lee (letter to Fraley, 15 June 1989) mentioned a further typical example. In her native country, Australia, where "behaviorological activity is virtually nonexistent," one of her psychology colleagues recently published a paper reporting the "discovery" that reinforcers have to be identified empirically. That point is of fundamental scientific importance. It is also an essential point reiterated in the behaviorological literature from the beginning (see Skinner, 1938) and has always been included as an elementary principle in introductory behaviorological texts (e.g., Skinner, 1953; Fraley, 1996a).

On 22 January 1991 an English language broadcast in China provided yet another example of educational psychologists "discovering" a half–century–old behaviorological principle. Some educators in Hunan Province reported documenting a "new" teaching method that yielded substantial improvements in students' academic performance. The "new" method was positive reinforcement. Students were positively reinforced for exhibiting the desired academic behaviors. In 1938 the historical behaviorology literature reported laboratory documentation of the basic relation in the positive reinforcement process (Skinner, 1938). By 1953 the process had been elaborately tested and documented, and its wide applicability was discussed in engineering detail in the literature (Skinner, 1953). And by the 1960s entire books were detailing its specific adaptations in educational practice (e.g., Skinner, 1968). (At the time of this discovery, the Chinese were completing a ten–year long attempt to update a 30–year loss of contact with the West; the Western *psychological* sources for their update would have been ill–prepared to inform them about this application. See Ledoux, 1997d.) Even the half–century–old *basics* of behaviorological science often have to await "discovery" by psychologists who then invalidly attribute the favorable outcomes to their own discipline. But in most such cases, the technological practices in question would not have followed as logical implications of the kinds of basic assumptions upon which psychology rests.

Some people counter examples like these by insisting that ultimately what is important is how well humans deal with their world, not *who* makes the discoveries or gets the credit. But such arguments are economic nonsense for a discipline that must compete in the cultural marketplace for its resources in order to continue to make its contributions. Furthermore, in pirating intellectual merchandise from behaviorology, seldom are the practices simply borrowed and properly used (though under false labels). Separated from their quality–controlling philosophy and underlying scientific principles, the practices become distorted until eventually they lose their effectiveness. Then they are discredited and discarded.

Additionally, the *kinds* of threats facing the global culture (Skinner, 1978, Ch. 2; 1982; 1984; 1987a, Ch. 2), and even our species (Marcattilio & Nevin, 1986; Ulman, 1986), implied urgency in getting those threats reduced. That urgency provided a prompt leading some participants toward the behaviorology movement. Under the circumstances some early behaviorologists did not believe that time was available for mainstream psychology's bit by bit rediscovery of behaviorological principles so that eventually those principles might be applied, by way of the psychological establishment, to our cultural problems. A separate discipline was needed, and needed right away so that it could help insure a viable future for humanity.

Perhaps global human culture is already fatally and irrevocably flawed (Skinner, 1987a, Ch. 1; Ulman, 1988). Or, instead, perhaps time for meaningful change is short. Organized psychology has from its inception been allowed to be keeper of the behavioral science upon which our culture depended. Psychology has had the mission to furnish both the scientific foundations upon which to build workable behavioral technologies and the analytical power to correct flawed policy in behavioral matters. Other cultural agencies such as organized religion, government, and education function (with some help from psychology) as instruments of organized eclectic behavioral lore. But organized behavioral *science,* traditionally represented by psychology, has had the mission to resist mystification of the human condition and provide more culturally propitious alternatives. Behaviorologists, voting with their feet, judged psychology to have failed in *that* mission.

However, the organized verbal community of psychology *had* succeeded in conditioning legions of people, including many of its critics, to feel inhibited about bluntly exposing that failure. Behavioral psychologists remain sensitive to their vulnerability within psychology. But behaviorologists, in circumventing psychology, have by design developed a discipline that requires neither persuading psychologists to change nor avoiding analyses criticizing the cultural role of organized psychology—although the choice of the most appropriate and effective ways to engage in that criticism remains an important strategic issue.

Perhaps psychology tried to do too much. Studies of mind do not spawn the practical behavioral technologies needed throughout the culture for solving major behavior problems. Behaviorology does that. A disciplinary division of labor seemed appropriate to the early behaviorologists, especially in view of the failure of psychology to prove its worth as an explicitly studied behavioral foundation science. Here is just one example of the conditioned neglect of psychology as a worthwhile foundation science: Among all the graduate degree programs in 17 different fields that focused on human behavior, listed in the *1990–1992 Bulletin* of the *West Virginia University Graduate Catalog*, none were found to require *any* courses in the psychology department, although three required their own versions of traditional psychology courses. Fourteen of those seventeen departments posted no requirements for any coursework centered on psychological subject matters. The trainers in most behavior–related fields do not appear to regard as worth their students' time and money whatever contribution psychology might make as a basic science foundation for their respective fields.

This neglect extends to the lack of representation of psychology in the general scientific literature in the culture. Skinner, who worked to change psychology into a worthwhile natural science, was troubled by that neglect because it reduced the contributions from his work. In a paper entitled "Whatever Happened to Psychology as The Science of Behavior," Skinner (1987b) complained that the editors of *Science* magazine tended to avoid publishing psychology articles and observed that apparently they "no longer regard psychology itself as a member of the scientific community" (p. 784). To the extent that Skinner's interpretation was correct, behaviorologists tend to side with the editors. Focusing more narrowly, perhaps the editors of *Science* are reluctant to entertain significant *behavioral* contributions because they construe these to represent psychology. Can natural scientists who maintain a close and affirmative affiliation with what is being construed as a pseudo–scientific discipline expect other than to stand "damned by association" within the community of natural sciences?

Also, the literature of psychology has included distorted views of behavioral principles and products put forth as straw men to suffer invidious comparisons with cognitive and mentalistic concepts. Such continuing misinformation reduces the effectiveness of behavioral contributions to cultural evolution. One well known example has been the consistently inaccurate treatment in psychological commentary concerning the aircrib invented by Skinner (see Skinner's foreword in Ledoux & Cheney, 1987; also Skinner, 1983a, pp. 385–386).

Summary of capacity for contributions. Behaviorologists pursued their separatist course partly to create an independent literature. That literature would report behaviorological contributions accurately. This would allow those works to find their way to effective cultural applications through authoritative print sources more respectful of their validity. But behaviorologists did not pursue independence simply to gain control of their own work, their own literature, and their own training programs. A more global objective was to afford the independent disciplinary status necessary for effectively interacting with other facets of the culture in providing behaviorological contributions.

(5) Control of Disciplinary Infrastructures

Difficulties arise in resolving the many *kinds* of contingencies in the mix necessary to bond a scientific discipline. Organized disciplines do not operate only under scientific contingencies. They also maintain political, economic, and social contingencies to regulate their members' professional lives. Historian Daniel Bjork noted that in the public view the essence of psychology is mystery rather than fact, and offered this speculation (letter to Fraley, 14 February 1989):

> Perhaps most American psychologists don't really *want* a science at all. Rather they want a profession. That is another way of saying they want status most of all. Moreover, in behavioral terms, isn't "status" more reinforcing than "science"—especially in America.... Reduce it to science and the media loses interest.

Psychologists themselves have struggled over this and related issues. Their struggles precipitated a divisive crisis within the APA (discussed in detail in a later chapter).

Even though a guild and profession focused majority might benefit in important ways from a scientific minority's products, it cannot let that minority gain control of the political, economic, and social infrastructure of the organized verbal community if that infrastructure is what sustains that majority. Although scientific psychologists of all kinds were, increasingly over the years, adversely affected, a disproportionately large number of *behaviorists* in psychology felt exploited in this way. Many behaviorists had spent years bringing to the attention of their more mainstream colleagues how effective and applicable their evolving behavioral technologies could be. But this often left the contributions of mainline psychologists open to invidious comparisons whether that was intended or not.

Since a traditional operating dictum in a scientific verbal community is that those with the demonstrably most effective repertoire are entitled to inherit leadership, a *political* suppression of any such minority can result. Giles (1984) posed the following question to some "diplomatic" behavior therapists whom he deemed to be too deferential toward their mainstream psychology colleagues. Referring to how, in their publications, those behavioral therapists tended to obscure the behavioral science that actually informed their work, Giles asked them: "With the evidence so substantially in favor of behavior therapy, why do you state your conclusions in such guarded fashion?" Giles reported that "without exception" they responded that "they perceived aversive consequences from taking a strong position in favor of behavior therapy." Furthermore,

> ...in general, they were fearful of incurring antagonism from non–behavioral clinicians; of being labeled rigid, biased and hostile; of bitter replies in the literature...of rejection of papers submitted for review or greater difficulty in obtaining tenure or alternative employment. *Some of the respondents were able to document loss of employment or refusal of promotion as a result of their orientation.* (p. 24; emphasis added)

A more explicit example concerned a behavior analyst attempting to operate as a psychology faculty member. With respect to the attacks that are sometimes mounted to preserve psychology, such professors of behavior analysis are no safer (and perhaps are less so) than behavior therapists. As reported in the article "Court Battle" (1991), Dr. W. Joseph Wyatt, who edits and publishes *Behavior Analysis Digest,* had been denied tenure at Marshall University,

> ...because he was a behavior analyst... In recommending against Wyatt's tenure the psychology chairman held, in essence, that being behaviorally oriented had rendered Wyatt incapable of understanding psychology generally. "He argued that because behavior analysis was not psychology's 'mainstream' my knowledge base was insufficient to allow me even to teach introductory psychology..."
>
> The chairman also held that Wyatt's research was unacceptable because it was published in behavioral journals and presented at the Association for Behavior Analysis...
>
> This approach touched anti–behavioral nerves with several of Wyatt's colleagues. One claimed to have thoroughly studied (and rejected) behaviorism, but could not name the terms of the three–term contingency... (p. 2)

These challenges, which some might label intellectually dishonest, were met by Wyatt in the courts. He said, "We all must stand for something, and for me behavior analysis and a faculty member's right to it as a legitimate point of view were worth taking a stand for" (p. 3). The county circuit court agreed with him and ruled on the issue; as a result,

> ...Wyatt, with the judge's order in hand, will return to Marshall University's faculty.... (p. 3)

While justice prevailed in the end, the energy that goes into these fights is not available for efforts that benefit the culture in more direct ways. The separation of competing epistemologies into their own academic disciplinary homes should reduce such battles for control of a shared disciplinary infrastructure.

Three additional examples of similar suppression were provided in detail by E.A. Vargas, Spangler, Stone, and Wishon (1988).

Summary of disciplinary infrastructures. These kinds of battles for control of the disciplinary infrastructure—especially that of organized psychology—helped propel some behaviorists toward the incipient behaviorology movement and its political solution of organizing the discipline separately.

Summary of Chapter Three

Different classes of contingencies, each class affecting individuals to varying degrees, controlled personal commitments to the behaviorology movement. Among the kinds most frequently identified as having been important in individual cases were the five discussed in this chapter. These pertained to paradigmatic incompatibility (mainly with psychology), control of arrangements to train future behaviorologists, potentially better approaches to professional job markets, improvements in one's capacity to make scientific contributions to the culture, and control over the organizational infrastructure of scientific verbal communities.

The next chapter, Chapter Four ("The Transition Period: Organizing the Discipline and Developing its Infrastructure") will present a comprehensive review of the activities to establish the organized discipline of behaviorology, and will examine the cultural engineering by which the newly named discipline was formalized and debuted in the scientific community.

Chapter 4:

The Transition Period: Organizing the Discipline and Developing its Infrastructure

After the introductory Chapter One, Chapter Two of this account of the emergence of behaviorology examined the nature and origins of the behaviorology concept. Chapter Three examined contingencies supporting individual commitments to a disciplinary independence movement. This chapter, Chapter Four, presents a comprehensive review of the subsequent activities to organize the behaviorology discipline. It examines the cultural engineering by which the newly named discipline was formalized, rendered operational, and debuted in the scientific community at large.

By the late 1980s, on the basis of differences in stimulus controls, verbal repertoires, and reinforcers, the followers of both disciplines, psychology and behaviorology, could validly acknowledge that dual memberships in these disciplines impose unrealistic demands at least on trainees. Not only had the task of bringing one's behavior under control of both subject matters become too demanding, but the contradictory nature of those two basic analytical approaches was continuing to evoke mutual rejection of their repertoires. Behaviorologists could not include the concepts of mainstream psychologists in their work, because to behaviorologists mentalism is non–natural, and nerve functions seem both irrelevant and part of a yet another discipline. For economic as well as paradigmatic and philosophical reasons, psychologists could tolerate, in the contexts of their discipline, little work designated as behaviorological (or any name of similar connotation) regardless of whether or not they claimed that work. As Murray Sidman, responding to a question from the floor during a panel discussion, told the 1986 convention of the Southeastern Association for Behavior Analysis, a separation of the science of behavior from psychology should have occurred some time ago.

Personal Steps toward Independence

In 1989, with Julie Vargas as president, the Association for Behavior Analysis (ABA) sent a questionnaire (see ABA, 1989) to its 3,460 members; 560 (just over 16%) responded. One item asked all members to indicate the "conceptual orientation" that best described their position. Choices included an assortment of popular terms and phrases without regard to their overlapping meanings. That item (with the number of responses to each category) included cognitive (4), cognitive–behavioral (56), interbehavioral (20), behavioral (264), radical behavioral (180), and behaviorological (15), (plus "other" and "NA"—not applicable [25]). For the first time, the already self–identified behaviorologists in ABA at that time were, as a group, afforded the opportunity to indicate their discipline publicly. More importantly, the item revealed to the ABA membership in general that a new and different disciplinary option had become available to them.

Some subsequent ABA membership forms also requested explicit self–identification of disciplinary affiliation. On the membership form used to develop the 1991 ABA Directory, 122 *non*–TIBA (The International Behaviorology Association) members of ABA selected "behaviorology" as their disciplinary identity (later forms listed options less explicitly). This large number surprised the much smaller group working to establish behaviorology as an independent discipline. One speculation held that many ABA members, preferring not to be identified with psychology as their basic discipline, were merely responding to the name without knowing its implications or connotations. To resolve that issue, a letter on TIBA stationery was sent to all 122 of those ABA members. It invited them to the next TIBA convention and included the following paragraphs:

> According to ABA membership records you have identified yourself as a person who respects the discipline of behaviorology in your professional work. This letter comes to you from The International Behaviorology Association (TIBA), the professional organization dedicated to preserving and developing that discipline.
>
> The behaviorology movement is specifically focused on the evolution of behaviorology as an *independent* natural science discipline. The discipline of behaviorology is guided by a strict radical behaviorist philosophy of science. TIBA exists to organize this discipline and to focus its mission of applying this science to the diverse facets of the culture. Most TIBA members are members of The Association for Behavior Analysis, which consists of a large and broad coalition of persons who fall into the general "behavioral" category, but who represent a variety of philosophical perspectives and who entertain various notions about how best to organize behavioral science for its cultural mission.
>
> If you are interested in pursuing your professional work (in any applied field) as a person whose professional activity is informed by the basic scientific discipline of behaviorology, you are invited to contact [...TIBA].

Following some details about membership, the letter ended in this way:

> We hope to see you at the [TIBA] convention. We will also be happy to respond to your inquiries about becoming a member of this movement to establish the independent discipline of behaviorology.

The arrival of only a few responses seemed to confirm the speculations that most of the behavior analysts who did not want to be classed as psychologists were not ready to affect a personal affiliation with an explicit alternative. But the letter informed a large number of persons of the implications and connotations of the behaviorology label to which they had been attracted. Thus TIBA functioned in timely fashion to further secure its informal control over the name of the discipline that it had been organized to protect—and to preserve the technically precise meaning of that name against the drift that can accompany popularization.

Responding to a shortage of text materials that represented an independent behaviorology in name and concepts, behaviorologists teaching in universities began to organize their instructional materials for publication as explicit "behaviorology" texts. By mid–1989 several such efforts were under way. Ernest Vargas became the first to devote a sabbatical leave (fall term, 1990) to such work. Bernice Stewart and Julie Vargas were completing a book (Stewart & J. Vargas, 1990) on child care written explicitly from a behaviorological perspective. Lawrence Fraley was organizing the materials for his behaviorology course into a textbook called *General Behaviorology* (current version: Fraley, 1996a). And others began inserting the name behaviorology into the titles of textual materials that they were authoring for local use in courses that they were teaching.

In 1991 TIBA formed an Academic Affairs Committee. It had three charges: (a) to explore, initiate, and coordinate activities relevant to establishing departments of behaviorology in institutions of higher education; (b) to initiate and coordinate efforts to establish programs of studies leading to degrees in behaviorology; and (c) to design, implement, and operate an evaluation mechanism by which behaviorologists in various kinds of institutional settings can be assessed with respect to the professional quality of their behaviorological productivity.

The early behaviorologists encouraged one another to identify openly their relation to behaviorology. Guy Bruce successfully did so in applying for, and obtaining, his first postdoctoral position as director of the Learning Skills Program at Monmouth College (IL). Discussion among TIBA members focused on ways to introduce behaviorological courses free of control by competing disciplines. The objective was to establish programs, and ultimately departments, of behaviorology as soon as practicable. Stephen Ledoux described potential training programs and coursework in behaviorology for the undergraduate and masters levels (see Ledoux, 1997c). He also included a certificate program that could be employed to provide behaviorology training to post–graduate professionals already dealing with behavior.

A few successive approximations to disciplinary homes had occurred, for example, when university–based training programs under the title "behavior analysis" had been established independent of existing psychology departments. Perhaps the best known one was at the University of Kansas. Another example began in 1989 at North Texas State University (NTSU). There, after seven years of effort, the training program headed by Sigrid Glenn, and founded on a strict radical behaviorist philosophy, received formal approval to award a masters degree in "behavior analysis." That program resided within the Center for Behavioral Studies, a university unit entirely separate from the college which housed that institution's traditional psychology department.

The "behavior analysis" label attached to such programs prolonged the ambiguity evoked by that name. In the NTSU case Glenn herself was soon to become active in the professional activities of the American Psychological Association (APA; see *Division 25 Recorder, 24/25*, p. 6). Still, this program increased the small list of universities at which an entering graduate student could go either to a natural science program and study behavior in its functional context, or to a separate and different program where one could study the varieties of psyches still thought by many to have something important to do with behavior and to exist in obscure, perhaps neurological, recesses of the "mind."

The Relevance of Contemporary Professional Organizations

Persons who thought that behaviorists of any kind should affiliate with an *existing* professional organization, and not further divide the general behavioral movement, often criticized the early behaviorologists. That raised the question of how the behaviorologists, in light of their goals and values, viewed the existing organizational options confronting them during the late 1980s. This section reviews the more prominent of those available options.

Division 25, APA. Division 25 of APA (American Psychological Association) had been operating under the title "The Experimental Analysis of Behavior." It was composed of behavior–analytic psychologists too attached to organized professional psychology to sever that relation easily, or in many cases even to approximate doing so. That could be done by joining the more removed ABA (Association for Behavior Analysis) instead. Some members of Division 25 had *concurrently* joined ABA while others had joined the Association for the Advancement of Behavior Therapy (AABT). But many of those dual affiliators continued both to call themselves psychologists and to behave as if an effective behavioral science could and should ultimately develop through a continuous evolution of traditional psychology.

Some APA Division 25 loyalists, when operating within the more "separatist" organizations (ABA and AABT), have contributed to a quiet but persistent tension between (a) groups more committed to total separation from the organized discipline of psychology and (b) groups more ambivalent about separation. Efforts to neutralize revolutionary zeal in the separatist movements have succeeded to the functional extent that neither ABA nor AABT publicly, explicitly, and officially proclaims clear justification for its independent existence. Nor does either organization take decisive, effective, formal, publicly visible, irrevocable steps to further distance itself from organized psychology. However, by 1991, whether intentionally or not, ABA had approximated such a step on the level of guild interests by deciding to begin accrediting "behavior analysis" programs (see Hopkins, 1991; Shook, 1993). Still, most of the eligible programs existed in university psychology departments and were construed to be *psychology* programs.

Since the inception of the APA Division 25, its leaders have tended to concentrate efforts on describing the nature of the science and philosophy that would have to prevail in a psychology discipline capable of fulfilling its putative cultural mission. At the same time, unlike the behaviorologists, those leaders have not inferred, because of the nature and strength of the encountered resistance, that stepping out of psychology is the most feasible approach to their long–range objectives.

Stepping out of an old discipline and recognizing a new one, while sometimes necessary to leave behind an untenable organizational morass, can exact significant professional costs from those who lead the departure. And because the time scale by which new disciplines emerge can span or exceed the remaining professional lifetimes of those who take that step, they may foresee little personal recovery of their former professional statuses. Like potential revolutionaries in any traditional setting, those in the APA ranks, in facing the quandary inherent in the option to jump to the behaviorology independence movement, had to gauge their respective capacities to be sustained by reinforcing effects inherent in promises of a future that they might help to construct but not live to experience. The contingencies of conservatism in issues like this tend to be stronger for older professionals who have little professional life remaining. This perhaps partially explains why the more established and respected professionals, who also tend to be older, often resist the appeal of such revolutions.

Further complicating matters, APA Division 25 leaders had moved to co–opt the name "behavior analysis" to imply that organized psychology had proprietorship over whatever professions, fields of study, or scientific disciplines are connoted by that phrase. (Such moves threaten the conceptual and organizational property rights that some attempt to claim under a "behavior analysis" label *independent* of nearby corresponding psychology properties, for example, the masters degree program at North Texas State University.) One move to appropriate that phrase involved changing the name of the *Division 25 Recorder* to *Behavior Analysis* for at least two full volumes between 1986 and 1989. Some Division 25 members floated a proposal that the division also change its name to Behavior Analysis. In the same vein, Division 25 had maintained a committee for "Behavior Analysis as a Separate Specialty [of psychology]" headed in 1988 by James Johnston. In reporting to the Division 25 Executive Committee, Johnston's committee recommended that "the Division tie in with *other groups of psychologists* (ABA, AABT) who might be interested in this issue" thus openly implying that ABA and AABT were psychological organizations ("Minutes of," 1988, p. 130; emphasis added).

Such efforts by the behavioral psychologists notwithstanding, the leaders of organized psychology as a whole appear to have been ambivalent about owning behavior analysis at that time. The president of Division 25 was "largely ignored" when he contacted the APA office about listing behavior analysis as a separate specialty within psychology ("Minutes of," 1990, p. 10).

The moves to incorporate behavior analysis into psychology might have exerted pressure, on those behavior analysts who were ambivalent about separation, to form closer affiliations with organized psychology. But these events also re–emphasized philosophical integrity as a variable of demarcation between (a) disciplinary coalitions like either psychology or behavior analysis and (b) the discipline of behaviorology.

By the late 1980s, the phrase *behavior analysis* had come to denote behavioral practitioners who operate individually with a variety of supporting philosophies of science and who also grouped together under the behavior analysis banner at least partly due to political and economic contingencies. On the other hand, behaviorologists shared radical behaviorism as their common philosophy of science. During the early years of their movement, described in this account, they did not compromise their philosophy of science to enhance a social, economic, or political position within organized science.

The Association for Behavior Analysis (ABA). Previously called the Midwestern Association of Behavior Analysis (MABA), ABA traces its origins to an eight year interval of informal and formal meetings begun in 1966. The history of that period, briefly reviewed here, comes mostly from a history article by Margaret Peterson (Peterson, 1978) who was involved in starting that movement.

ABA was begun, however gradually, by people frustrated in their attempts to operate scientifically under organizational arrangements controlled by others who were respecting a different science—a kind of motivation that would later share in driving the behaviorology movement. Significantly, like TIBA, ABA also began with a strong commitment to the philosophy of radical behaviorism and to the kind of science that radical behaviorism supports. Peterson, in her article, consistently used the terms behavior analysis, behavior analyst, behaviorist, and behavioral:

> ...in the restricted sense of the orientation most directly related to the work of B.F. Skinner and characterizing the work [then] currently published in the *Journal of the Experimental Analysis of Behavior* (JEAB) and the *Journal of Applied Behavior Analysis* (JABA). (p. 3)

The psychologists who had long dominated the Midwestern Psychological Association (MPA) had been rejecting submissions from behavioral people for presentations at MPA conventions (p. 3 [stand–alone page numbers like this in this chapter are from Peterson, 1978]). This snubbing precipitated an all–day meeting of concerned behaviorists during MPA's 1971 annual convention. The agenda pertained to organizing a "behavioral group." Peterson explained:

> MPA continually proved to be an inefficient mechanism for behavior analysts to exchange and report research interests. These difficulties eventually led to the development of an independent behavioral movement within MPA. (p. 3)

This early effort was merely an attempt to organize for political leverage *within* MPA. The need for separation only gradually became apparent.

If, in emerging from these early beginnings, ABA had evolved into the organizational center of an independent scientific discipline that was quality–controlled by the philosophy of radical behaviorism, then the behaviorology movement probably would not have arisen two decades later. Aside from historic interest, why ABA did *not* follow such a course is of substantial *practical* importance in steering the evolution of organized behaviorology; hence the following degree of detail.

Within the MPA minority, consisting of concerned behaviorists, two strategies emerged: First the group would try to change the operation of MPA by taking over some of its leadership positions. Some positions were subsequently obtained, but any resulting changes in the way the organization operated were deemed insufficient. A survey among the dissatisfied behaviorists revealed "overwhelming" support for a second strategy that was subsequently adopted: The group would conduct its *own* behavior analysis conferences in conjunction with MPA conventions.

MABA held its first such conference in 1974. But costs and room scheduling problems forced the meeting to be held at the University of Chicago rather than at the MPA convention hotel elsewhere in the city. At the group's second convention, held in 1975 concurrently with MPA (but at another hotel just across the street), one important development was the declaration of a new purpose. In addition to continuing to press MPA for more cooperation, the statement of purpose also declared that the new behavioral organization would "provide a meeting place for behavior oriented *non*–psychologists" (p. 5; emphasis added). This was in no way intended to threaten the political dominance of the psychologists who maintained a substantial majority in the break–away MABA.

However, problems with MPA continued. MPA insisted on "complete censorship rights to all sessions MABA wished to hold or schedule" (p. 7). As a result, at a critical meeting held during that second convention, the MABA Organizing Committee reviewed its relations with MPA. A survey had revealed that few of MABA's people were actually attending sessions at both conventions. This suggested that the cost being incurred by MABA to make that possible for its members was not justified. Also, hotel accommodations for the joint meetings with MPA were difficult to secure. So the committee decided to pursue the task of effecting a *total* organizational separation of MABA from MPA. But that move was intensely debated, and the decision to do so cost the fledgling MABA organization some of its members, including one of its most energetic leaders, Gerald Mertins, who was then serving as MABA coordinator. Mertins left MABA to continue his efforts to influence MPA directly from within.

MABA held its 1976 convention in tandem with that of MPA rather than concurrently. MABA had stepped away from MPA, but only one pace. This step was a successive approximation that tested the water but did not yet pit MABA's exclusive drawing power against that of MPA. Nor did that step completely alienate MPA people by operating with total independence as a direct competitor, though that would soon happen.

The fourth MABA convention, in 1977, saw increasing commitments by MABA leaders to growth, both national and international, as well as, significantly, to guild issues. A resolution emerged that MABA pursue licensing and professional certification—a step beyond the mere accreditation of training programs. That resolution arose not only because these "have proven economically and politically beneficial to professions" (p. 14) but also because "if MABA does not take an active role, such decisions will be made by persons in other disciplines and legislative bodies who may attempt to licence or govern behavior–analytic practices" (p. 14). (Just such an attempt occurred in Florida in 1991, and is discussed in Chapter 5.) Though probably not fully analyzed at the time, this commitment to guild issues formally committed MABA to growth in part as a *political* organization.

In planning for the 1978 convention, the MABA Council endorsed the concept of growth in various ways. It changed the organization's name to The Association for Behavior Analysis. It extended ABA's influence internationally. It established regional affiliated organizations. And it accepted an organizational focus on social issues, furthering the need for the kind of organization that could attain political effectiveness. In general, the MABA leaders acted on the concurrent and rational assumption that organizational and political power would best accrue through the recruitment of large numbers of people. That notion may have gained special strength from the financial worries that the organization had faced throughout its formative years, which made the economies of scale seem especially attractive. MABA was small and operated with volunteer help and meager funds. But it had originated in a larger organization (MPA) which had a big–budget tradition and large–scale fiscal operations. In spite of the poverty that circumstances now imposed, the early MABA leaders were accustomed to thinking about organizational money matters from a bigger organizational perspective.

The long–range organizational implications of these various moves toward guild issues, rapid growth, and support of social causes were probably not obvious. Steps taken to build a scientific discipline, and moves taken to enhance political, social, or economic advantages, often have incompatible implications to which people are not sensitive at the time. Importantly, the MABA founders had been especially concerned about good science and had wanted to create an organization that would better support it. Nathan Azrin, an early MABA president, had expressed a hopeful visionary projection (from Peterson, 1978):

> What we are witnessing with MABA may be not only a distinctive type of regional convention organization, but also the birth of a new discipline... separate from Psychology, Psychiatry, Education, and other related areas. Perhaps this perspective will give special impetus to the growth of the area, more so than has been possible when behavior analysis has been required to mold its development to conform to the format of the other disciplines. (p.15)

However, the organization drifted toward a policy of mass recruitment of members. Inevitably the need for income from dues and the need for a collective political voice conflicted with efforts to impose scientific and philosophical skill requirements on new applicants. The organization increasingly emphasized action on social and cultural fronts which could unintentionally divert attention from important scientific and philosophical issues. This was an emphasis that would appeal to potential recruits with more of a bent for social and political action than for the science that could best inform those actions. And with membership came control through unrestricted voting rights.

While affecting an *organizational* separation from psychology, the early failure to bear the cost of dissociating conceptually and scientifically from psychology permitted some followers to keep a foot in both disciplinary camps. This also kept the door open for ABA to continue recruitment of large numbers of behaviorally inclined *psychologists.* Most such persons would remain loyal to the organized discipline of psychology and would not work to support a separate discipline. They would support ABA only as a semi–autonomous piece of organized psychology and as a general behavioral cause–and political–action group.

Ever since MABA became ABA, tensions have continued in ABA between different factions: One group preferred that behavior analysis remain a disciplinary facet of psychology. Another group wanted a separate discipline called *behavior analysis* with its own philosophy, science, and behavioral technologies apart from those identified with psychology. But by the late 1980s, after long erosion of any such potential once there, the dream of a separate "behavior analysis" discipline centered in ABA seemed remote. This was especially so with the large number of psychologists and others loyal to psychology residing in ABA as voting members who could not be expected to endorse their own discipline's exclusion.

Some members on both sides of the argument had made heavy professional investments in the implications of their respective positions. Therefore they were not in a position to acquiesce, so a moot debate continues. Consider, for example, the equality of the substantial personal professional investments of the people in behavior analysis training programs, some within, and some outside of, organized psychology. ABA members at North Texas State University or at the University of Kansas, where behavior analysis training is *apart* from psychology, are in no more of a personal position to acquiesce on this issue than are ABA members from universities where behavior analysis training is embedded *within* psychology departments, such as at Auburn University, West Virginia University, or Western Michigan University.

Behavioral psychologists, dedicated to changing psychology to a more behavioral discipline, have had an option of supporting either ABA or Division 25 in APA. Political leverage might be gained by threatening the larger psychology establishment with defection by participating in ABA. This is similar to an abused spouse initiating divorce proceedings and temporarily moving out in what sometimes is actually a threatening gesture aimed at ultimately saving the relationship. When the split begins to look permanent or is taken too seriously, the party engaged in the ploy makes moves of reconciliation (see the discussion in a later section about the American Psychological Society for other examples of this strategy). However, little evidence suggested that the massive APA, with nearly 65,000 members (Hayes, 1987b, p.41), had grown concerned about the gestures of independence by the few percent (Division 25, 1990) of its members in the behavioral minority.

A reasonable conclusion seems to be that the ABA of today cannot serve as the organizational locus of an entirely independent and singular discriminable discipline—nor has that been possible since the early days of MABA. This is due to a series of early assumptions, decisions, and commitments by its leaders, as well as because of moves within organized psychology against an independent behavior analysis discipline. To a debatable degree, which some members seek always to reverse, ABA has attained an *organizational* independence from the psychology establishment. But persons committed to retaining behavior analysis as a conceptual facet of psychology continue to share heavily in the control of ABA.

The reluctance of some devoted ABA supporters to accept the view that ABA represents a disciplinary mix, instead of an integral discipline called behavior analysis, was underscored when one of the authors of this document submitted a final draft of a paper (Fraley, 1988c) to *The Behavior Analyst.* In that paper he had described behavior analysis as "a branch of psychology represented by an APA division much influenced by behaviorological science." The editor subsequently telephoned to say that the paper had been forwarded to the printer with that statement deleted at the editor's discretion. One stated reason was to save space. Another was because the editor disagreed that that should be the case, and was uncomfortable about acquiescing to the psychology establishment on that point.

Another example surfaced early in February 1989 on the ABA ballot to elect a Council representative at–large. One candidate's statement of goals for ABA included strengthening the identity of behavior analysts—credentialling them as such and accrediting their training programs. The candidate lamented the fact that the special skills of behavior analysts are "too readily claimed by the special educator, counselor, psychologist or other 'imposters'…" At that time both the editor and the candidate mentioned in these examples were associated with training programs that had the phrase "behavior analysis" in their titles yet operated apart from psychology departments.

The founders of ABA, however, were mainly psychologists who had adopted the phrase *behavior analysis* and taken their organization outside of APA. But they had not also taken its scientific and philosophical property outside of the *concept* of psychology. Psychologists remained welcome in ABA. And so many of them joined ABA that for psychologists with territorial tendencies to claim "behavior analysis" as one of the areas either within psychology, or under the umbrella of its influence, seemed natural and appropriate (see J. Vargas, 1989, for some relevant data).

As of this writing ABA is playing out a perhaps necessary historical role by occupying a transition niche in the evolution of behavioral science. Organized in ABA, *behavioral* psychology, including behavior analysis, constitutes an evolutionary branch between the trunk of organized mainstream psychology and the emergent organized discipline of behaviorology (also, see Ledoux, 1997a). At least a few of the ABA founders apparently viewed ABA's emergence as the organizational expression of an independent disciplinary movement. But that was neither the functional reality of its beginnings nor of its existence since that time. Even Azrin, whose hopeful appraisal of disciplinary independence was quoted earlier, was later counted among those who preferred that behavior analysts remain within psychology. He even argued against behaviorists leaving the APA for the equally psychological APS (American Psychological Society) saying, "behavioral interests are not served by actions that encourage individuals or Division 25 to weaken the involvement with APA" (Azrin, 1988, p. 140). Many ABA members hesitate, for apparently rational reasons, to let philosophical and scientific commitment jeopardize a personal professional position mediated either by organized psychology or by an indefinite discipline called behavior analysis. ABA contains a smaller number of behaviorologists (or persons prepared to assume that identity).

ABA continues to serve what many behaviorologists see as an important purpose. If not as a disciplinary locus protective of a particular science and its special philosophy, then ABA serves as a scientific coalition. ABA provides a meeting ground for behavioral professionals of different types. At the same time, the various behavioral *disciplines*, organized elsewhere to foster their own conceptual integrity, more clearly define themselves and work to resolve any conflicts attendant to their mutual existences. In such a role ABA, as a general behaviorally oriented organization, operates more as a widely representative science forum and social/political advocacy body supporting behavioral causes, most of which are ardently supported by the behaviorologists in ABA. In the advocacy role ABA *complements* mainly scientific disciplinary organizations such as TIBA

(Ledoux, 1989). All early TIBA leaders and most of its members retained their formal affiliations with ABA. In her 1989 ABA presidential address, Julie Vargas (1989), in a data–based examination of the nature of ABA, revealed a kind of organization left suited by its history for precisely the kind of mission described here.

E.A. Vargas (1988) had earlier elaborated on the respective roles of TIBA and ABA. In part, he wrote that we behaviorologists

> ...can spend our time talking and becoming active over matters such as credentialling, women's rights, rights to effective education, and other social policy matters. Or...we can spend our time talking about habituation, foraging behavior, experimental work in the classroom, clinical applications of behaviorological principles, contingency analysis of cultural phenomena, five–term contingency analysis, verbal behavior, and other science matters.
>
> Other organizations, for example, the Association for Behavior Analysis to which many of us belong, already deal with advocacy issues. Such a role well fits an organization such as ABA. ABA's members divide themselves on basic scientific and epistemological issues, as denoted by such labels as interbehaviorists, radical behaviorists, cognitive behaviorists, and methodological behaviorists. These groups would never agree on a basic disciplinary foundation. Furthermore they represent different disciplinary backgrounds in their interest about behavior analysis. There are psychologists and behaviorologists, social workers and sociologists, educators and clinicians—and a stray member here and there from other disciplines, for example, philosophy. Many, if not most, of these professionals did not join ABA to step away from their home discipline and set up a new one. They joined ABA to exchange views on mutual interests. They share, for example, common ethical concerns. Though a psychologist and a behaviorologist would disagree whether it is language or verbal behavior that should be studied, they would agree that all students and patients should have the right to effective treatment. These common social policy concerns can be pursued within an organization such as ABA. Our scientific disciplinary needs can be fully met only by our own organization. (p. 3)

By 1991, a scientific/technological trend, congruent with this analysis of organizational evolution, was detectable within ABA. For instance, in its 1991 publicity flyer, the Society for the Advancement of Behavior Analysis (SABA, ABA's tax–free satellite organization) was defining behavior analysis as "a science–based helping *profession* based on the application of basic principles of learning to the solution of behavior and performance problems" (emphasis added; see Fraley, 1992b). Calling behavior analysis a profession, which is defined by the kinds of problems its practitioners attempted to solve, skirted the issue of how to describe and organize a verbal community around the underlying science that implicitly informed such work. But more importantly, the behavior analysis leaders were defining that movement in guild terms rather than discipline terms. Their action was perhaps a tacit recognition of a kind of shift in the behavior analysis movement that carried it further away from any posture of competition, with movements like behaviorology, for the organizational locus of the underlying basic natural science.

Those events did not occur without resistance. The appearance of this guild–focused definition brought strenuous objections from the science–oriented faction within

ABA, and the president of ABA subsequently disavowed it (Morris, 1991). The following year, the *Behavior Analysis Digest,* a publication edited and distributed independently of ABA by Joseph Wyatt, responded to this debate by publishing its own definition of behavior analysis as "a natural science approach to the study of behavior, and the application of science–based interventions to problems of individual, social, and cultural importance" (Behavior Analysis..., 1992). This marked the first time that members of the organized behavior analysis movement had emphasized the adjective "natural" in a scientific definition of their activity. The behaviorologists had, from the beginning, accepted their own natural science approach as a basic assumption of their self–definition. But the behavior analysts, in nursing their relations with the heavily metaphysical mainstream psychology community, had never before so blatantly defined themselves in language that emphasized that facet of their contrast with the more traditional psychologists. In doing so, some of them were nudging themselves away from psychology and closer to behaviorology.

However, ABA's 1989 membership questionnaire (ABA, 1989) had also asked respondents how they would characterize ABA *then,* and how they would predict it *in 5 years* and *in 10 years* hence. With percentages of respondents listed in that order (i.e., 1989, +5, and +10), responding members characterized their organization as follows: as a scientific society (27.2%, 25.5%, 23.9%), as an academic organization (34.2%, 28.8%, 25.9%), as advocacy oriented (9.6%, 12.8%, 14.3%), as practitioner oriented (28.0%, 31.9%, 34.7%), and as other (1.0%, 1.0%, 1.2%). These responses predicted a slow drift toward a less scientific and less academic organization that would be more focused on clinic–related issues. Such a trend may have appeared likely in part due to immigration from the more clinically oriented Association for the Advancement of Behavior Therapy (AABT). Long–term changes in AABT (discussed in the next section) continued to make that organization increasingly less appealing to consistently behavioral practitioners.

For behaviorologists to try to change ABA into a behaviorological disciplinary organization did not seem feasible, or even appropriate. This was for the same kinds of reasons that made the attempt to recast psychology into a suitable home for their discipline seem not only inappropriate but futile. Many ABA members spoke ambiguously about their respective disciplinary orientations. Others seemed ambivalent. ABA members needed individually to analyze the contingencies governing their involvement with ABA. They would have to consider the incompatible basic analytical approaches represented respectively by psychology and behaviorology. And they would have to chart their own best courses for future disciplinary and professional progress.

Ironically, by the early 1990s, moves with strong independence implications (discussed in detail in Chapter 5) were coming from the clinically oriented ABA members rather than from the more scientifically oriented group. Behavior analytic clinicians, who objected (a) to being state licensed as "psychologists" and (b) to required supervision by psychologists as a condition of practice, were seeking to be licensed as "behavior analysts." This would require state recognition of behavior analysis as an independent discipline (Shook, 1993). While political and economic issues had attenuated the independence moves by the more science focused members, these issues were now propelling the clinical group toward disciplinary independence.

In summary, the founders of ABA included a number of radical behaviorists who were prepared to experiment with disciplinary separation. But political and economic contingencies favoring quick numerical growth soon produced a large coalition of "behavioral" people among whom disciplinary unity was increasingly infeasible. Soon the issue of commonality in science and philosophy, beyond that generally connoted by the term *behavioral,* was overshadowed by other causes shared among the members. Appropriately, under the circumstances, ABA began to entertain advocacy issues rather than assuming the organizational role of protector of the scientific and philosophical integrity of a particular basic discipline—though passionate advocates of an independent behavior analysis discipline continued to resist these trends on scientific grounds. By the early 1990s they had gained support from clinicians seeking independent credentials for behavior analysts. Apart from the question of whether behavior analysis is a kind of psychology or an independent discipline, ABA is organized for, and heavily committed to, the pursuit of social causes and professional issues. As such it complements more than competes with the more purely science focused TIBA.

The Association for the Advancement of Behavior Therapy (AABT). Over the years most members of AABT have been practicing clinical psychologists who have found behavioral techniques useful. The integrity of the organization centers on a particular field of application, namely clinical practice. The relation of AABT to organized psychology is less revolutionary than that of ABA. Membership in AABT does not significantly jeopardize one's status as a psychologist with respect to basic disciplinary foundations. In AABT, where many members regard themselves as either psychologists or practitioners of the medical specialty of psychiatry, the more mentalistic members impose compromises on their more behaviorist colleagues (see Giles, 1984). This weakens any countercontrols that behavioral practitioners might mount against the drift toward cognitive or mentalistic verbal behavior. Werner Matthijs, the Belgian behaviorologist, and others familiar with the European Association of Behavior Therapy (EABT), have described that organization in the same way (personal communications). Al Kearney (1988) reported in his presentation at the first TIBA convention:

> The cognitive movement has gained such great ascendancy and strength in AABT that, at the World Congress of Behavior Therapy, Joseph Wolpe was prompted to suggest publicly that the name of AABT be changed to the "Association for the Promotion of Eclectic Recipes."

Given these realities plus its applied focus on clinical applications as opposed to the development of the basic science, the early behaviorologists construed AABT to be even less suitable than ABA to serve as the organizational home of a new discipline featuring a consistent philosophical, scientific, and technological integrity. The founders of the behaviorology movement therefore did not seriously consider attempting to organize under the auspices of AABT.

In general, besides the uncertainty about which discipline should inform a clinician's practices, within psychology departments three kinds of contingencies detract from the quality of clinical training that behaviorologists would deem adequate (see Michael, 1980, for an extended discussion): (a) The prevailing perception of virtue in eclecticism (Ledoux, 1997a) results in surveys of the conceptual foundations of various schools of analysis, and training in the behavioral perspective is necessarily diminished when treated merely as one of those approaches. (b) The enthusiasm for applied research in such programs can lead to curricula which de–emphasize conceptual fundamentals to allow time for accelerated and extended involvement with applied practice. And (c) faculty members in clinical programs, themselves products of such training, can lack interest or skills in the conceptual foundations of a behavioral science. A professional organization peopled by such faculty members and their students, or former students, appeared unprepared to play a significant role in the emergence of an independent basic science of behaviorology. Even behavioral psychologists, echoing Wolpe's lament, have been voicing complaints in conversation about what they see as AABT's creeping disrespect even for the principles of *behaviorally influenced psychology.*

The American Psychological Society (APS). During the mid–1980s a substantial political rift developed within APA when the applied, clinically oriented practitioners, with their numerical superiority, assumed increasing political control of the giant APA to further what were primarily their guild interests. The rift seemed to be exacerbated by traditional biases against clinicians among more theoretical and conceptual APA members: They often deemed clinicians to be less well trained in the scientific and philosophical fundamentals, and more prone to scientific drift under both the practical exigencies of clinical practice and the strong personal financial contingencies that often pervade clinical operations. These more scholarly types, whose salaries were often provided through universities, were typically free of the kind of economic contingencies that prevail in the working environments of those who must survive on client fees. The more scholarly, academic types within APA, representing the scientific and philosophical mix typical of psychology, became increasingly concerned about their relative loss of control over the disciplinary literature, training programs, credentialling, and even definition of the psychology "discipline" itself. In the subsequent political battles, waged over efforts to reorganize APA, these numerically inferior forces, representing more attention to scientific fundamentals, continually lost.

Steven Hayes (1987a, 1987b, 1987c), from his platform as president of the behavioral Division 25 of APA, described the mounting crisis and marshaled support to resist the guild–focused clinicians. He helped organize the APS as a separatist group initially called the Assembly for Scientific and Applied Psychology (ASAAP), and threatened to lead that group out of the APA if political parity could not be achieved within the APA. The resistance movement operated under the joint auspices of ASAAP and the Council of Graduate Departments of Psychology. That resistance movement, defending what its leaders described as "good science," gained widespread support from various units within APA, but not an overall political majority.

More importantly, because Hayes and his close followers had long been identified with the tiny behavioral minority within psychology, perhaps such a new organization, with Hayes and his close followers taking a leading role in its development, might be more behavioral than APA. Persons identifying themselves as "behavioral" constituted only a small percentage of the APA membership (Epstein, 1987a, reported that Division 25 membership had dropped below 2% of the APA total). But the ratio of behavioral members to non–behavioral members *within* the new APS movement appeared to improve only slightly.

While still formally within APA, the movement scheduled its own separate conference for June 1988. Movement leaders invited over 100 psychologists thought to share their concerns. The regularly appearing news and information article in the APA Division 25 journal, *Behavior Analysis* (1988, *1*, 23), noted that "approximately 10% of the invitees are in one way or another affiliated with behavioral psychology." This implies, of course, that about 90% were *not* behavioral. Although the behavioral faction might have accomplished a slight ratio gain as a result of the APA rift, that gain did not appear to be significant.

During these developments Hayes remained active in the leadership of APA Division 25, which he apparently hoped would defect to APS (see Hayes, 1987a–c). Division 25, focusing on the "experimental analysis of behavior," had always attracted more scientific and scholarly people than guild–focused practitioners. But by 1988 the appeal of Division 25 was waning significantly within the increasingly guild–oriented APA. Although APA had tens of thousands of members, Division 25 received only seventy new applications for membership during all of 1987. A 1988 report to the Division 25 Executive Committee stated "only 15 out of 3460 applications this quarter to APA were for Div. 25" ("Minutes of," 1988, p. 125). Within APA this was a market share of less than one–half of one percent. Hayes (1988b) described the deteriorating situation this way:

> Year by year Division 25 shrinks in size. We are now down several hundred members from our peak; our total membership will probably sink below 1,000 in the next few years [a prediction that proved correct; see Division 25, 1990]. We just lost one of our Council seats and at the current rate will lose our last one within several years. Our leadership is leaving. Even former Presidents of the Division are no longer Division 25 members. The Division 25 convention hospitality suite, which used to draw hundreds, now draws only handfuls. The convention program, which used to receive several dozen submissions, now receives almost none. Basic behavior analysts often literally have to be begged to present a paper in our convention program. (p. 138)

In January 1989 a circulated brochure described the new academic and scientific psychology organization. (By that time it had become independent of APA and been renamed the American Psychological Society.) The brochure listed 64 important psychologists who had joined as "founders." Very few could be identified as behaviorists of *any* variety (e.g., the 1986 ABA membership list included only two of them, Stephen Hayes and Duane Rumbaugh). To attract the large numbers of followers necessary for the kind of political struggle being waged, the behavioral psychologists once again needed to maintain a togetherness with cognitivists, "humanists," and others of most any ideological persuasion. A coalition partner had only to pass as seriously "scientific" (as psychologists define that term). APS leaders increasingly employed the descriptive phrase "scientific psychology" apparently to emphasize their differences with the implicitly less scientific guild–focused factions that they sought to leave behind in the APA.

Signs of a political struggle to capture a large membership continued to appear, some aimed at recruiting ABA members. Hayes, who had become treasurer of the new APS, had long been an ABA member and participant in ABA conventions. But he sent a letter to ABA informing its leaders that he and his usual traveling party, having grown dissatisfied with ABA, would not attend the 1989 ABA convention. That action, however intended, was widely interpreted as an appeal for others to join him in abandoning ABA in favor of the new APS movement in psychology. But ABA membership records across the following two years revealed no sign of such a shift.

At about the same time, B.F. Skinner, along with many important psychologists, received a request from the APS psychologists. They wanted him to join in formally endorsing their new movement and the APS organization. After some delay, in March 1989, the *APS Observer* featured a section entitled "Letters of Greeting" that included the following entry signed by B.F. Skinner (1989c):

> Many years ago, E.G. Boring predicted that the future of the APA would depend upon whether those members who would eventually compose a very

> large majority, because there would be more places for them in American life, could control their own interests and aspirations and make sure that the scientific side of the Association would continue to occupy an important place. I do not think they have done so, and a fresh start is therefore needed. The American Psychological Society seems to me to be the natural next step in the furtherance of psychology as a science. (p. 8)

Though requested as one of a large set of such endorsements, the APS literature focused special attention on Skinner's letter.

The emergence of APS was particularly interesting to the leaders of TIBA insofar as APS, like TIBA, was purportedly established to foster good science. But APS members were also being subjected to strong contingencies in classes other than scientific. For instance, in its first 24 weeks of existence, APS membership rose to 4000 regular members plus 1000 students. Its leaders were contemplating establishing a "Washington presence," and they recommended that the APS budgets for 1989 and 1990 include $100,000 and $250,000 respectively for that purpose. (For more details, see the *APS Observer, 2* [2], 1989.) By the start of 1993, advertisements for new members, mass mailed to university faculties including those in behavior–related departments, saliently touted insurance programs, travel and lodging discounts, financial services, discounts on profession–related purchases, and potential access to prizes and awards. These materials also heavily emphasized a strong APS mission of government lobbying.

Clearly, aside from whatever the "scientific psychology" label was intended to imply about the development and evolution of science, APS was formally bringing its members under a wide variety of non–scientific contingencies and appealing to potential new members on those bases. Furthermore, while APS might shun practitioners with self–serving guild focused interests who did not seem appropriately respectful of scientific foundations, APS still reflected an intense preoccupation with maintaining the status enjoyed as a result of the cultural entrenchment of organized psychology.

Many behaviorologists had little difficulty agreeing that the APS movement may indeed be "the natural next step," as Skinner said, *for psychology.* But that agreement was quite aside from considerations about their own science. The struggle over guild issues, which precipitated the APS revolution, remains a problem in psychology for psychologists. It is not a particular problem in behaviorology (though the APA/APS struggle helped clarify some important matters for behaviorologists). Furthermore, the lines of fracture that have been produced in organized psychology by that issue are not lines of fracture that threaten the behaviorology movement. That is by design; the behaviorology movement was conceived and constructed to minimize guild–related contingencies. The scientific psychologists' whole revolutionary struggle was directed against those kinds of disruptive economic contingencies and their scientific and political implications within psychology.

Whether or not the APS movement ultimately succeeds, psychology, emerging either split or whole, will continue as the disciplinary home, or homes, of thousands of persons who defend and practice a science quite unlike behaviorology in nature and capacity. And the psychologists can be expected to multiply themselves prodigiously. Behavioral psychologists who support APS might, with the help of their majority non–behavioral allies, eventually impose some effective countercontrols on colleagues deemed conceptually shallow or economically distracted. But the APS alliance portends no relief for its behavioral faction with respect to the types of philosophy and science predominating in the discipline of psychology. ABA convention programs show that even Steven Hayes soon resumed his annual participation in the ABA conventions (e.g., in 1992 the program listed him as a participant in five convention events).

Except as a somewhat parallel organizational experiment to be observed and evaluated, the APS movement appears to be irrelevant to the behaviorology movement. One residual question of interest pertains to the behavioral psychologists who sought to further the interests of good science by bolting to APS *instead* of taking the opportunity to move away from psychology and join the behaviorology movement. Did they make the right move? Hayes's own growing dissatisfaction with APS as an organizational sanctuary for his science was revealed in a question that he raised about the future of APA Division 25. In his scathing denunciation of APA (Hayes, 1991), in which he explained his recent departure from that organization, he asked:

> ...where will a Division 25 live? It is not a scientist group, nor a practitioner group, nor a scientist–practitioner group. It is a *disciplinary* group. *Yet we have no disciplinary organization left within psychology.* (p. 21, emphases added)

Earlier in that article he had allowed that "APS could still come through if its upcoming reorganization is brilliantly done. ...I still have hopes" (p. 21). But apparently he did not have many, in view of his unequivocal declaration that his discipline had *no niche within organized psychology* (which at that time clearly included APS). All things considered, Hayes seemed to be living through the kind of implications that several years before had led the behaviorologists to make their own kind of decisive organizational move.

A New Professional Organization

An organization originally called The Behaviorology Society came into existence on 24 May 1987 when nine radical behaviorists met on the eve of the thirteenth ABA convention in Nashville, Tennessee. Gathered for the meeting (which was tape–recorded and major portions subsequently transcribed—see Ledoux, 1987b) were Lawrence Fraley (West Virginia University), Sigrid Glenn (NTSU), Douglas Greer (Columbia University), Joe Layng (Enabling Technologies, Inc., Chicago, IL), Stephen Ledoux (State University of New York at Canton), Jack Michael (Western Michigan University), Mark Sundberg (Sundberg & Associates, Concord, CA), Ernest Vargas (West Virginia University), and Julie Vargas (West Virginia University). The meeting was organized and chaired by E.A. Vargas.

Members of the group were already in general agreement on the need to recognize formally the distinctive nature and independence of this scientific discipline. The agenda included (a) potential names for the organization, (b) the current situation of the basic science of behavior, and (c) the implications of the culture–wide monopoly, with respect to behavior–related matters, enjoyed by the cognitive/mentalistic coalition of researchers, practitioners, sympathetic administrators, and politicians.

The participants also considered the relation of any new organization to ABA. This was a sensitive issue because some persons in attendance had extensive professional investments in ABA, and a few continued to assume that ABA might yet become the organizational locus of an integral and independent scientific discipline. Those conservative in that regard prevailed in rejecting possible names for the new organization that contained the term "international" or "association." The founders did intend that the organization evolve with an international character. But some objected to the grand connotation of that term, deeming it pretentious since the incipient organization had fewer than ten members, all Americans. Also, ABA was stressing *its* international operations (though until the behaviorologists had subsequently done so with respect to their organization, ABA did not begin appending phrases to that effect to its name). Using "international" or "association" might have hinted at organizational competition, which some present would not tolerate, and all were anxious to avoid.

After adopting a name, *The Behaviorology Society,* those present constituted themselves as the Society's Executive Board. Julie Vargas was unanimously elected to serve as the first chairperson. The Executive Board then asked her to organize the drafting of several statements: purpose and goals, cultural mission, relationship to other organizations, membership arrangements, and other statements deemed important. She was to circulate a draft of those constitutional documents among the Society members for review and critique. The members adopted plans for future meetings. By the time the meeting adjourned, the discipline of behaviorology had been given formal recognition under the auspices of an organization of its advocates and practitioners. So passed the 24th of May, 1987.

Seven months later, on 28 December 1987, an all–day meeting was held in Waltham, Massachusetts. Invitations to participate were extended to the five Executive Board members within a day's driving distance of the Boston area. Julie Vargas chaired the meeting, which Lawrence Fraley, Stephen Ledoux, and Ernest Vargas also attended. This subset of the original group functioned as an Executive Board subcommittee. It had been empowered by the larger group at the founding meeting to take action on early organizational matters. Circumstances had gradually convinced the members of the subcommittee that the name should accurately describe the nature of the planned organization. Also the admission to membership of some persons from other countries was imminent. So the subcommittee decided to change the name of the organization to *The International Behaviorology Association* contingent upon subsequent approval by the members. The subcommittee would also ask the members to approve other actions taken, including scheduling the first convention of TIBA for August 1988.

Until more members became available to help with the organizational work and the tasks could be further subdivided, some of the early members accepted assignments to rather broad responsibilities: Ernest Vargas was to concentrate on membership matters; Stephen Ledoux would organize the first convention, and also focus on international activities; Lawrence Fraley would plan for publication activities; Julie Vargas would investigate the problem of how to develop teaching and training opportunities for the new discipline. She would also consider how behaviorological instructional materials might be created, and would explore the possibility of a handbook for the discipline.

More importantly, TIBA leaders were sensitive to the implications of the various organizational structures, operations, and mission–related assumptions discussed earlier in this chapter. Clearly, no existing organization was suited to providing an organizational home of the kind needed for this movement. Therefore, those attending devoted much of the meeting to designing a structure for the new organization that would keep members' behavior focused on the basic mission objectives. For example, any organization of persons with specialized repertoires can lose its way if an overzealous devotion to ballot box democracy is combined with a relaxation of standards for the admission of new members. Scientific organizations fall prey to that trend when the recruitment of large memberships, thought necessary for gaining status and influence through political and economic power, is accomplished at the expense of qualitative standards for the discipline–related repertoires of the recruits. The result can be control invested in a scientifically and philosophically divergent electorate. TIBA would chart the course of its growth to avoid that unacceptable trade. As E.A. Vargas (1988) wrote:

> The strength of TIBA will lie not in size, but in the commitment of its members: how extensively they dedicate themselves to the science of behaviorology, the effort to improve that science, and to the means by which that science can be improved.... Such work concerns not only the products of science, but the infrastructure to facilitate the production of those products. TIBA constitutes part of that infrastructure, as would a journal, a department of behaviorology, and other resources that become tools to move the science forward. Our scientific work depends on its supportive base. (p. 4)

The TIBA Board members attending the Waltham meeting saw their task as designing an organization that could optimize and maintain the quality of the science—especially its capacity for cultural applications. So they adopted an organizational structure (which the full TIBA Executive Board accepted prior to the first convention) featuring four membership categories. Three were non–voting categories: (a) Student, (b) Affiliate (conceived at that time as a category for interested persons, typically from other disciplines or fields, and often with minimal if any behaviorological skills themselves, who, for a variety of reasons, want to maintain close contact with the organization, receive its publications, etc.), and (c) Associate (for persons with an extensive behaviorological repertoire and a good record of professional accomplishments). The fourth category, Fellow (later changed to "Full"), was to be acquired by Associates through invitation extended by the Fellows.

Matters of importance would be resolved through voting by the Fellows. In this way the direction of the organization would remain in the hands of those members of the discipline who, over a long period of time, would have demonstrated substantial effective behavior under relevant philosophical, scientific, and political contingencies. Nevertheless, *this restriction of voting rights was a calculated risk.* The reservation of all voting privileges for a subset of people was understood to invite power seizing coups. The organization would have relatively few Fellows in its early stages, so the capacity to exert healthy counter–controls over an individual moving aggressively to establish personal control over the organization would therefore be limited. But at this time, all parties to these considerations endorsed the importance of maintaining appropriate balances of views and functional counter–controls among the Fellows.

The Associate membership category was designed to be the main category for accomplished behaviorologists, while Fellows were to exhibit a substantial extra increment of work on behalf of both the discipline and the TIBA organization. Fellows also supported TIBA by paying significantly higher dues from the outset (which they voted to double for just themselves in 1992). In December 1988, after the first convention, a new Executive Board further decided that all new, non–student TIBA members would enter at the Affiliate level. After a year of disciplinary contribution and organizational service, qualified behaviorologists could advance from affiliate status to the Associate level and beyond.

The subcommittee at the Waltham meeting assigned priority to scientific and philosophical integrity centered in the discipline of behaviorology. It rejected development strategies dependent on numerical strength *acquired by lowering the scientific standards for membership.* In a world pervaded by cognitive and mentalistic assumptions, the behaviorological vanguard could better tolerate thin ranks than tenuous resolve. The adopted organizational design separated the concept of membership size from the concept of organizational control. *The organization could accommodate any number of members,* but a personal share in controlling the organization was supposed to accrue only in proportion to one's recognized professional contributions. (See "A Small Selection of Photographs," in the book containing Ledoux, 1997e [this book], for a photo of the Waltham meeting participants.)

First TIBA convention—1988. TIBA held its first convention, TIBA–1, on 9–11 August 1988 at Clarkson University in Potsdam, New York. John Nixon, Director of Clarkson's Institute for the Study of Applied Behavior Analysis (ISABA), had extended an offer for ISABA to serve as the host. Local arrangements were coordinated by Stephen Ledoux, who was employed at the State University of New York campus in nearby Canton. Ernest Vargas developed the program of presentations and sessions.

The convention served as a forum for detailed discussions about the scientific and organizational foundations of behaviorology and directions for its development. The purposes were (a) to consolidate the integrity of the discipline by bringing the members more strongly under control of its properties, (b) to refine the definitions of the discipline including its scope and mission, (c) to plan for the continued evolution of the discipline, and (d) to prepare TIBA, the scientific and professional organization of the discipline, to support these goals through its own development and activities.

The Executive Board subcommittee responsible for planning the convention preferred a small single–track convention of persons prepared to work for the discipline and for TIBA. They thought the intimacy possible among a smaller number of committed people would support a higher quality of scientific exchange and encourage fuller and more candid contributions. The capacity of the preferred meeting room imposed a limit of thirty participants (booked by advanced registration only).

News of the upcoming convention was reaching people too late in many cases to secure travel support or to avoid conflicts with previously scheduled professional events. Many could only express interest and asked to be kept informed. A couple mentioned having been advised (by colleagues who thought the new movement pointlessly divisive) *not* to attend. McIlvaine Parsons wrote a thoughtful letter to say that he sympathized in general with moves to strengthen "behaviorist approaches" but he could not lend his support to movements which fractionalize "operant psychology."

The convention program (TIBA, 1988), which was tape–recorded, featured papers on components of the discipline, its history, and its future development. The first morning session, entitled *Philosophical and Experimental Foundations of Behaviorology,* opened with Ernest Vargas's talk titled "Difficulties and Opportunities." Carl Cheney followed with "Impacting Behavior with Science." And Jack Michael concluded with "What Is and What Is Not Our Subject Matter." The afternoon session, entitled *Philosophical and Technological Foundations of Behaviorology,* featured R. Douglas Greer, then Laura Dorow (presenting for herself and Nan McCorkle who was unable to attend), a contingent from the Los Horcones community, and Al Kearney. They respectively related behaviorology to applied settings in general, to schools, to experimental communities, and to clinical practice. (Joe Layng, also scheduled to speak, did not attend the convention nor participate further in the behaviorology movement.) The final session, entitled *Past, Present, and Future of Behaviorology,* occurred the morning of the second day. It began with a presentation called "Behaviorology: Where We Have Been and Where We Are Now" (an early version of the present paper) by Stephen Ledoux and Lawrence Fraley. A combined open forum, business meeting, and planning session followed that last paper. The discipline itself absorbed most of the discussion. Topics included TIBA journals and other publications, academic programs and departments, administrative and organizational features of the discipline, and future meetings. (At future conventions, scientific papers on topics of general interest would occupy a much larger part of the program while separately scheduled formal business meetings would deal with most organizational topics.)

Twenty people attended the convention. That number enabled the group to sit around a large circle of tables and engage in spirited discussion and debate. Most took economical lodging in an adjacent Clarkson University dormitory made available to participants. The participants represented a mix of disciplinary backgrounds and current fields. But they shared an affinity for the discipline of behaviorology, or at least for their respective concepts of it which, not surprisingly, proved to differ somewhat. In addition to the previously mentioned presenters of papers, also attending were Scott Beach, Guy Bruce, John Eshleman, Sigrid Glenn, Jeffrey Kupfer, Robert Spangler, John Stone, Jerome Ulman, and Julie Vargas. Also present was Juan Robinson who spoke for the Los Horcones Community, in Mexico, which holds a group membership in TIBA and sent a three–person delegation. (See "A Small Selection of Photographs," in the book containing Ledoux, 1997e [this book], for a photo of most of the TIBA–I participants.)

During the extended and serious discussions about the behaviorology movement a number of issues surfaced. While not all were fully resolved, at least a tentative organizational position emerged with respect to most of them. None of the issues proved so divisive as to derail the movement. Debated questions included these: What is the relation between behaviorology and behavior analysis, both as sciences and as organized movements? Is holding concurrent memberships in TIBA and ABA inconsistent? Can TIBA and ABA be complementary, and if so, would either need to change? If TIBA, especially in its early years, de–emphasizes numerical strength (and thus political clout) in order to consolidate its scientific and philosophical integrity and establish an enduring foundation, then how, other than politically, might it exert its effect and influence? Is the endorsement and participation of important and well known people critical to the recognition of the behaviorology movement? Through what mechanisms can behaviorologists develop a distinct identity and a unique set of definitive characteristics for behaviorology? And finally, what ethics should govern in cases of behaviorologists who deemed it necessary to de–emphasize or hide their scientific orientation when operating within their respective positions of professional employment?

Some convention participants most committed to a separate and distinct discipline of behaviorology shared a common intuitive notion that potentially divisive issues, especially those pertaining to relations with other disciplines and organizations, would sooner or later be resolved in their favor by events taking place *within those other settings.* If they were correct, organized behaviorology could afford to let nature take its course, with respect to some of those matters, rather than having to purchase gains through *immediate* and perhaps pressured conversions to a common wisdom.

Among the participants at that first convention, perhaps the most fundamental difference, with the most far reaching implications, was centered on the essential nature of the fledgling movement. Was it limited to the development, protection, and dissemination of effective natural science as a personal behavior repertoire in individuals? Or was it also primarily an *organizational* effort to produce a new and independent scientific verbal *community*, that is, to forge a new organizational product to serve as the organizational home of this science within the culture? This issue was about whether the behaviorology movement would evolve into a new scientific cultural agency or whether it would function more as a kind of retreat for the scientific refurbishing of persons who would do their work within other scientific verbal communities to which the benefits would then accrue. One variant was this: Were the energies and resources of this movement to be spent as direct and indirect contributions to the improvement of other organized disciplines, or would this movement stand alone ultimately to assume the cultural mission of organizing an independent discipline around this science, an endeavor in which others had lagged or faltered? Though in retrospect, the participants obviously brought these differences to that first convention in 1988, this issue was too subtle and complex to emerge explicitly, and it was not articulated on that occasion where it emerged, if at all, only as biases in the address of other issues. Debate on this potentially divisive matter would open later, mainly through the literature (e.g., see Fraley, 1988d & 1991).

In any case, the first convention was lively. Debates were vigorously pursued. Many offers to work in specific ways for the discipline or for the TIBA organization were tendered and accepted. As the convention concluded, all participants, to differing degrees, declared or implied that their further personal involvement would be worthwhile.

Prior to the first convention, the group chairperson, Julie Vargas, had contacted members of the founding group through a mailing of information about the sub–committee's preferences for organizational structure, dues, and transitional procedures. Also included was a ballot listing all nine members of the original group, from which they were to elect a president, a secretary, and a treasurer as the first formal officers of TIBA. Use of the ballots indicated acceptance of the organizational procedures. Members returned the secret ballots to a secretary at West Virginia University who had agreed to receive them and provide a report on the election outcome. Julie Vargas announced the results toward the end of the convention: Ernest Vargas had been elected Secretary, Lawrence Fraley, Treasurer, and Jack Michael, President (each for a term that would end in January 1992).

Michael had recently assumed the office of acting psychology department chairperson at Western Michigan University. During the convention discussions about the behaviorology movement he had taken the position that he was a psychologist who wanted to continue the effort to change psychology. He wanted to regard himself as a "behaviorological psychologist." Some found that acceptable because they regarded psychology as a *field* of study (although Michael's own view of what psychology should become did not comport to that model). Others deemed that position inconsistent, and the label "behaviorological psychologist" self–contradictory, because they construed behaviorology and psychology to be separate basic disciplines featuring incompatible sciences and philosophies that preclude such dual allegiance. Yet another view held that, while psychology and behaviorology were indeed fundamentally different and largely antithetical, psychology represented a scientifically and philosophically ill–informed *approximation* of behaviorology. In some of these various comparisons both psychology and behaviorology provided analytical repertoires applicable to behavior–related phenomena, but they remained incompatible paradigms. Some people were still weighing the issues. Others reasoned that organizing a separate behaviorology was the *alternative* to further serious efforts to convert the tens of thousands of mentalistic psychologists to a new and improved science (see Fraley, 1988d, for details). In any event Michael expressed his appreciation for the honor of the presidency, cited lack of time to pursue the duties of TIBA president, and declined the office.

Those in attendance from among the original nine founders immediately met and on a new ballot chose Stephen Ledoux as the first formally elected president to serve TIBA under its accepted organizational practices. His first duty was to assume the convention moderator's position being relinquished by Julie Vargas. The three new officers (Ledoux, Vargas, and Fraley) became the first Fellows of the organization. They also functioned as the first formally elected Executive Board thereby initiating the newly approved organizational structure and operating procedures.

Before adjourning, the members endorsed the international character and thrust of the behaviorology movement. They also indicated substantial support for holding some future meetings and conventions outside the United States. The delegation from the Los Horcones Community in Mexico volunteered to study the feasibility of their hosting the second TIBA convention. Their offer was enthusiastically accepted. (The second TIBA convention, TIBA–2, was subsequently held there in January 1990.)

When Clarkson University settled its account, TIBA discovered the first convention to have unexpectedly produced a profit of about $1000. TIBA began to invest this in its fledgling publications and other professional activities. For about $150 per person, the participants had paid the registration fee, received lodging, and even a couple of meals. Clarkson University had invested and recovered about $2000 on the convention. Something about TIBA's special approach to launching the behaviorology discipline was implicit in these figures.

The TIBA Statement of Purpose. Before the convention closed, those present also extended general approval to a July 1988 draft of the TIBA statement of purpose, which Stephen Ledoux had authored and taken through many revisions. That version received further polish during the next year. At an Executive Board meeting on 26 May 1989, the following refined version was approved and incorporated as part of the TIBA By–laws ("TIBA By–laws," 1989):

> TIBA is a professional organization dedicated to representing and developing the philosophical, analytical, experimental, and technological components of the discipline of behaviorology, the comprehensive natural science of the functional relations of behavior including determinants from the environment, both socio–cultural and non–cultural, as well as determinants from the biological history of the species. Therefore, recognizing that behaviorology's principles are generally relevant to all cultures and species, the purposes of TIBA are:
>
> A. to foster the philosophy of science known as radical behaviorism;
>
> B. to nurture experimental and applied research analyzing the effects of physical, biological, behavioral, and cultural variables on the behavior of organisms, with selection by consequences being an important causal mode relating these variables at the different levels of organization in the life sciences;
>
> C. to extend technological application of behaviorological research results to areas of human concern;

D. to interpret, consistent with scientific foundations, complex behavioral relations;

E. to support methodologies relevant to the scientific analysis, interpretation, and change of both behavior and its relations with other events;

F. to sustain scientific study in diverse specialized areas of behaviorological phenomena;

G. to integrate the concepts, data, and technologies of the discipline's various sub–fields;

H. to develop a verbal community of behaviorologists;

I. to assist programs and departments of behaviorology to teach the philosophical foundations, scientific analyses and methodologies, and technological extensions of the discipline;

J. to promote a scientific "Behavior Literacy" graduation requirement of appropriate content and depth at all levels of educational institutions from kindergarten through university;

K. to encourage the full use of behaviorology as the essential scientific foundation for behavior related work within all fields of human affairs;

L. to cooperate on mutually important concerns with other humanistic and scientific disciplines and technological fields where their members pursue interests overlapping those of behaviorologists; and

M. to communicate to the general public the importance of the behaviorological perspective for the development, well–being, and survival of humankind.

The first meetings of the new Executive Board. On 20 November 1988 the TIBA Executive Board, consisting of the first three TIBA Fellows (Lawrence Fraley, Stephen Ledoux, and Ernest Vargas), convened in Albany, New York at their own expense for a three–day meeting. Through approximately twenty hours of business meetings, they addressed a long agenda, including development strategies and tactics for the organization, organizational structure, and operating style. They worked to develop the discipline of behaviorology, and its professional organization, TIBA, in accordance with behaviorological principles. Like so many other aspects of the culture though, when subjected to behaviorological redesign, familiar organizational aspects had to be cast in new and unfamiliar ways by the designers.

The Executive Board devoted much time to the careful analysis of the behavior controlling implications of each proposed step, both immediate and long term. Three crucial issues emerged. First, how might TIBA further adjust its organizational structure and operating procedures to prevent the behavior of its people from drifting away from the organizational objectives? For example, the board devoted much time to finding ways of doing things that would avoid the leaders coming under economic contingencies that could jeopardize scientific standards. Second, how could TIBA balance the need for organizational stability against the need to prevent individuals or groups from retaining control and exploiting the organization to mediate access to their personal reinforcers? Third, how should TIBA manage growth? Since TIBA had to invent the organizational structure, and the arrangements for operating within it, as the organization developed, the proper pace of growth was critical. TIBA would have to develop its human resources individually and employ these resources productively. If the new movement merely became the object of the latest wave of popularity, then the transient "sincerity peddlers," who attach themselves to the latest scientific fad, could quickly inundate it. In the long run such people can have adverse effects on any movement that attracts their "loyalty."

The Executive Board recognized as its tasks (a) to develop the new disciplinary organization around the only current science with which to address effectively, at its level of analysis, the behavior–related problems of the global culture, (b) to protect the integrity of that verbal community, and (c) to provide for the constructive evolution of that science while countering the powerful and omnipresent contingencies to compromise it. The first TIBA Fellows thus attempted to create a *behaviorological* organizational product by design. They acted upon the premise that the newly organized discipline of behaviorology would ultimately eclipse psychology in providing effective behavioral technologies to address problems throughout the culture. This was already true in cases where stringent accountability was being enforced. Persons who *had to produce* effective behavior–related outcomes quickly operated in a more behaviorological fashion. But, for the time being, the general paucity of accountability in behavior–related operations throughout the culture allowed a variety of alternatives, usually pseudo–scientific and maintained under non–scientific contingencies, to prevail. The behaviorology movement would have to be initiated, constituted, maintained, and operated ultimately to assume the cultural niche reserved for an effective science of behavior. Many of the independent variables critical to that ultimate disciplinary dominance were controllable by the early TIBA Fellows as design variables—a circumstance felt as a substantial responsibility. Nevertheless, how best to arrange those variables with respect to any particular issue was seldom immediately clear.

The three participants practiced and refined the skills of reasoned argument necessary for consensus building, a process which hopefully would define the operating mode of TIBA. They reached many specific decisions, and a multitude of planning details fell into place: TIBA would develop its own general journal, named *Behaviorology.* TIBA would also pursue the proposal that it publish *The Analysis of Verbal Behavior,* an established journal, with Mark Sundberg continuing as editor (however, Sundberg subsequently dropped membership in TIBA and sought to transfer control of his journal elsewhere while continuing his career–long efforts to change psychology). The organization would ratify By–laws for TIBA. And the organization would become incorporated, seeking the non–profit tax status proper for a scientific organization.

Subsequent meetings produced further actions. The Executive Board appointed Jerome Ulman as International Activities Coordinator (replacing Stephen Ledoux who had served in that capacity prior to his election as President of TIBA). The Board also appointed Carl Cheney to the post of Publications Coordinator. As the three elected officers (Fraley, Ledoux, and E.A. Vargas) were initially the only TIBA Fellows, they also met not as an Executive board but *as* TIBA Fellows and extended invitations to Cheney and Ulman to become Fellows as well.

All five Fellows–and–officers were in Milwaukee for the 1989 ABA convention. They met again there, both as TIBA Fellows and as executive officers, for a total of about six hours. They approved the TIBA By–laws that Ledoux had drafted and other Executive Board members had edited. They made further plans for the second TIBA convention. And they reviewed progress on other fronts. Psychology–behaviorology relations, and the continuing question of what publicly to say about those relations, absorbed much of the discussion.

TIBA Publication Operations

To appeal to natural scientists of behavior, the behaviorology movement would have to offer a wide range of publication opportunities. The early behaviorologists were generally committed to developing a *complete* disciplinary model, including a full spectrum of professional publications.

TIBA Publications Board. In the fall of 1991, Cheney announced a TIBA Publications Board which he would chair (as Publications Coordinator). Also serving were Robert Crow (newsletter editor), John Eshleman, Lawrence Fraley (journal editor), R. Douglas Greer, Glenn Latham (journal managing editor), Nancy Marchand–Martella and Ronald Martella (*Behaviorological Commentaries* co–editors), Jerome Ulman, Ernest Vargas, and Julie Vargas. Cheney also began to function as TIBA 's coordinator of textbook production.

The TIBA Newsletter. The immediate need for communications to link the members of the new behaviorology movement had led to the early establishment of a newsletter. Volume 1, No. 1 appeared in the fall of 1988, edited by Carl Cheney. Called simply *"TIBA Newsletter,"* the first–page heading, composed by Lawrence Fraley, included the TIBA stationery logo previously designed by Stephen Ledoux and Scott Beach (featuring the name "Behaviorology" in five languages). After three issues in Volume 1, Volume 2 appeared in a more attractive layout under the editorship of Scott Beach who produced issues No. 1 and No. 2 during the spring and summer of 1990. As a major financial contribution to TIBA, Beach produced and distributed those two issues at his own expense. Unfortunately, he then contracted a serious illness during a foreign trip and could not continue. With Beach unable to produce issue No. 3 in Volume 2, Lawrence Fraley produced that issue while a new editor was sought. Robert Crow agreed to assume the editorship, and the newsletter operation was transferred to Crow, at the Louisiana State Medical Center in New Orleans, beginning with Volume 3. Following the Winter 1991 issue (Vol. 4, No. 1), TIBA changed the name from *TIBA Newsletter* to *Selections.* Late in 1992 Kathleen Orlando, then a TIBA student member at West Virginia University, took over the editorship.

A journal for TIBA. Shortly after forming in 1987, TIBA organized an investigation into all aspects of the feasibility of a TIBA journal. This investigation continued throughout 1988 (the year the TIBA newsletter began publication).

Many considerations and recommendations arose from that investigation. While journal contents would have to make worthwhile scientific contributions, a journal would also play an important role in defining, anchoring, and establishing the discipline. The contemplated reviewing arrangements were rigorous and included substantial assistance to authors in shaping high quality articles. By the selective nature of the subscription list (including all TIBA members) TIBA could assure authors that a critical audience of behaviorological colleagues would receive their published works.

An additional proposal was that each author receive a copy–ready master of his or her article in the form published in the journal (along with a suitable cover sheet saliently identifying the journal of origin). Using these materials, authors could acquire high quality reprints prepared through their own local and hopefully inexpensive copying services. Authors would be encouraged to distribute these among their respective colleagues and to other parties potentially interested in their work. In this way, authors could construct further professional networks linked to behaviorology.

In May 1989 the Executive Board reviewed and reiterated elements of journal policy: The journal would feature a balance of article types and would maintain quality through careful reviewing procedures. By the fall of 1989 about a dozen authors had made commitments to submit specific works.

A variety of issues arose and had to be addressed: Would behavioral psychologists, behavior analysts, or various other behaviorists, all committed to other than the behaviorological way of advancing the science, want to publish in this journal? Would they find themselves comfortable contributing to this journal and thereby lending an implicit measure of personal support to the particular long–term strategy represented by the behaviorology movement?

Another potential problem concerned the founders of TIBA who, as active professionals, had long established production patterns. As a matter of practicality, how difficult would those patterns be to change? Would other established behavior–related journals compete for their work? And, would rational organizational engineering outpace emotional predisposition? For instance, might a behaviorologist discover that his or her professional lifetime of efforts to promote better science and philosophy within the broadly defined domain of organized psychology not be as readily transferred to the support of an independent discipline as that person might have assumed?

An additional issue had implications for project management: In spite of other potential difficulties, the importance of the journal *was* understood. So, not unexpectedly, people therefore were cautious in taking concrete steps in support of it, taking time to satisfy themselves on the many points of concern about qualitative matters.

A more strategic issue revolved around the tension between member recruitment and journal establishment. To advertise the new movement and the science that it represented would necessitate publishing behaviorological articles in other more established, mass–circulation journals and in mass–marketed books. But that would make those works unavailable to a TIBA journal. Yet, the longer TIBA went without a journal, the more tenuous and uncertain the development of the movement appeared, especially in the view of outsiders who might be contemplating joining it. Publication outlets can be very important, especially to the kind of scientifically productive person often regarded as valuable to recruit. The TIBA leaders had to consider whether to disseminate the available behaviorological articles by publishing them in the books and journals of other disciplines, which would inform a wider audience about the behaviorological science and its organized movement, or whether, at least temporarily, to commit those products to enhance the movement's publication–related infrastructure.

Finally, as TIBA proceeded to define and refine its operations, it dedicated 25 percent of its dues income to fund what was regarded as another important and innovative aspect—a formalized program of research support. Could TIBA fund concurrently a journal and a substantial research support program? At its May 1992 meeting the TIBA Executive Board determined that both programs could and should be pursued concurrently. The journal effort would go forward.

All of these were worthy issues. In the end they did not prevent the establishment of the journal or significantly delay it. They are reported here to reveal how important journals do not spontaneously and abruptly arise out of the complex scientific, social, political, and economic communities that such journals represent; the actual origins of such journals are more complex and far more interesting.

In January 1992 Lawrence Fraley, who had headed the journal feasibility study and had been serving as Editor *Pro Tem,* was named Editor for a two year term. During 1991–1992 he expanded the editorial team to include associate editors: R. Douglas Greer for experimental studies, Nancy Marchand–Martella for applied studies, and John Eshleman for conceptual studies. Shortly thereafter Gloria Paige was also added as the Book Editor. The Managing Editor's function was consolidated under Glenn Latham and with his supervision the production team prepared to do the final styling of manuscripts and produce camera–ready copy of journal issues for the printer. By the summer of 1992 a set of manuscripts that had passed successfully through the reviewing process had been forwarded to Latham for that kind of final preparation.

The debates about journal issues and attendant activities brought into focus the need to further bureaucratize the organization. The founders of TIBA had created it as an engineered product, and had done so in a very short time relative to the long, slow, and more natural evolution of similar organizations. For them, designing and operationalizing TIBA embodied an exercise in behaviorological organizational engineering. Furthermore, those who had set TIBA into motion were monitoring it. And as engineers are wont to do, they continued to tinker with it, sometimes though direct interventions—especially E.A. Vargas whose training included a sociologically based specialization in complex organizations. Yet room for such continuing interventions was not an aspect of the normal, designed operating mode of TIBA. Perhaps the time had come for the designers to relax some of the direct control that they had retained informally more or less in the form of what might be called "inventor's privilege." But much was at stake. Could the organization operate more independently in accordance with its intrinsic nature? Would the clock run smoothly and keep good time if the clock makers ceased their tinkering and closed the case? Adjustments would continue to be required, but whether or not they could more often be made to occur through the normal self–correcting mechanisms built into the operating arrangements of the organization remained an unresolved question.

The International Behaviorologist. During the summer of 1991, with the *TIBA Newsletter* in its third volume and the journal still under development, Carl Cheney, as Publications Coordinator, took the lead in establishing what was initially called *Behaviorological Commentaries.* This publication featured letters, essays, and point–of–view pieces, and was edited by Ronald Martella and Nancy Marchand–Martella, although Nancy would soon transfer to the journal leaving Ronald as the sole editor. By its magazine–like nature and its featured subject matter, this publication fit between the newsletter and the journal, giving TIBA a three–faceted publication front. This journal maintained short–process peer reviewing. It also left copyrights with the authors who could then republish their material elsewhere without special permission. In 1993, coinciding with Ronald Martella's announced intention to relinquish the editorship, the Executive Board changed the name of this publication to *The International Behaviorologist* (TIB). However, the future of the publication remained ambiguous; manuscripts accumulated but as of this writing no issue of TIB has appeared. This extended delay has resulted from uncertain financing, a failure to achieve consensus on editorial policy, and latent concerns about the kinds of articles that should be featured.

Occasional publications. During 1992, members of the TIBA Publications Board were discussing a further expansion of publication operations to include the occasional publication of special works unsuited by excess length or other characteristics for inclusion in newsletter, magazine, or journal. These might include special purpose booklets or full sized books of various kinds.

Little Tests for TIBA—The History of Some Policy

In the early stages of an organization, a multitude of new issues arise. Many of these are inconsequential, some are important, and a few are loaded with potentially calamitous implications for an organization. Unfortunately, the relative significance of these various matters is *not* indicated in the often ordinary, mundane, and unheralded circumstances in which they arise. Yet the early establishment of a simple precedent or policy in resolving any such issue can unknowingly set an organization on a possibly disastrous course from which it cannot later easily deviate. This possibility poses a managerial challenge. As previously noted, for example, early decisions within ABA eventually loomed as a major obstacle to the emergence of ABA as the locus of an independent discipline in spite of its origins and organizational separation from psychology.

In the spring of 1989 two seemingly small issues surfaced that possibly represented such tests of disciplinary character for TIBA. These examples are described here, capturing in the record those passing moments of confusion and uncertainty plus the actions taken to resolve them. This is done to suggest potential adverse implications which might thereby have been avoided in the future of TIBA.

Use of the* TIBA *label. The first issue had implications for the relation of the organization to its members. A two–page journal article (Fraley, 1988c) featuring a behaviorological theme appeared with TIBA listed as the author's affiliation. The newly formed TIBA was publicized, but articles labeled this way could be interpreted incorrectly as official TIBA statements. After some discussion the TIBA Executive Board addressed the issue in language later included in the TIBA By–laws (1989/1990):

> The name of the organization may not be used by any member in a way that implies endorsement by the organization unless such an official endorsement has been extended by TIBA and the member is acting in accordance with the provisions of that endorsement. (1990, p. 16)

In this way TIBA reserved, as a group resource, the property rights to an increasingly strong conditioned reinforcer. TIBA withdrew those rights as resources for personal control by individual members. (For the underlying principles, see Skinner, 1953; compare Chapters 20 & 21.)

Use of the* Behaviorology *label. The second issue, concerning use of the behaviorology label, had implications for the autonomy of the discipline. TIBA members wanted behaviorological training opportunities to develop. The question of how to start new courses and programs had been a prevailing concern of TIBA leaders. Historical circumstances had left many people who were sympathetic to the behaviorological movement trapped in academic departments of psychology. There, any course that they taught would be labelled formally as a *psychology* course, and any behaviorally oriented programmatic track would be interpreted as a facet of psychology.

The behaviorology movement had taken the significant step of organizing itself outside of psychology. At the moment of constitution, the TIBA founders had created a critical discontinuity between the behaviorology movement and a debilitating legacy from which they thought it could not otherwise subsequently extract itself. But although behaviorology had been recognized, defined, and organized as a discipline independent of psychology, the differences were not yet as well defined in these early times as they would later become. Also, existing differences were not yet clearly perceived among members of the cultural community at large. The new movement seemed to have materialized just beyond the outer rim of psychology. Created free, it was now challenged to propel itself safely away in spite of some strong contingencies that could draw it back into the psychology vortex.

At the spring 1989 meeting of the Northern California Association for Behavior Analysis, some TIBA leaders had led a discussion session about the behaviorology movement. While there, a psychology faculty member described a new psychology course to be taught during the following fall term. These TIBA leaders returned from California with a request that TIBA condone that person's using the term "behaviorology" in the title of that course. On the one hand TIBA leaders wanted to see behaviorology taught under its own disciplinary title as part of the effort to maintain and further develop disciplinary independence. On the other hand, they wanted courses with behaviorological content to be developed. And they were also anxious to reinforce the enthusiastic behaviors of newly interested people who were offering to take concrete steps. A round of discussions arose among the TIBA leaders as they attempted to identify, measure, and pursue the conflicting implications. Significance in this episode resided less in the immediate aspects of the issue than in how members were reading and reacting to the somewhat remote and obscure implications attached to what at the time seemed a rather minor and passing event.

In the strict or conservative view, any course, regardless of title or content, taught within a psychology department and identified with a psychology prefix or designator, would formally define that topic and subject matter *to be* an element or facet of psychology. This had already happened repeatedly with "behavior analysis" despite continuing though unsuccessful efforts by many influential behavior analysts to deny organized psychology's claim to behavior analysis. Eventually, behaviorology courses would safely arise in departments and programs bearing explicit *behaviorology* titles, but that could only occur after such departments came into existence.

Explicitly identified behaviorology courses could also safely operate in any existing department if the integrity of that department were based upon any *applied* field. This is because no specific basic behavioral disciplinary affiliation is assumed for the faculty who work in such departments. Each applied behavior–related field, from advertising to zoo keeping, is open to whichever behavioral discipline can become established and accepted as the foundation behavioral science supportive of the field's operations. Courses with "behaviorology" in their title were appearing in such areas both internationally and domestically. The applied field of education is a typical example. For instance, in 1991 the Graduate Studies Department of the Xi'an Foreign Languages University in Xi'an, China (PRC) offered a course titled "Behaviorology and Education." Concurrently, the English Department of that university offered an undergraduate version of the same course titled "Behaviorology and Teaching" (Ledoux, 1997d). Even if other competing disciplines such as psychology are already being taught in such an applied field, the discipline of behaviorology can be introduced, and it can contest for the role of supportive philosophical and scientific foundation.

A few academic departments, however, are of a different nature. Though they pertain to something about which to think (behavior, in these examples), they are not organized primarily around *specific classes* of its occurrence (i.e., they are not organized the way, for example, that a criminal justice department is organized around the study of the occurrence of *illegal* behavior). Instead they offer programs that might be classified as more purely foundational or basic. Each features a disciplinary integrity established more around its particular epistemology than around specific kinds of environmental occasions to which it might be relevant. Examples include departments of behaviorology, psychology, and theology—each of which focuses on many of the same behavior–related events as do the others. While sharing a focus on a similar subject matter in general (behavior), their substantial differences pertain to the respective ways in which their followers think about behavior. In their manifestation as foundation disciplines, apart from applied studies that often accompany them, such departments prepare students to think in a particular way about behavior in *any* applied setting. (Each such setting might in turn give rise to its own academic department of applied studies, for example, social work, or a department of labor relations in a business school). To the extent that recognized elements of the basic discipline of behaviorology are allowed to appear under the rubrics of *foundational* disciplinary competitors, behaviorology surrenders its epistemological identity as a unique discipline—that is, as a unique way to think about subject matters to which it might be relevant.

In the contrasting lenient or liberal view—because many of the best potential behaviorologists worked in psychology departments and were the people upon whom the movement might have to rely for many of its developmental products—tolerating psychology labels, and perhaps also even explicit claims to behaviorology by psychologists, may be necessary in order to get early behaviorological products. The movement needed those products and might not otherwise obtain them. Perhaps no realistic alternative was available. Maybe the pressure to develop behaviorology–labelled courses and tracks within explicitly labeled psychology units would simply overwhelm any resistance that TIBA could muster. So why crystallize the issue by fighting to an inevitable and publicly visible loss?

Another argument held that displaying the behaviorology name and developing behaviorological products under the formal designation and auspices of organized psychology, at least to a limited extent, would not matter enough to make a fuss about it, especially if any such courses or materials incorporated the behaviorology/psychology disciplinary difference as an explicit theme. Perhaps moving out of psychology later might not be as difficult as some seemed to think. Also, behaviorologists could successfully assert that behaviorology, though some of its parts were temporarily trapped in psychology units, was represented there only by prisoners of circumstance who were not really psychologists but something different.

The discussions meandered back and forth between counter–posed questions (presented here rhetorically): Are behaviorologists abandoning the concept of disciplinary independence? Why not, as a necessary short–term tactic, take an occasional step away from what remains the ultimate goal? Could not the new movement lose far more than it stands to gain from the emergence of behaviorology–titled courses within departments recognized as the disciplinary keepers of competing epistemologies? Will the new movement run aground on the shoals of stubborn allegiance to impractical ideological notions? Will it be destroyed by the careless neglect of its own principles?

Within a short time TIBA reached a resolution. The minor moment faded into the history of the movement. TIBA would *not* condone appearances of the name "behaviorology" in contexts that could imply that behaviorology is a part of any other discipline. TIBA would condone behaviorology–titled courses in the training departments of applied *fields,* a context in which epistemological competition is appropriate. Behaviorological materials would be developed and tested in such settings, but caution would prevail. Where ambiguities might arise behaviorologists expected explicit, unambiguous clarifications on the issue of disciplinary separateness. In psychology–titled departments behaviorologists could develop and test explicitly behaviorological teaching materials provided that these clearly and adequately informed students that behaviorology was an independent discipline and not part of psychology. But no course or curricular track in a psychology department would bear a formal behaviorology title. (See Ulman, 1990b, and Fraley, 1990b, for related examples.)

If this was a little test, had TIBA passed? Many such issues were arising, each with its hidden implications of unknown potential. This section presented just a couple of incidents to suggest that critical organizational circumstances often stem from origins that might have gone unrecognized and unheralded in the stream of mundane affairs.

Within a few months another psychologist, this time on the East Coast, was calling to say that he was designing his introductory psychology course for the fall 1989 term. He wanted reactions from TIBA leaders to some materials about behaviorology that he planned to include in that course. The materials did *not* make explicit that behaviorology and psychology were entirely different disciplines, nor was it clear that the caller fully understood that. The textual materials also implied incorrectly that the essence of the name behaviorology was in its greater connotation of clinical respect for certain ethical principles popular with the public than was true of the name psychology. TIBA leaders were pleased to have had some relevant policy already in place. After discussion of the matter, the caller agreed, in response to feedback from the behaviorologists, to mention the emergence of behaviorology as a separate discipline but to teach as "behavioral psychology" or "behavior analysis" much of what otherwise would have been erroneously ascribed to behaviorology.

During the discussions about what TIBA policy should be, Fraley, whose applied–field teaching job was in an educational *psychology* department, recalled for TIBA leaders a relevant incident involving one of his courses. He had developed it as an explicit introduction to behaviorology, though the official course title was "Introductory Behavior Analysis." A couple of years earlier, while away on summer vacation, his cognitively specialized department chairperson had reassigned that course. It was to be taught that summer by another faculty member who for years had collaborated with the department's cognitive majority faction. That person had long acted as a strong opponent of the behaviorology movement within the department. He had publicly denounced his own somewhat behavior–analytic, clinically oriented training as having been much too narrow. During that summer term, he taught Fraley's course after having advertised it on campus using flyers similar to those Fraley had been using. But in class he substituted methodological, clinically oriented textual materials and taught a strict psychology course with a behavior–analytic slant.

TIBA leaders were quick to recognize that the same thing could easily happen in the case of *any* formal behaviorology–titled courses established in departments committed to alternative epistemologies and disciplines. And the usurpation could be permanent.

Refinements to TIBA Status and Infrastructure

A disciplinary and professional data base. In the fall of 1989, Ernest Vargas, as Secretary of TIBA, began to organize a data base for the discipline of behaviorology.

Vargas's design included far more than the customary membership directory for a professional organization. For example, records of the publications of all TIBA–member behaviorologists would be electronically configured for retrieval according to different search variables. TIBA would thus maintain in a highly usable way the complete body of discipline–related literature that its members produced. Vargas enlisted John Eshleman and Scott Beach to work on the technical development of the necessary computer software. They made plans to get the system operating while the TIBA membership was still small. Within two years Eshleman demonstrated to TIBA an elaborate custom–designed electronic format to accommodate such a data base. In the spring of 1992 TIBA Secretary Julie Vargas collected relevant data from each TIBA member and began the process of inserting this data into the new system.

Formal establishment. As Treasurer of the organization, Lawrence Fraley drafted a one–page "Document of Constitution" for TIBA, dated 26 May 1989 , and secured its ratification by signatures of the five TIBA Fellows. On 7 August 1989 TIBA received a certificate of incorporation from the State of West Virginia, the treasurer's home state. And on 3 November 1989 Fraley submitted a formal application to the Internal Revenue Service (IRS) for TIBA's exemption from Federal income tax as a non–profit scientific organization. The IRS subsequently approved this application.

Cash–flow management. TIBA's cash flow was based mainly on member dues. TIBA Treasurer Fraley designed and put into effect a membership renewal scheme wherein the membership year of each TIBA member was determined by the month on which that member first joined the organization. This renewal arrangement had the advantages of (a) distributing the annual work of the treasurer more evenly, (b) keeping the organization's cash flow steady across the calendar year, and (c) allowing the earlier detection of membership trends and changes. In 1992 Jerome Ulman, who followed Fraley as treasurer, transferred the financial operations of TIBA to an electronic database. This brought the behavior of the TIBA leaders under much stronger stimulus control of various money–related variables.

Scientific Contingencies Committee. At the 1991 ABA Convention in Atlanta, Ernest Vargas, the Acting President of TIBA while Stephen Ledoux was teaching in China, organized the first TIBA Scientific Contingencies Committee. It brought together a group of young professionals charged with developing recommendations to the Executive Board about how TIBA might arrange contingencies to increase and maintain the scientific productivity of its members. Chaired by Marta Metcalfe, the committee included Guy Bruce, Mark Clingan, John Eshleman, and Doreen Vieitez (Clingan did not renew his TIBA membership and briefly faded from TIBA involvement until he rejoined in 1993 after securing a position at Vanderbilt University in Nashville). This important committee was formed with young professionals on the assumption that TIBA would evolve and prosper in the long run though the lifetime commitments of its younger members who should be heavily involved in fashioning the contingencies that would bind the organization.

Conventions. About a year after TIBA was founded, it began holding two–to–three day long, single track annual conventions. In August 1988, Clarkson University was the site of the first convention, described previously.

Comunidad Los Horcones in Hermosillo, Sonora, Mexico, was the site of TIBA–2 on 4–8 January 1990. Community members coordinated the site. And Ernest Vargas organized the program and chaired the sessions. The convention, with a theme of "cultural design and development," drew about 20 attendants. The first souvenir TIBA–logo badges appeared at this convention thanks to Scott Beach who had designed and produced them. They reappeared at later conventions.

Ball State University in Muncie, Indiana, was the site of TIBA–3 on 4–6 January 1991. Jerome Ulman coordinated the site, organized the program, and chaired the sessions. The convention drew about 17 attendants. The B.F. Skinner Memorial Lecture series began at this convention with historian Daniel Bjork presenting "Toward a biography of B.F. Skinner: Rationale and interpretation" (see Bjork, 1993). The first souvenir TIBA–logo mugs appeared at this convention and reappeared in new designs at later conventions.

The Clarion Hotel in New Orleans, Louisiana, was the site of TIBA–4 on 3–5 January 1992. Robert Crow coordinated the site, while Carl Cheney organized the program, and Grace Baron chaired the sessions. The convention drew about 32 attendants. Fred Keller prepared "Education by torchlight" as the B.F. Skinner Memorial Lecture (see Keller, 1993). But he developed a case of the flu, and his paper was delivered by Julie Vargas. The Executive Board settled into the practice of meeting on the days before and after the convention. (See "A Small Selection of Photographs," in the book containing Ledoux, 1997e [this book], for a photo of the authors of this paper at TIBA–4.)

The Stone House Club Inn in Little Compton, Rhode Island, was the site of TIBA–5 on 18–20 March 1993. Grace Baron coordinated the site, while Anne Kupfer organized the program and chaired the sessions. The convention drew about 25 attendants. Joseph Cautela presented "General Level of Reinforcement" as the B.F. Skinner Memorial Lecture (see Cautela, 1994). The rest of the program, which included poster presentations (now a regular program feature), was also heavily research–focused, more so than any previous convention program. By this convention, TIBA was matching contributions from individuals to support undergraduate student attendance. Also by this convention TIBA had decided to continue to schedule its conventions in the month of March, around B.F. Skinner's birthday if possible.

Conventions continue as annual events. (One of the appendices in Ledoux, 1997e [in this book] provides basic details on the 1994, '95, '96, and '97 conventions.)

Research support. In a somewhat bold and innovative move during TIBA–4 in New Orleans, the TIBA Executive Board dedicated 25% of the organization's income from dues to the support of scientific research projects. TIBA members would be able to apply for funds to support their behaviorological research. Ernest Vargas developed this concept and presented it to the Board for endorsement. The Board delayed refinement of the proposal and the procedural details for a future meeting. A year later at the 1993 TIBA convention, the Research Funding Committee chaired by Anne Kupfer began to make research grants in response to proposals submitted by TIBA members.

Fine–tuning of membership criteria. The mid–year Executive Board meeting of 23 May 1992, held in San Francisco to coincide with travel to the 1992 ABA convention, saw an important formal adjustment in the membership area: Acting on a proposal from the Membership Committee, the Executive Board emptied the category of TIBA Fellow. All existing TIBA Fellows moved into a new category called "Full Member." Affected by this change were the three initial Fellows (Fraley, Ledoux, and E. Vargas) plus Cheney, Ulman, and J. Vargas. A new requirement was also added: Full Member status would require not only work for the TIBA organization and higher dues (requirements for the former Fellows) but also producing and promulgating a minimum of one scientific data–based product every three years. This stressed the importance of Full Members being directly involved in scientific activity, and attempted to make it so.

The vacated Fellow category was retained, but redefined as a more honorary status. During the discussion of how the now empty Fellow membership category would be defined, a long–standing difference of opinion about the nature of the behaviorology movement surfaced indirectly: Some suggested that TIBA Fellowship might be bestowed as an honor on persons who had conducted good science but who had not joined TIBA nor supported the behaviorology movement. This was consistent with the basic notion that TIBA existed merely to support the science, and to do so without regard to where, organizationally, the scientific activity occurred—and without regard to the views of the recipient about how best to organize scientific disciplines.

Opposed to that position were those who viewed the behaviorology movement not only as a developer of the science but also as an organizational solution to the problem of how best to insure the constructive evolution and vitality of the science within the context of the culture. Those who construed TIBA to have a cultural as well as a scientific mission (see Fraley, 1991) wanted the category to contain only Fellows who had ascended up the TIBA membership ladder and who endorsed the establishment of an independent behaviorology discipline. That, they argued, would be in keeping with the TIBA committment to shape repertoires rather than give prizes.

The Executive Board did not settle this issue at that meeting, although majority sentiment appeared to favor ascension to Fellow via the established TIBA membership track. The Board did agree that Ernest Vargas, as Membership Committee Chair, would receive suggestions about criteria for the Fellow category and develop relevant proposals for future consideration by the Executive Board.

Leadership. A small number of people, contributing a variety of necessary and useful skills, founded the behaviorology movement. That small band advanced in a coordinated way on several fronts important to the success of the movement. Assessing the respective contributions of those people would be difficult. Nevertheless, it soon became obvious to those who worked on the early stages of the movement that one person was filling a particularly important role. The accidents of history had brought to the behaviorology movement a specialist in the organization of human resources—a coordinator who accomplishes exceptional feats mediated through the behavior of others. That is, the movement had a functional leader. Good ones require little in the way of formal authority, although that is helpful. True, people in the behaviorology movement came predisposed to emit a lot of behavior on behalf of an independent discipline. But to appreciate how so much of it came to be emitted in such a timely and coordinated fashion one must take into account the special repertoire in managing complex organizations brought to this movement by Ernest A. Vargas. (In 1991 he was elected to become TIBA's president for a three–year term beginning January 1992.)

Summary of Chapter Four

After a sufficiently definitive concept of behaviorology had come to control *descriptive* verbal behavior, a small band of self–declared behaviorologists took concrete steps to organize a new and independent verbal community around that discipline. Manifestation as a scientific professional organization came in the form of TIBA, but its relation to other behavior–related organizations raised many questions that could only be answered on the basis of careful analyses of the relations of TIBA to each of them. In the years 1987–1992 TIBA established a governance structure, largely through agreement on by–laws and the subsequent non–profit incorporation of TIBA. The organization established policy through which it exercised control over its intellectual property. And TIBA designed and partially developed a three–level publication program, successfully conducted the first several TIBA conventions, and—importantly—largely resolved ambiguities about the integrity of the discipline and its relations to other disciplines and fields. Personal commitments were then possible on the basis of more explicitly and starkly contrasted principles—and people could, and did, sort themselves accordingly. TIBA established an operating style that cast the appeal of the movement in such a way that only those prepared to support it, and to accept the implications of doing so, tended to add themselves to its ranks. The TIBA leaders concentrated on behaviorological designs for the organized discipline that would strengthen the focus on science, and prevent drift under political, economic, or social contingencies. Slowly, *and by design,* TIBA tried to bureaucratized itself as its designers relinquished direct control over its operations. Systematically, the behaviorologists were installing behaviorology in the community of natural sciences.

The next chapter, Chapter Five ("The Continuing Debate: Reactions from the Behavioral Community at Large") will review the prevailing cultural milieu and analyze the support for, and opposition to, the growing behaviorology movement. While the behaviorologists were moving steadily ahead to refine the concept of their discipline and organize the scientific verbal community that would exercise intellectual proprietorship over it, the general "behavioral" community continued an increasingly moot debate on the concepts of a behaviorology movement and discipline.

Chapter 5:

The Continuing Debate: Reactions from the Behavioral Community at Large

After the introductory Chapter One, Chapter Two of this account of the emergence of behaviorology examined the nature and origins of the behaviorology concept. Chapter Three examined contingencies supporting individual commitments to a disciplinary independence movement. Chapter Four presented a comprehensive review of the activities to organize the behaviorology discipline and examined the cultural engineering by which the behaviorology discipline was formalized and installed in the community of natural sciences. This chapter, Chapter Five, reviews the prevailing cultural milieu and analyzes the support for, and opposition to, the behaviorology movement.

The behaviorologists were refining the concept of behaviorology and organizing a scientific verbal community to protect and extend this discipline. Meanwhile, the general behavioral community continued an increasingly moot debate on the concept of a behaviorology disciplinary movement.

Continuing Debate on the Movement

The International Behaviorology Association (TIBA) was not affiliated with the Association for Behavior Analysis (ABA). TIBA had been established independent of any other existing organization, discipline, or applied field. However, during the 1987 ABA convention, which began the day following the original founding meeting of the behaviorologists, both informal discussion and scheduled formal discussion focused on the behaviorology movement. This was partly a result of recent articles in *The Behavior Analyst* (ABA's journal) plus some ABA convention sessions mentioning behaviorology.

The question of change strategies. At that convention the title of one well–attended symposium, organized and chaired by Guy Bruce (at the time, a graduate student advisee of Ernest Vargas), was "Behaviorologist, Behavior Analyst, or Psychologist? A Question for the Young Professional." This symposium featured B.F. Skinner as a discussant. Numerous members of the audience supported an independence movement, but others raised objections, including Skinner whose objections went beyond his dislike for the name. But Robert Epstein, who also objected to the name, rose to offer several reasons, with which the behaviorologists agreed, to reorganize the discipline concerned with behavior.

Among those present various arguments arose. Some objections to a separate discipline came from persons who apparently viewed psychology as too big, too powerful, and too well established to be affected by what they saw as splinter movements. Behaviorologists deemed this concern to be irrelevant because they had abandoned the objective of changing psychology (scientifically and organizationally) into a suitable disciplinary home for behaviorology. Instead psychology would be circumvented. Another argument along pragmatic lines resisted the behaviorology movement because organized psychology currently controlled access to critical resources such as jobs, grants, licensing, and reimbursement through insurance. However, behaviorologists did not deem such established control to be immutable. And they saw such concerns as relevant only to those professional opportunities directly controlled by organized psychology, not to professional opportunities in the multitude of other behavior–related fields also in need of an effective basic science. In those diverse fields, the applied practitioners seldom claim expertise in any particular behavioral foundation science and are more open to whatever foundations best support their applied work. Furthermore, within their organized professions they tend to rely less on legally codified prescriptions for traditional cognitive psychology than is done in professions directly controlled by, and generally construed to be parts of, organized psychology.

To many of those attending the 1987 ABA convention, the possibility of a behavioral science separate from psychology seemed remote. So did a mission affecting the culture more broadly than was implicit in those few applied areas in which formal psychology has attained a controlling monopoly in the employment market (e.g., clinical psychology). For some of those people, the struggle for the science of behavior would remain, as it has always been, one of trying to reconstruct and redirect psychology. So, at the Bruce symposium, some speakers again suggested the traditional and well–failed change strategies: (a) attack cognitive/mentalistic psychology in publicly visible ways, especially in print and debate; (b) gain control of conventional courses and then teach them behaviorally both in method and content; (c) write and publish new textbooks reflecting the behavioral perspective on all of the conventional aspects of psychological subject matter; and (d) continue to insist that behaviorally oriented individuals are not only psychologists, but are, in fact, the best ones. And, of course, *try not to lose your job as a result of doing these sorts of things,* especially when operating within units formally organized under the psychology banner. (That is realistic advice; to people's use of these old strategies, psychologists often respond with actions threatening their jobs. For example, see "Court Battle," 1991; Vargas, *et al.,* 1988; and Giles, 1984, discussed in an earlier chapter.)

However, the concerted 60–year effort to pursue those well–worn change strategies has not succeeded. That may seem a short time in the historical context of the evolution of science. But the growing need for effective behavioral science was accelerating exponentially and, in the view of most behaviorologists, was becoming too urgent to allow that struggle to have its protracted play. This was especially so because the contingencies prevailing in psychology rendered demonstrations of the relative effectiveness of behaviorological *science* somewhat irrelevant. A subsequent survey of undergraduate "learning" courses in psychology departments, a traditional source of new radical behaviorist students, exemplifies the scope of the failure of those change strategies. In reporting that survey, Lattal, McFarland, and Joyce (1990) bewail the lack of coverage of even introductory "behavior analytic" material in these courses. The reasons they cite for this situation include: (a) few radical behaviorist faculty are available in psychology departments, (b) those that are available seldom have control of learning courses, (c) few radical behaviorist textbooks and laboratory manuals are available, and (d) those departments require what they call a greater "breadth" and "diversity of viewpoints" in these courses than behavioral psychologists see as justified. Lattal *et al.* reiterated the behavioral psychologist's standard rebuttal to this requirement for "diversity":

> Departments of Biology do not present evolution and creationism as alternative accounts of life nor do Physics Departments present relativity and astrology as alternatives for understanding cosmology. (p. 128)

The place reserved for behaviorists in psychology. Lattal *et al.* (1990), as is characteristic of behavioral psychologists, did not address certain relevant questions: Why should a majority that practices one discipline relinquish control over its learning theory courses to a group that entertains an entirely different discipline? Why should that majority even allow the views of the other group to consume space in a learning foundations course meant to serve *its* discipline? After all, one could argue that behavioral "psychologists" do not represent a legitimate minority within psychology because their discipline is *not* psychology. Mainline psychologists, in squeezing out behavioral science and philosophy in practical if not yet official ways, tacitly respect that argument.

An example more explicitly addressing respect for separate disciplines arose in 1988 in the educational psychology department at West Virginia University where behaviorologists Lawrence Fraley, Ernest Vargas, and Julie Vargas had been employed for more than 20 years. The traditional educational psychologists, who were in the majority, suddenly had a brief opportunity to design, unilaterally, the department's new doctoral program, an unusual circumstance arising in the college out of some arcane internal politics. Their program design excluded from its requirements *any* course taught either by Fraley, Vargas, or Vargas on the grounds that the behaviorological science taught by those three people (under "behavior analysis" and other non–behaviorology course titles) did *not* represent psychology nor merit a place in the core of an educational *psychology* program. The three behaviorologists subsequently took successful steps at the university level to compel a reversal of their psychology colleagues' snubbing action directed at their discipline. They did this in order to secure professional operating room. But they nevertheless agreed with the psychologists that those psychologists should keep their discipline to themselves. The three took the position that such problems of disciplinary incompatibility require organizational solutions at the college and university administrative levels. The problem is that, with very few exceptions, American institutions of higher education, like those world–wide, have no academic departments devoted exclusively to the natural science of behavior, especially human behavior. (For further discussion of graduate level training in radical behaviorism being crowded out by required diversity in psychology programs, see Michael, 1980.)

Following the 1987 ABA convention, one behavior–analytic psychologist, Peter Harzem, who had been chairing a partly behavioral psychology department at Auburn University, joined the debate by publishing an article on the virtues of being a psychologist (Harzem, 1987). He offered a restatement of Skinner's earlier but still relevant thesis that, because modern technology has multiplied the dire implications of human errors in judgment, a commensurate behavioral technology must be developed to regain control in the culture (Skinner, 1971, Ch. 1). Harzem mapped out a cultural mission for such a science similar to that previously specified by Fraley (1987). But instead of endowing a separate discipline with that mission as Fraley had done, Harzem again argued, notwithstanding half a dozen decades of accumulated evidence to the contrary, that it could and should all be accomplished by the minority behavioral community based within organized psychology. Harzem also appeared to write as if the discipline that he described, and the mission that he delineated for it, represented psychology *per se.* This was an implication that behaviorologists (as well as most psychologists) see as a distortion of reality because a vast majority of psychologists (the 95% or more who are non–behavioral) do *not* and probably *cannot* accept such a behavior–analytic definition of that discipline.

In the fall 1988 issue of *The Behavior Analyst,* two spokespersons for the supposedly eclectic (but generally cognitive/mentalistic) psychology mainstream (Proctor & Weeks, 1988) replied to Harzem in a "wrist slapping" rebuttal critical of what they construed to be Harzem's myopic scientific elitism. Proctor and Weeks touted the "cognitive revolution" in psychology. They reviewed some of its putative research accomplishments. They noted what they considered to be its positive impact on a number of different fields. And they presumably refuted Harzem's premise that psychology was failing in its cultural mission—a mission to which Proctor and Weeks allowed that behavioral psychologists could contribute, but which certainly did *not* necessitate an overhaul of psychology along more behavioral lines as Harzem had advocated. They characterized Harzem as uninformed about the significant movements in his own discipline (psychology) and arrogant in his implications about the superior effectiveness of behavior analysis.

Proctor and Weeks pointedly directed three items of advice (1988, pp. 138–139) to Harzem and his fellow behavior–analytic psychologists: (a) "Behavior analysts should cease denying the reality of the cognitive revolution and familiarize themselves with the major advances that have occurred in psychological research…" (b) Behavior analysts should quit talking to themselves in "in–house" journals about things of which they are already quite convinced and instead should publish in mainstream psychology journals. (Ironically the refusal of those journals, since the 1950s, to accept behavioral articles had contributed significantly to the initial movement of many behavioral people from mainstream psychology in the 1970s. Also, in an article rebutting Proctor and Weeks, Lee [1989] appealed to the principle that journal specialization follows, and merely reflects, the increasingly discriminative characteristics of a maturing science.) And (c) "Behavior analysts should join the rest of the psychological community in the ongoing pursuit of scientific knowledge, without having the predetermined agenda of 'supplanting cognitive explanations'."

In short, Proctor and Weeks added their endorsements to the similar demands of other representatives of organized psychology. They laid out, once again, the ground rules by which behavior analysts are expected to conduct themselves if they are to be citizens of the psychology verbal community. Their message and its tone exemplified the social punishment that mainstream psychologists inflict on behavioral psychologists who resist the norms imposed by the overwhelming cognitive/mentalistic majority.

Invalid attacks on radical behaviorism. A year after the Proctor and Weeks article, and along the same lines, Michael Mahoney published, in *The American Psychologist,* a more concerted attack on radical behaviorism in psychology (Mahoney, 1989). Like many semi–behavioral psychologists, Mahoney typically misrepresented radical behaviorism. Essentially he implied wrongly that the mediating internal processes with which cognitive, humanistic, and psychotherapeutic psychologists preoccupy themselves fall beyond any adequate conceptual and analytical reach of the functionalist umbrella of radical behaviorism. He implied that those processes require a more comprehensively founded "scientific psychology." Behaviorologists disagree. The sciences of both verbal behavior and emotional behavior (including related respondent behavioral components)—each informed by the philosophy of radical behaviorism and now being organized outside of psychology within the discipline of behaviorology—deal effectively with any real and relevant evidence adduced by the cognitive, humanistic, and psychotherapeutic schools of psychology.

In the first place, behaviorologists recognize that all *real* events in those domains of concern are variables in functional relations. On the other hand, ontological criteria deny existence to some of what those psychologists seek to understand (a classic example is subconscious mental activity invented to explain behavior). Next, with all of those mental and emotional constructions purged of their residual mysticism and recognized as *behavior,* cognition becomes verbal behavior, and the humanistic impetus becomes emotional behavior. And the behaviorologists *have* powerful sciences of *those* phenomena. As behaviorologists then develop effective behavioral technologies involving events in those domains of concern, they see the many substantial preoccupations of psychologists as either basically irrelevant or unimportant to those domains. So, in those contexts, behaviorologists neglect those preoccupations. That neglect is not because behaviorology cannot deal with such things, but because it *can* deal with them—and has sorted them into appropriate places in the grand scheme of things.

However, Mahoney's article, if weak as a comparative review of paradigms, was much more important as propaganda. His perspective did not reach beyond psychology, and he wrote as if everything "behavioral" was implicitly under the psychology umbrella. Appealing to his own interpretations of history and citing various authoritative sources, Mahoney (1989) developed positions to these effects: (a) Radical behaviorists in psychology, in their extremist zeal to disavow personal agency, have clung to anachronistic science. That group "isolated itself from and came to lag behind changing perspectives on the nature and practice of optimal scientific inquiry. ...radical behaviorists...in turning their backs on the lessons of philosophy, have found themselves unnecessarily tethered by their own first assumptions" (p. 1373). (b) Radical behaviorists are self–righteous and intolerant, and have thus become "scientistic" followers of an unworthy approach to science, which renders them poor citizens of the psychological scientific community. (c) "Respected scientists" have had to revise radical behaviorist accounts of learning to take into account new complexities in cognition. (d) Only those who abandon the extremism of radical behaviorism can share in the disciplinary progress of psychology so saliently manifested by the "cognitive revolution." Worthwhile behavioral contributions to psychology have come from methodological and "metaphysical" behaviorism, and continue to come from methodological or "liberal" behaviorists who incorporate, or take into account, the explicitly "mediational" concepts of behavior from cognitivist theory. Few important psychologists any longer care about radical behaviorist views. And (e) today relatively few genuine radical behaviorists can even be found. The integrity of radical behaviorism [in psychology] is weakening in the face of dramatic revisions compelled by the views on other fronts elsewhere in paradigmatically balanced psychology. So speaks Mahoney.

Mahoney's article, appearing in the prestigious and widely read *The American Psychologist,* jarred the behavioral psychology community. In implying to behavioral camp followers that their fortunes would be more promising elsewhere, Mahoney's article perhaps influenced disaffiliations among persons who were insecure in their commitments to radical behaviorism and to the strict natural science of behavior that it informs. Mahoney implied that remaining a radical behaviorist within psychology is (a) surely a matter of embarrassment and (b) certainly not the path to any viable professional future in that disciplinary coalition.

Some behaviorologists found themselves in agreement with *both* of Mahoney's implications, though not for his reasons. The article obviously stung many behavioral psychologists who set about organizing rebuttals (e.g., Catania, 1991). Perhaps as well as anything that behaviorologists have said, articles like those of Proctor and Weeks (1988) and of Mahoney (1989) indirectly suggest the impracticality of behavioral people trying either to maintain their scientific integrity within organized psychology or to change psychology into an effective science for the kind of cultural mission that most behaviorologists deemed important.

Some organizational and intellectual realities. The behaviorologists were confronting an organized psychology discipline populated by intelligent, articulate individuals. These persons had a lifetime of credible training and experience implying to them that their discipline was valid and effective. Furthermore, their ethical training produced a strong belief in the kind of scientific and philosophical eclecticism necessary to construe psychology as an integral discipline. Mainstream psychologists, of whom Mahoney and Proctor and Weeks were typical examples, accepted little of behavior analysis (especially in its radical behavioristic expression) and even less of behaviorology. They revealed little comprehension of the complexity and sophistication of what they called behavior analysis or of its fundamental philosophical, scientific, and technological differences with the discipline that they knew as psychology. They did not seem to understand that behavioral people cannot merge their concepts with those of traditional psychology while, at the same time, maintaining their own behavioristic scientific probity because those propositions are incompatible. Not only was the scientific integrity of behavioral individuals eroded in the psychology community, but the behavioral people were not, and could not have been, understood there.

In addition, behavioral programs, operating merely as options, specializations, or areas of emphasis *within* departments of psychology, are more vulnerable than would be true of departments devoted exclusively to a behaviorological discipline. Harzem (1987) did not address this point. Yet Harzem's own program, like any behavioral specialization existing as but one epistemological face in a larger multifaceted program, has no guarantee of security beyond the next faculty meeting, the next change in chairperson, or the next new dean. Chairpersons easily redirect academic programs that displease them simply by reassigning the courses to politically reliable faculty members who can be expected to make desired changes. A simple faculty vote within a psychology department to de–emphasize an internal behavioral movement, or an administrative decision to shift resources to other specializations, remained easily arranged dispositions of minority movements that have no formal status beyond mere areas of interest in much "broader" psychology programs. This can happen even when the minority is correct about the greater effectiveness of its science. On the other hand, to eliminate a whole discipline, including its established academic department, from a higher education institution is more difficult. A group of faculty members, or their administrative leaders, might easily dispose of some individual or minority faction at the department level. But another order of difficulty is encountered when an institution attempts to declare that an integral discipline is no longer to be part of its curriculum.

Perhaps Harzem's position reflects contingencies affecting individuals who have achieved *personal* success as members of epistemological minorities in various disciplines. But inherent in such a strategy is the peril of attenuating revolutionary fervor that often accompanies personal success. Behaviorologists have lost faith in reliance on personal success as the mechanism by which to protect their science within the psychology milieu.

An example from theology parallels the plight of behaviorists in organized psychology (Basil, 1987/88). A number of prominent Catholic theologians, religious educators, and church officials, attending a forum for secular humanists and liberal Catholics, successively criticized basic principles, policies, and practices of organized Roman Catholicism. Observers questioned why the speakers had not left the church. As individuals, they had not only "let go of the Pope, the Bible, and church tradition" (p. 6) but had also convincingly justified their having done so. In response, Dan Maguire, a professor at Catholic University, is reported to have insisted that the "essential moral creed" of Christianity, which he respects, has never been "incarnated" in historical Christianity. But as Basil (1987/88) noted,

> It was not clear to many in Washington, however, why Maguire and some of the other speakers thought that it was worth belonging to a religious institution that had never "incarnated" its "essential moral creed." Perhaps, being born Catholic, they want to remain attached to their family's roots or to the admittedly fascinating rituals of their church—regardless of its dogma. Perhaps they hope to overturn two thousand years of authoritarian religious rule "from the inside," as it were; then they would have a ready–made and powerful institution to promote humanistic ideals on a world–wide scale. ...But it should be pointed out that this strategy could backfire. By remaining within a church whose very foundations they attack, these dissident Catholics could be making traditional authoritarian Catholicism stronger. After all, one could argue that the church has been able to co–opt the voices of some of its harshest critics. No matter how free–minded these fringe Catholics are, their primary message will always be that they support the church. (p. 6)

From the perspective of the behaviorology movement, a self–analysis similar to the one for liberal Catholics would seem to be in order for behavioral psychologists. They are persons who retain disciplinary allegiance to psychology, but who (a) have let go of mind, (b) regard as irrelevant the physiological mechanisms included under cognition, and (c) have turned away from many traditions of allegiance to organized psychology. Perhaps they should consider the supportive implications of even their opposition if expressed *from within,* and *as members of,* the institution that they oppose. Catania (1991), chastising Mahoney (1989) for his misrepresentations of radical behaviorism, wrote that if Mahoney's views:

> ...*really* represented the position of contemporary psychology, it should come as no surprise that some radical behaviorists have moved to more congenial environments... (p. 68; emphasis added)

(Catania immediately added "but intellectual ghettoes are as objectionable as racial or ethnic ones." Behaviorologists might agree with Catania's observation about intellectual ghettoes, but not about who, implicitly, is trapped in one.)

This issue continued to maintain tensions even among the early behaviorologists who differed with one another about both the degree and the appropriate kinds of supportive cooperation in which to engage with majority psychologists. Often, to gain access to students so that they could provide behaviorological training, behaviorologists had to participate in a psychology program. That program not only would claim credit for the products of that training but also would prosper in various ways through the professional involvements of the behaviorologists. Some argued that this amounted to organized psychology exploiting behaviorologists in ways that maintained organized psychology at the expense of independence for behaviorology. Others counseled patience, and argued that the preliminary work being done under the psychology umbrella was crucial for the future of behaviorology and so should not be jeopardized by premature and costly rebellion. Without resolution, some raised rhetorical questions about indulgences in self-serving rationalization while others countered with concerns that unwise emotionalism might be getting too intense.

A public separatist review. The 60-year effort begun by Skinner to make-over psychology had failed, and conditions aversive to behavioral people were continuing in force. But as Ernest Vargas observed at the conclusion of Bruce's 1987 ABA symposium, those same contingencies had previously forced the issue of separation and independence on radical behaviorists, and their experiments with separation on those occasions had worked well. He added that the only way to determine whether separation will continue to work was to continue to use it.

At the symposium Vargas also briefly reviewed the historical highlights of those earlier occasions for separatist activity: Behaviorists had experienced difficulties getting their articles accepted in the traditional psychology journals which usually required the group designs and the related statistical significance tests typical of mainline psychology. (To understand the kinds of studies that the behavioral people were doing, see the approaches to research explained in Sidman, 1960.) So radical behaviorists successfully founded separate journals independent of the psychology establishment, including the *Journal of the Experimental Analysis of Behavior* (JEAB) and the *Journal of Applied Behavior Analysis* (JABA). When the professional interests of behaviorists were no longer adequately met by any of the existing divisions of the American Psychological Association (APA), behaviorists began a separatist movement within APA by founding a new division of their own, Division 25, titled "The Experimental Analysis of Behavior." When later the APA and its regional organizations were not adequately meeting their convention and other needs, even with their own division, behavior analysts gradually pursued a larger scale separatist course by eventually founding ABA.

Finally, when, among other things, the lack of training and application facilities (which normally comes as part of a disciplinary home) threatened the contributions and even the continuation of their scientific verbal community, and weakened the quality controls needed to preserve it, behaviorologists acted. They moved to complete and refine the definition of an effective and natural science of behavior, and to organize an independent verbal community around it.

A comparison with the Cultural Materialism movement. A comparison between this separatist trend from psychology and the course pursued by cultural materialists and others within anthropology (Harris, 1979) may be instructive. Cultural materialists, like behaviorists, have entertained an unusual philosophical and analytical perspective within their "parent" discipline—one sharing some basic principles and assumptions with behaviorology (see E.A. Vargas, 1985). However, the coalescence of their discriminable integrity within anthropology does not appear to have precipitated the degree of conflict that has surrounded the behaviorists in psychology, nor have the cultural materialists sponsored an emergent independence movement. Cultural materialists as a group have not professed difficulties in publishing in the traditional anthropology journals nor of being denied adequate convention participation by the professional organizations of anthropology. The cultural materialists have been able to remain within anthropology and have continued working to revise and improve that discipline. Perhaps this is because more traditional anthropologists have not widely construed them to be operating with a different basic science or philosophy, but only to have reached some unusual insights and conclusions. This approximates the relation between the behavioral and mainline psychology communities in the 1940s and 1950s.

The discipline of behaviorology is heavily focused on controlling behavior. Its members base its rights claims to intellectual property on the effectiveness of products manifested at the level of control. In comparison, the science based on cultural materialism has not yet fully advanced to the level of control with respect to *its* subject matter. It remains largely interpretative and analytical, having passed through descriptive stages and having attained the capacity for accurate predicting and some control. As yet, however, cultural materialism does not exhibit effective technologies, based on its own principles, for designing and developing new cultures, or even new cultural practices. (See Fraley, 1988c, for a more analytically detailed examination of this point; see Beach, 1988, for hints of progress.)

Perhaps cultural materialism has not yet demonstrated control because the culture has not yet imposed much of a necessity for doing so within the scope of applied concerns entertained by anthropologists. The predictions of cultural materialists might be more accurate, and their analyses more parsimonious, than those of more traditional anthropologists. However, the implications of any such contrasts have not been sufficiently adverse to provoke the traditional majority to opt for political and economic countercontrols within the discipline. Not enough is yet at stake. But what if a major lucrative market were to develop for such skills? What if the cultural materialists within anthropology no longer merely described and retrospectively predicted the courses of old cultures? What if they were to start *producing* superior cultures and cultural practices by design? Then mainline anthropologists (just as mainline psychologists) could not be expected to acquiesce calmly to their own eclipse.

One early attempt at anthropological control involved the Vicos Hacienda project in the 1950s (see Holmberg, 1967). In that project anthropologists actually did design and implement new cultural practices. They assisted the residents of the hacienda, who had been vassals of the land, to funnel the fruits of their labors more efficiently back into their society. The project was deemed controversial within the anthropology community. Colleagues criticized project leaders for using their scientific powers to impose their own cultural values on the hacienda community.

Such rifts might presage similar rifts from efforts in the significant area of designing the cultural aspects of off–Earth settlements. Space settlements will require cultural practices respecting new kinds of values that will also have to be conditioned by design—in some cases values not shared by the designers themselves. The new practices would enable people to thrive under the alien physical and socio–cultural conditions in space, on moons, or on planets (see Beach, 1991a, 1991b; BACD, 1991).

In the 1960s, at the height of the debate about Vicos Hacienda, the anthropology community was unable to deal effectively with the issue of the putative sanctity of values. Since then, developments in behaviorological science have placed the management of values in a technology based on natural science. That is because values are behavioral effects of the contingencies under which people operate. Specifically, values are reinforcers, and most are selectively conditioned by the consequences of behavior and functionally facilitated by the concomitant emotional respondents called *feelings.* And behaviorological science and technology have worked these areas well. (For more detail, see Skinner, 1953, 1971, 1974; Krapfl & Vargas, 1977; and E.A. Vargas, 1975, 1982.)

In general, the greatest cultural needs are felt at the scientifically mature level of effective control. Throughout the culture the greatest value is attached to effective outcomes at that level. Thus more professional reinforcers are at stake among scientific groups competing for the professional markets defined in terms of effective *control* over behavior. For example, in just one area, consider the enormity of the resources that our culture is prepared to invest in whichever scientific discipline can develop the most effective technology of teaching (Skinner, 1968; also, see Barrett, 1991). Behaviorological scientists have repeatedly demonstrated what they construe to have been convincing wins in such implicit contests (e.g., see Johnson & Layng, 1992). No surprise occurs, then, when educational psychology is the locus of much interdisciplinary conflict centered around what some educational behaviorologists regard as attempts to suppress their more successful science. (For some details and examples on the educational issues, including the U.S. Federal government's massive "Project Follow Through," see *all* the articles in the Youth Policy Institute's July/August 1988 issue of *Youth Policy.*)

An original separatist move. Small scale separatist moves by behaviorists within psychology had actually become necessary on much earlier occasions than those Vargas included in his summary at the 1987 ABA convention symposium. For instance, Skinner's early psychology course at Harvard, Psych. 7, was too divergent for the conventional psychology faculty. Under the new name "Natural Science 114: Human Behavior," the course moved to the general education area where it proved successful with a wide range of students. These students tended to be focused on the realities and practicalities of the culture, and faculty resistance subsided. Skinner (1983a) reported:

> ...it was a much more appropriate title. I had not given my students a general survey of psychology; *I had taught a very different subject.* The new title also attracted students whose major interests were in the social sciences or humanities but who needed a sophomore–level Natural Science course, and they were just the students who needed to know more about a science of behavior. (pp. 23–24; emphasis added)

Skinner (1983a, p. 44) subsequently converted that course material into his 1953 book *Science and Human Behavior.* That book features principles induced from an experimental analysis of behavior, and develops the conceptual foundations of a discipline strikingly different from that introduced in typical beginning psychology courses.

Skinner's Oscillations

For a number of years behaviorologists had been feeling an increasing disappointment at the progressive deceleration of the general ABA–centered behavioral movement toward disciplinary independence for the science of behavior. In 1987–1988, as those observers finally acted to establish an independent behaviorology discipline, they were sensing a rapidly accelerating reversal of the general behavioral movement back into the fold of organized psychology (a trend which their actions may have retarded).

Back to psychology. An incongruous event that occurred at the end of the 1987 ABA convention perhaps in part propelled this reversal back toward psychology. B.F. Skinner unexpectedly added a ten–minute addendum to his previously prepared major address—one in a series of annual presentations serving as the traditional final session of the annual ABA conventions. Skinner had spent his entire professional life building the case for a behavioral science revolution and explicitly providing the leadership for it through his research and writings. In contrast with this, Skinner told his audience that he thought a separate discipline was a mistake, that behavior analysis was a kind of psychology (and should *become* psychology), and that organized psychology was where the behavioral movement should remain. He had wanted a revolution, but now he was declaring that it was to occur *within* psychology, not as a departure from psychology.

Although Skinner subsequently oscillated on this issue (two years later he announced his reversal of this view, discussed in a later section), at this moment he seemed to declare unequivocal favor with one path away from a junction at which he had been poised throughout a lifetime of strategy deliberations. He had spent his professional life arguing alternately that psychology should be changed and that it should be abandoned. His lifelong bias was for changing it. He had explicitly taken that stand as early as 1928 when he wrote "...my fundamental interests lie in the field of Psychology, and I shall probably continue therein, even, if necessary, by making over the entire field to suit myself" (Skinner, 1979, p. 38).

Speculatively, a variety of potential sources may have raised the special prepotency of that recurring preference just at the time of the 1987 ABA talk. These sources include: (a) convention sessions (such as the previously described Bruce symposium that involved Skinner) which had focused on the issue of a separate discipline and sharpened many relevant variables; (b) a resolution to redouble a thus–far unsuccessful effort, perhaps triggered by misgivings about the appropriateness of that cause (a public declaration of recommitment postpones any impending verdict of failure and, as a self–management practice, renders oneself liable for the social punishments reserved for those who do not keep to their commitments); and (c) the pressure exerted by respected psychology colleagues whose counsel favored staying within psychology.

Regardless of possible reasons for his declaration, Skinner's remarks contributed to the already advanced erosion of the capacity of ABA to spawn an independent scientific discipline. Ironically, he had chosen to make these statements at a meeting of an organization which was originally established to demonstrate a measure of independence from psychology for the behavioral movement, and which he had for years fervently supported. Although ABA had attained its *organizational* independence from psychology, *disciplinary* independence had remained elusive. The concept of an independent behavioral discipline had always promised security for the separate existence of ABA. But Skinner's saying that the struggle can only proceed from *within* psychology implied the extent to which the behavior analysis independence movement had failed. As he urged the behavior analysts to keep trying to change psychology into a worthwhile science, part of the audience believed that Skinner was appealing on behalf of a cause already lost. In any case, Skinner's surprising and seemingly self–contradicting declaration elicited strong visceral responses from just about everybody. Depending on the histories of the affected individuals, the personal reactions represented a wide range of emotions.

As he made clear in his autobiography (1979 & 1983a), Skinner had neglected the politics of organized disciplines in favor of successful scientific pursuits. But his voice had grown influential. His recommendations about organizing the discipline, always heavy with political implications because so many people attended closely to whatever he said, constituted a weighty political resource for those whose objectives were served by whatever position he took.

Skinner was adding his powerful endorsement to the concept that "behavior analysis" *is* psychology. Most behaviorologists had already taken that position as part of their effort to discriminate clearly between behaviorology and behavioral psychology which had staked a strong claim to "behavior analysis." The APA, for its part, had implicitly accepted that collaborationist perspective when its behavior–analytic Division 25 in 1987 briefly changed the name of the division journal to *Behavior Analysis.* Prominent behavioral psychologists with memberships in ABA were commonly referring to behavior analysis as a kind of psychology and to behavior analysts as psychologists (e.g., see "Minutes of," 1988, 1990). Edmond Fantino (1988), as editor of JEAB, explicitly described behavior analysis as an aspect of psychology. And numerous behavior analysis training programs were imbedded in psychology departments.

By the time Skinner gave his talk, most behaviorologists correspondingly saw little hope for an independent science of behavior analysis. (In his speech, Skinner did not pursue *that* implication of his position.) The trend toward a psychology–free credential by the clinical faction in ABA (Shook, 1993), with its implications for an independent behavior analysis discipline, had not yet had a significant impact on the general thinking of behavioral people. In any case, Skinner's speech encouraged psychology–oriented followers to distance themselves even farther from what some had seen, partly through his leadership, as the goal of a separate scientific discipline. Skinner's 1987 disavowal of that goal allowed any followers who might have been feeling the political heat of an independence–oriented rebellion to resume overtures to psychology that previously might have been deemed unfashionable. Some behaviorologists welcomed that self–culling insofar as it reoriented toward psychology a lot of people whose ambivalent faltering might have clogged the machinery of the behaviorology movement.

An affiliation with ABA no longer connoted one's disciplinary identity because the phrase "behavior analysis" had become so imprecise. Increasingly, ABA members felt compelled to declare their respective professional and disciplinary identities, some with and some away from psychology. And within two years, by 1989, the ABA leadership was explicitly evoking such declarations from its members by way of official questionnaires and new fill–in items on the ABA membership forms (as described in Chapter 4).

The Ulman–Skinner letters. An accidental fall at his home put Skinner in the hospital and prevented him from attending the 1988 ABA convention, though he returned in 1989. During the two years between the 1987 and 1989 conventions, a number of people interacted with Skinner on how best to preserve the science that he had developed and about the position that he was taking with respect to an organized disciplinary home for it. Skinner's reluctance to leave psychology was based on several practical considerations: Aside from his expressing a personal distaste for the name behaviorology, he was making the following points (recorded here as noted in his 23 January 1989 letter of response to Jerome Ulman's endorsement of a separate discipline): (a) Behavior analysis is already spread too thinly across too many organizations, so a new one, further fragmenting the movement, is not needed. (b) Colleges and universities are unlikely to create departments of behaviorology for some time. (c) Behaviorology would have little chance of gaining recognition from the National Science Foundation (NSF), at least for a long time. And (d) psychology can yet be redefined, and one useful approach to that end is to continue with good experimental scientific work that will yield ever more convincing scientific data in support of the behavioral perspective.

The dilemma confronting Skinner and other behaviorists who had long struggled to change psychology was underscored by an anecdote that Julie Vargas (Skinner's daughter) related in a letter (20 October 1988) to Fred Keller:

> Last week I was up in Cambridge for two days and a TV crew came to discuss shooting...for a 26 half–hour series on psychology. It was to be an introductory course, like a beginning textbook, they explained. They wanted my father in three of the series, a brief appearance in two and a major part of the one on learning. Brief means a couple of minutes and "major" means 10 minutes—maybe 15 or even 20.... Out of 26 half–hours, or 780 minutes, about 20 minutes or roughly 3% was devoted to the science of behavior.

A little farther along she added "I can't convince my father that being a little piece of 'psychology' does not bode well for our science." The letter ended with "I just wanted to let you know that TIBA is progressing well and to show you our brochure."

During the 1988 Christmas holidays, in discussing with Julie Vargas how best to preserve the science that he had developed, Skinner allowed that he might tolerate the term behaviorology. By January 1989, he was referring in various conversational contexts to "the behaviorologists" and their movement. In a letter to Ulman (6 March 1989), Skinner conceded that the name behaviorology is not as bad as "otorhinolaryngology." Ulman had said that initially he too had found the name behaviorology a bit strange and offered a remedy: "In the privacy of your bath, try saying *behaviorology* aloud at least 50 times." To this Skinner, in his 6 March 1989 letter, replied "I am grateful for the enthusiasm and loyalty of the behaviorologists. I'll try saying the word to myself in the bathtub and see how good a predictor you are." Still, Skinner had not yet completely abandoned his presumption of organized psychology as keeper of his science and philosophy. By April 1989, the American Psychological Society (APS) was publishing the solicited letter from Skinner (presented in an earlier chapter) lending endorsement to that movement.

The following passages from one of Ulman's letters to Skinner (24 February 1989) represent the kinds of views being advanced to Skinner by persons committed to disciplinary independence (subsequent to their inclusion here, the Ulman–Skinner letters were published in *Behaviorology;* see Ulman, 1993). After conceding that neither universities nor the NSF are likely to recognize behaviorology anytime soon, Ulman addressed many issues beginning with what he thought was Skinner's misplaced confidence in the new APS:

> In my view, APS is merely a protestant form of the same old religion, a splinter group from the Assembly of the Personal Agency, consummate defenders of "autonomous man." What motivates the overwhelming majority of APS, I suspect, is opposition to the exclusive guild concerns of the clinical majority in APA, not the promotion of a science of behavior as you and I understand it.
>
> Given the character of its membership, the "science" we can expect APS to advance is exactly the kind you have argued against throughout your career—hypothetical–deductive methodology, statistical inference rather than experimental analysis, the philosophy of logical positivism, and the type of theorizing that, as you so aptly stated in 1950, "appeals to events taking place somewhere else, ...and measured, if at all, in different dimensions (e.g., in the real nervous system, the conceptual system, or the mind)." ...Any behavioral

> psychologists in their [APS] ranks (if the behavioral constituency approaches even 10%, I would be greatly surprised) simply serve to give a behavioristic veneer to the ersatz science of psychology.
>
> In general, our participation in any *psychological* organization presupposes at least tacit acceptance of a common program. Because psychologists cannot agree on a radical behavioral program without themselves becoming something other than psychologists, a psychological organization must of necessity abandon radical behaviorism in favor of theorizing based on mind, cognition, and/or the conceptual nervous system. In short, the program of the psychologist is the defense of the psyche; the program of the radical behaviorist, its demise.
>
> What must at all cost be defended and nurtured are those cultural contingencies—as rare as they are exquisite—responsible for the development of the natural science of behavior. By comparison, it matters little to behaviorologists whether we will soon see behaviorology departments sprouting up around the country or receive a nod of approval from the NSF. That is, the integrity of the discipline takes precedence over the number of people who may or may not come to feel comfortable about recognizing behaviorology as an independent life science. What does matter, I am sure, is that our scientific work be carried out within that protective social environment we call the discipline of behaviorology.
>
> ...I am afraid that this travail [the effort to reform psychology] is Sisyphean and will only wear us down and ultimately exhaust our extremely limited resources. We simply cannot afford to continue our scientific work as a specialty within the psychology establishment. To remain there any longer portends to be a recipe, not only for our continued servitude, but for eventual extinction of the very contingencies necessary for the survival of our science and the philosophy upon which it is based. Yes, as you advise, more active experimental work is needed, there are many issues that need to be explored, and there is much to discuss about the implications of our work. But psychologists since the time of Watson have not merely ignored us, they have contemptuously rejected our experimental research. And there is no apparent reason to suppose they will behave any differently in the future.
>
> ...The founders of The International Behaviorology Association, ...recognize selection by consequences as the most important causal mode in the life sciences and are committed to pursue the use of the contributions to behaviorology found in the works of B.F. Skinner for integrating the concepts, data, and technologies of the discipline's various subfields. With rigorous membership qualifications for its leadership, a newsletter already in production..., a journal under development, and TIBA chapters forming internationally, we are prepared to stay the course.

Skinner's reply (6 March 1989), a few lines beyond one page, was cordial and appreciative. But, after saying that he did not take the APS very seriously, Skinner, though without his usual literary vigor, let stand his previous position that *psychology* represents the study of behavior—including the behavior of the brain, not as the mysterious generative source of behavior, but as part of the thing called the behaving body. He complained that the cognitive psychologists have been doing inappropriate kinds of things *in the name of psychology.* And he lamented the fact that others, who also understand what is going wrong, too often let them get away with it. He briefly reviewed the list of his own rebuttals to the cognitive views, the views that he thought had led psychology so far afield (from a behavior science). Skinner made the point that he had no objection to legitimate interests by psychologists in how the body worked, but that psychology needed to switch its emphasis to the kind of science that makes possible practical behavior–technology applications.

Behaviorologists continued to raise the issue with Skinner in various ways. For example, taking advantage of inescapable realities, Julie Vargas from time to time reportedly brought to Skinner's attention factual data implying futility in continuing a disciplinary affiliation with psychology. On 28 April 1989, Ulman sent one more eloquent letter to Skinner, reiterating the reasons for disciplinary separation. In this letter he argued the points with new examples and facts. He countered the notion that staying with psychology protected previous gains and represented the shortest path, however bleak, to a secure home for our discipline. Ulman concluded in this way:

> ...As long as we remain within the church, for whatever reason, the longer we must abide by its commandments, chief among which is an unquestioning respect for the divinity of the psyche (or any of its cognate hypostases—mind, cognition, experience, etc.). I feel that we can best move forward, not by arguing with psychologists about what may or may not be going on in the black box; writing letters to hostile, psyche–intoxicated editors; nor playing no–win political games in psychology departments. We have done all of that for over 50 years and it has gotten us nowhere. I say, psychologists made their own metaphysical bed, now let them lie in it. We have much more useful things to do; namely, to advance the independent discipline of behaviorology in all of its facets—philosophical, analytical, experimental, and technological—and, most importantly, disseminate our successes to the public.

Regardless of whatever fueled the great engine of organized psychology, it did not require a more effective science. The nature and course of organized psychology had remained little affected by the protracted proffer of a more effective basic science by its politically insignificant behavioristic minority. The radical behaviorists' long–nourished anticipations of an overhauled psychology had matured fruitlessly. No promising new change strategies arose to mask the increasingly hollow echo of old ones being reiterated. With few exceptions the leadership in organized psychology, whether in APA or APS, remained unalterably cognitive and mentalistic, and the discipline of psychology was organized and operated to reward members for following that lead.

A declaration of independence. By the time of the 1989 ABA convention in late May, Skinner had again had enough of psychology. In spite of his wavering in 1987, his estrangement had developed across a long if intermittent history. He had made it explicit as early as 1938 in *The Behavior of Organisms.* In 1972, when a colleague had asked if operant people should form a separate discipline, Skinner (1980, pp. 71–72) had noted, "I have been coming close to that view." He went on to list four major fronts of disciplinary activity that he thought had taken psychology astray.

Then, as his major address at the close of the 1989 ABA convention, Skinner presented his declaration of disciplinary independence, titled "A World of Our Own" (Skinner, 1989a). Reviewing the ancient origins of cognitivism and the more recent origins of behaviorism, he described how cognitivists increasingly have hidden their ancient and invalid assumptions by adopting descriptive language from other respected fields. He reviewed and analyzed samples of what he construed to be the current cognitive/mentalistic nonsense that pervades the literature of psychology. He defined a proper behavioral discipline to include the concerns of ethologists and dwelt on the importance to such a discipline of the mechanism of selection at all levels of analysis. He spoke of the neglect in cognitive psychology both of the concept and implications of selection. On the cognitive/behavioral dichotomy in the search for the origins of behavioral events, Skinner had this to say (quoted from a tape recording of his talk):

> Let's just imagine that all of these people who are trying to find out what is inside the skull, whether it is mind or brains (it doesn't matter), ...[are] all completely successful. Let's suppose that people who introspect see the same thing.... And let's suppose that cognitive theories have all been meshed well together...[into a] super– or mega–theory. Everybody agrees! This is it! And let's assume that brain science has come up, not only with what happens when you slice a brain in two, or when you inject a drug into it, but [with descriptions of its nature] down to the finest detail, so that we know what is happening when someone says "hello." And let's suppose that is exactly what you see when you introspect and is exactly what cognitive theorists say is in there. What would you have? You would have a biochemical system. It would be completely orderly. It would simply do what it does because of its structure.

Here Skinner implicitly dismissed the notion of a personal autonomous agent and alluded to the controlling environment in which occur the events that subsequently stimulate (that is, functionally control) the internal neural activity. When the body behaves, that exhibited behavior is simply the only one possible in the interaction between that body as currently structured and the controlling environment as currently structured. (For elaboration, see Fraley, 1992a.) These kinds of behavior–producing interactions feature the accessible independent variables over which the kind of control called intervention can be gained; they provide the basis for behavioral engineering. Skinner asserted that behaviorists should remain interested in behavior–related neural events within the body. But he further argued that the *behavioral* people are the best prepared to specify that for which the neural scientists could productively look.

After presenting some historical details about *his own earlier acceptance of principles portending a separate discipline,* Skinner noted that he nevertheless:

> ...went on saying that the science of behavior was psychology. And [he added] I am convinced now that I was wrong. I think they are very different fields.

Perhaps alluding in part to his brief addendum after his 1987 ABA address, he confessed to having "been slow in throwing off the notion that a science of behavior is the future of psychology."

Here are some related conclusions heard elsewhere in his talk:

> ...We've got an exclusive field here. No one is anywhere near us.
>
> ...I believe that this field is an extraordinarily important one and has no rivals.
>
> ...It seems to me perfectly evident that those of us who are thinking well in the terms of behavior analysis are miles ahead of those people.
>
> ...Now I think this *is* a world of our own.

After Skinner's earlier call, made during his 1987 ABA talk, for followers of his science to stay in psychology, he did not attempt to publish a paper based on that speech (as had been his usual practice). But a couple of weeks after his 1989 "independence" talk, Skinner accepted an offer by Lawrence Fraley, tendered as editor *pro tem* of the incipient behaviorology journal, to prepare and provide a paper copy of the 1989 "independence" speech transcribed from a tape recording. Skinner would edit it and prepare a version for publication in the new TIBA journal (to be named *Behaviorology*). Talking later to a family member during the Christmas season of 1989, Skinner again noted that, while he had been slow to turn away from psychology, he thought that our discipline should have been established independently a long time ago. And he mentioned the paper on that theme which he was preparing for *Behaviorology*. He subsequently submitted the paper to *Behaviorology*, and it was included in the first issue (Skinner, 1993).

In August 1990, during a speech at the APA convention only a week before his death, Skinner reiterated the evaluation of psychology to which his science inevitably leads. Holland (1990) reported the scene:

> To the ballroom full of psychologists he said that, with the selection of consequences as the cause of our body (natural selection) and our behavior (environmental contingencies), there is no role left for a creator or for an initiating self or mind. So cognitive science "is the creationism of psychology." (p. 32)

Yet in the end Skinner would leave ambiguous his endorsement of a future course for the discipline built around the science he originated. On 17 August 1990, the day before his death, Skinner finished editing a final paper (based largely on that talk to the APA) entitled "Can Psychology be a Science of Mind" (Skinner, 1990). In it he reviewed the polyglot disciplinary topography of psychology. Then he explained one last time why psychology would have to undergo substantial paradigmatic change to fulfill its putative cultural mission. Referring to his selectionist–based science as "behavior analysis," the closing sentence of that final article brought to an end, without resolution, his life–long struggle to change psychology: "...but whether behavior analysis will be called psychology is a matter for the future to decide" (p. 1210).

But the decision had *already* been made—by the behaviorologists: The science Skinner originated would be called neither behavior analysis nor psychology. It would be called behaviorology. And the behaviorologists had reached two additional conclusions: (a) Not only does psychology not represent Skinner's science but, more importantly, it is unlikely *ever* to do so; and (b) Skinner's reasons for entering into organized psychology had had nothing to do with any appeal of the psychology paradigm, and *he had never come to behave philosophically or scientifically as a psychologist.*

The Issue of Covert Reform

Many others were proving even less able than Skinner to overcome the powerful contingencies that bound them to the professional situations in which they had struggled for most of their careers, in some cases with personal success. Apart from differences of opinion about the best approach to bring an effective science of behavior to our culture, the fact remained that psychology was professionally well organized and well established. Its group–arranged contingencies afforded many professional advantages plus a substantial protective umbrella for the professional and economic interests of the people in its different philosophical/scientific verbal subcommunities. Any radical behaviorist could stay within organized psychology, enjoying those benefits, while the perennial behavioral movement to change psychology from within afforded that person the imprimatur of an organized cause for being there. Outside observers could not effectively sort out the relative effects of the various kinds of contingencies sharing in the control of decisions to remain within, and to support, psychology.

During October 1989, Sam Deitz, Editor Elect of *The Behavior Analyst,* was speaking on educational reform at two successive regional ABA Chapter conferences. He told those audiences that behavior analysts should stop trying to attach credit for their accomplishments to their theoretical foundations and simply work to get their *practices* accepted as the normal way of doing things. After all, Deitz claimed, no educational practice is derived uniquely from only *one* theoretical position. As evidence for that conclusion, he noted that in practical situations cognitive and behavioral people make *similar* suggestions. Through that line of reasoning he arrived at this point: Offensive theory need not be touted at the expense of cooperative progress.

Certainly, the prevailing contingencies in many simple situations compel similar practical reactions from persons of differing theoretical persuasions. But that is because their differing scientific and philosophical repertoires are not evoked in such simple situations. Most people will respond cooperatively to a breach in a dike by throwing more sandbags on the leak regardless of differences in their respective scientific and philosophical repertoires or, for that matter, their religious, political, economic, or social ones as well. For that level of responding, people need neither philosophical nor scientific repertoires. But when an appropriate course of action is less obvious, those kinds of verbal repertoires become necessary to supplement other behavior–controlling stimuli. And unique practices, based on integral theoretical approaches, often *do* follow. For example, complex educational practices informed by behaviorological principles frequently differ in important and effective ways from those based upon cognitive/mentalistic principles and assumptions. To appreciate those differences one need only examine contrasting education textbooks like the J. Vargas (1988) behaviorological text, or the Fraley (1996a) behaviorological text, with a cognitive/mentalistic text such as the one by Biehler and Snowman (1990). Or consider the contested revolution precipitated in education during the 1960s and 1970s by the behaviorologically inspired emphasis on behavioral objectives. (For a representative textbook on behavioral objectives, see J. Vargas, 1972.)

The give–away of the products of a discipline, while de–emphasizing or hiding their conceptual origins (as Deitz advocated), may facilitate personal accommodations. But most behaviorologists saw in that strategy the peril of their discipline being extinguished. The expectation that at some future cultural awakening, or in some grand episode of enlightenment, the discipline will either be recognized properly, or will have become recognized to *be* psychology, requires that it retain its integrity until the time of its promised resurrection or prevalence. But in the view of most behaviorologists, the mechanisms of the preservation and survival of the discipline are precisely what gets eroded, suppressed, and precluded in the Deitzian prescription for its interim latency.

Adjustment Problems of Individuals Contemplating the Separatist Movement

Organized professions within one cultural agency often engage the sanctions of another cultural agency, namely law, to extend or maintain their privileged access to professional service markets. In contemplating their professional and disciplinary options, individuals outside such a legally fixated profession sometimes can find themselves confronting legally codified job classifications, legally restricted access to credentials, and legally mandated requirements for specified training.

Members of the Florida Association for Behavior Analysis (FABA, an affiliate of ABA) confronted this issue in 1990 (Taylor, 1990). Proposed revisions to state law would have required behavior analysts in Florida to become licensed under one of five existing groups within five years. The groups were school psychologists, psychologists, clinical social workers, marriage and family therapists, and mental health workers. These groups claimed to know and use "behavior modification" and "behavior analysis." But their members were mostly psychology trained. Their repertoires in behaviorological science and technology were minimal compared to the training expected of FABA members. So FABA members being licensed under codes designed for any of those groups would have amounted to a mislabeling. And if not licensed, FABA members would have had to work under the supervision of someone so licensed—a situation as odious as it would have been inappropriate. FABA members pursued two courses of action: They successfully obtained an exemption for "behavior analysts" from the new law, and they began drafting their own licensing law. Such actions are to be expected when separate disciplines are involved.

For those behavioral individuals who have not been compelled by law to call themselves "psychologists," an alternative basic discipline, behaviorology, and the disciplinary coalition called behavior analysis have both become available. But other behaviorists have continued to have vested interests in professions for which organized psychology remains the *legal* keeper of the intellectual property rights. Often deemed necessary to protect the public from quackery, that legal mechanism carries the risk of a blindly enforced respect for outmoded ideas. Efforts to win scientific and philosophical arguments with assistance from the strong arm of the law require great sensitivity to that risk. Verbal fixation, even if legally sanctioned, is antithetical to science. The implications of bolstering the relations between scientific ideas and attractive opportunities for economic gain through alliance with the agencies of government and law deserve careful study, especially with respect to long term effects. (For another examination of these perils, see Booth, 1989.)

Some individuals turned away from both the risks and the difficulties of disciplinary independence. Among them some persisted in arguing defensively that radical behaviorists simply entertain a *different point of view* within the more securely and comfortably established discipline of psychology. They seemed not to differentiate, to the extent others did, between (a) separate disciplines and (b) differing points of view within one discipline. For example, when geologists argued over the existence of continental drift, it was an argument *about how best to interpret their incomplete data.* But both sides operated out of the same analytical framework founded in physics, chemistry, biology, and mathematics—with a particular collective conceptual integrity called geology. And because they shared the same philosophical and scientific foundations and examined the same tectonic phenomena, *they were all geologists.* But behavioral and cognitive individuals within organized psychology do not operate out of the same analytical framework nor do they share a common scientific and philosophical foundation (Hineline, 1984). Theirs is not merely a rift resulting from insufficient data, and therefore it cannot be healed through efforts to "get all the relevant facts." The geologists, in the presence of accumulating data, could finally agree about continental drift. But even in the presence of copious and adequate data behavioral and cognitive/mentalistic people still tend to disagree because they do not behave under the stimulus control of data in the same way.

Could cognitive/mentalistic people even *afford* to agree? Lawrence Fraley readdressed this subtle question during a brief talk at the 1996 ABA convention (Fraley, 1996; also see Sagan, 1995):

> ...the natural scientists of behavior who tried to persuade psychologists to change their science and philosophy failed to recognize that psychology, for the most part, was not a scientific discipline, but only a *scientized* discipline. Psychology began as the study of that interface between the metaphysical and physical worlds thought to reside in the mind of man, and that assumption still underlies much of contemporary psychology. Most people in our culture have been conditioned over a lifetime to view a domain beyond the natural world as real, and they deem explanatory reliance on its elements to be rational. The traditional psychology community has drawn much of its membership from that vast population, and represents a subset of it—a cadre devoted to a scientific study of how the natural and non–natural worlds conjoin in a mind that functions as a channeling device between those worlds.
>
> Many such people are devoutly religious persons with whom religious students feel a special affinity, and psychology training programs attract many such students. On their Sabbath, those psychology professors and their student followers pray to a deity...for interventions among variables in the physical world. They assume that a person's communication with that deity is channeled by way of a mini–deity functioning as a vital force within the body. In its religious context it is called the soul or human spirit....
>
> On Monday mornings when these people return to their traditional psychology classrooms, the soul is temporarily renamed; it becomes the "self," and the remainder of the week is spent on a secular scientific analysis of how it might work. Some psychologists, who take no part in the religious aspects, stay focused on what they see as a more *secular* self–agent. But they remain equally mystical.
>
> During those kinds of studies, however, no findings are tolerated that substantially contradict the underlying metaphysical assumptions. That is why traditional psychology can be regarded as a scientized community rather than a scientific community. Those mystical assumptions are not inferred *from* scientific evidence. They are brought *to* the scientific evidence, which is then gleaned for any support that it can lend to those assumptions. This means that in the traditional psychology community, the persuasiveness of evidence, so compelling among the natural scientists, loses cogency in proportion to its threat to those mystical assumptions.
>
> Skinner and his followers never had a chance of making over psychology by demonstrating that practices informed by their natural science were more effective. Their practices, when deemed effective, were merely co–opted and re–described in psychological language so that they seemed new rather than appropriated. (Other effective practices actually originate independently in both communities under common prevailing contingencies. In that case there is no need for either side's science, although once essentially the same practice

> has appeared in both camps, it is given very different descriptions and interpretations in the respective behavioral and psychological communities.)
>
> Should accumulating evidence force a traditional psychologist to the brink of either abandoning mysticism or discounting valid and reliable evidence, the typical traditional psychologist treats the dilemma as a Hobson's choice—there is no real option. Any science that contradicts the fundamental mystical assumptions is abandoned. People who got into science in the first place in order to shed some scholarly light on the details of their deepest philosophical assumptions (including, especially, those of a religious nature) are not going to abandon those foundations if that science starts causing trouble. Instead, they abandon the science, which at that point is merely an intellectual tool that initially looked helpful, but has proven to cause more difficulties than it is worth.

Behaviorologists understand the mentalistic approach, and have reason to do so. The programs in which many behaviorologists were trained required that they engage in substantial cognitive and mentalistic study. Furthermore, the basic assumptions underlying all of psychology are part of the cultural lore familiar to most people. Psychology embodies a scientized incorporation of secular cultural lore and the metaphysics prevalent in religion—all matched as closely as possible to whatever the physiology–based neural scientists can say about how nervous systems function. Behaviorologists also understand the mentalistic approach because the analytical mechanisms of behaviorology are particularly suited to overcoming some of the riddles that, unsolved, allow mentalism to seem more reasonable. But the reverse is seldom true. People with the typical cognitivist/mentalist training usually lack comprehension of the behaviorology repertoire. Furthermore, they face an additional major repertoire deficit insofar as they construe their professional tasks to be those that behaviorologists have defined for themselves. Overcoming that deficit could take years of new study requiring substantial relearning of basics. Radical behaviorism and the science that it informs are complex and difficult to learn. Such costs are usually too great for an established professional person to bear. Denying their worth has always been easier than mastering them.

Rationally, instead of bearing those costs, a person might resist, in some cases by ignoring scientific evidence and eschewing open academic debate. Often the resistance takes the form of resort to available counter–controlling arrangements embodied in the politics of scientific verbal communities or to remedies available through appeal to other cultural agencies (e.g., law) for help and protection.

The behavioral psychologists, such as those at the 1987 ABA convention who sympathized with a continuing effort to change psychology from within, will perhaps carry on the attempt to persuade listeners who cannot readily afford the implications of the message. But behaviorologists, by organizing independently, are free of the contingencies to expend themselves on that continuing classic exercise in futility. Each behavioral individual must deal at the personal level with the question of what kind of professional contribution to make, and in which disciplinary and organizational framework to make it. One can work primarily to serve one's self, one's group, or one's culture in its best long–range interests. The cost of personal commitment in any one of those domains might be forfeiture of reinforcers available in the other two (for discussions of this issue, see Wood, 1976, and Vargas & Fraley, 1976).

At this writing, many behaviorally oriented scholars have no realistic alternatives to operating within units representing organized psychology and must find ways of surviving there. The shaping of behavioral individuals under contingencies of accommodation with mainstream psychology can produce self–punishing compromises of scientific and professional integrity. The escape from these is sometimes a forced and often convoluted rationalization. The person might try to find some virtue in being suppressed or in being forced to pretend a devotion to eclecticism. A more aggressive defense of one's disciplinary integrity can require complex and sophisticated repertoires of academic and political conflict that few individuals have had an opportunity to acquire and refine. Without the skill to conduct an effective kind of fight (and often without much hope that attempts will yield more than a glorious career demise), persons trapped in organized psychology can be left privately resentful at what has happened to them. Among that subset some might seek relief by reciting comfortable half–lies about the cleverness of subtle infiltration or the sacrificial devotion of existence as a behavioral mole. Meanwhile, they could hope that their occasional limited victories or accomplishments would yet save their science.

Behaviorologists did not enjoy any special immunity from such self–protective contingencies of accommodation. Nor could one argue that personal interests played no part in behaviorologists' respective commitments *to* the separatist movement. However, behaviorologists simply arranged to avoid having to contact many contingencies of accommodation. The behaviorologists' approach to professional and scientific probity was to arrange not to have to share a discipline in the first place—especially with multitudes who (a) were untrained in behaviorological science, and yet (b) were organized for the political and ideological defense of the strongly conditioned reinforcers of their own discipline.

Psychologists might force unattractive compromises on some behaviorists within organized psychology, making the separation issue complex for them. But the behaviorologists tried not to forget how complex the separation issue could also be for those behaviorists unaffected by contingencies of personal self–protection or self–interest. Aside from any special strength that aversive contingencies and various self–interests might lend to rationalizations about eclecticism, other behaviorists *were* taking into account the same complex and extensive mix of relevant variables that behaviorologists had considered. However, unlike the behaviorologists, they were oppositely concluding that their discipline must develop *within* psychology. They were hoping eventually to monopolize the present disciplinary coalition that comprises psychology.

As most behaviorologists have always agreed, where best to develop this discipline *is* a difficult judgment call. Intelligent people differ. Individuals respond to such a mix of variables according to their respective personal and professional histories and current circumstances. And they behave accordingly.

The Adjustment of the At–Large Behavioral Community

As TIBA and the behaviorology movement developed within the broader behavioral community, some resistance, perhaps loosely coordinated, continued. It was generally confined to individuals whose investments and values committed them either to organized psychology or to the semi–independent "behavior analysis" movement. During and after 1989, following the earlier flurry of rather open debate, these resistors could clearly see that a certain group would seriously continue its pursuit of an independent behaviorology discipline. Some behavioral opponents then responded in ways that to the behaviorologists seemed like extinction procedures: Public mention of the behaviorology movement did not occur in some contexts that would normally have included it. Articles referring explicitly to behaviorology seemed to meet extra difficulties wending their way through the publication process. Reports surfaced about people being advised to ignore the behaviorologists (these were first–hand or second–hand reports, but they had the usual behavioral effects nonetheless). Some uncommitted individuals who had been maintaining collegial exchanges about the movement through correspondence with behaviorologists ceased their responding. A couple of people explicitly mentioned pressure from colleagues to do so, and reported that they were discouraged by the responses of some colleagues to any mention of the behaviorology movement.

Yet at the same time, other behavior analysts were pointing anew to the irreconcilability of the two disciplines. McDowell (1991) advanced the unusual argument that the differences between behavior analysts and psychologists stem from their *ontological* differences: They do not recognize the same realities. "This difference is so fundamental that I think it unlikely that the two disciplines can be reconciled" (p. 29). McDowell provided numerous examples. Nevertheless, he recommended, as have other behavior analysts, still another attempt at "enlightenment" to demonstrate to an implicitly psychological audience the kind of quality science and philosophy that should prevail.

Opportunities to answer opponents' questions did occur. For example, to encourage such exchanges, Deborah Shanley asked Lawrence Fraley, Stephen Ledoux, and Ernest Vargas to appear as panelists in a discussion session at the tenth annual conference of the Berkshire Association for Behavior Analysis and Therapy (BABAT) at the University of Massachusetts at Amherst on 14 October 1989. The topic was the interrelations among TIBA, ABA, and AABT (the Association for the Advancement of Behavior Therapy). The session, with Joseph Morrow as moderator, attracted a crowd of about thirty people. Three rather prominent persons in the audience accounted for much of the audience participation. Their work, though in different fields, was informed by behavioral psychology, and they had professional ties and loyalties to ABA. At least two of them were explicit advocates of continuing with attempts to change organized psychology. They were enthusiastic about the kind of organizational independence ABA manifested. And ABA was where they thought their attempts to change psychology could be based. At the session they challenged the efficacy and appropriateness of the behaviorology movement. They raised questions about TIBA (a) competing with ABA, (b) enjoying little political power, and (c) having few members. Respective answers focused on organizational complementarity, the apolitical purposes of TIBA, and the value of getting right before getting big.

In general, behaviorologists would have preferred the early support of more people. But TIBA did not need the broad–based political power to which some critics pointed as a deficiency. In fact, a relatively small number of followers during this early organization and design phase had some benefits. TIBA leaders were experimentally and developmentally applying their own science to designing and establishing a new kind of scientific/professional verbal community of some complexity and sophistication. And they were doing so without benefit of comfortably sufficient prescriptive precedent. With their science under so many threatening contingencies, taking each next step correctly was more easily accomplished with a smaller–scale model. And for some people, being able to do that outweighed the importance of swelling the ranks.

One of the BABAT conference questioners did press for clarification as to whether the behaviorology movement was based on new science or simply represented a disciplinary reorganization. That was a difficult question, because the answer is complex: Through the new movement, old science *had* emerged within new organizational arrangements. While a new verbal community had been established, its founding members spoke an older scientific language. But the movement, through reorganization, relieved constraints that had been hindering the continued development of new and better science. Thus behaviorologists fully expected that in the more propitious professional atmosphere of the new disciplinary organization, the science of behaviorology *would* evolve constructively away from what prevailed in behavioral psychology, behavior analysis, and behavior therapy. Subsequently, TIBA would design certain organizational arrangements (discussed in an earlier chapter) precisely to evoke more new scientific activity by members.

During the same period, typical signs of permanence continued to accumulate with respect to behaviorology. The TIBA letterhead appeared frequently over items of official correspondence. TIBA had established the annual behaviorology convention, the TIBA newsletter, *Selections,* and *Behaviorological Commentaries,* as regular events. And ABA was asking all members to indicate on the membership form which discipline, psychology, behaviorology, or some other discipline, informed their work. At the same time, opponents of behaviorology were leaving unanswered some difficult questions implying the appropriateness of the behaviorology movement which behaviorologists had raised in the literature and at meetings.

Meanwhile, routine and often innocuous public acknowledgments of the behaviorology group gradually began to reappear in contexts where they might be expected. Typical of these was a statement in the newsletter of the Cambridge Center for Behavioral Studies reporting that a "...consortium, chaired by Barbara Etzel, has representatives from the Cambridge Center, ABA, Division 25 of the APA, and TIBA" (Recruiting diversity..., 1993).

Psychologists Tighten Control on Behavior Analysis Journals

Concerned radical behaviorists launched the behaviorology movement in part on the conviction that the behavior analysis movement could neither guarantee the integrity of radical behaviorist philosophy and the science that it informs, nor adequately support the further growth and development of these. The erosion of the radical behaviorist character of the behavior analysis movement could be seen in the changing character of behavior analysis literature.

Behaviorism. The journal *Behaviorism,* founded by Willard Day, had for years been the philosophical journal of the behavioral movement in the United States. It was the principal literary medium of the radical behaviorist philosophy of science. When Peter Killeen and George Graham replaced Willard Day as co–editors of that journal, they set forth in their first editorial the evolutionary trends that they would pursue (Graham & Killeen, 1985). After commenting on the necessity of scientific evolution, they acknowledged the production of variation through the mechanisms in organized science, declared the importance of meta–scientific reviews of disciplines by the philosophers of science, and began to mention their new directions. They would "facilitate...the generation of new variants of behaviorism, and the selection of promising variants for further development" (p. 1). This, they noted, would restrict the focus and emphasis to "measurable public behavior." Among topics specifically encouraged for authors were *"theories of learning"* and *"the role of cognitive variables"* (emphasis added). The editorial board would be continued under the old policy restricting membership to "psychologists" and "philosophers."

Given a lenient interpretation, none of this new focus would necessarily *have* to fall outside of a behavior–analytic framework, nor, as far as scientific and philosophical principles are concerned, even a behaviorological one. But to some behaviorologists and behavior analysts, these statements and characteristics seemed restrictive, peculiar, and neglectful of the verbal integrity of the radical behavioral community for which, and to which, the journal had long spoken. Those provisions would afford comfort and imply welcome both to traditional psychologists and to those in the behavioral movement anxious to nudge the movement away from a separate, independent disciplinary home for radical behaviorism and back under the umbrella of organized psychology. Early in 1989 the two editors sent out renewal notices on which the phrase "behavioral psychology" was defined to "include the experimental analysis of behavior as well as recent developments in *philosophy of mind"* (emphasis added).

At about this same time the behaviorological community was saddened by news of Willard Day's fatal heart attack. As people paused to reflect on Day's professional lifetime of support for quality behavioral science and philosophy, many regretted the apparent disciplinary regression in the journal that he had founded and edited for many years. Although Day had never taken his journal out of the psychology community, he had maintained its integrity as a journal serving the radical behavioral minority. The new editors seemed to be courting a wider audience at the expense of that integrity. Earlier, at the 1988 ABA convention, Lawrence Fraley had spoken with Willard Day about the behaviorology movement. Day listened carefully with his usual great interest. He responded that any movement dedicated to preserving the integrity of radical behaviorism appealed to him. In addition, he had asked to be kept informed.

By 1991, editor George Graham was introducing Volume 19 (1) of what had been *Behaviorism* with a prefacing editorial in which he wrote:

> Between 1985 and 1990 the editorial scope of the journal expanded rapidly under catholic editorial tastes and pressures within psychology for eclectic theorizing. So *Behaviorism* in 1990 did not appear as *Behaviorism.* It appeared under the current name of *Behavior and Philosophy.* This is how it will continue to both call and describe itself: a vehicle...for the philosophical reflections of psychologists and the psychological ruminations of philosophers. (unnumbered preface page)

In 1992 Howard Sloane, a TIBA member, became Executive Director of the Cambridge Center for Behavioral Studies which publishes *Behavior and Philosophy.* Sloane was generally known as a supporter of the original concept of this journal. With his leadership of the Center, many behaviorologists hoped to see a reversal of the trend away from radical behaviorism in *Behavior and Philosophy.*

***Journal of the Experimental Analysis of Behavior* (JEAB).** In 1987, Edmond Fantino began his tenure as editor of JEAB. In his introductory editorial (Fantino, 1988), he defined behavior analysis to be *within psychology* and behavior analysts to *be psychologists.* He described one change that he would introduce to the journal as "broadening the conceptual scope of articles that appear in the journal" (p. 1). Fantino suggested that behavior analysts have shied away from "cognitive phenomena," though he did mention some exceptions, and he declared that "behavior analysts certainly have not been at the forefront of the recent movement in cognition." This he lamented because he believed behavior analysts could contribute functional analyses of "language and cognition."

Fantino's enthusiasm to reassociate the behavior analysis movement with mainline psychology could easily be inferred (a) from his implication (the matter of justification aside) that a valid movement in the field of cognition had been in progress, and (b) by his statement to the effect that, by returning to the psychology fold, behavior analysts would find those cognition studies worthwhile and could begin to get a piece of the contributory action. However, when Fantino described the potential nature of those behavior analytic contributions, he suggested that they could offer alternative analyses of the data adduced in cognitive psychology. Thus, hidden beneath the overtures of disciplinary balance and cooperation were implications that (a) cognitivists lack a science adequate to interpret validly their own data, and that (b) the behavior analysts could follow with better analyses of language and cognition—as if, perhaps, to co–opt the "cognitive revolution."

By 1989 the journal was clearly reflecting Fantino's concept of a cognitive–behavioral blend in which behavior analysis had been relegated to a still important though quite insufficient aspect of an implicit psychology discipline (White, McCarthy, & Fantino, 1989). In 1991, the radical behaviorist Charles Catania (1991), in an open rebuttal to Michael Mahoney (1989), noted that JEAB included papers "...even on those research lines that you regard as forcing the revision of and challenging radical behaviorist accounts (p. 67)" (though his examples pre–dated Fantino's tenure as editor). Catania, a self–identified behavioral *psychologist* and skilled career–long miner of the psychology literature, implicitly accepted such a mix of contents as worthwhile. Behaviorologists grant the possibility of discovering worthwhile fragments in the psychology literature. They object only on what are fundamentally economic bases to the inefficiency of a literature laced with irrelevant and often invalid paradigmatic influences (see J. Vargas, 1990). Unfortunately, Fantino did not address the ultimate fate of behavior analysis and its literature as an insecure enclave within the larger verbal community of psychology.

Division 25 Recorder. The journal of APA Division 25, *Division 25 Recorder* (and briefly renamed *Behavior Analysis*) was always strictly a psychology journal. When the rift in the American Psychological Association (APA) resulted in the formation of the independent American Psychological Society (APS) in 1988, APS leader and advocate Linda Parrot was editing the *Recorder.* Parrot's APS advocacy was shared with her spouse Steven Hayes, another APS leader and once Division 25 president. In APA Division 25 Executive Committee meetings Hayes, against opposition, supported moving that Division from APA to APS. Presumably this would have moved the *Recorder* to APS as one of the transferred assets ("Minutes of," 1988). In the meantime, within the new APS, plans were announced to begin a new journal modeled after *Science* magazine (Salzinger, 1988, p. 118). Yet the fact remained that control over both *Behavior Analysis* (a.k.a. *Division 25 Recorder*) and any new journals of APS would apparently remain within the discipline of psychology regardless of which organization owned them. This was because both APA Division 25 and the new APS were strictly psychology–related organizations. They were populated by persons who saw themselves as psychologists and who regarded behavior analysis merely as a facet of psychology. Publications subsequently emerging from APS reflected the mainline psychology perspective of the vast majority of its members. Readers found these to be less behavioral than materials that continued to be published by the "behavioral" division (Division 25) of APA.

Conclusion on journal control. The general drift toward a cognitive–behavioral blend in the behavioral psychology literature seemed an inevitable aspect of the strategy to show the psychologists some better science by pretending merely to represent a part of their own psychology discipline. The change in character of these various journals was also rational for economic reasons, because minority "behavioral" journals sell poorly in the vast psychology marketplace. The changes were also probably an inevitable aspect of the effort to merge the selectionist and transformational paradigms and thus consolidate the psychology verbal community. But this drift in the character of the traditional behavioral literature left many authors, especially the behaviorologists, looking for alternative publication outlets. The effort within TIBA to publish *Behaviorology* seemed timely.

Internal Issues Debated

Early participants in the behaviorology movement were much in agreement. Yet among themselves they debated several issues, some of which are described in this section. Some pertained to the nature with which individuals wanted to endow the movement. But debated more frequently, and often more vigorously, were the *strategies* by which the movement should develop.

Contest? To what extent or in what ways, if any, were behaviorology and psychology in a real contest, and should their relation be characterized as such? This question about the behaviorology movement continued to preoccupy the early behaviorologists. (It would subsequently become a main theme in the lead article of the first issue of *Behaviorological Commentaries* [Fraley, 1991].)

People in the culture at large have presumed that psychology is the discipline to fill the cultural niche reserved for whichever discipline can best support effective behavioral technologies. Behaviorologists regard that as a mistake, because it is behaviorological science that has most demonstrated effective technological applications. So organized behaviorology *is* left to compete with organized psychology for what should be behaviorology's appropriate stall space in the cultural marketplace.

If psychology and behaviorology could *divide* the subject matter—with behaviorology focused on environment–behavior relations and psychology concerning itself with internal mediations of behaviors—then any adversarial relation could give way to a more complementary or supplementary relation. But some behaviorologists did not want to abandon the study of relations between bodies and behavior to psychology. A few early behaviorologists, Carl Cheney for example, were actively researching relations between *physiological* and behavioral variables. In general, whenever alternating the level of analysis—between behavior/environment functional relations and the internal workings of the body that mediate the production of behavior—becomes necessary, behaviorologists prefer interdisciplinary transfer between behaviorology and physiology, which keeps the analyses within the realm of the natural sciences.

Nevertheless, such a division along subject matter lines appealed to many early behaviorologists as a gesture of political appeasement. To the extent that psychologists would accept it, behaviorologists would avoid provoking a territorial fight with a politically and economically well established giant. The behaviorologists actually have had little scientific respect either for the rampant cognitive theorizing of psychologists or for their efforts to correlate those theories with real physiological events adduced by the physiology–based neural scientists. This is mainly because behaviorological science provides parsimonious alternative explanations that render many of those cognitive/mentalistic theories improbable in the first place (see Skinner, 1953).

In addition, behaviorologists sought to leave behind with the psychologists more than just a domain of subject matter irrelevant to behaviorological concerns. Behaviorologists have always objected to the *non–natural* aspect of psychology, that is, the fundamental metaphysical concepts of life, behavior, and the human species that no person or group has ever succeeded in effectively disabusing within psychology and which have been conducive to the psychologists' prevailing mentalism.

Some behaviorologists remained unwilling to settle for any resolution of that territorial dispute in ways implying that the behaviorology community accepted psychology as an equal, worthwhile, and respectable partner at the roundtable of the natural sciences—a partner that merely focused on subject matters different from those studied by the behaviorologists. Of course, the behaviorologists did not include in that concept of organized psychology the scientific contributions of those behavioral psychologists whom they thought belonged in behaviorology. But many behaviorologists believed that in the long run such respect for psychology, whether believed to be true or feigned for strategic reasons, would evoke an adverse judgment from the grand community of natural sciences at large. That community would simply lump behaviorology together with what would eventually become discredited behavioral pseudo–science. Though some behaviorologists appeared not to share this concern, in general they offered little articulation of their view.

The fear that the behaviorology movement could easily become preoccupied in premature fights with the much larger psychology community was not without basis. Critical organizational resources would be consumed and a hostile organizational giant would be aroused. The opposing views in open contests with organized psychology represented the age old tension between prudence and integrity (some saw it as the shrewd versus foolish variety). Perhaps some behaviorologists covertly anticipated that the psychology verbal community would, in fact, *eventually* develop a better scientific paradigm, apply it to its own internal disciplinary house–keeping, settle the implicit territorial disputes both with physiology and behaviorology, and claim a legitimate place beside behaviorology at the natural science roundtable. Others merely seemed reluctant for personal reasons to suggest that some important, capable, and very nice people had been wasting their scientific time with psychology.

Would behaviorology, its followers eschewing mentalism as they did, be *allowed* to gain scientific prominence within the culture? That is (the issue of logical subject matter divisions aside) would organized psychology in conjunction with a mentalistic culture at large (bolstered by some current legal codes) move to prevent the prominence of any integral and entirely natural behavior science? Would psychology instead act to preserve a metaphysical interface wherever behavior is studied? The purely natural science of Darwinian biology had faced a similar challenge and, with continuing vigilance, has prevailed. But could behaviorology duplicate that accomplishment? Could behaviorology affect a quiet and peaceful emergence as the independent natural science of its own culturally important subject matter? Or should it prepare vigorously to defend, more fundamentally, the very *concept* of applying natural science to behavior within this culture—a course that might produce conflict with organized psychology? Skinner had anticipated a contest at this fundamental level and had described the issues attendant to it in some detail (see Skinner, 1953, pp. 17–22).

Discipline/field/status relations. The emergence of the behaviorology discipline stimulated debate among the behaviorologists about the definition of "discipline." Difficulties arose because peoples' discipline–related concepts differed. Effective communication depends on terms defined in common, but agreements about concepts of discipline proved elusive. Some people (e.g., Fraley 1988d, 1990a) thought that they could distinguish a mega–repertoire consisting of an extensively shaped answer to the general question of how best to know, and called, simply, a "discipline" (...of something). Such a repertoire was construed to include several components. Two verbal components were (a) a philosophy of science and (b) a set of scientific principles. A third component (c) consisted of an accumulated set of prescriptions or practices of the kind usually implied by a term such as *behaviorological technology.* Through the technological practices, the principles of the science were related to, or applied to, a particular subject matter, and the data thereby adduced could evoke the induction of further scientific principles. Other people, though, did not clearly discriminate philosophical, scientific, and technological elements in given cases. Nor could parties to the discussion reach agreement on which aspects of such a mega–repertoire were entirely verbal. Some also questioned the asserted functional relations among philosophical, scientific, and technological behaviors.

However, the frequently appearing phrases "organized discipline" and "scientific verbal community" seemed to be synonymous. Many also tended to use the terms *field* and *discipline* interchangeably in common parlance. According to one attempted discrimination, the locus of the variables definitive of a discipline resided in the behavioral repertoire of the person (e.g., behaviorology). The variables definitive of a field resided in the environment, or more specifically, in the piece of the environment said to be the subject matter of concern (e.g., law or education). One worked *in* a field *with* the disciplinary repertoire that one had brought to it. The following comment, which appeared in the first issue of *Behaviorological Commentaries* (Fraley, 1991), is a partial elaboration of this distinction:

> Within our culture there are only a few distinctly different *major* approaches to analytical thought *about behavior.* Here's what I mean by that: If I am preparing myself to become a teacher (which happens to be *my* applied area), my culture offers me only a few major ways to think about the relevant behavioral events that I will encounter in the field of teaching. To name the obvious and familiar ones, I can think behaviorologically, essentially relating environmental variables to behavioral events, with a heavy explanatory reliance on selection mechanisms at several levels of analysis; alternatively, I can think psychologically, relating behavioral events to internal cognitive transformational processes, which may or may not include appeals to metaphysical influences; and I can think purely metaphysically by relating behavioral events more or less exclusively to metaphysical variables in other–world domains.
>
> Since, in my field of education, all students have long been required to study psychology in order to acquire their basic analytical approach to behavior, almost all educators are psychologists as far as their basic analytical philosophy–science paradigms are concerned. But then, so are almost all nurses,

> lawyers, clinicians, advertisers, and practitioners in hundreds of other applied fields. The culture offers students hundreds, maybe thousands, of *fields* in which to apply their respective basic few ways of thinking about behavior.
>
> Behaviorology is not one of those applied fields; it is a basic scientific discipline, including repertoires of science and philosophy, which can be applied to the problems in *any* of those many applied behavior–related fields. And importantly, *so is psychology.* This does not refer to those applied fields that also go unnecessarily under the expropriated title of "psychology", but rather in the sense of a basic science and philosophy as a fundamental and comprehensive way of thinking about any behavioral phenomena. (pp. 10–11)

Given that difference, a person would bring a disciplinary behavioral repertoire to bear on the problems encountered in a field. One implication, however, was that a person's complete professional description would often require two terms. One would indicate the discipline with which the person solved problems. The other would indicate the field in which the person worked and encountered those problems. The need for such labelling is implicit, for example, in efforts to talk accurately about educators. A satisfactory description often requires that a given educator be designated as a behaviorologically informed educator or as a psychologically informed educator. (For an example of material that is heavily psychological but also substantially informed by a metaphysically based discipline, see the text by Scoresby & Price [1991], two educators at Brigham Young University, an institution sponsored by an organized religion.)

On the sociology of science front (see Fraley, 1988d), these concerns gave rise to another sort of issue: At the start of the 1990s, several important and respected people, whose repertoires could be called behaviorological, had not yet endorsed the separatist approach of the behaviorology movement (though some had joined TIBA as affiliate members). They were continuing to work for change within organized psychology, and they regarded themselves as "psychologists." But what did that mean in any particular case? All of them seemed to want change in the mentalistic disciplinary tradition of psychology, but toward what definition of psychology was such a person working? In a psychology purged of mentalism, would the subject matters include the behavior–environment relations *to which behaviorology had already laid claim?* Those people would have to make clear their own positions with respect both to their disciplines and to their concepts of how subject matters were to be divided among recognized disciplines for study and practice.

Theoretically, the positions taken by those people had implications for the behaviorology movement. Separate disciplines could hardly exist with one called psychology and one called behaviorology and both defining their subject matters identically. But if the behaviorologists were correct about the futility of changing psychology, some of the potentially adverse implications of such territorial conflicts would not be realized because psychology would *not* change. Behaviorologists argued about the extent to which attempts to analyze the professional status of radical behaviorists in psychology were even necessary. Some thought such analyses were presumptuous; they intruded on those peoples' right to fashion their own careers. Others thought such analyses were important to the behaviorology movement; no matter what radical behaviorists did, their actions and the implications of those actions should be clearly understood by all parties. Discussion continued about how the organized behaviorology movement should relate to a person who was scientifically behaviorological yet who remained in psychology while wanting to maintain some tie to the behaviorology movement.

As the behaviorology movement slowly pulled away on its independent course, those in TIBA who had persisted in seeking some sort of straddling posture found that position increasingly untenable. (However, as of this writing, straddlers have tended not to drop out of TIBA, perhaps because of the Affiliate membership category available to everyone.) They had argued, in effect, that the behaviorology movement should lever from *within* organized psychology for change in the nature of psychology. But that was not to be, and ultimately each such person would probably move, however gradually, to one camp or the other.

Many such persons had *not* joined TIBA. Mutually respected colleagues looked at one another across the widening gap sometimes with annoyance, and increasingly with sympathy and occasionally regret. Among all who might have liked to share in the independence venture, pleas for understanding were cautiously exchanged between those who had subsequently committed to doing so and those who had not. Long term trends seemed to point to worsening conditions for those who stayed behind within psychology. Perhaps additional behaviorological people would yet shift to the independence movement. In the meantime, behaviorologists considered which approach would better promote or facilitate such moves: Should those potential affiliators be confronted with (a) explicit, challenging, and thought provoking analyses or (b) with a happy face that explained little but teased with the implication that professional life as an independence–oriented behaviorologist is reinforcing?

Science club versus cultural mission. The need for behaviorologists to focus on the evolution of their science became increasingly evident. As the 1990s began, the future of behaviorology as an independent discipline clearly became more secure with each extension or refinement of the science. Not only would more science be needed but it also had to evolve with its own scientific character unique to behaviorology. The more effective and unique their science became, the better would be the position of the behaviorologists to pursue the mission of providing the culture with the technologies of an independently organized natural science discipline of behavior.

However, an introspective preoccupation with the science could de–emphasize if not neglect that cultural mission. Some behaviorologists, in their enthusiasm to get on with such a science development program, appeared willing to put aside most issues pending at the interface between the discipline and the ambient culture, such as maintaining a full publication program or establishing behaviorology departments in universities. Some even appeared ready to neglect or de–emphasize the separateness of their discipline in presentations to the outside. They would seemingly have the movement take on more the character of a science club focused on science *per se*, but with little attention to how the behaviorology *movement* related organizationally to the various facets of the culture.

Other behaviorologists thought that such neglect might be imprudent, especially if carried to what they feared might be an excess. For example, they wanted to see the scientific outcomes and other products of behaviorologists function to strengthen and support their own organized behaviorology discipline and its cultural mission. They did not want to see the scientific works or other products of behaviorologists in TIBA co–opted to support or strengthen organized psychology. After all, many people found themselves under strong and mostly economic contingencies to maintain links to organized psychology. And under those circumstances people, perhaps under the guise of acting as change agents, could easily find themselves consolidating their position by allowing the benefits of their behaviorological products to accrue to the psychology establishment.

While TIBA remained a scientific organization without a pursued cultural mission, some members raised the question of what place a research–focused TIBA reserved at its scientific roundtable for those who would apply the science to the analysis of social issues. These could be as diverse as contemporary philosophy, corrections, death and dying, education, organizational behavior management, or verbal behavior, to name but a few. The implications that their work was not as welcome nor as respected within TIBA as that of data–based researchers weakened the bonds between TIBA and some of the more applied analysts of behavior. Concerns began to arise about the implicit skew in what had begun as a more balanced disciplinary verbal community in which conceptual analysts and application specialists were equally appreciated for their work in mediating the impact of the science on the culture.

In concentrating somewhat exclusively on a science development program, some TIBA leaders also wanted to keep the TIBA membership low. Each member might then know all others on a first–name basis, and at conventions, especially with intimate single–track formats, each participant would engage all others. In such ways, limited membership could improve social and scientific exchanges among members and help consolidate the scientific efforts *of that small group* of people.

However, limiting membership to gain these enhancements for so few could put severe limits on how quickly and thoroughly behaviorologists could deliver the needed depth and range of behaviorological products to the culture. For while TIBA leaders focused on developing science with only a small membership, threats to worldwide cultural survival (e.g., over–population and ozone depletion) loomed, as did many other cultural problems (e.g., control by an often costly and excessive use of punishment, and misplaced respect for non–natural constructs of many kinds such as the reliance of the legal system on the putative free will of "autonomous man"). Theoretically, applied behaviorology could help solve them all. And those behaviorologists who viewed neglect of the cultural interface as imprudent construed many of these concerns to be enlarging exponentially and overtaking humanity on a time scale shorter than the time scale on which *a small group* might successfully address them. Hence they argued for greater organizational efforts in the membership and cultural interface areas.

Those behaviorologists who stressed the importance of the cultural interface made suggestions. In practical terms, to support the relation of the behaviorology movement to the culture at large might require, for instance, a higher organizational priority for TIBA's publication agenda than occurs under a primary focus on scientific development. The publication priority needs to be high enough to ensure a continuous flow of high quality journal and magazine articles. These would properly display behaviorology while providing TIBA's rank–and–file members with valuable returns on their organizational investments including, reciprocally, further extension and refinement of their science. To get such a result, TIBA would probably have to appeal more proactively, rather than just by passive example, to convince additional behaviorological scientists (laboratory and applied), scholars, and students of the appropriateness of the behaviorology movement, persuading such people to join TIBA and/or to contribute to its literature. TIBA has neither sought nor required a large political base through which to have an impact on the culture. But it does need to serve as the medium of organizational expression for behaviorologists and behaviorological scientists who, if not operating under the auspices of TIBA, might remain vulnerable to having their work co–opted in service to antithetical or competing disciplines. Such suggestions have not, as of this writing, had much impact.

A small organizational membership also facilitates control of the organization by its smaller cadre of leaders. But to address this or any other concern, an expanded recruitment that would bring in less committed people was not a goal. The recruitment issue pertained to other existing behaviorologists (by function if not yet by name) who thus far were neglected by organized behaviorology. Cultural impact aside, the vitality of TIBA's science agenda required a greater participation by these people.

The difficulty resolving these issues took its toll. As *Behaviorology* (with the exceptions of most of the Presidents' presentations and the B.F. Skinner Memorial Addresses) rejected otherwise reasonable manuscripts because they were not data–based research papers, its regular publication schedule became intermittent after three issues. *The International Behaviorologist,* in which such manuscripts might have been published, had not materialized primarily for lack of funding in an organization with a preference for keeping membership small. And potential submissions to it may have decreased anyway as members experienced pressure to refocus their priorities onto data–based researches (an effort that apparently was still not yet productive enough to insure the viability of a pure research journal).

David Krantz Revisited

Today, behaviorologists look back twenty years to David Krantz's (1971) carefully constructed and well presented critique of the era in psychology when serious separatist rumblings began (reviewed in Chapter Two). The interpretations by Krantz, and others who have echoed his biases, have lost much of their cogency. The issue of commensurability has been settled despite some continued grumbling: Some psychologists study the fictional construct called "information" along with its processing by *autonomous* minds, psyches, or other behavior–originating agents thought to exist within organisms. In these efforts they study events *different* from those that concern behaviorologists and they do so from a philosophical perspective that puts them beyond the bounds of natural science. Natural science does not recognize discontinuities in any functional chain of causal events such as those implicit in concepts of free will or autonomous selves. Other psychologists dwell on emotional behavior, endowing it with special importance and often with metaphysical interpretations. To behaviorologists, feelings are respondent behavioral effects, which, like so many others, can be engineered to prescription. Still other psychologists treat behavior as a natural phenomenon but depend heavily on inferred hypothetical cognitive constructs which seem necessary given the conceptual structure of the science with which they attack problems. The latter kind of psychologists differs with behaviorologists mainly about the *appropriate* science. The former kinds differ mainly about *philosophy* of science. And both, consequently, differ with behaviorologists about what aspects of the subject matter upon which to focus. Any of these classes of difference justify organizational separation of the respective verbal communities.

One can now recast the issue of behaviorological isolationists allegedly reducing the effectiveness of their science by ignoring the potential contributions from other schools.

Some people contemplate a kind of scientifically respectable cognitive science existing as a specialization within physiology along the theme of brain science. Scientists within that subset, whose main thrust is to seek physiological evidence for their inferred hypothetical cognitive constructs, would perhaps describe themselves using psychological labels. But, regardless of how scientifically legitimate such a seemingly over–theorized field might become, that field would not require the interest of behaviorologists—only their acknowledgment. On the other hand, a person who does not fully respect a natural science philosophy nor master the science implicit in applying selection concepts to behavior is left with scientistically rendered, traditional, non–natural assumptions. No valid basis exists for behaviorologists (or other natural scientists) to treat those assumptions as scientifically worthwhile, nor whatever disciplines they represent as scientifically qualified alternatives to behaviorology (also see Frase, 1970, p. 337, and Sidman, 1986a, pp. 214–215, concerning the lack of disciplinary integrity in psychology).

The argument that cognitivists and mentalists have novel and important things to say to behaviorologists now seems to amount to little more than the easy observation that persons under different stimulus controls might look at different things, a fact that carries no concomitant guarantee that effective reports will follow. Occasionally psychologists, looking at events to which behaviorologists have given little or no attention, report something of worth to behaviorologists. But in such cases rarely if ever has it seemed to be something that behaviorologists could not have produced were they to have addressed those same issues. Julie Vargas (1990), concluding her analytical rebuttal to Salzinger's (1990) argument that behavioral people should read cognitive literature because they would find it useful, wrote that:

> ...reading cognitive studies is, for a behaviorologist, like looking through a bargain basement. You must search through many unsuitable items before finding something you can use. When reading time is limited, why not go where the density of valuable finds is higher—directly to behavioral work? (p. 201)

When some behavioral people continue to insist that culling cognitive literature is fruitful, questions arise: Do their discoveries really withstand behaviorological tests for quality scientific products, or are the discoverers being overly enthusiastic (see J. Vargas, 1990)? Are their searches, and public proclamations of delight at making discoveries, mostly tactics in a social strategy of accommodation with their host cognitive/mentalistic communities? Could the discoveries that *are* of real value to behaviorologists have resulted *only or exclusively* from applications of a cognitive or mentalistic paradigm? Or were they produced *in spite of* those repertoires (which in those instances did not happen to get in the way)? Behaviorological colleagues have little basis for criticism when an individual's culling through cognitive literature survives the critical scrutiny implicit in such questions. Many behavioral scholars, having spent much of their professional lifetimes scrutinizing psychological literature for useful items, have grown skilled at finding them. But the behaviorologists raised the question of how much more fruitful their labors would have been had the discipline of psychology been capable of producing a more uniformly worthwhile literature.

Krantz also dwelt on the role of professional courtesy in the relations between professionals in different disciplines. Professional courtesy in some appropriate form will always have its place. But psychologists, in mistakenly regarding behavioral people as a part of psychology, have rationally expected the sort of professional courtesy from behavioral people that they would expect from other psychologists, a courtesy apropos of collegial *disciplinary peer* relations (see the discussion of Proctor & Weeks, 1988, in an earlier chapter). But the view that behavioral people should have continued to express deferential professional courtesy to those who have devoted their professional lives to a different discipline—in some cases featuring philosophies that tolerate non–natural science—and to have done so in such a way as to prolong the suppression, eclipse, or neglect of the natural science of behavior, was an argument that by 1990 had worn thin for most contemporary behaviorists, and especially for behaviorologists.

Increasingly, behaviorologists appeared more comfortable and confident with their own discipline. In their own respective ways they behaved more frequently as if behaviorology–suppressing deference were not polite, but self–demeaning; as if it did not extend courtesy, but implied weakness; as if it confused and misled students; and as if it damaged natural science in general, because all natural science is compromised when it is betrayed in any one area. Increasingly, deference yielded to the recognition that long–range interests of the culture were ill–served by delays in critical scientific progress needed immediately. Part of behaviorology's coming of age was simply that behaviorologists, in exhibiting professional courtesy, would begin to avoid doing so in ways that were once a harmful but necessary aspect of the abandoned strategy to fit into, and to change, the cultural megalith of organized psychology.

Besides, for most people who were affected by this issue, normal collegial relations within universities already afforded a more appropriate paradigm for collegial courtesy. Universities exist within the culture in part to test the efficacy of grand ideas over long periods of time. No guarantee exists, nor should exist, that all such ideas are mutually compatible. Pretenses to false compatibility by persons who represent different and antithetical disciplines do not respect the founding principles of academic institutions. Given the cultural mission of the academy on behalf of the culture that supports it, both parties have a right to be there. They can respect each other not for the quality of their respective ideas but in mutual recognition of their respective participation in fulfilling the purposes of the academy. That is the *only* valid basis for respect between disparate intellectual traditions. It conserves the integrity of each party because it is a respect based on cooperation, not integration.

In the prevailing view among behaviorologists, organized psychology has long been deemed too big and politically powerful to be changed from within by anything that behaviorologists might do at its scientific debating round–tables, especially since many non–scientific factors contribute to the organizational integrity of psychology in the first place. Those mainstream psychologists who are distressed by any perceived threat of potential competition (whether real or not) presumably would be pleased to see behaviorological revolutionaries expend themselves in that effort. And why not? Psychology is not only organized to contain or co–opt such efforts but also to train multitudes of traditional cognitivists for each behaviorally inclined person produced. Fortunately for behaviorologists, their movement has rendered that whole approach as unnecessary as it is futile.

The tiny behavioral sub–community operating within organized psychology has produced a limited number of behaviorally trained and skilled people. To distinguish between this somewhat estranged minority of behavioral scientists and the vast remainder of people working in organized psychology, authors usually denote that minority in psychology by calling them "behavioral" psychologists. Conversely, behavioral authors have attached adjectives such as "mainline," "mainstream," "traditional," "cognitive," and "mentalistic" when referring to members of the majority. But the behaviorology movement was in part born out of the conviction that remaining in psychology and calling oneself a psychologist, while denoting oneself as "behavioral," was inappropriate. Some, however, have had to continue to do that, at least temporarily, if for no other than the practical reason of remaining employed.

Those natural scientists of behavior, particularly the radical behaviorist "Skinnerians" who have struggled to maintain a disciplinary home base within organized psychology, have nevertheless maintained a literary isolation from mainstream psychology (which Krantz described in detail). That was done largely as a matter of scientific necessity. Coleman and Mehlman (1992) found that "the contrasting self–citation and mutual–citation practices that were reported by Krantz ...have largely persisted in the 20 years from 1970 to 1989" (pp. 47–48). Yet, at the same time, on the political front the behaviorists in psychology had to work at cross purposes to their scientific selves by redoubling their communication efforts with the psychological establishment. As a typical example the final general session concluding the 1992 ABA convention, entitled "Science Agenda for the 1990s,." featured the assembled presidents and science officers of the American Educational Research Association (an organization in which traditional psychology prevails), ABA, APA, APS, and, AABT (see the Eighteenth ABA Annual Convention Program, p. 164).

People could not validly be criticized for the histories that brought them to a behavioral view, nor for circumstances that led some to continue viewing organized psychology as the appropriate setting in which to pursue studies of behavior. But this protracted professional experiment—in the pattern of the protracted political experiment of Nationalist China—in which some behavioral psychologists isolated themselves *as psychologists* off the coast of mainland Psychology and claimed to *be* the only real psychology, appeared to the behaviorologists to be doomed. In *this* case however, behaviorologists believed that reabsorption into mainstream psychology would hurt the culture by significantly contaminating and warping their science. Not only would the extent to which that science need be taken into serious account by mainline psychologists be diminished, but the capacity of the resulting compromised residual version of that science to provide its contributions to the culture would be diminished also.

Summary of Chapter Five

Chapter Five reviewed the cultural milieu and analyzed the support for, and the opposition to, the growing behaviorology movement as the community at large witnessed its coalescence on the scientific professional scene. It examined some of the self–management problems facing those who were taking the lead in forming a verbal community around the behaviorology discipline. And it described and analyzed their actions and interactions on disciplinary issues.

As the behaviorology movement materialized as an accomplished fact, the contingencies on members of the behavioral community at large shifted subtly in important ways. The period during which hypothetical issues were posited for harmless conceptual analyses gave way to a new era featuring personal confrontations with an issue that required a career decision. The objections of resisters now focused more on *practical* issues. But with an alternative to affiliating with the verbal community of psychology now available, people found as ever more onerous their having to accept their disciplinary citizenship being policed by mainline psychologists as the price to remain in psychology. While some behavioral people shifted to the behaviorology movement, others flirted with that movement and still others renewed their resignation to abide.

The behaviorologists eschewed intense recruitment drives and worked to consolidate and further establish their organized verbal community. Leaders debated alternatives about how best to do that and how to relate to outsiders. They fought to a draw with the behavioral psychologists for Skinner's final endorsement regarding proprietorship of the intellectual property. During this same period the literature of the "behavior analysis" movement slipped increasingly under the influence and control of organized psychology.

Increasingly, with respect to interdisciplinary relations, the behaviorologists recast old problem definitions and old perspectives: They no longer accepted some of the old challenges—and they discerned new ones. Their values were changing. Their mission was changing.

The next chapter, Chapter Six ("Interdisciplinary Context: A Cultural Role for the New Discipline," presented integrally with the conclusion Chapter Seven and the endnotes and complete references) will examine the prevailing views of the early behaviorologists on where their discipline fit both among the community of natural science disciplines extant in the culture and in the cultural marketplace. It will also comparatively explore the different levels of analysis characteristic of behavior–related natural science disciplines, and examine cultural resistance to behaviorology.

Chapter 6:

Interdisciplinary Context: A Cultural Role for the New Discipline

After the introductory Chapter One, Chapter Two of this account of the emergence of behaviorology examined the nature and origins of the behaviorology concept. Chapter Three examined contingencies supporting individual commitments to a disciplinary independence movement. Chapter Four presented a comprehensive review of the activities to organize the behaviorology discipline and examined the cultural engineering by which the behaviorology discipline was formalized and installed in the community of natural sciences. Chapter Five reviewed the prevailing cultural milieu and analyzed the support for, and the opposition to, the behaviorology movement. This chapter, Chapter Six, the last of the five main parts of this account, examines the prevailing views of the early behaviorologists on where their discipline fit both among the community of natural science disciplines extant in the culture and in the cultural marketplace. It also comparatively explores the different levels of analysis characteristic of behavior–related natural science disciplines, and examines the cultural basis of resistance to behaviorology.

The early behaviorologists faced many questions about where their discipline fit with respect to other established disciplines and fields. This was only natural since they accepted the relationship of their discipline to other behavior–related fields as one of supplying an effective foundational science and technology of behavior.

The Cultural Context of Behaviorology

Early behaviorologists defined and formulated behaviorology in a way that allowed it to function well in a quality controlling capacity at the hub of a metaphorical wheel representing scientific contributions to global cultural development. At that hub are all existing basic behavior–related disciplines. They exhibit different philosophical approaches, some mutually incompatible and each contesting for control. That includes behaviorology (with its particular natural science philosophy) as well as its disciplinary competitors. The spokes are the various behavior–related fields, which share in defining and imparting identity to human culture. The lengthening of the spokes occurs as those fields develop through the effectiveness of their respective behavioral technologies. The expansion of the rim connotes the expansion of our culture in all of its diversity. The whole process functions only as well as the basic repertoires at the hub can support it. Behaviorologists asserted their independence in order to address that central mission better.

In the broad context of science, the place of behaviorology is determined in three ways: (a) by the qualities that make it a natural science (as opposed to a non–natural or pseudo–science), (b) by the kind of analyses that it features to best address the problems to which it is directed, and (c) by the nature of the subject matter under study. Being a *natural* science like chemistry, physics, or biology means that the epistemology and ontology of behaviorology respect a continuity in any functional chain of material events that define time. Natural science allows no breaks in that chain of events—that is, no discontinuities in the functional chain of material events that accumulate, link by link, in what is called a *natural history.* In a non–natural science, those linkages of material events are said to be broken on occasions of intervention by non–material, or metaphysical, events (e.g., the non–spatiotemporal activities criticized by Hayes & Brownstein, 1986).

Disciplinary repertoires that posit or tolerate non–physical *mentalistic* entities, believed to intervene and play a causal role in determining behavior, classify as non–natural behavior sciences (if the term "science" is even deemed applicable in such cases). Hence they are frequently designated as "soft" sciences (generally understood as a polite euphemism for epistemologically sub–standard). The phrase "social sciences" was originally coined to describe sciences focused on interactive behaviors among people. But it has also come to denote multi–paradigmatic approaches as well, including some that entertain appeals to metaphysical phenomena (Skrtic, 1991). Not only has this issue yielded internal struggles in psychology, but also in other social sciences like anthropology and sociology (despite efforts to recast sociology as a natural science, e.g., Burgess & Bushell, 1969; Hamblin & Kunkel, 1977; and Homans, 1961).

Culturology

The subsequent discussion of behaviorology among the life sciences features the term "culturology" which is used here to fill a gap in the labeling of the domains of concern across the life sciences from molecules to cultures. That term, like behaviorology, has had various origins (e.g., see White, 1949, pp. 115–117 & 409–415; Stephen Ledoux had also composed it independently in 1986). Culturology, like behaviorology, is etymologically appropriate: "the study of culture." Just as the discipline of behaviorology has a scientifically informed philosophy of science, known as radical behaviorism, a similar philosophy of science is developing among certain schools within the broad field of anthropology, for example, the cultural materialism of Marvin Harris (Harris, 1979). While the people who represent those schools of thought will ultimately declare their philosophies and name their own discipline, *culturology* appears here as the interim name for that discipline for its convenience in avoiding long and possibly inaccurate labels such as "anthropology informed by cultural materialism."

Behaviorology Among the Life Sciences

The natural sciences traditionally divide between physical sciences and life sciences. Behaviorology and other foundation life sciences rely heavily, though not exclusively, on the causal mode of selection in their explanatory frameworks. In contrast, foundation physical sciences, such as physics and chemistry, have depended more on mechanical causality. (See Skinner, 1987a, Ch. 4, for details on this distinction.)

The scientific study of life, especially human life, stretches across several levels of analysis. On one end is the discipline of biology, chiefly studying, across the entire history of each species, the physical and chemical activities of individuals from the sub–cellular level to the level of the organism. "Behavior" as subject matter in biology can be approached from those physiological foundations. But what can be learned about behavior on that basis tends to be insufficient for *practical* purposes in social and environmental contexts, and often needs to be supplemented by appeals to behavioral science at a different paradigmatic level. This happens, for example, when attention turns from *how* a body behaves to *why* an organism behaves. Behaviorological engineering is difficult to support when it is based on scientific principles induced from strictly biological investigations of behavior. However, some biologically informed animal behaviorists have found reason to expand their physiologically based studies of behavior to consider behavior/environment relations—thus contributing to a science of behavior from their side of the disciplinary overlap with behaviorology.

On the other end of the life science continuum is the discipline of culturology, chiefly studying the social behavioral/cultural activities, especially of verbal species, at the level of the group or population. "Behavior" as subject matter in culturology is essentially the study of group–produced effects, for example, the combined or synergistic effects of concerted individual behaviors. The shared practices of a people that give their group its cultural identity are of interest in culturology as well. Importantly, the group behaviors of interest to culturologists can endure beyond the range of individual lifetimes. Naturally, in conducting their studies culturologists concern themselves to some extent with the behavior of individuals. In doing so they share some concerns with behaviorologists.

Between biology and culturology is the discipline of behaviorology, chiefly studying the functional relations between the environmental milieu and the behavior of individuals. With this focus behaviorology overlaps many behavior–related concerns in both biology and culturology. See Figure 1.

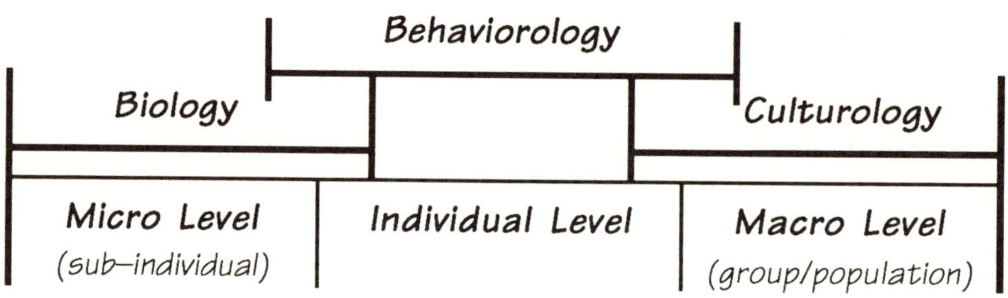

Figure 1. Disciplinary coverage for the three main levels of analysis in the life sciences.

Biology provides essentially a micro or sub–individual analysis of life, while culturology provides a macro or supra–individual analysis. Between them behaviorology provides an analysis chiefly focused on the environment/behavior relations of individuals within each individual's lifetime. Behaviorology takes into account relevant determinants from (a) the biological history of the species, (b) the behavioral history of a given individual, (c) the current physiological state of the given individual, and (d) the current environmental context, including cultural factors that might share in the control of the individual's behavior. Behaviorology is thus the study of all behavior–controlling functional relations between the environment and the organism, *as both environment and organism change.* Figure 1 illustrates these disciplinary relations. (The study of ecosystems, species evolution, and the behavior of animals in groups by some animal biologists implies that a disciplinary overlap also exists between biology and culturology. So Figure 1 might be redrawn as a triangle with extended sides that cross each other. Each side would represent one of these domains and its associated discipline. The areas where the lines cross would then represent the overlap in the interests of the intersecting disciplines.)

Individual and Group Levels of Analysis

The disciplinary boundaries presented here remain somewhat flexible. The discreteness of any discipline is generally recognized in proportion to the quality of the products produced by its members. Valid disciplinary identity exists, not due to special sanctions or protections guaranteed by political, legal, or economic contrivances, but because others, acting upon the scientific foundations of alternative disciplines, cannot do the job better. The disciplinary regions mapped here are not construed as territorial claims staked or recognized. They are merely domains of phenomena, available for scientific study, with respect to which adequacy in scientific address has been demonstrated by the mentioned groups.

The play of this qualitative principle can be seen in the overlap between behaviorology and culturology. Consider the following example (Hayes, 1988a) which clarifies the difference between the behavior of individuals and a maintained cultural practice. Referring to the strikingly repulsive jokes that most everyone hears being passed among people, Hayes invited the reader to suppose

> ...that a situation emerges in which joke telling is expected. You may find to your dismay that the only joke you remember is one of these disgusting jokes. You may repeat it. Noting the reaction, you may never say it again. In the meantime, however, you have infected your audience with this terrible joke. They may go through the same cycle. Thus, we may have a wave of horrible jokes swiftly propagated across the country, even though this behavior may fail to be maintained, even for a short while, in each individual engaging in the practice. (p. 16)

The two levels of analysis are evident: At one level the behavior of an individual can be analyzed with respect to (a) why that person exhibited that behavior, (b) at what rate and to what end the behavior occurred to that individual, and (c) the fate of that behavior in the repertoire of that individual. Alternatively, the *cultural practice of repulsive joke telling* can be analyzed separately at a different level of analysis. Note, for example, that the joke telling, as a cultural practice, can continue (a) beyond the tenure of that particular kind of verbal behavior in the repertoire of any one individual and (b) beyond even the lifetime of any one of its mediating individuals. The strength of a cultural practice also differs from the strength of the contributory behavior of any individual participant, and it is measured in different ways.

Those who study cultural practices at the descriptive level chart their spread among the members of a culture, measure their strengths, and record their durations. And they can, of course, do all of those things without concern about the specific controls on the behavior of the individuals who had roles in mediating those practices. With that implied division of scientific labor, behaviorologists and culturologists can work concurrently and maintain differentiated disciplinary identities.

However, when objectives advance from the levels of *description and prediction* to the level of *control,* scientists concerned with culture must then design and develop new cultures (or change existing ones) by producing practices not yet occurring. Throughout the history of their discipline, culturologists have traditionally eschewed intervention. Mainly, they have identified, described, analyzed, and traced. And they have produced some accurate predictions. But the production of new cultural behavior requires control over the behavior of the individuals who contribute to the cultural practices of concern. At that level of operation, the disciplinary distinctions can become blurred, because culturologists would need the intervention capabilities of behaviorology. (Fraley [1988c] elaborated on this point and pursued the disciplinary implications.)

Operating at the level of *control* represents a much more recent trend in culturology. Circumstances increasingly impose this trend in spite of traditional disciplinary ethics that oppose intervention. With respect to method, contingencies of reinforcement can be imposed simultaneously on all members of a group so that the individual responses occur concurrently and yield group effects. Something like this might be approximated by universally applied food rationing. Another class of group effects results when a given kind of contingency successively impinges on different individuals at different times. The illusion of motion known as the "wave," which spectators at American football games sometimes generate in stadiums, is an example. The previous joke–telling example also represents a variation in this class of effects.

Not only is a predictive science of *group–produced* effects (as opposed to a science of individually produced effects) possible, but so is a *controlling* science. Such a science has to some extent developed in support of the activities of anthropologists and sociologists, and it could develop further. Although group effects are necessarily produced by the summation of the behavior of individuals, a science of group effects *can* support intervention technologies in which the analytical repertoire of the cultural engineers does *not* penetrate to the level of individuals. For instance, composers and conductors can reliably produce prescribed group effects without knowing the details of how any particular orchestra member plays his or her instrument. That is because the audience–appreciated properties of the group effect are characteristics of the combined products or activities of the behaving performers. The contributing individual producers of that group effect are not each producing a small one–person version of the group effect appreciated by the audience. What an individual contributes is different—often extremely so—from the appreciated group effect.

The orchestra example, which is typical, shows how one cannot pursue the ontological status, or reality, of the behavioral group effect *intact* back to its stimulus–controlled behavioral origins. Similarly, you can try to approach a distant Olympic flag generated by a stadium section of card holders. But you ultimately arrive at any one of many persons each holding up a colored piece of cardboard. The flag, which is so clearly perceived from afar, can no longer be detected; a person holding a colored square does not evoke a flag–seeing response by an observer. Yet, the level of the behavior of those individual card holders is the only level at which interventions pertinent to the group effect can be *functionally* effective. Only when intervention attempts, intended to alter the properties of the flag–seeing response in remote observers, reach down to affect the behavior of all or some of the card holders can those group level interventions possibly work (e.g., card–change cues *producing* a change of cards that together shows a different flag). Insofar as any group behavioral intervention must have its ultimate effect on the behavior of those individuals whose combined activities yield the group effect, any capacity for intervention (i.e., control) that develops at the group level of analysis must functionally reach for its effect to a control over the behavior of individuals—a behavior technology province well–worked by behaviorologists.

In producing effects at the group level, behavior engineers must arrange to evoke the behavior of many individuals. But in many cases they give little attention to the resulting behavior *of particular individuals.* Instead, they attend to the resulting group effect, and deliver stimuli and consequences in a blanket fashion. Group level engineers, whether conductors, economists, parliamentarians, social revolutionaries, or general culturologists, can impose adjustments that yield changes at the group level. And, as has been illustrated, they can do so while treating the whole analytical level of the affected individuals as a scientific "black box." Culturologists thus do not have to be behaviorologists to operate at the scientific level of control from the perspective of their group level of analysis. Yet that level of intervention lacks the sensitivity for fine–tuning the group effect, which requires changes to the behavior of *specific individuals.*

Behavior scientists have long recognized that efforts to affect the behavior of groups are more successful when informed by an understanding of just how and why *individuals* behave under the imposed arrangements (see Skinner, 1953, Ch. 19). With that additional capacity at the behaviorological level, culturologists can fine–tune their engineering. They can trace many of the breakdowns or circumventions of group–level interventions to anomalies at the individual level as, for example, when a single card holder in the stadium raises a card of the wrong color. And then they can deal with those anomalies. If intervention technologies were limited only to group–level controls, imagine the plight of a social engineer whose plan for large scale waste management does not work well because one waste hauler, in spite of the engineered policies, regulations, and social ethics—all manipulated at the group level—is cutting costs by dumping his individual loads into a river from a remote bridge, loads so toxic that they nullify the whole engineering effort. That hypothetical cultural engineer, unenlightened as to the workings of events at the individual level, would not know in a technical sense how or why such anomalous dumping could occur. So he or she would not be able to down–focus the engineering effort to the individual level to fix that specific fault which is degrading the desired group effect. A culturologist, if really skilled *only* at group level engineering, could only continue to impose blanket contingencies in the hope that potentially errant individuals will share an appropriate response with others to at least some of those contingencies. Obviously, good cultural engineering requires skills at both the individual and group levels of analysis. And those responsible for cultural engineering must be prepared to operate, or cooperate, across the combined range of those levels of analysis as situations demand.

In the meantime, those behaviorologists who are additionally concerned with the engineering of cultural practices focus on controlling the behavior of the individuals whose behavior contributes to cultural practices. The behaviorological literature is rich in basic material applicable to that sort of science, for example, *Walden Two* (Skinner, 1948), and the culture–related chapters in *Science and Human Behavior* (Skinner, 1953) and *Beyond Freedom and Dignity* (Skinner, 1971). The Los Horcones community in Mexico has long provided a living laboratory. Ledoux (1985) has addressed some concerns of experimental communities. And Beach (1988), in an article suggesting that the design, construction, and operation of experimental communities might be called "sociocultural systems engineering," provides a sample of the type of disciplinary blending endorsed above. (The relevance of this blending, for culture design in space settlements, was addressed in the previous chapter.)

A Niche in the Cultural Marketplace

The technological advances, especially of the past century, have left a disturbing discrepancy between the technical capacity to affect the environment and the control over the behavior with which people would do so (for typical examples see Fraley, 1981, 1987; Lamal, 1986; Skinner, 1987a, Section 1; Skinner, 1989b). For decades numerous and diverse fields, seeking basic scientific help in closing that gap, have turned to psychology and continually found its mainstream lacking in the technical foundations capable of supporting their work. As Skinner (1987b) put it, "unable to offer a useful conception of its subject matter, psychology has not formed good relations with other sciences" (p. 785). Most of those fields now ignore psychology. For example, the *1990–1992 Graduate Catalog* at the University of West Virginia revealed that, outside of psychology–operated graduate programs, fewer than one in five behavior–related graduate programs required any coursework in psychology subject matters. One unfortunate effect of that otherwise rational disregard has been the neglect of the work of Skinner and his colleagues which, having been lumped indiscriminately with the rest of psychology, has undeservedly shared the neglect.

Yet dozens of non–psychology fields exist that are essentially applied behavioral areas if one considers their announced cultural missions and the behavior–related skills implicit in their training objectives. The early behaviorologists saw great potential for the cultural impact of their discipline in precisely these areas. These fields—many listed here with selected references to related articles or books, often authored from the behaviorological perspective—include advertising, applied anthropology (see Glenn, 1988; Harris, 1979; Lloyd, 1985; Malott, 1988; and E.A. Vargas, 1985), architecture, criminal justice (Fraley, 1988a, 1988b), economics, education (e.g., Barrett, 1991; Holland, 1960, 1967; Johnson & Layng, 1992; Keller, 1968; Skinner, 1968; E.A. Vargas, 1996; J. Vargas, 1977, 1988; West & Hamerlynck, 1992), environmental studies and ecology, ethics (Krapfl & Vargas, 1977; E.A. Vargas, 1975, 1982), entertainment, ethology, gerontology (Skinner & Vaughan, 1983), history, human factors engineering, industrial and labor relations, journalism, law (Fraley; 1981, 1983), management (Daniels, 1989), nursing (and other health related fields, e.g., pediatrics [Christophersen, 1988; Stewart & J. Vargas, 1990]), occupational health and safety engineering, organizational restructuring (Vargas & Fraley, 1976), peace studies, philosophy (Chiesa, 1994), physical education/sports/leisure studies, political economics, political science, public administration, religious studies (Burhoe, 1981; Schoenfield, 1993), social activism (Ulman, 1983, 1986), social work (Thyer, 1987) and all its sub–fields such as substance abuse and rehabilitation, sociology, urban studies, women's studies, and others. Whether they face problems that require a revolution or a band–aid, practitioners in all of these fields would find the principles of behaviorology not merely relevant to their work but, in most cases, the essential scientific foundation for timely achievement of their behavior–related purposes.

The behaviorologists generally agreed that behavior–related fields were scientifically adrift with respect to foundation behavioral science. They also thought that their movement would benefit these fields by avoiding the legacy of a discipline that most of these fields had rationally rejected. Scientific integration with these fields seemed more facilitated by an independent behaviorology displaying its own academic, scientific, and professional integrity.

Belief and Intolerance in America

Though its name helps, accurate public perceptions of behaviorology developed slowly. Daniel Bjork, a scholar of cultural and intellectual movements, has hypothesized from a historian's perspective about the reflexive rejection of many behaviorological concepts within American culture (letter to Fraley, 14 February 1989). Speculating about why Proctor and Weeks (1988) called behaviorology an anachronism, Bjork posited that "eclectics have won out over the true believers throughout American history and have dominated our cultural scene since at least the early nineteenth century." Bjork elaborated as follows:

> Belief and intolerance have been historically associated in America with the Old World. Mainline psychology, like mainline American culture, sells eclecticism and tolerance.... There is also a long history of mainline American culture dismantling or simply smashing any group or individual who believed to the point of intolerance. Witness the fate of the Puritans. Behaviorologists, if I read them correctly, are by their very scientific beliefs intolerant of the lingering mentalism in psychology.

The parallel, of course, is with any natural science. Behaviorologists' scientific beliefs make them intolerant of mentalism just as, for instance, modern astronomers' scientific beliefs make them intolerant of astrology, physicists of mysticism, biologists of creationism, and so forth. Bjork continues:

> Mainline psychologists, reflecting the values of the larger American culture, simply have no tradition of belief. And when they meet real belief in behaviorologists they do the "American" thing and attempt to discount or eliminate it.
>
> Eclecticism is especially American. The separation of behaviorology as a separate discipline is perceived not simply as non–academic and anti–intellectual, but as un–American...because it refuses to tolerate eclecticism as the base for the discipline. Behaviorology is dismissed as an Old World Cult—an anachronism more fitting in the Jesuit world of the late Middle Ages.
>
> When you embrace eclecticism, you dismiss disciplinary purity. Behaviorology becomes a contemporary reminder of Old World fanaticism.

Bjork also saw the behaviorology movement confronting an American public that was biased against many behaviorological concepts perhaps as part of a widespread disdain for the natural sciences in America. (Nevertheless, Americans are strongly attached to the *products* of the natural sciences. Having referred to America's current stage between theocracy and sociocracy as "vacillocracy," Beach [1991c] mentioned that the motto America actually follows at present could be stated as "In God we trust, but on Science we depend." Such a motto portends deficiencies in science support; see Sagan, 1995, about the dangers of those deficiencies.) The efforts of behaviorologists to protect and maintain the integrity of their disciplinary verbal community, so necessary to good science, thus accidently precipitated some rejection. (Behaviorologists were not alone in experiencing such rejection; see Ratner's discussion of the earlier efforts to reject Darwin and evolution from biological science [Ratner, 1936/1984].)

Bjork's analysis also suggests why non–behaviorologists easily exploit the public to arouse disapproval of behaviorology while relevant issues such as scientific validity and effectiveness go ignored. Earlier sections of this work have provided several examples of language implying that behaviorologists exhibit this "un–American" intolerance and disrespect for the supposed virtues of eclecticism: Epstein's disapproval of allegiance to an "unattractive credo," Burns's accusation about "rejectionism," Proctor and Weeks's reference to the "arrogance" and "scientific elitism" of behaviorists, the theme of Wendt's assault on Keller's program at Columbia University, and Krantz's attribution of "conceptual imperialism" to behaviorists. One anonymous reviewer of a draft of this work claimed that behaviorologists have behaved in an "anti–intellectual fashion" that is "not academically defensible." Aside from the question of validity in these accusations, any of these sentiments, cast as culturally protective admonitions, function as general anti–science weapons. This was especially so when these weapons were aimed at an emerging natural science discipline in a culture (a) much preoccupied with metaphysical alternatives that distract many of its members from issues that affect them, and (b) much infatuated with the popular pseudo–sciences that entertain them (Sagan, 1995).

A modern scientific discipline is a rare and elaborate verbal product requiring a long, careful, and invariably difficult course of development. It remains subject to easy mutation by extraneous contingencies of many kinds. Such a discipline can be protected and further refined only with the help of a stringent intolerance for unconducive contingencies. "Belief" in the discipline is merely the strength of the control exerted by its elements over the behavior of its practitioners as they engage in technological behaviors to affect the environment (see Fraley, 1984, for an in–depth analysis of the concept of belief). Statements asserting belief are based upon tacts of the reliability in those controlling relations. In simple terms, if one notices that one's science works well and reliably to produce effective behavior in difficult situations, then one attains the state to which people refer as one's strong *belief* in that science.

The application of modern experimental science to the old questions about behavior has essentially dissociated behaviorology from any philosophically mentalistic lineage. This has made feasible a new focus on the practical *control* of behavior. The resulting natural science discipline has severed the simplistic reliance on faith in piously proffered explanations and substituted the experimentally derived data base. A data base functions as a special kind of controlling environment in which modern behaviorologists have sought order and described relations. Applying those relations, behaviorologists have extrapolated to accurate predictions and developed technologies affording control. (Some suggest that natural scientists like behaviorologists, rather than abandoning faith, have transferred it to the data base.)

The important concepts of how to shape and maintain a scientific verbal community are themselves behaviorological products. Those science–protecting concepts, invidiously likened by critics to excessive displays of faith, are *not* continuously derived from the tradition of Middle Age fanatical ideologies. Like modern physics and other basic natural sciences, organized behaviorology is a verbal community whose members necessarily eschew eclectic compromises with alternative paradigms. That tradition, while respecting the ancient principle of avoiding alien influence, is of more modern resurgence among the scientific communities where it has been a necessary strategy to preserve natural science in cultures steeped in metaphysical indulgence. The behaviorology of the 1990s has as yet had insufficient history to overcome such cultural biases against it. Even Darwinian biology, after more than a century, has not entirely solved this problem.

The tradition of American tolerance coupled with the suppression of overzealous believing developed for sound practical reasons. The Old World systems of belief were based on religious and abstract philosophical epistemologies, largely divorced from reality, nature, and practicality. Strong believing of those kinds might have had therapeutic value in the lives of the believers, and probably furthered the economic and other personal interests of the purveyors of faith who contrived and maintained those belief systems. But such strong beliefs contributed nothing to the coherence and integrity of the new American cultural amalgam. On the contrary, they proved divisive. American cultural development, having to depend upon such ideologically diverse human resources as were available, required that *those* kinds of strong personal beliefs be socially punished until they no longer prevented critical culture–building cooperation.

Unfortunately, American culture has *indiscriminately* generalized this special suppressive facet of Americana to certain highly valuable belief systems of an entirely different type for which the American culture has great need. Those, of course, are disciplines based on epistemologies of natural science. Those repertoires *do* reflect reality; they *are* natural; and they *do* share in the control of technological behaviors yielding practical and much needed results. The products of *those* disciplines *support* the cultural integrity. The commitment and intolerance exhibited by behaviorologists, often mistakenly regarded as excessive, were simply the care necessary to develop and maintain any modern scientific verbal community. Physicists, chemists, and other natural science communities exhibit the same care.

One problem that raises public bias against behaviorological concepts, principles, and technologies is that these represent the latest products from the sciences which remove humans ever further from a seemingly preferable though false pedestal. Earlier findings had already shown, for example, that the Earth is not the center of the universe (Copernicus and Galileo), and that our bodies are products of the laws of nature (Darwin). Now behaviorological science shows that our very being, our behavior, is lawfully related to the ways nature works. A public that is comfortable with the opposite views sees these facts as threatening and moves against the supporting sciences.

Another problem is that behaviorology is not as yet fully discriminated as a modern science by a public that has little understanding of the nature of science, especially with respect to behavior. For the time being, that public sees behaviorology merely as another facet of a skeptically regarded tradition most saliently represented by psychology and psychiatry. As Bjork put it (letter to Fraley, 14 February 1989):

> The American public perceives psychology as a strange amalgam of science, fad, and hocus–pocus. Its essence is mystery not fact.... At bottom, psychology may still be perceived as more religion than science.

Americans have never wasted much time on philosophical matters, and for the most part their eschewing of that whole domain has worked to their advantage. Ironically, in carrying that pattern to the excess of punishing defenders of behaviorological integrity, the American academic community suppresses the very discipline that is needed to understand, and gain more effective control of, philosophy in relation to both natural science and culture in general (see Fraley, 1990a). If the human species is to survive its interactions with its own environment, natural science and its philosophy must come to *characterize* the culture both to countercontrol abuses (e.g., see Gould, 1981) and to enhance further natural science advances. Progress remains limited as long as the steps necessary to protect natural science are misconstrued as harmfully divisive aspects of the culture and are punished to suppression.

Behaviorologists expect, however, that if effective results can gradually have an increasing impact on cultural survival, the misperceptions will slowly change; the suppression will decrease, even end. More appreciation for natural science in general and behaviorology in particular will become common. Individual behavior, cultural practice improvement, self control, and cultural survival will all be enhanced by the intensifying development of the now emerged discipline of behaviorology.

Summary of Chapter Six

Behaviorology serves the culture as a basic natural science discipline that can productively inform the work of practitioners in a wide variety of behavior–related fields. Many of those fields have little reliance on other basic behavior disciplines, especially psychology, and represent a needy market for behaviorological foundations. The behaviorological level of analysis puts that discipline between biology, which features a more micro–level of analysis, and culturology, which features a more macro–level of analysis—although behaviorology overlaps both biology and culturology. The bias against behaviorology within American culture reflects both the age–old conflict between faith and reason and the more recent American tradition of punishing pockets of apparently excessive faith, in the interest of forging a cultural integrity out of ideologically disparate human resources. The culture cannot be saved without massive interventions based on the products of the natural sciences—and most needed are the contributions of the natural science of behaviorology.

This chapter, Chapter Six, was the last of the five main *parts of this account of the emergence of behaviorology. It accompanies Chapter Seven which provides a brief conclusion to this account and which is followed by endnotes and references.*

Chapter 7:

Conclusion

This account of the emergence of behaviorology had five main parts, Chapters Two through Six. Chapter Two examined the nature and origins of the behaviorology concept. Chapter Three examined contingencies supporting individual commitments to a disciplinary independence movement. Chapter Four presented a comprehensive review of the activities to organize the behaviorology discipline and examined the cultural engineering by which the behaviorology discipline was formalized and installed in the community of natural sciences. Chapter Five reviewed the prevailing cultural milieu and analyzed the support for, and the opposition to, the behaviorology movement. Chapter Six emphasized the prevailing views of the early behaviorologists on where their discipline fit both among the community of natural science disciplines extant in the culture and in the cultural marketplace. This chapter, Chapter Seven, provides a conclusion for this account of the emergence of behaviorology; it is followed by the endnotes and the references for all the chapters in this account.

This multi–part work has addressed the questions that naturally arise with respect to the emergence of a new discipline. It has described (a) the nature of behaviorology as a science, (b) the facts and circumstances of its origins as a concept, (c) its formal organization as a new and independent disciplinary verbal community, (d) the behavior of its leaders as they conducted a behaviorological development project to establish this discipline, (e) the place of this discipline within the scientific community at large and within the culture in general, and (f) the cultural bases of resistance to behaviorology. This work not only has included the *chronicle* of the emergence of this discipline, but also it has described the *nature* of its development.

Powerful technologies are developing from this behaviorology discipline. They can effectively support a wide variety of behavior–related fields. But enthusiasm about the effectiveness of these technologies is sometimes accompanied by disdain for their behavioristic origins. As one psychology student in an introductory behaviorology course recently asked in a hopeful vein, "May one simply adopt the behavioral technologies based upon this science without accepting the underlying science, assumptions, and philosophy?" Addressing that kind of question, Eshleman and Vargas (1988) admonish that our

> ...technology should not lose its behavioristic character. More explicitly, as practitioners of a behaviorological technology, we should not disguise its origins. Not only does such disavowal impart an apologetic air to our professional activities, which then denigrates those activities (along with us), but it also reinforces any tendency, on that part of a verbal community that is hostile, to continue punitive actions. At worst, others in the community join in on the condemnations—believing the arguments they make against a behaviorological technology without knowing why they make them. At best, the rest of the community remains ignorant as to where credit should accrue,

> with consequent effect on delivery of resources for professional work by behaviorologists. Such selling out in order to buy in leaves everyone holding the bag, including, eventually, the community we try to help. (p. 30)

Behaviorology is not the first discipline that has had to separate from another field in order to advance. Psychology itself is one example. Fraley (1987) notes:

> Psychology was a revolution based on experimental methodology; behaviorology is one based on a science of philosophy. Today's behaviorologists have more valuable contributions to make to the culture than rehabilitating psychology.... Behaviorists should now move forward, ...unburdened, toward the fulfillment of their own cultural destiny and adapt an effective behavioral science to the varied institutions and agencies of our culture. (p. 125–126)

Future readers, should their lives have unfolded within the context of a culture pervaded by behaviorology, might have difficulty appreciating a past era of antithesis to behaviorological science. That people would not have readily invested in a repertoire that effective—one that obvious and well demonstrated in its validity and implications, one that elegant in its parsimonious reduction of false complexities—could tax the comprehension of those who live in such a future. But behaviorology being taken for granted is not presently among our cultural assets.

The most effective behavioral science ever to emerge appeared among the behaviors of only a small number of people. A subset of these continued to work on the socio–cultural arrangements to protect, develop, and share it. Its importance was enough to evoke the commitments of entire professional lives, but to different and sometimes incompatible courses of action.

The smaller group whose members called themselves behaviorologists confronted a wide world of people most of whom were drifting down culturally destructive paths because they lacked a science of behavior that was sufficiently effective and sufficiently relevant to help them avoid doing so. The behaviorologists also confronted other behaviorists who entertained elements of behaviorological science but who acted to invest their pieces of the intellectual treasure in other ways. While the outcome of the struggle to strengthen a discipline of behaviorology could not be predicted at that time from the data base of those circumstances, behaviorologists acted in part because they already knew that future. They knew it as a tenuously resolved vision, a vision that emerged as a product of many variables inhering in their particular special histories.

If the behaviorologists' judgment proves to have been correct, and if they shall have prevailed in the effort to make common the behaviorological repertoire, then the culture—and eventually the whole planetary biosystem—will have benefited, perhaps most importantly by surviving. The early behaviorologists believed, of course, that this was what was at stake, or they would not have incurred the costs of organizing the behaviorology movement.

Endnotes

Parts of this work were presented at the fourteenth Association for Behavior Analysis convention in Philadelphia, PA, May 1988, and at the first convention of The International behaviorology Association in Potsdam, NY, August 1988. The work was then published alone as a book (Fraley & Ledoux, 1993), and the present 1997 version of the work is based upon this book version. Stephen Ledoux included an earlier historically unique draft of the work in a 1992 book of readings. Ledoux had made extensive stylistic adjustments, such as reducing the use of the passive voice, to ease translation from English into some other languages. These changes have been retained in the present version of the work in the 1997 revised and expanded version of that 1992 book of readings, now titled *Origins and Components of Behaviorology* (Canton, NY: ABCs). The paper received further minor content revisions before inclusion in *Origins and Components of Behaviorology.*

The authors thank Jerome Ulman for providing copies of the Ulman–Skinner letters so that parts could be included in this paper (the complete set of letters was subsequently published in *Behaviorology;* see Ulman, 1993). The authors also thank their many interested colleagues who provided helpful comments on earlier drafts of the manuscript, including detailed reviews by Daniel Bjork, David Feeney, Vicki Lee, Werner Matthijs, Jerome Ulman, and Ernest Vargas. Address correspondence regarding this paper to the first author at the College of Human Resources and Education, 609–C Allen Hall, West Virginia University, Morgantown WV 26506–6122 USA.

References

Association for Behavior Analysis (ABA). (1989). Survey results. *The ABA Newsletter, 12* (3), 19–20.
Azrin, N. (1988). Con statement. *Behavior Analysis, 23* (3), 139–140.
Ator, N.A. (1986). Behavioral biology. *The Behavior Analyst, 9,* 123–125.
BACD. (1991). *The Behavior Analysis and Cultural Design Newsletter, 1.* [Behavior Analysis and Cultural Design special interest group of ABA.]
Baer, D.M. (1987). Do we really want the unification of psychology? A response to Krantz. *New Ideas in Psychology, 5,* 355–359.
Barrett, B.H. (1991). The right to effective education. *The Behavior Analyst, 14,* 79–82.
Barry, A.E. (1986). Behavior, psychology, and praxics: Where does science fit in? *The Behavior Analyst, 9,* 225–226.
Basil, R. (1987/88). Catholicism and change. *Free Inquiry, 8* (1), 5–6.
Beach, S. (1988). *Genesis Two: An Ethnographic Description.* Fair Oaks, CA: Scott Beach, Cultural Engineering and Design Associates.
Beach, S. (1991a). The Martians are coming. *Behaviorological Commentaries, Serial No. 1,* 25–28.
Beach, S. (1991b). Behaviorology and space settlement. *CONTACT Newsletter, 2* (2), 2–3.
Beach, S. (1991c, Fall). Personal and historical transformations. Lecture notes presented to Government 112, California State University at Sacramento.
Behavior Analysis… (1992). *Behavior Analysis Digest, 4* (1), 1.
Biehler, R.F. & Snowman, J. (1990). *Psychology Applied to Teaching (Sixth Edition).* Boston, MA: Houghton Mifflin.
Bjork, D.W. (1993). Toward a biography of B.F. Skinner: Rationale and interpretation. *Behaviorology, 1* (1), 7–11.
Booth, W. (1989, February 3). A clash of cultures at meeting on misconduct. *Science, 243,* 598.
Bowler, P. (1983). *The Eclipse of Darwinism: Anti–Darwinian Evolution Theories in the Decades Around 1900.* Baltimore, MD: Johns Hopkins University Press.
Branch, M.N. & Malagodi, E.F. (1980). Where have all the behaviorists gone? *The Behavior Analyst, 3,* 31–38.
Burgess, R.L. & Bushell, D. (1969). *Behavioral Sociology, the Experimental Analysis of Social Process.* New York: Columbia University Press.
Burhoe, R.W. (1981). *Toward a Scientific Theology.* Belfast, Ontario, Canada: Christian Journals Ltd.
Burns, G.L. (1988). Radical and paradigmatic behaviorism: Alternative theory construction methodologies. *Behavior Analysis, 23* (2), 66–72.
Catania, A.C. (1973, May). The psychologies of structure, function, and development. *American Psychologist,* 434–443.
Catania, A.C. (1987). Some Darwinian lessons for behavior analysis: A review of Bowler's *The Eclipse of Darwinism. Journal of The Experimental Analysis of Behavior, 47,* 249–257.

Catania, A.C. (1991). The gifts of culture and of eloquence: An open letter to Michael J. Mahoney in reply to his article, "Scientific psychology and radical behaviorism." *The Behavior Analyst, 14,* 61–72.

Cautela, J.R. (1994). General level of reinforcement II: Further elaborations. *Behaviorology, 2* (1), 1–16.

Cheney, C.D. (1988, August). Impacting behavior with science. Paper presented at the first convention of The International Behaviorology Association, Potsdam, NY.

Cheney, C.D. (1991). The source and control of behavior. In W. Ishaq (Ed.). *Human Behavior in Today's World* (pp. 73–86). New York: Praeger.

Cheney, C.D. (1992). Activity anorexia [Review of *Solving the Anorexia Puzzle: A Scientific Approach*]. *The Behavior Analyst, 15,* 157–160.

Chiesa, M. (1994). *Radical Behaviorism: The Philosophy and the Science.* Boston, MA: Authors cooperative.

Christophersen, E.R. (1988). *Little People (Third Edition).* Kansas City, MO: Westport Publishers.

Coleman, S.R. & Mehlman, S.E. (1992). An empirical update (1969–1989) of D.L. Krantz's thesis that the experimental analysis of behavior is isolated. *The Behavior Analyst, 15,* 43–49.

Comunidad Los Horcones. (1986). Behaviorology: An integrative denomination. *The Behavior Analyst, 9,* 227–228.

Court Battle. (1991). Behavior analyst wins court battle. *Behavior Analysis Digest, 3* (1), 2–3.

Daniels, A.C. (1989). *Performance Management (Third Edition, revised).* Tucker, GA: Performance Management Publications.

Deitz, S.M. (1986). Splitters and lumpers. *Division 25 Recorder, 21,* 66–68.

Division 25. (1990). Division 25 membership. *Division 25 Recorder, 26* (1), 5–7.

Drash, P.H. & Freeman, B.J. (1973). *Behavior Modification, Behavior Therapy, and Operant Conditioning: An Historical Survey and a Bibliography of Books in Print, 1900–1972.* Baltimore, MD: Behavioral Information and Technology.

Epstein, R. (1984). The case for praxics. *The Behavior Analyst, 7,* 101–119.

Epstein, R. (1985). Further comments on praxics: Why the devotion to behaviorism? *The Behavior Analyst, 8,* 269–271.

Epstein, R. (1987a). The debate about praxics: Some comments meant especially for students. *The Behavior Analyst, 10,* 127–131.

Epstein, R. (1987b). In the yellow wood. In S. Modgil & C. Modgil (Eds.). *B.F. Skinner: Consensus and Controversy* (pp. 333–335). New York: Falmer Press.

Eshleman, J.W. & Vargas, E.A. (1988). Promoting the behaviorological analysis of verbal behavior. *Analysis of Verbal Behavior, 6,* 23–32.

Fantino, E. (1988). Editorial. *Journal of the Experimental Analysis of Behavior, 49,* 1–2.

Ferster, C.B. & Skinner, B.F. (1957). *Schedules of Reinforcement.* Englewood Cliffs, NJ: Prentice–Hall.

Fraley, L.E. (1981). The spread of behavior analysis to the applied fields. *The Behavior Analyst, 4,* 33–41.

Fraley, L.E. (1983). The behavioral analysis of Mens Rea (doctrine of culpable mental states). *Behaviorists for Social Action Journal, 4* (1), 2–7.

Fraley, L.E. (1984). Belief, its inconsistency, and the implications for the teaching faculty. *The Behavior Analyst, 7,* 17–28.

Fraley, L.E. (1987). The cultural mission of behaviorology. *The Behavior Analyst, 10,* 123–126.
Fraley, L.E. (1988a, May). Behaviorological corrections: A new concept of prison from a new discipline. In J. Ellis (Chair), *Correctional behavior analysis.* Symposium conducted at the fourteenth annual convention of The Association for Behavior Analysis, Philadelphia, PA.
Fraley, L.E. (1988b). Covert mini–courts within judicial and law enforcement operations. *Behavior Analysis and Social Action, 6* (2), 2–14.
Fraley, L.E. (1988c). Introductory comments: Behaviorology and cultural materialism. *The Behavior Analyst, 11,* 159–160.
Fraley, L.E. (1988d). You're a what? *TIBA Newsletter, 1* (1), 5–7.
Fraley, L.E. (1990a, January). The science of philosophy. Paper presented at the second annual convention of The International Behaviorology Association, Comunidad Los Horcones, Hermosillo, Sonora, Mexico.
Fraley, L.E. (1990b). Thrust and parry. *TIBA Newsletter, 2* (2), 7–8.
Fraley, L.E. (1991). The behaviorology movement. *Behaviorological Commentaries, Serial No. 1,* 3–13.
Fraley, L.E. (1992a, January). Uncertainty about determinism. Paper presented at the fourth annual convention of The International Behaviorology Association, New Orleans, LA.
Fraley, L.E. (1992b). Behavior analysis and behaviorology. *Behaviorological Commentaries, Serial No. 2,* 22.
Fraley, L.E. (1996a). *General Behaviorology* (fall edition). Morgantown, WV: Lawrence E. Fraley (609–C Allen Hall, WVU, Morgantown WV 26506–6122 USA).
Fraley, L.E. (1996b, May). An academic home for a natural science. In H. Ferris (Chair), *Should we have graduate programs in behavior analysis.* Symposium conducted at the twenty–second annual convention of The Association for Behavior Analysis, San Francisco, CA.
Fraley, L.E. & Ledoux, S.F. (1993). *The Emergence of the Discipline of Behaviorology.* Canton, NY: ABCs.
Fraley, L.E. & Vargas, E.A. (1986). Separate disciplines: The study of behavior and the study of the psyche. *The Behavior Analyst, 9,* 47–59.
Frase, L. (1970). Boundary conditions for mathemagenic behaviors. *Review of Educational Research, 40* (3), 337–347.
Gaydos, G.R. (1986). On praxis and praxics. *The Behavior Analyst, 9,* 229–230.
Giles, T. (1984). Probable superiority of behavioral intervention—III: Some obstacles to acceptance of findings. *Journal of Behavior Therapy and Experimental Psychiatry, 15,* 23–26.
Glenn, S.S. (1988). Contingencies and metacontingencies: Toward a synthesis of behavior analysis and cultural materialism. *The Behavior Analyst, 11,* 161–179.
Gould, S.J. (1981). *The Mismeasure of Man.* New York: W.W. Norton.
Gould, S.J. (1987). *An Urchin in the Storm.* New York: W.W. Norton.
Graham, G. & Killeen, P. (1985). Behaviorism: The next generation. *Behaviorism, 13,* 1–2.
Hake, D.F. (1982). The basic–applied continuum and the possible evolution of human operant social and verbal research. *The Behavior Analyst, 5,* 21–28.
Hamblin, R.L. & Kunkel, J.H. (Eds.). (1977). *Behavioral Theory in Sociology, Essays in Honor of George E. Homans.* New Brunswick, NJ: Transaction Books.

Harris, M. (1979). *Cultural Materialism: The Struggle for a Science of Culture.* New York: Random House.

Harzem, P. (1987). On the virtues of being a psychologist. *The Behavior Analyst, 10,* 175–181.

Hayes, S.C. (1987a). Bracing for change. *Behavior Analysis, 22* (1), 7–10.

Hayes, S.C. (1987b). The gathering storm. *Behavior Analysis, 22* (2), 41–47.

Hayes, S.C. (1987c). Moving ahead. *Behavior Analysis, 22* (3), 85–90.

Hayes, S.C. (1988a). Contextualism and the next wave of behavioral psychology. *Behavior Analysis, 23* (1), 7–22.

Hayes, S.C. (1988b). Pro statement. *Behavior Analysis, 23* (3), 138–139.

Hayes, S.C. (1991). Why APA does not deserve our support. *Division 25 Recorder, 26* (2), 19–21.

Hayes, S.C. & Brownstein, A.J. (1985). Mentalism and the "as–yet–unexplained": A reply to Killeen. *Behaviorism, 13,* 151–154.

Hayes, S.C. & Brownstein, A.J. (1986). Mentalism, behavior–behavior relations, and a behavior–analytic view of the purposes of science. *The Behavior Analyst, 9,* 175–190.

Hineline, P.N. (1984). Can a statement in cognitive terms be a behavior–analytic interpretation? *The Behavior Analyst, 7,* 97–100.

Hineline, P.N. (1991). Modesty, yes; humility, no. *The Behavior Analyst, 14,* 25–28.

Hishinuma, E. (1989). The future of radical behaviorism: Brief comments on Glenn's Editorial and Drash's "On Terms." *The Behavior Analyst, 12,* 93–95.

Holland, J.G. (1960). Teaching machines: An application from the laboratory. *Journal of the Experimental Analysis of Behavior, 3,* 275–287.

Holland, J.G. (1967). A quantitative measure for programmed instruction. *American Educational Research Journal, 4,* 87–101.

Holland, J.G. (1990). Selected for consequences. *Division 25 Recorder, 24/25* (3), 32.

Holland, J.G. & Skinner, B.F. (1961). *The Analysis of Behavior.* New York: McGraw–Hill.

Holmberg, A.R. (1967). The research and development approach to the study of change. In P. Bohannan & F. Plog (Eds.). *Beyond the Frontier* (pp. 307–318). New York: Natural History Press. (Originally published in 1958 in *Human Organization, 17* [1], 12–16.)

Homans, G.C. (1961). *Social Behavior: Its Elementary Forms.* New York: Harcourt, Brace, & World.

Hopkins, B.L. (1991). ABA to begin accrediting graduate programs of study in behavior analysis. *The ABA Newsletter, 14* (3), 19–21.

Hunter, W.S. (1925). General anthroponomy and its systematic problems. *American Journal of Psychology, 36,* 286–302.

Johnson, K.R. & Layng, T.V.J. (1992). Breaking the structuralist barrier: Literacy and numeracy with fluency. *American Psychologist, 47* (11), 1475–1490.

Johnston, J.M. & Pennypacker, H.S. (1980). *Strategies and Tactics for Human Behavioral Research.* Hillsdale, NJ: Erlbaum.

Kauffman, J.M. (1989). *Characteristics of Behavior Disorders of Children and Youth (Fourth Edition).* Columbus, OH: Merrill.

Kearney, A. (1988, August). Behaviorological principles for the framework for clinical practice. Paper presented at the first convention of The International Behaviorology Association, Potsdam, NY.

Keller, F.S. (1968). "Good–bye teacher…" *Journal of Applied Behavior Analysis, 1,* 79–89.

Keller, F.S. (1986). A fire in Schermerhorn Extension. *The Behavior Analyst, 9,* 139–146.

Keller, F.S. (1993). Education by torchlight. *Behaviorology, 1* (2), 1–8.
Keller, F.S. & Schoenfeld, W.N. (1949). The psychology curriculum at Columbia College. *American Psychologist, 4,* 165–172.
Krantz, D.L. (1971). The separate worlds of operant and non–operant psychology. *Journal of Applied Behavior Analysis, 4,* 61–70.
Krapfl, J.E. & Vargas, E.A. (Eds.). (1977). *Behaviorism and Ethics.* Kalamazoo, MI: Behaviordelia.
Kuhn, T. (1970). *The Structure of Scientific Revolutions (Second Edition, Enlarged): International Encyclopedia of Unified Science, 2* (2). Chicago, IL: The University of Chicago Press.
Lamal, P.A. (1986). On facing reality. *The ABA Newsletter, 9* (3), 6.
Lamal, P.A. (1988, spring). Thinking straight about psychology and behaviorism: A review of Stanovich's (1986) *How to Think Straight About Psychology. The Behavioral Educator,* 9–10.
Lattal, K.A., McFarland, J.M., & Joyce, J.H. (1990). What is happening in psychology of learning courses? *The Behavior Analyst, 13,* 121–130.
Ledoux, S.F. (1973). *The Experimental Analysis of Coverants.* M.A. thesis, California State University, Sacramento.
Ledoux, S.F. (1977, June). Behaviorism and "mind." Paper presented at N'est–ce Pas? Society meeting, Melbourne, Victoria, Australia. Printed in S.F. Ledoux (Ed.). (1979). *Behaviorism and Mind and Much More (Second Edition)* (pp. 109–154). Churchill, Victoria, Australia: GIAE.
Ledoux, S.F. (1985). Designing a new *Walden Two*–inspired community. *Communities, No. 66,* 23–31, 84.
Ledoux, S.F. (1987a). Expanding the happy few: A review of *The Critical Years* by Doris Durrell. *Behavior Analysis and Social Action, 6,* 44–47.
Ledoux, S.F. (1987b). Highlights of the founding meeting of The Behaviorology Society. Unpublished manuscript.
Ledoux, S.F. (1989). The interorganizational question and ABA. *TIBA Newsletter, 1* (2), 1–2.
Ledoux, S.F. (1997a). An introduction to the origins, status, and mission of behaviorology: An established science with developed applications and a new name. In S.F. Ledoux. *Origins and Components of Behaviorology.* Canton, NY: ABCs. Reprinted with revisions from (1992) *Behaviorological Commentaries, Serial No. 3,* 11–31.
Ledoux, S.F. (1997b). An introduction to the philosophy called radical behaviorism. In S.F. Ledoux. *Origins and Components of Behaviorology.* Canton, NY: ABCs. Reprinted with revisions from (1992) *Behaviorological Commentaries, Serial No. 4,* 3–10.
Ledoux, S.F. (1997c). Behaviorology curricula in higher education. In S.F. Ledoux. *Origins and Components of Behaviorology.* Canton, NY: ABCs. Reprinted with revisions from (in press) *The International Behaviorologist, 1.*
Ledoux, S.F. (1997d). Behaviorology in China: A status report. In S.F. Ledoux. *Origins and Components of Behaviorology.* Canton, NY: ABCs. Reprinted with revisions from (1992) *Behaviorological Commentaries, Serial No. 4,* 24–36.
Ledoux, S.F. (1997e). Appendices. In S.F. Ledoux. *Origins and Components of Behaviorology.* Canton, NY: ABCs.
Ledoux, S.F. & Cheney, C.D. (1987). *Grandpa Fred's Baby Tender or Why and How We Built Our Aircribs.* Canton, NY: ABCs.

Lee, V.L. (1987a). Radical behaviorism and behavior analysis: A review of *Behavior Analysis and Contemporary Psychology. The Behavior Analyst, 10,* 95–101.

Lee, V.L. (1987b). The structure of conduct. *Behaviorism, 15,* 141–148.

Lee, V.L. (1988). *Beyond Behaviorism.* Hillsdale, NJ: Erlbaum.

Lee, V.L. (1989). Comments about the isolation of behavior analysis. *The Behavior Analyst, 12,* 85–87.

Leigland, S. (1985). Praxics and the case for radical behaviorism. *The Behavior Analyst, 8,* 127–128.

Lerner, E.J. (1991). *The Big Bang Never Happened.* New York: Times Books.

Lloyd, K.E. (1985). Behavioral anthropology: A review of Marvin Harris' *Cultural Materialism. Journal of the Experimental Analysis of Behavior, 43,* 279–287.

Logue, A.W. (1988). A behaviorist's biologist: Review of Philip J. Pauly's *Controlling Life: Jacques Loeb and the Engineering Ideal in Biology. The Behavior Analyst, 11,* 205–207.

Lovie, A.D. (1987). Ethnographic discourse analysis and J.B. Watson: The behaviorist as propagandist. In W.J. Baker, M.E. Hyland, H. Van Rappard, & A.W. Staats (Eds.). *Current Issues in Theoretical Psychology* (pp. 151–164). Dordrecht: Elsevier.

Mahoney, M.J. (1989). Scientific psychology and radical behaviorism. *American Psychologist, 44* (11), 1372–1377.

Malagodi, E.F. & Branch, M.N. (1985). Praxics and behaviorism. *The Behavior Analyst, 8,* 123–125.

Malott, R.W. (1988). Rule–governed behavior and behavioral anthropology. *The Behavior Analyst, 11,* 181–203.

Marcattilio, A.J. & Nevin, J.A. (1986). The threat of nuclear war: Some responses. *The Behavior Analyst, 9,* 61–70.

McDowell, J.J. (1991). Irreconcilable differences and political reality in these dark ages. *The Behavior Analyst, 14,* 29–33.

Michael, J.L. (1980). Flight from behavior analysis. *The Behavior Analyst, 3* (2), 1–21.

Michael, J.L. (1985). Behavior analysis: A radical perspective. In B.L. Hammonds (Ed.). *Master Lecture Series, Volume 4: Psychology of Learning* (pp. 99–121). Washington, DC: American Psychological Association.

Michael, J.L. (1989). *Verbal and Nonverbal Behavior: Concepts and Principles.* Kalamazoo, MI: Psychology Department, Western Michigan University.

Minutes of the Division 25 Executive Committee Meeting. (1988). *Behavior Analysis, 23* (3), 121–131.

Minutes of the Division 25 Executive Committee Meeting. (1990). *Division 25 Recorder, 26* (1), 9–11.

Moore, J. (1981). On mentalism, methodological behaviorism, and radical behaviorism. *Behaviorism, 9,* 55–57.

Moore, J. (1984). On privacy, causes, and contingencies. *The Behavior Analyst, 7,* 3–16.

Morris, E.K. (1991). Message from the president. *The ABA Newsletter, 14* (4), 1–6.

Morse, L.A. & Bruns, B.J. (1983). Nurturing behavioral repertoires within a non–supportive environment. *The Behavior Analyst, 6,* 19–25.

Nessel, J. (1982, May). Understanding psychological man: A state of the science report. *Psychology Today.* In M.G. Walraven & H.E. Fitzgerald (Eds.). (1984). *Annual Editions—Psychology 84/85* (pp. 4–16). Guilford, CT: Dushkin.

NTSU. (1988, May 14). *North Texas State University Spring Commencement.* Denton, TX: North Texas State University.

Peterson, M.E. (1978). The Midwestern Association of Behavior Analysis: Past, present, and future. *The Behavior Analyst, 1* (1), 3–15.

Proctor, R.W. & Weeks, D.J. (1988). The virtues of scientific psychology: A reply to Harzem. *The Behavior Analyst, 11,* 131–140.

Ratner, S. (1936, January). Evolution and the rise of the scientific spirit in America. *Philosophy of Science, 3,* 194–122. In A. Montagu (Ed.). (1984). *Science and Creationism* (pp. 398–415). New York: Oxford University Press.

Recruiting diversity into behavior Analysis. (1993). *The Current Repertoire, 9* (2), 4.

Sagan, C. (1995). *The Demon–Haunted World: Science as a Candle in the Dark.* New York: Random House.

Salzinger, K. (1988). Living in interesting times: A serial. *Behavior Analysis, 23* (3), 118–120.

Salzinger, K. (1990). Cognitive problems, behavioral solutions. In L.J. Hayes & P.N. Chase (Eds.). *Dialogues on Verbal Behavior* (pp. 183–196). Reno, NV: Context Press.

Samaan, M.K. (1973). *Behaviorology: The Humanist Alternative.* Sacramento, CA: California State University Library.

Schoenfeld, W.N. (1993). *Religion and Human Behavior.* Boston, MA: Authors Cooperative.

Scoresby, A.L. & Price, A.H. (1991). *Readings in Child Development.* San Francisco, CA: McGraw–Hill, College Custom Series.

Sherbowsky, D. (1935). *An Outline of Behaviorology—The Psychology.* New York.

Shook, G.L. (1993). The professional credential in behavior analysis. *The Behavior Analyst, 16,* 87–101.

Sidman, M. (1960). *Tactics of Scientific Research.* New York: Basic Books. Reprinted, 1988, Boston, MA: Authors Cooperative.

Sidman, M. (1986a). Functional analysis of emergent verbal classes. In T. Thompson & M. Zeiler (Eds.). *Analysis and Integration of Behavioral Units* (pp. 213–245). Hillsdale, NJ: Erlbaum.

Sidman, M. (1986b). The measurement of behavioral development. In N.A. Krasnegor, D.B. Gray, & T. Thompson (Eds.). *Developmental Behavioral Pharmacology* (pp. 43–52). Hillsdale, NJ: Erlbaum.

Skinner, B.F. (1938). *The Behavior of Organisms.* Englewood Cliffs, NJ: Prentice–Hall. Seventh printing, 1966, with special preface. Reprinted, 1991, Cambridge, MA: The B.F. Skinner Foundation.

Skinner, B.F. (1948). *Walden Two.* New York: Macmillan.

Skinner, B.F. (1953). *Science and Human Behavior.* New York: Macmillan.

Skinner, B.F. (1956). A case history in scientific method. *American Psychologist, 11,* 221–233.

Skinner, B.F. (1957). *Verbal Behavior.* New York: Appleton–Century–Crofts. Reprinted, 1992, Cambridge, MA: The B.F. Skinner Foundation.

Skinner, B.F. (1968). *The Technology of Teaching.* New York: Appleton–Century–Crofts.

Skinner, B.F. (1969). *Contingencies of Reinforcement: A Theoretical Analysis.* New York: Appleton–Century–Crofts.

Skinner, B.F. (1971). *Beyond Freedom and Dignity.* New York: Knopf.

Skinner, B.F. (1972). *Cumulative Record: A Selection of Papers (Third Edition).* New York: Appleton–Century–Crofts.

Skinner, B.F. (1974). *About Behaviorism.* New York: Knopf.

Skinner, B.F. (1977). Why I am not a cognitive psychologist. *Behaviorism, 5* (2), 1–10.

Skinner, B.F. (1978). *Reflections on Behaviorism and Society.* Englewood Cliffs, NJ: Prentice–Hall.

Skinner, B.F. (1979). *The Shaping of a Behaviorist.* New York: Knopf.

Skinner, B.F. (1980). *Notebooks B.F. Skinner.* Englewood Cliffs, NJ: Prentice Hall.

Skinner, B.F. (1982, May). [untitled response to question]. In J. Nessel. Understanding psychological man: A state of the science report. *Psychology Today.* In M.G. Walraven & H.E. Fitzgerald (Eds.). (1984). *Annual Editions—Psychology 84/85* (pp. 4–16). Guilford, CT: Dushkin.

Skinner, B.F. (1983a). *A Matter of Consequences.* New York: Knopf.

Skinner, B.F. (1983b). Can the experimental analysis of behavior rescue psychology? *The Behavior Analyst, 6,* 9–17.

Skinner, B.F. (1984). The shame of American education. *The American Psychologist, 39,* 947–954.

Skinner, B.F. (1987a). *Upon Further Reflection.* Englewood Cliffs, NJ: Prentice–Hall.

Skinner, B.F. (1987b). Whatever happened to psychology as the science of behavior. *American Psychologist, 42,* 780–786.

Skinner, B.F. (1989a, May). A world of our own. Major address presented at the fifteenth annual convention of the Association for Behavior Analysis, Milwaukee, WI. Printed, 1993, *Behaviorology, 1* (1), 3–5.

Skinner, B.F. (1989b). *Recent Issues in the Analysis of Behavior.* Columbus, OH: Merrill.

Skinner, B.F. (1989c). [untitled letter]. *APS Observer, 2* (2), 8.

Skinner, B.F. (1990). Can psychology be a science of mind? *American Psychologist, 45,* 1206–1210.

Skinner, B.F. (1993). A world of our own. *Behaviorology, 1* (1), 3–5.

Skinner, B.F. & Vaughan, M.E. (1983). *Enjoy Old Age.* New York: W.W. Norton.

Skrtic, T.M. (1991). *Behind Special Education.* Denver, CO: Love.

Staats, R.W. (1986). Left and right paths for behaviorism's development. *The Behavior Analyst, 9,* 231–237.

Stewart, B. & Vargas, J. (1990). *Teaching Behavior to Infants and Toddlers: A Manual for Caregivers and Parents.* Springfield, IL: Charles C. Thomas, Publisher.

Taylor, S. (1990). Hard won exemption allows Florida behavior analysts to continue to practice. *The ABA Newsletter, 9 (2),* 12–13.

The coherence of psychology. (1989). *APS Observer, 2* (5), 10–11.

Thorndike, E.L. (1911). *Animal Intelligence.* New York: Macmillan.

Thyer, B.A. (1987). Contingency analysis: Toward a unified theory of social work practice. *Social Work, 32,* 150–157.

Thyer, B.A. (1991). The enduring intellectual legacy of B.F. Skinner: A citation count from 1966–1989. *The Behavior Analyst, 14,* 73–75.

TIBA. (1988). Convention program for the first convention of The International Behaviorology Association, Clarkson University, Potsdam, NY.

TIBA By–laws. (1989). The International Behaviorology Association, Office of the Secretary, 609 Allen Hall, West Virginia University, Morgantown, WV 26506. Reprinted, 1990, *TIBA Newsletter, 2* (3), 13–16.

Ulman, J.D. (1983). Toward a united front: A class analysis of social and political action. *Behaviorists for Social Action Journal, 4* (1), 17–23.

Ulman, J.D. (1986). Working class strategies for world peace. *Behavior Analysis and Social Action, 5,* 36–43.

Ulman, J.D. (1988). Just say no to commodity fetishism: A reply to Rakos. *Behavior Analysis and Social Action, 6,* 25–31.

Ulman, J.D. (1990a). Paradigmatic behaviorism: Hierarchically schematicized eclecticism. *TIBA Newsletter, 2* (1), 6.

Ulman, J.D. (1990b). A memo to the Dean regarding behaviorology. *TIBA Newsletter, 2* (3), 1–3.

Ulman, J.D. (1993). The Ulman–Skinner letters. *Behaviorology, 1* (1), 47–54.

Vargas, E.A. (1975). Rights: A behavioristic analysis. *Behaviorism, 3* (2), 120–128.

Vargas, E.A. (1982). Hume's "ought" and "is" statement: A radical behaviorist's perspective. *Behaviorism, 10* (1), 1–23.

Vargas, E.A. (1985). Cultural contingencies: A review of Marvin Harris's *Cannibals and Kings. Journal of the Experimental Analysis of Behavior, 43*, 419–428.

Vargas, E.A. (1987). "Separate disciplines" is another name for survival. *The Behavior Analyst, 10*, 119–121.

Vargas, E.A. (1988). Organizing for the future of the discipline. *TIBA Newsletter, 1* (1), 2–5.

Vargas, E.A. (1990, May). Behaviorology: The range and domain of its paradigm. Paper presented at the second annual convention of The International Behaviorology Association, Comunidad Los Horcones, Hermosillo, Sonora, Mexico.

Vargas, E.A. (1991a). Behaviorology: Its paradigm. In W. Ishaq (Ed.). *Human Behavior in Today's World* (pp. 139–147). New York: Praeger.

Vargas, E.A. (1991b). Verbal behavior: A four–term contingency relation. In W. Ishaq (Ed.). *Human Behavior in Today's World* (pp. 99–108). New York: Praeger.

Vargas, E.A. (1993, May). Review of Philip Pauly's *Controlling Life: Jacques Loeb and the Engineering Ideal in Biology.* Book review presented at the nineteenth annual convention of the Association for Behavior Analysis, Chicago, IL.

Vargas, E.A. (1996). A university for the twenty–first century. In J.R. Cautela & W. Ishaq (Eds.). *Contemporary Issues in Behavior Therapy: Improving the Human Condition* (pp. 159–188). New York: Plenum.

Vargas, E.A. (In preparation). *Educational Behaviorology.*

Vargas, E.A. & Fraley, L.E. (1976). Progress and structure: Reorganizing the university for instructional technology. *Instructional Science, 5*, 303–324.

Vargas, E.A., Spangler, R.S., Stone, J.E., & Wishon, P.M. (1988, May). Behaviorists in non–behavioral places: Practicing a discipline without a profession. Paper presented at the fourteenth annual convention of the Association for Behavior Analysis, Philadelphia, PA.

Vargas, J.S. (1972). *Writing Worthwhile Behavioral Objectives.* New York: Harper & Row.

Vargas, J.S. (1977). *Behavioral Psychology for Teachers.* New York: Harper & Row.

Vargas, J.S. (1988). *Behaviorology for Teachers.* Morgantown, WV: L.E. Fraley.

Vargas, J.S. (1989). The road less travelled by. *The Behavior Analyst, 12*, 121–130.

Vargas, J.S. (1990). Cognitive analysis of language and verbal behavior: Two separate fields. In L.J. Hayes & P.N. Chase (Eds.). *Dialogues on Verbal Behavior* (pp. 197–201). Reno, NV: Context Press.

Vitulli, W.F. (1969). Psychology or behaviorology? A plea for descriptive accuracy. *American Psychologist, 24*, 958.

Watson, J.B. (1913). Psychology as the behaviorist views it. *Psychological Review, 20*, 158–177. Reprinted in T. Shipley (Ed.). (1961). *Classics in Psychology.* New York: Philosophical Library.

Wendt, R. (1949). The development of a psychological cult. *American Psychologist, 4*, 426.

West, R.P. & Hamerlynck, L.A. (Eds.). (1992). *Designs for Excellence in Education: The Legacy of B.F. Skinner (Limited Edition).* Longmont, CO: Sopris West.

White, L.A. (1949). *The Science of Culture: A Study of Man and Civilization.* New York: Farrar, Straus, & Giroux.

White, K.G., McCarthy, D., & Fantino, E. (1989). Cognition and behavior analysis. *Journal of the Experimental Analysis of Behavior, 52,* 197–198.

Wood, S.W. (1976). Responsibilities of the college teacher: A behavioral perspective. In L.E. Fraley & E.A. Vargas (Eds.). *Behavior Research and Technology in Higher Education* (pp. 11–20). Reedsville, WV: Society for The Behavioral Analysis of Culture.

Wyatt, W.J., Hawkins, R.P., & Davis, P. (1986). Behaviorism: Are reports of its death exaggerated? *The Behavior Analyst, 9,* 101–105.

Youth Policy Institute. (1988, July/August). *Youth Policy, 10* (7).

Quoted*

§

...I have tried too long to follow Watson in saying that psychology is the science of behavior. I am now convinced that is wrong. Psychology has always been concerned with internal explanations. To show how futile that is, let us imagine that it has been successful. Let us suppose that all those who examine mental processes introspectively now agree on what they see. Let us suppose that what they see confirms a set of theories upon which all cognitive psychologists now agree. And let us suppose that brain science, looking inside the behaving organism in a different way, has found what convincingly can be called the same thing. Shall they then have discovered the causes of human behavior or simply more about what is behaving? (p. 3)

...We have been accused of building our own ghetto... Rather than break out of the ghetto, I think we should strengthen its walls. No field of science has ever been more clearly defined than this world of ours. In no other world are there more fascinating things to be explored. No world has a greater potential for solving the problems that face the world today, above all saving the planet Earth. (p. 5)

§

*From: Skinner, B.F. (1993). A world of our own. *Behaviorology, 1* (1), 3–5.

A Small Selection of Photographs

Photo compliments of Carl D. Cheney

Authors of "Origins, Status, and Mission..." at TIBA–IV, New Orleans, LA, USA, January 1992 [Left to right: Lawrence E. Fraley and Stephen F. Ledoux]

Photo by Stephen F. Ledoux

Participants at the Executive Board subcommittee meeting, Waltham, MA, USA, December 1987 [Left to right: Lawrence E. Fraley, Ernest A. Vargas, Julie S. Vargas and Stephen F. Ledoux]

Most participants at the first TIBA convention, Potsdam, NY, USA, August 1988.

Douglas Greer	Ernest Vargas	Jack Michael		John Stone	Scott Beach	
		Lawrence Fraley		Laura Dorow		
Jerome Ulman	Al Kearney		Robert Spangler		Carl Cheney	
Sigrid Glenn	Guy Bruce				Julie Vargas	Juan Robinson
Stephen Ledoux		Jeffrey Kupfer		John Eshleman	Linda Armendariz	

Behaviorology Curricula in Higher Education

Stephen F. Ledoux

The By–laws of the professional organization of behaviorologists, *The International Behaviorology Association* (TIBA), state that one of several purposes of TIBA is "to promote a scientific 'Behavior Literacy' graduation requirement of appropriate content and depth at all levels of educational institutions from kindergarten through university" (TIBA, 1989, p. 3). To carry out this and other TIBA purposes, large numbers of fully trained behaviorologists are needed.

Some General Behaviorology Training Concerns

Since comprehensive professional training historically occurs at colleges and universities, behaviorologists' initial efforts regarding training programs should address curricula at that level. Therefore, this paper focuses on behaviorology curricula in higher education, including curricula at the Associate (A.A.), Baccalaureate (B.A.), and Master of Arts (M.A.) / Master of Science (M.S.) degree levels.

Consensus

The success of curriculum development efforts depends in part on consensus regarding the repertoires of behaviorologists and the curricula to generate those repertoires. So, one purpose of this paper is to contribute to the development of that consensus.

Achieving consensus on repertoires and curricula can facilitate the development of additional academic homes and programs of behaviorology in which to implement such curricula. Descriptions of the repertoires of behaviorologists provide standards against which professional organizations evaluate curricular programs for certification or accreditation. Consensus statements about the desired repertoires—in the form of a variety of general and specific program descriptions as presented here, or in other forms—could assist behaviorologists as they prepare proposals to establish or expand programs in their own academic units. Behaviorologists could point to the consensus as an appropriate indication of disciplinary maturity, organization, and solidarity, and these are important characteristics that would likely be taken into account by those to whom behaviorologists present program proposals.

Parts of the curricula in this paper were originally included in a requested proposal to the Institute for the Study of Applied Behavior Analysis (Potsdam, NY) concerning potential extensions of the Institute's curricula. The paper was then completed for presentation as the author's TIBA presidential address at the second TIBA convention (Comunidad Los Horcones, Hermosillo, Sonora, Mexico, January 1990).

Consensus can, and perhaps must, vary across academic levels. Given the foundational nature of the A.A. and B.A. levels, consensus at these levels is especially important and might be easier to obtain. Other natural science disciplines have reached a workable consensus on curricula at those levels. Given the increasing specialization for which graduate trainees prepare, programs at M.A. and doctoral levels are more variable, making standardization more difficult. Consensus for these higher levels usually involves more general guidelines with respect to the repertoire components that denote a specialization within a behaviorological repertoire.

Curricular Design Alternatives

The behaviorological literature already contains expressions of concern (e.g., Michael, 1980) about the contents of training programs for professionals in the science of behavior founded by B.F. Skinner. Most such articles, however, were written while behaviorological science shared a history (Ledoux, 1997a) with another discipline. They focused on training problems that arose *from* that residence, such as the requirement that some training time be devoted to courses with cognitive/mentalistic contents (see Fraley & Ledoux, 1997, for a full discussion). These articles addressed the question of what should be done with our *share* of the training time (which often shrank even as the scientific content to be covered expanded). This paper explicitly addresses the chief alternative by posing the question of what we want to do with behaviorology training time when we behaviorologists are responsible for *all* of it. How should behaviorologists be trained?

One approach to designing curricula starts by describing an ideal finished product: the repertoires whose refinement and manifestation denote a behaviorologist. In this approach, a curricula organizer might specify a comprehensive list of behavioral objectives relevant to the topics in the subject matter of behaviorology and design curricula around that list.

At the first TIBA convention, Michael (1988) presented a tentative list of important topics in behaviorology. His list included both respondent and operant conditioning, and virtually all known subtopics. Behaviorologists might add to this list the appropriate philosophical, analytical, technological, and other relevant topics to create a master list. That master list could be organized under conceptual headings that could become parts of course titles, including "Conceptual Foundations" (philosophical, analytical, interpretative, and historical), "Experimental Foundations" (basic and applied measurement, methodology, and research), and "Technological Foundations" (effective applications in general and in specific areas). This might be the approach of choice, especially when designing curricula in a situation free of those current administrative contingencies in higher education that constrain effective educational practices.

The approach of this paper differs. For convenience, it uses the firmly established and administratively sanctioned degree structure of higher education in the United States of America (i.e., A.A., B.A., M.A./M.S., and Ph.D.) as a familiar foundation, while acknowledging other equally viable systems. More specifically, the curricular designs presented here take into account various (and sometimes constraining) academic and administrative contingencies. An example of a constraining contingency would be the requirement that all students conform their speed of progress on a set of course materials to a particular amount of time (for instance, three contact–hours per week for a 15–week semester). At the same time, the curricular designs presented here seek to provide, through as much practice of behaviorologically sound educational methods as possible, some of the evidence upon which to base improvements to administrative contingencies, improvements that bring those contingencies and improved educational methods into conformity.

This design option then proceeds by bringing together aspects of the programs and courses through which behaviorologists currently teach approximations of the complete behaviorological repertoire in various educational settings. These programs and courses appear here as a series of curricular structures. While specifically *not* designed for any particular institution, the description of these curricular structures may ease the task for others who are designing programs by providing a set of patterns and components that they can adapt to their own situation. To the extent that the curricular structures and components described herein derive from the current teaching activities of behaviorologists, some consensus is automatically inherent.

Facets of Program Design

Program design involves at least three facets: (a) *curricular* concerns which center on course descriptions, course sequences, and component courses of degree programs, (b) *resource* concerns which center on staff, facilities, and materials, and (c) *instructional* concerns which center on staff skills and instructional design and programming for each course. The design option presented here emphasizes the curricular concerns, and acknowledges that resource concerns are specific to the educational institution in which a program designer operates.

With respect to the instructional concerns, this design option reiterates the demonstrated value of implementing the educational methods derived from behaviorological science (see Johnson & Layng, 1992; J. Vargas, 1988). This design option also supports the improvements to administrative contingencies implicit in that science. For instance, on the basis of the type and the extent of the repertoire that is conducive to effective educational design, Vargas and Fraley (1976; also see Vargas, 1996) proposed dividing the content and process functions of teachers between subject–matter experts (persons with an extensive repertoire in a particular subject matter) and educational design experts (persons with an extensive repertoire in educational behaviorology). Such a division would provide an important foundation for further improvements to administrative contingencies that could enhance the effectiveness of education throughout an institution's programs. For instance, while design and content experts make equally vital contributions to the success of a course, one design expert can pair up with several content experts to achieve those results with many courses.

Curriculum Related Issues

The four programs described in detail here (of which three award certificates and one is the B.A. diploma) are not the first programs with behaviorological *content.* Most such programs, however, are embedded within the curricula of other disciplines or fields. For example, in the early 1970s, Joseph Morrow started offering an undergraduate, behaviorological science "Certificate in Behavior Modification" within the psychology department at California State University, Sacramento (see Ledoux, 1997a). Other examples are (a) the graduate training offered by Lawrence Fraley (see Fraley, 1996), Ernest Vargas, and Julie Vargas in education at West Virginia University, Morgantown, and (b) the graduate training offered by Jerome Ulman in special education at Ball State University, Muncie, IN. These are more appropriate because a number of basic *disciplines,* behaviorology among them, can inform an applied behavioral *field* such as education or special education, and some disciplines can do so more effectively than others.

Some programs are administered independently of other disciplines and fields. One example is the M.S. program with behaviorological content at North Texas State University (Denton) that Sigrid Glenn directs within a university unit separate from the departments of other disciplines or fields. In terms of resources, credibility, and stability, the establishment of programs *within academic departments of behaviorology* is preferred, perhaps with behaviorology departments being administered within larger academic units also responsible for other *life* sciences such as biology and culturology (i.e., natural science anthropology; see Fraley & Ledoux, 1997, Ch. 6).

Overview of the Certificate and B.A. Programs

The programs will be described here as if *they already existed so as to avoid excessive use of the subjunctive.*

These programs provide one of various ways to organize comprehensive behaviorology training according to differing student needs. Students might include (a) those who want to fulfill a Behavior Literacy graduation requirement, (b) those who are majoring in behaviorology at the A.A. or B.A. (or M.A./M.S.) level so as to investigate or enter a career as a behaviorologist, and (c) those who are working or studying in another human–service or human–development field for which they want behaviorological input.

Behavior Literacy. The first program leads to a *Behavior Literacy Certificate* (BLC, or simply "Literacy Certificate"). The BLC requires nine semester hours (three courses) including six hours (a two–term sequence) of Introduction to Behaviorology. The third course, The Behaviorology of Child–Rearing Practices, is important, for it ties behaviorology in detail to a vital component of the daily life of virtually every person, behaviorologist or not. The third course thereby demonstrates in a practical way the value of Behavior Literacy. If this third course is unavailable, then (a) its topic should be incorporated into the remaining required courses (even though this would mean covering less detail in this and all other topics), and (b) a special certificate would not be warranted. The criterion of completing an especially demanding, three course, higher education Behavior Literacy graduation requirement justifies granting a certificate. (Other literacy graduation requirements, such as Computer Literacy requirements, rarely demand more than a two course sequence and may never earn a certificate.)

The ABC. The second program leads to a certificate called the *Affiliate of Behaviorology Certificate* (ABC, or simply "Affiliate Certificate"). This certificate requires three courses beyond the BLC, for a total of six courses. The ABC is an intermediate step, at the undergraduate level, between the minimum behavior literacy repertoire, represented by the BLC, and the two more advanced programs, one for majors and one for professionals, both of which incorporate this 18 semester–hour program. In essence, the ABC is similar to an undergraduate minor. With relevant changes in course numbers and levels (as indicated in the requirements for the ABC), this program could constitute a reasonable lower division or two–year college major at the A.A. level.

The PSBC. The third program leads to a certificate called the *Professional Studies in Behaviorology Certificate* (PSBC, or simply "Professional Certificate"). This is a 30 semester–hour program with four courses beyond the ABC. The PSBC provides basic training for non–behaviorological professionals. This specifically includes persons working or studying in another human–service or human–development field. The PSBC is designed to add a solid foundation in behaviorological science to their professional repertoires so that they may take into account implications of behaviorological science for their work. Whether they hold a graduate degree, an undergraduate degree, or as yet no degree, such professionals may seek this certificate because it is similar to a minimal major in behaviorology (like a second, or double, undergraduate major); meaningful benefits accrue without needing further graduate studies outside their original areas of professional interest. Alternatively, they could seek a graduate behaviorology degree. (However, while the repertoire acquired through the PSBC is appropriate for bringing behaviorology to bear on work in various applied behavioral fields, the more extensive repertoire acquired through the B.A. program is the preferred background for further study in behaviorology.)

The B.A. The fourth program adds nine courses to the ABC requirements and represents a strong, 45 credit–hour undergraduate major culminating in a baccalaureate degree. This program is designed to lay a thorough foundation both for entry–level employment in fields where behaviorology is the appropriate foundation science and for further graduate level studies in behaviorology.

Program Parameters

Program requirements reflect the familiar arrangements of courses each having three contact credit–hours attached, with three laboratory hours replacing one contact hour, in a 15–week semester. (These parameters, while not the best known arrangements, are used because they are the kinds of parameters program designers will likely face when they begin a program proposal. Improvements can be a part of a proposal or can follow at a later time.) Also, the course numbers used here reflect lower division credit (100/200 level), upper division credit (300 level), shared upper division/graduate credit (400 level), and graduate credit (500/600 level). To fulfill the requirements for elective courses, a variety of additional behaviorology courses that could serve as electives are included in the list of course descriptions.

As is typical of natural science training curricula, and to make these program descriptions more useful to program designers, the courses in the programs of this natural science follow systematic sequences. Repertoires gained in early courses form systematic foundations for the contents of later courses. So the courses are listed in a preferred enrollment sequence, with prerequisites noted explicitly. Instances where concurrent enrollment (corequisite) could be allowed to replace a prerequisite are listed as well. (The preferred enrollment sequences could not consistently reflect the arithmetic sequence of the course numbers because the actual numbers were arbitrarily selected to keep, if possible, thematically related courses numerically close.)

Specific Program Requirements

Behavior Literacy Certificate. The following fulfill a comprehensive higher education Behavior Literacy graduation requirement:

1. **Behaviorology 101:** Introduction to Behaviorology I. (Includes Lab on basic principles and methods.)

2. **Behaviorology 102:** Introduction to Behaviorology II. (Includes Lab in simple applied research and methods. Prerequisite [Pre]: Beh. 101.)
3. **Behaviorology 201:** The Behaviorology of Child–Rearing Practices. (Pre or co-requisite [Co]: Beh. 102.)

Affiliate Certificate. The first three requirements are equivalent to those for the Behavior Literacy Certificate. Additional requirements follow those three:

1–3. (As in the BLC.)

4. **Behaviorology 320:** History and Philosophy of Behaviorology. (Pre/Co: Beh. 102.) [In an A.A. program, the course number would indicate the lower division level, e.g., 220.]

5. **Behaviorology 325:** Behaviorology and Culture. (Pre: Beh. 102.) [In an A.A. program, the course number would indicate the lower division level, e.g., 225.]

6. **Behaviorology 335:** Survey of Behaviorology Applications. (Includes Lab/fieldwork in measurement and applied methods and research. Pre: Beh. 201.) [In an A.A. program, the course number would indicate the lower division level, e.g., 235.]

Professional Certificate. The first six requirements are equivalent to those for the Affiliate Certificate. Additional requirements follow those six:

1–6. (As in the ABC.)

7. **Behaviorology 355:** Verbal Behavior I. (Pre: ABC.)

8–9. Electives: two behaviorology courses relevant to the student's professional area (see course descriptions).

10. **Behaviorology 496:** Professional Paper. (Pre: Beh. 355 and one of the electives; also, Pre/Co: the other elective.)

B.A. Program. The first six requirements are equivalent to those for the Affiliate Certificate. Additional requirements follow those six:

1–6. (As in the ABC.)

7. **Behaviorology 365:** Advanced Behaviorology I. (Pre: ABC.)

8–9. Electives: two Behaviorology courses (see course descriptions).

10. **Behaviorology 340:** Behaviorology in Education. (Includes a Lab on course and educational materials design. Pre: ABC.)

11. **Behaviorology 395:** Teaching Practicum in Behaviorology. (Pre: Beh. 340 plus the course in which the student is to assist.)

12. **Behaviorology 345:** Experimental Behaviorology: A Survey. (Includes Lab in course–related experimental research. Pre: ABC.)

13. **Behaviorology 355:** Verbal Behavior I. (Includes a Lab on verbal behavior [VB] research. Pre: ABC.)

14. **Behaviorology 385:** Behavior Technology: A Survey. (Includes Lab/fieldwork in course–related applied research. Pre: Beh. 345.)

15. **Behaviorology 495:** Personal Project or Paper, *or* **Behaviorology 496:** Professional Paper. (Pre: Beh. 355 and one other behaviorology course; also Pre/Co: another behaviorology course.)

General Program Requirements and Conventions

In these programs a course counts toward requirements by meeting an appropriate level of behaviorologically based educational evaluation criteria. These criteria combine percentage, frequency, and other applicable measures, in overlapping parts of an instructional sequence. For example, percentage measures would apply more during the acquisition of new behaviors to meet the original specification (mastery) of any particular educational objective of a course, and would then overlap with frequency measures that apply more to the performance improvement and maintenance specification (fluency) of those educational objectives. Such measures would be involved with each objective as a student progresses through the series of objectives for a course.

Differences in usage, however, require a clarification about the term *mastery.* In some circles, mastery means setting a criterion, perhaps at a high level, for students to meet for a particular grade, as an alternative to grading students on a statistical curve. But in the context of behaviorology training, and in the more general context of behaviorology–derived practices in education, mastery implies much more than just meeting a set standard. In these contexts mastery requires at least (a) that material has been prepared for presentation in numerous small steps providing for, and demanding, a high density of successful and properly consequated student responses, (b) that students are not allowed to move on to another component until they are competent on previous components, and further (c) that the material has been approached systematically so that acquiring a repertoire in later components *relies* upon having already acquired a competent repertoire in earlier components. (Through this last requirement, mastery automatically contributes to fluency.)

Based on their understanding of mastery and fluency, behaviorology program operators will specify both the mastery–generating instructional design as well as the criteria by which a student's passing a course will fulfill a program requirement. However, these programs operate within some administrative structure, and so will be required to state their design and criteria in terms amenable with the practices of that structure. (Discussion about improving those practices extends beyond the scope of this paper.)

Since administrative practices differ among institutions, an approximation of the relation between passing a course and fulfilling a program requirement provides an adequate starting point for program designers: For a course to count towards requirements, a student must pass it at the "A" level, representing a 90% mastery criterion combined with an appropriate fluency criterion. If a "B" or "C" is earned (80% and 70% respectively), the course might count for general academic credit but not toward these certificates or degrees until remediation to the "A" level has been completed. For a grade less than "C," the student must repeat the full course, completing it at the "A" level (by remediation if necessary) before it can count towards fulfilling requirements.

Assuming that the methods of educational design used to teach these courses invoke the principles of behavior being taught, these standards should pose no unreasonable barriers for the typical student in higher education. Ideally, students should complete a course at their own pace, based on established yet evolving mastery/fluency criteria, and then move right along to the next course, regardless of calendar terms. This pacing may differ from the classic self–pacing of PSI (Personalized System of Instruction; see Keller & Sherman, 1982). Some research (see Buskist, Cush, & DeGrandpre, 1991) indicates that the classic self–pacing of PSI may not be absolutely required for educational success.

Program Validation

TIBA, through its Academic Affairs Committee, is undertaking to provide some form of certification or accreditation for behaviorology programs. TIBA might then review those programs every few years. For a program to be called a behaviorology program, it would meet the criteria set by TIBA. As more actual programs come on line, numerous minor variations from recommended programs will occur. This type of variation is normal, usually reflecting continuing advances in the discipline as a whole, and should disturb no one. For instance, the courses and requirements for a physics degree at Stanford differ from those at Yale, but no one has claimed one or the other to be inadequate on that basis. With respect to behaviorology, the programs described here are merely part of a larger number of programs that could fall within a range of acceptable criteria.

A *range* of criteria is appropriate for a discipline based on selection. The programs delineated in this paper would change over time also, within a range of acceptable criteria. These programs would change both as behaviorologists become more effective with respect to behavior–environment relations, and as solutions to curricular problems arise in the practice of designing and operating actual programs.

Graduate Level Programs

Master's Program. With the PSBC or, preferably, the B.A. program as a prerequisite, a masters–level program might require 30 additional credits over nine or ten courses such as these (see the course descriptions for details on examples):

Beh. 475: Verbal Behavior II. (The course description includes a laboratory component on VB research. Pre: Beh. 355.)

Beh. xxx. An M.A. program includes at least one course, or preferably a two course sequence, on **research methods and measurement** that covers a measurement–based analysis of behavior at the level of the specific properties of behavior, and that uses more up–to–date sources to cover the behaviorological material contained in works like Sidman's (1988) *Tactics of Scientific Research* and Johnston and Pennypacker's (1980) *Strategies and Tactics of Human Behavioral Research.*

Beh. xxx. An M.A. program includes at least one **experimental research** course involving laboratory responsibilities (e.g., Beh. 450).

Beh. xxx. An M.A. program includes at least one **applied research and fieldwork** course involving research and/or technological responsibilities (e.g., Beh. 490).

Beh. xxx. An M.A. program includes at least one **seminar** course (e.g., Beh. 430, 440, or 465).

Beh. xxx. An M.A. program includes three to five elective courses (9–15 credits, depending on the credit value of the thesis, to bring the total number of credits to at least 30) determined in consultation with the student's advisor and considering the need for both generality and specialization at this level.

Beh. 600: Master's Thesis/Practicum. With 1–6 credits, as determined by the student's thesis committee in advance, and based on the scope of the work, this course should be taken in the final term prior to completion of all degree requirements.

A student may seek an M.A./M.S. degree in behaviorology without any previous behaviorology training. One starting point to plan graduate studies under this circumstance is to rely on the sequence of courses inherent in the system of prerequisites for required masters–level courses.

Ph.D. Program. Doctoral programs should require a third course, with a laboratory component, on advances in the analysis of verbal behavior. But beyond that, the more specialized nature of doctoral programs takes discussion of their contents beyond the scope of this paper.

Behaviorology Courses

Descriptions of Principle Courses in these Programs

Various behaviorology courses are described. These include a range of potential elective courses since electives are among the proposed requirements. Logical prerequisites are also listed. With the exception that either Beh. 495 or Beh. 496 fills the same explicit requirement, course numbers with an asterisk (*) indicate courses explicitly specified for the B.A. program.

Beh. 101*: Introduction to Behaviorology I. *Introduction to Behaviorology* is a two–course sequence, for both majors and non–majors, on the science of the variables controlling the behavior of humans and other animals. This first course of that sequence introduces the student to the range of components that comprise the discipline of behaviorology including (a) its philosophy of science and selection paradigm, and (b) its experimental methods, theory, and technology. The philosophy and paradigm include the criteria for natural science, the fallacy of inner causes, the significance of control and selection, the status of private events, and the behavior of the scientist. Methods include basic single–subject designs and measurement. Theory includes the fundamental natural laws describing the antecedent and postcedent relations between behavior and its controlling variables; these include such basic principles as added and subtracted reinforcement and punishment, extinction, simple schedules, stimulus control, and establishing operations. Technology includes the basic practices used to apply behaviorological principles to change accessible variables so as to change and especially to expand behavior repertoires through behavioral engineering. Basic techniques include differential reinforcement, shaping, fading, chaining, modeling and imitation, and time out. Other topics include superstitious behavior, emotion, escape and avoidance, and deprivation and satiation. The course includes a laboratory component on the basic principles and methods.

Beh. 102*: Introduction to Behaviorology II. *Introduction to Behaviorology* is a two–course sequence for both majors and non–majors. This second course of that sequence begins by introducing the student to the basic application of behaviorological principles and techniques to the prevention and solution of mild to moderate (non–incapacitating) behavior problems in the most common settings (e.g., child rearing, education, business and industry and organization management). The course includes a laboratory component on applied behaviorology research and methods, starting with the student changing his or her own behavior. The course also introduces analyses of complex behaviors and the variables of which they are a function, such as event–shaped and verbally–mediated behaviors, social behavior, verbal behavior, stimulus equivalence relations, multi–term contingencies, personal control, group control, cultural design, and various controlling agencies (such as in economics, education, government, law, religion). The course also includes analyses of (a) the preference for design rather than accident or chance in the control of both individual behavior and, especially, cultural practices, and (b) the relevance of science to ethics and morality. (Pre: Beh. 101.)

Beh. 201*: The Behaviorology of Child–Rearing Practices. This course covers, in two parts, the science and technology of behaviorology applied to the child–care repertoires of parents. The first part covers some methods applicable throughout pre–adult years which encourage the *prevention* of the common behavior problems of these years. Some common problems that can be avoided are associated with bedtime, eating, dressing, shopping, and automobile travel. Some methods to prevent these problems include "catch 'em being good," let kids help, monitor kids, orderly routines, time out, and other forms of discipline. The second part covers some methods applicable to helping distraught parents change problem behaviors that have occurred (i.e., "cure" techniques, rather than prevention techniques). Other topics include toilet training, language, intelligence, creativity, achievement, reading, Aircribs, and morality. (Pre or Co: Beh 102.)

Beh. 320*: History and Philosophy of Behaviorology. This course is an in–depth treatment both of the history of the emergence of behaviorology as a discipline and of the philosophy of science of this discipline, tracing the development of the philosophy since the early twentieth century, comparing and contrasting it with other philosophies of the times, examining its role in the emergence of the behaviorology discipline, and considering its implications for experimental and applied work at the individual and cultural levels. (Pre or co: Beh. 102.)

Beh. 325*: Behaviorology and Culture. This course is a probe of the relevance of behaviorology to cultures and their survival and improvement (a) by examining such previously progressive concepts as freedom and dignity and the current effect of these on the development of more effective cultural practices, and (b) by examining a range of scientifically based and improved cultural practices working in concert and producing a better world as represented in the behavioral "utopian" literature. The course includes coverage of the implications, relevant to the present and future of behavior science and its professionals, the culture, and the world at large, that are inherent in the later writings of B.F. Skinner (i.e., *Reflections on Behaviorism and Society* [1978] and later works). (Pre: Beh. 102.)

Beh. 335*: Survey of Behaviorology Applications. This course surveys the application of behaviorological principles and techniques to therapy and clinical behaviorology with respect to the common and uncommon solutions for moderate to severe (incapacitating) abnormal behavior problems in common and uncommon settings. The course includes the measurement and classification of the behaviors it surveys. The course also includes lab/fieldwork in measurement and applied methods and research. (Pre: Beh. 201.)

Beh. 340*: Behaviorology in Education. This course is an examination of the interaction between instructional design and human behavior in educational settings from two vantage points: (a) the theoretical, historical, and philosophical aspects of the facts of teaching and learning, including the reasons for effective and non–effective methods, the role of technology in teaching, and the teaching of thinking, motivation, creativity, and discipline, and (b) the practical aspects of the teaching effort, including teaching as the management of the learning environment, the measurement and evaluation of behavior change, the educational techniques of behavior change, and the expansion of the learner's behavior repertoire as a function of teaching. The course includes a laboratory component in which the student prepares and tests teaching materials, designs a course, and addresses the issues of systematic mastery, fluency, and cybernetics in instructional design. (Pre: ABC.)

Beh. 345*: Experimental Behaviorology: A Survey. This course surveys complex behavior–environment relationships including stimulus equivalence classes and complex schedules of reinforcement, as well as other complex antecedent and postcedent factors of which behavior is a function. The course includes a laboratory component on the complex relationships surveyed. (Pre: ABC.)

Beh. 350/450: Behaviorology Research Lab: General. In this course the student will assist in the ongoing work of two to four current research experiments, in two or more different laboratories or under two or more different project researchers in the same laboratory. For each of the two or more projects, the student will become familiar with the background experiments and issues of the project, the current work of the project, and some of the potential directions of the project. (Pre: Beh. 345.)

Beh. 355*: Verbal Behavior I. This course is an introduction to B.F. Skinner's scientific approach to considering language as verbal behavior (VB), including coverage of multiple control and the elementary relationships between the controlling environment and verbal behavior, plus investigation of the development and applications of this approach from its appearance, through evaluative and technological research reported in the literature, to the present. The course includes not only an introduction to the book *Verbal Behavior* (Skinner, 1957) but also reviews of the book (the book itself being more thoroughly covered in a more advanced course). The course includes a laboratory component on VB research. (Pre: ABC.)

Beh. 360/460: Non–Humans and Verbal Behavior. This course covers the research, controversy, and further developments in the non–human language field, emphasizing the work with sign language and primates as well as the implications of this research to understanding human verbal behavior. (Pre: Beh. 355.)

Beh. 365*: Advanced Behaviorology I. This course is a theoretical analysis of phylogenic and ontogenic contingencies. Topics related to this analysis include the design of cultures and the environments that produce the designs, the question of purpose in light of the experimental analysis of behavior, the concern with problem solving behavior and the related issues of event–shaped and verbally mediated behavior, the critique of theories alternative to this analysis, the question of whether or not "theories" of learning are necessary, and the problem of freedom and control as it relates to the control of human beings. (Pre: ABC.)

Beh. 370/470: Advanced Behaviorology II. In this course the student will learn to evaluate criticisms of behaviorological science. The course includes review of critical commentary, and response to that commentary, such as is available in the "Canonical Papers of B.F. Skinner" issue of *The Behavioral and Brain Sciences* (7, 4, 1984) and/or other similar sources. (Pre: Beh. 365.)

Beh. 375/475: Verbal Behavior II. This course provides comprehensive coverage of all aspects of verbal behavior (VB) as presented in the original work on this topic (i.e., the book, *Verbal Behavior,* by B.F. Skinner, 1957) and in more recent literature updates. The course includes a laboratory component on VB research. (Pre: Beh. 355.)

Beh. 380/480: Human Development. This course is an analysis of the phylogenic and ontogenic contingencies operating in the subject matter of the field of human development. (Pre: Beh. 355.)

Beh. 385*: Behavior Technology: A Survey. This course provides training in two major repertoires that are needed for effectiveness in the work of behavioral engineering: (a) training *about* the techniques stemming from the laws of behavior that are used to generate, maintain, increase, and decrease behavior in applied settings, and (b) training *in the actual use,* or application, of these techniques as reported in the research literature. The course includes a lab/fieldwork component in course–related applied research. Pre: 345.)

Beh. 390/490: Behavior Technology Fieldwork: General Experience. In this course the student will assist in ongoing behaviorological engineering work at two to four different field settings such as clinics, schools, and other institutions. Data gathering and paper presentation will be included. (Pre: Beh. 385.)

Beh. 395*: Teaching Practicum in Behaviorology. This course introduces the student to the application of scientific teaching methods (e.g., self–paced, systematic mastery and fluency designs, precision teaching, and instructional designs that are cybernetic) while the student practices these methods by assisting comprehensively in the teaching of another behaviorology course (such as Beh. 101 and Beh. 102). May be repeated for credit. (Pre: Beh. 340 plus the course in which the student is to assist.)

Beh. 440: Seminar: A Survey of the Contributions of Behaviorology. This course is a seminar on selected materials from relevant sources elaborating on the actual and potential contributions of behaviorology to a wide variety of applied behavioral fields and other disciplines. (Pre: ABC.)

Beh. 465: Seminar: Current Issues in Behaviorology. This course considers the major current issues in behaviorology as represented in current and recent issues of the discipline's journals, and in recent books in the discipline. (Pre: ABC.)

Beh. 485: Directed Reading in Behaviorology. This course provides directed reading on discipline–related topics or sources not comprehensively covered in other courses. (Pre: ABC.)

Beh. 495*: Personal Project or Paper. This course is a project (with a report), or a paper (with the goal of publication), relating behaviorology to (and/or improving, with a behaviorological perspective) the popular cultural view of a topic selected by the student and the faculty member in consultation. (Pre: Beh. 355 plus others that are program specific.)

Beh. 496*: Professional Paper. This course is a library and/or field research paper, with the goal of publication, relating behaviorology to the student's preferred applied behavioral field, including the importance, relevance, and contributions of behaviorology to the selected area. (Pre: Beh. 355 plus others that are program specific.)

A Selection of Additional Courses

Several additional behaviorology courses are probably more valuable to the advanced student, according to his or her specific career focus. So these courses are more likely to be found in graduate programs. Here, however, course numbers reflect both undergraduate and graduate status in order to show the relation of such courses to the courses already described. The amount of course credit earned will range from one to three, depending on variables inherent in the subjects actually covered. Here is a sample of such courses (an appendix in Ledoux, 1997b, describes the experimental and applied course *sequences*):

Beh. 346/446, 347/447, 348/448, 349/449: The Experimental Analysis of [a Selected Topic]. This course is an examination of the background experiments and issues of [the topic], the current work on [the topic], and some of the potential directions of research on [the topic]. (Pre: Beh. 345.)

Beh. 351/451, 352/452, 353/453, 354/454: Behaviorology Research Lab on [a Selected Topic]. In this course the student will assist in ongoing experimental research on [the topic], including the preparation of reports for publication. (Pre: Beh. 350/450 and the course on The Experimental Analysis of [the same Topic].)

Beh. 386/486, 387/487, 388/488, 389/489: Behavior Technology in [a Selected Setting]. This course is an examination of the concerns and issues relevant to technological applications in [the selected setting] and of the prevalent techniques (and their supporting research) that are used in [the selected setting]. (Pre: Beh. 385.)

Beh. 391/491, 392/492, 393/493, 394/494: Behavior Technology Fieldwork in [a Selected Setting]. In this course the student will assist in ongoing behaviorological engineering work in [the selected setting]. Data gathering and paper presentation will be included. (Pre: Beh. 390/490 and the course on Behavior Technology in [the same Setting].)

Beh. 430, 431, 432, ..., 439: Seminar on Behaviorology and [a Selected Topic]. This course provides a seminar on [the selected topic] in behaviorology. (Pre: ABC.) [These would be topics not covered in depth in another course. Examples of potential topics include ethics or epistemology.]

Beh. 441, 442, ..., 449: Seminar: The Contributions of Behaviorology in [a Selected Area]. This course provides a seminar on the contributions, both actual and potential, of behaviorology to [the selected area]. (Pre: Beh. 440.) [The selected area would be one that is not already covered in depth in another offered course. Such areas could involve the impact of behaviorology specifically in a particular human service, human development, or other applied behavioral field.]

Practical Curricular Development

The interaction of the local circumstances of a particular educational unit with program preferences, such as those inherent in the programs described here, will likely result in curricula well suited for that particular educational institution. Those curricula need not, even should not, mimic the details of the programs described here. These programs were devised without reference to the kinds of conditions that affect curricular design at the local level and which differ from one institution to the next.

Behaviorologists, through TIBA, their professional organization, will build and act on consensus concerning the curricula that produce more and better behaviorologists. Since TIBA will have arranged to certify or accredit training programs, behaviorologists involved in program design and development will presumably consult TIBA for guidance during the process.

Endnotes

In an effort to build further consensus, this paper was submitted to *Behaviorology* for full peer review (even though as a presidential address it was to be automatically accepted). On the basis of the full peer review, the paper was accepted by *Behaviorology.* Later, with incomplete explanation, the paper was transferred to *The International Behaviorologist* (TIB). As of the publication of *Origins and Components of Behaviorology,* the 1997 book of readings that included this paper with minor revisions, the first issue of TIB, in which this article was scheduled to appear, had not yet been published. (The bibliography in this book includes items that may be usable in some of the courses described in this paper. The paper had earlier received minor revisions for inclusion, by permission of *Behaviorology,* in the 1992 edition of this book of readings.)

The author thanks Guy Bruce, John Eshleman, Lawrence Fraley, Julie Vargas, an anonymous reviewer, and the participants at the presentation of the presidential address version for their helpful comments on earlier drafts. Address correspondence regarding this paper to the author at SUNY–CTC, Canton NY 13617–1096 USA.

References

Buskist, W., Cush, D., & DeGrandpre, R.J. (1991). The life and times of PSI. *Journal of Behavioral Education, 1* (2), 215–234.

Fraley, L.E. (1996). *General Behaviorology* (fall edition). Morgantown, WV: Lawrence E. Fraley (609–C Allen Hall, WVU, Morgantown WV 26506–6122 USA).

Fraley, L.E. & Ledoux, S.F. (1997). Origins, status, and mission of behaviorology. In S.F. Ledoux. *Origins and Components of Behaviorology.* Canton, NY: ABCs.

Johnson, K.R. & Layng, T.V.J. (1992). Breaking the structuralist barrier: Literacy and numeracy with fluency. *American Psychologist, 47* (11), 1475–1490.

Johnston, J.M. & Pennypacker, H.S. (1980). *Strategies and Tactics for Human Behavioral Research.* Hillsdale, NJ: Erlbaum.

Keller, F.S. & Sherman, J.G. (1982). *The PSI Handbook: Essays on Personalized Instruction.* Lawrence, KS: TRI Publications.

Ledoux, S.F. (1997a). An introduction to the origins, status, and mission of behaviorology: An established science with developed applications and a new name. In S.F. Ledoux. *Origins and Components of Behaviorology.* Canton, NY: ABCs. Reprinted with revisions from (1992) *Behaviorological Commentaries, Serial No. 3,* 11–31.

Ledoux, S.F. (1997b). Appendices. In S.F. Ledoux. *Origins and Components of Behaviorology.* Canton, NY: ABCs.

Michael, J. (1980). Flight from behavior analysis. *The Behavior Analyst, 3* (2), 1–21.

Michael, J. (1988, Aug.). What is and what is not our subject matter. Paper presented at the first convention of The International Behaviorology Association, Potsdam, NY.

Sidman, M. (1988). *Tactics of Scientific Research.* Boston, MA: Authors Cooperative.

Skinner, B.F. (1957). *Verbal Behavior.* New York: Appleton–Century–Crofts. Reprinted, 1992, Cambridge, MA: The B.F. Skinner Foundation.

Skinner, B.F. (1978). *Refections on Behaviorism and Society.* Englewood Cliffs, NJ: Prentice–Hall.

TIBA. (1989). By–laws of The International Behaviorology Association (approved: 1989 May 26). Reprinted, 1990, *TIBA Newsletter, 2* (3), 13–16.

Vargas, E.A. (1996). A university for the twenty–first century. In J.R. Cautela & W. Ishaq (Eds.). *Contemporary Issues in Behavior Therapy: Improving the Human Condition* (pp. 159–188). New York: Plenum.

Vargas, E.A. & Fraley, L.E. (1976). Process and structure: Reorganizing the university for instructional technology. *Instructional Science, 5,* 303–324.

Vargas, J.S. (1988). *Behaviorology for Teachers.* Morgantown, WV: L.E. Fraley.

Behaviorology in China: A Status Report

Stephen F. Ledoux

During the 1990–1991 academic year, I taught some English but mostly behaviorology courses in the People's Republic of China. I accompanied my spouse as part of a faculty exchange between her university, St. Lawrence University, and the Xi'an Foreign Languages University (XFLU) in Xi'an, Shaanxi. While there I held discussions, the chief source of information, with as many of the behavior science professionals as I could reach at different higher education institutions in Xi'an.

Upon my return many colleagues (both Western and Chinese) asked me to describe, *from my experience,* the status and directions of the natural science of behavior in China. Most of these colleagues, particularly those from China, requested that the description include the behaviorological context, a request with which I have tried to comply through references. Of course, "from my experience" means that, since preparing this report was not the point of my stay in China, I did not gather numerical data relevant to the expressed opinions and perceived trends mentioned herein. Perhaps those making future visits will collect appropriate data and report what more, or what else, those data tell us.

Circumstances (in some cases, the language barrier) kept the number of professionals I could contact small (fewer than ten). So I cannot guarantee that my comments or those of my sources represent the general views of China's behavior science professionals. But my sources were of the opinion that they did. They cited some interwoven factors to support that contention. (As the level of discussion did not involve data presentation, these factors are still speculative in nature.)

One such factor involves a culture–based propensity, unless the speaker has earned senior status, to qualify statements even when these have only a minimal chance of being wrong. For example, in casual conversation a junior faculty member is likely to say "*Perhaps* it has been raining" (emphasis added) when the window panes are observed to be wet, while a senior faculty member would forego the qualifier. This propensity is combined with a similar hesitancy to speak up in the first place unless you are sure you are right. My sources attributed these to the relatively large amount of "perhaps" culturally–determined embarrassment (loss of "face") experienced when one is in error in a context with a high population density as is common in China. Confidence that one is right, and hence a greater willingness to speak up, along with a reduction in qualifiers, gradually accrues with experienced seniority. As a result, what those with senior status say is acted upon out of respect for the speaker's status. The probability of verifying the statement is often reduced accordingly; the speaker is presumed to be right.

This paper developed as a response to the requests of some of the author's Chinese and Western colleagues who were interested in the professional experiences the author had during his teaching year in China.

My sources believed these related factors reflect the hierarchical nature of the organization of disciplines and institutions in China wherein senior members do most of the talking and junior members play more of a supporting role. The result is that Chinese professionals tend to qualify their answers to probing questions in inverse proportion to their academic and professional seniority. As seniority increases, the number of autoclitics (Skinner, 1957) decreases. For Chinese speakers, seniority, as opposed to variables implying statement accuracy, seems to exert more control over autoclitic emission than is common for Western speakers.

I gathered information I consider reliable under these circumstances because some of my sources were senior members of the behavior science disciplines. For example, one professional with whom I held revealing in–depth discussions holds seniority at least as great as that of the others, and enough to reduce qualifiers considerably. This source is Professor Fang Qiang. The entries on his business card provide some measure of his seniority. These include (a) Professor, Northwest Institute of Political Science and Law, Xi'an, Shaanxi, (b) Director, Committee on Legal Psychology, Xi'an Psychological Association, (c) Deputy Director, Committee on Criminal Remolding Psychology, Chinese Society of Science of Law, (d) Member of the Committee on Legal Psychology of the Chinese Psychological Association, and (e) Member of the Preparatory Committee on Psychology in Literature and Arts of the Chinese Psychological Association. Professor Fang did not have the opportunity to comment on everything. The comments he made, however, did confirm information from other sources when he and they covered the same topics.

The major points I discovered about behavior science in China are all interrelated. The most obvious point pertains to the nature of "psychology" in China, especially the recent historical problem of a break with some counterparts outside China, counterparts the Chinese consider important. This break left the Chinese discipline in need of updating. After working on the update for ten years, the Chinese thought the task completed. They are discovering that it is not and that what is still missing is what some call behaviorology. However, for behaviorology to be adopted to finish the update, the other major points I discovered must be considered. These pertain to the nature of higher education in China with respect to (a) its extent, (b) its requirement for demonstrated applications from "new" disciplines (partly as a function of its structure), and (c) the resistance resulting from retaining comfortable even if outmoded opinions about behavior science (including opinions about its paradigm and its philosophy of science). Each major point will be addressed in turn, after a description of the relevant aspects of my teaching context that hold implications for understanding and acting on the question of behaviorology in China.

Specific Context and Developing Behaviorology

My teaching situation exemplified some of the variables affecting the development of behaviorology in China. Hence, this section includes more than the usual details.

XFLU hired me to teach in two departments, English and Graduate Studies. Most of the college graduates in English from XFLU become language teachers, more than

80%, the majority in middle schools (similar to US high schools), according to department personnel. So the English Department asked me to teach an undergraduate teaching methods course to their "fourth grade" students (i.e., seniors) in the second semester. They called this course "Behaviorology and Teaching." Also, about 80% (by count) of the graduate students at XFLU *are* language teachers. So the Graduate Studies Department asked me to teach a graduate version of the teaching methods course at the same time. (I taught two sections due to the enrollment of other teachers as well as graduate students.) They called it "Behaviorology and Education." The content of both courses derived mostly from the textbook *Behaviorology for Teachers* (J. Vargas, 1988).

Most XFLU seniors take a traditional teaching methods course taught in their native tongue. This course surveys specific practices for particular circumstances (e.g., how to do vocabulary drills with second–year, junior middle–school students), plus theories and philosophies from various educational perspectives. That course spends little time discussing scientific foundations of teaching and learning. The "Behaviorology and Teaching" course replaced the traditional course for undergraduate English majors and (like its graduate–level counterpart) covered scientific foundations as well as the applications of these in education.

The Graduate Studies Department also asked me to teach a behaviorology course on verbal behavior (VB) in the fall 1990 semester, the first semester I was there. They gave the course the name "Verbal Behavior and Language Study." The purposes of the course were (a) to explore the behaviorological analysis of verbal behavior and (b) to examine the implications of this analysis for, and its applications to, the teaching of foreign languages. This department also offered a course called Psycholinguistics (only in the fall term of the academic year) which included coverage of Chomsky's language theories. Only English–speaking students could take these courses because the texts were in English for both of them. Due to subsequent demand, the Graduate Studies Department asked me to offer the VB course again in the following spring term.

Some students took both the Psycholinguistics course and the VB course. The comments from both students and faculty colleagues about Chomsky's theories are revealing. They told me that "Everyone in China who is involved in language training knows Chomsky's theories but, since applying them to language training is so difficult, if not impossible, few people show much interest in them; they are just something you are 'expected' to know."

When asked to teach these courses, especially the VB course, I expressed some concern: Starting with courses in advanced, specific application areas would sacrifice the more comprehensive understanding of fundamental principles and methodology that are necessary for skill development and successful work in applied areas. I further suggested that standard introductory courses would provide coverage of the main scientific principles and methods of behaviorology, preparing the way for advanced, applied courses, and that initially I should teach such an "Introduction to Behaviorology" course. But this suggestion received little attention, and I tried to find out why. The answer involves several interacting factors and helps show the complexity of some of the tasks facing those who would work to enable behaviorology to make its contributions to humanity's world–wide culture.

The Nature of Psychology in China

The use of the word *psychology* to translate the entries on Professor Fang's business card provides an initial insight into psychology and behaviorology in China. Professionals there use the word differently, to encompass far more, compared to the way professionals in Western countries use it. The Chinese use a word they translate as *psychology* to encompass the three sources they currently see for their discipline: traditional Chinese perspectives, the perspectives from the discipline in the Soviet Union (especially the work originating with Pavlov on reflex/emotional, that is, respondent, behavior), and Western perspectives.

The Chinese have included three parts in the Western component of their discipline: psychoanalytic (e.g., Freud), mainstream (that is, cognitive/mentalistic; e.g., Maslow and Piaget), and behavioral (that is, the science of behavior originated by Skinner). The Chinese report a special preference for the Pavlovian and Skinnerian work due to the natural science approach and experimental methods these two share.

In part, this preference for Pavlov and Skinner may be due to a particular aspect of Chinese history. The Chinese culture has been less burdened than Western culture has been by philosophically idealist dualism, a dualism that pervades Western culture. So Chinese culture has suffered less from the unscientific separation of phenomena into the different realms of mental and physical (soul/body, spiritual/material, mind/reality) that results from philosophical dualism. Western psychology traditionally prefers the non–physical aspect. (The Chinese language, while it has a rich variety of terms for most of the Western usages of the term *mind,* actually lacks a direct translation of mind as Western psychologists use that term—as a dualistic, uncaused metaphysical cause. Instead, for that usage, Chinese generally uses a word that, less appropriately, translates back into English better as "brain.") The combination of being less affected by the dualism problem plus China's modern preference for philosophical materialism enables Chinese professionals interested in improving the human condition to achieve greater progress at a faster pace than their Western *psychology* colleagues. The extent to which China's professionals make such progress depends on the extent to which they maintain their preference for philosophically materialist natural science when considering disciplines pertaining to human behavior. Progress also depends on maintaining an advanced level in the natural science of behavior; historical circumstances have, however, made this difficult.

The Break in Contact with the West, and the Quest to Update

The development of the Western components of the Chinese psychology/behavior science discipline has not been even. For thirty–odd years after the mid 1950s, Chinese psychologists were out of contact with the work, reports, and progress of their Western counterparts. Chinese psychologists spent the 1980s trying to rectify this situation. Their efforts to update the Western component of their discipline were many, including (a) short–term (one to three weeks) and longer–term (up to one year or more) personnel exchanges with their Western colleagues, (b) academic conferences both at home and abroad, (c) contact with current Western psychology journals and textbooks, and (d) Chinese students earning higher degrees (M.A. and Ph.D.) in top–rated psychology departments in the USA (e.g., Harvard). And they reported that they had believed that their efforts were virtually complete.

However, at the time of my visit, Chinese psychologists were coming to understand that their updating task was incomplete. They were seeing that their update had really been only of the psychoanalytic and mainstream components. Their update of the behavioral component had hardly begun because they did not realize that they were consulting sources that lacked the necessary information. The information they needed to complete their update has not resided in psychology or its literature since the 1960s. Increasingly in the 1950s, Western (American) psychology journal editors turned down behavioral studies partly because these studies lacked the technically required reports of statistical significance. In effect, those editors ignored the judgement (see Sidman, 1960 [1988]) that the *experimental* control methodology of behavioral research is scientifically more powerful than the *statistical* control methodology typically used in psychology. So behavioral researchers founded behavioral journals separate from the standard psychology journals and published their research in those behavior science journals as well as in their own behavior science textbooks. Their experimental methodology, with its emphasis on single subject designs, had produced, and continues to produce, discoveries of principles (see, for example, Fraley, 1996; Michael, 1982; Sidman, 1986a, 1986b; Whaley & Malott, 1971) and advances in practices and applications (see, for example, Beach, 1991; Christophersen, 1988; Clark, 1996; Cooper, Heron, & Heward, 1987; Epstein, 1981; Fraley, 1980; Johnson & Layng, 1992; Latham, 1994; Ledoux, 1982; Schlinger & Blakely, 1987; Sidman, 1989, 1994; Sidman, Wynne, Maguire, & Barnes, 1989; J. Vargas, 1988; West & Hamerlynck, 1992). These are all relevant to solving human problems and are related to further advances in extended analyses of complex human behavior (also see, for example, Cautela, 1994; Cautela & Ishaq, 1996; Fraley, 1988; Krapfl & Vargas, 1977; Skinner, 1957; Ulman, 1991; Vargas, 1996; Vargas & Fraley, 1976).

At the same time, in that decade of the 1960s, other developments were affecting the status of Western psychology. The so–called cognitive revolution, along with various economic and political contingencies (extensively analyzed in Fraley & Ledoux, 1997), gave rise to non–behavioral psychologists' increasing satisfaction with psychology's *transformation* paradigm. That paradigm is incommensurable with the *selection* paradigm of a natural science of behavior like behaviorology (see Vargas, 1991, for a thorough comparison of these paradigms; also see Fraley & Ledoux, 1997; Ledoux, 1997a). Psychology's transformation paradigm is also incompatible with the philosophy of science called radical behaviorism which informs behaviorology (for basics, see Ledoux, 1997b; for details, see Chiesa, 1994). Most of these developments happened after Chinese behavior scientists had lost contact with Western events.

As of this writing Chinese behavior scientists are realizing that they have been operating with a behavioral component that is over thirty years out of date. (They are also realizing that any dissatisfaction they may have had with the behavioral approach is as likely due to that factor as to any other.) By completing the update of this information, that is, by becoming familiar with behaviorology, Chinese professionals may decide to do some extensive re–evaluation of the relevance of the various components of their discipline, and perhaps even begin to shed the idealism–based parts.

Moves in this direction are already developing. Even the term Chinese professionals use for their behavioral component is noteworthy. That term is *Xingwei Xue* which the Chinese translate as *analysis of behavior, behaviorology, behavior analysis, behavior science,* or *science of behavior.* (Unfortunately, this means that the Chinese language has no current term that connotes what English connotes with the term behaviorology: a separate and independent natural science discipline.)

Chinese professionals also expressed dissatisfaction with what they describe as a lack of useful substance in the psychoanalytic and mainstream psychology components which they have already updated. They find very little that can be put to use to help deal with some of the practical issues that they face in their culture and society. Those Chinese scholars introduced to the wide range of research and applications reported in well–known *behavioral* journals (e.g., *Journal of the Experimental Analysis of Behavior, Journal of Applied Behavior Analysis, The Behavior Analyst, The Analysis of Verbal Behavior, Journal of Behavioral Education, Behaviorology,* and *Behaviorological Commentaries/ The International Behaviorologist*) express ample interest in behaviorology. They know that what they have in China is out of date, and they want to examine and thoroughly familiarize themselves with, and expand, behaviorological science and technology.

In summary, since the late 1950s, reports of virtually all the numerous, significant advances in research and applications in the science of behavior have increasingly appeared in journals and textbooks independent of the in–house texts and journals of organized psychology. So these developments have not appeared in the traditional *psychology* sources the Chinese consulted for their update. While Western psychologists have, since the 1960s, often claimed "Behaviorism is dead" (see Wyatt, Hawkins, & Davis, 1986), in self–contradiction they have also continued to claim it as their own. Yet all that time their version of behavior science *within* psychology was getting more and more obsolete. This obsolete version was all that was available to Chinese scholars for their update *from within Western psychology.* The information needed to complete the update is available in the literature of behaviorological science. For, as psychology's information became obsolete, the science in the West that Chinese behavior scientists have seen as the behavioral component of their discipline was becoming the separate, independent discipline of behaviorology, with its own disciplinary literature (see Fraley & Ledoux, 1997; Ledoux, 1997a; Skinner, 1989, 1993).

Developing Behaviorology: The Challenge for China's Higher Education System

The Extent of Available Training Opportunities

Chinese scholars face certain challenges in developing behaviorology in their country. One concerns the small number of training opportunities available in China's education system, at least as of 1990. Even though China's population is well over one billion, the Chinese report that they have few higher education institutions in China, relative to the population to be served (the historical reasons for this situation go beyond the scope of this paper). Only a few of those institutions offer training in Chinese psychology (behavior science). Even then, "Education Science" is the name of the discipline in which students earn degrees.

The following institutions are reported to be the only ones offering that training at this time: Those institutions that offer it at the B.A. degree level are: Beijing University, Beijing Teacher's College, and East China Teacher's College in Shanghai. Training at the M.A. degree level is offered by the Shaanxi Teacher's University in Xi'an, Hangzhou

University, South West Teacher's College in Chong Qing, and the Northeast Teacher's University in Lan Zhou. Doctoral level training is offered at Beijing University, Beijing Teacher's College, and the Psychological Institute of the Chinese Academy of Social Science in Beijing. (A few others may offer this training, such as Beijing Normal University, but the specifics of their programs were unavailable.)

The Requirement: Demonstrate Useful Applications First

Another challenge rooted in the circumstances of Chinese higher education is the apparent requirement that unfamiliar approaches (those that are "new" to China, in the sense of not currently being taught) demonstrate useful applications before receiving academic recognition, support, training in basics, and expansion. The difficulty here is that some of the most useful behaviorological applications are complex ones that *require* extensive attention to basics in the first place. How can this dilemma be resolved? Perhaps, by updating the old, still taught version of behavior science to behaviorology, this dilemma will simply be avoided. But that presents separate challenges, described in a later section, regarding the comfort of familiar, though outmoded, opinions.

The characteristics of my academic setting (described earlier) are typical results of the preference for applications first. These characteristics were: (a) the desire to have a behaviorology and education course taught that emphasized *applying* behaviorology to teaching methods and the high demand for this course, (b) the desire to have a VB course taught that emphasized *application* to language training and the high demand for and subsequent repetition of the VB course, (c) the low interest in Chomsky's theories "because they are not so useful/applicable," and (d) the current lack of interest in having *basic* behaviorology courses taught that introduce the discipline in depth rather than just emphasize a particular application area.

The effect of the education system's structure. The structure of Chinese higher education may itself be partly responsible for the "demonstrate useful applications first" condition. This structure is based on a need for applied specialists, the demand for whom is continually greater than the supply available from China's limited number of institutions. Most higher education institutions in China have an applied mission in a particular area (e.g., a petroleum institute, an architectural–engineering institute, or a foreign language university—the American concept of "general education" is not widely known). Such institutions often do not comprehensively teach (i.e., as "majors" themselves) the disciplines that inform their respective areas of application. Only a few higher education institutions in China have a mission broad enough to allow them to teach disciplines comprehensively. Some can do so for only one or a few disciplines (e.g., a music conservatory or a teacher's university). The few, more comprehensive universities can do so for many disciplines, usually providing training through graduate degrees. (The latter institutions often train the faculty for other institutions.)

Those institutions with applied missions are always sensitive to the possibility that other, perhaps "new," disciplines may provide contributions that can increase the effectiveness of personnel working in the applied area of the institution. When they find such a discipline, they "try it out" and the amount of success it shows generates commensurate demand. If a discipline "tried out" this way shows enough success, and generates enough demand, then those institutions with broader missions may begin teaching it comprehensively.

For example, if those who took the applied behaviorology classes at XFLU are more effective as teachers of foreign languages, then other teachers of languages and of other subjects may become interested in such courses. Other institutions may then start teaching similar courses, such as teacher's universities. In time, the major universities would begin offering comprehensive training in behaviorology, in part simply to supply properly trained faculty to the applied institutions.

Such a scenario began even while I taught the first VB course. The discussions about offering the behaviorology and education/teaching courses, and the VB course repeat, began halfway through that first term as the usefulness of behaviorology's analyses became apparent. Word of this usefulness quickly reached the Shaanxi Teacher's University (STU), next door to XFLU. That institution then asked XFLU to allow me to teach a section of "Behaviorology and Education" to its students and teachers in the spring term. (STU had to withdraw the request for financial reasons as the compensation XFLU requested, an amount in addition to my stipend for that section but typical in such situations, was more than STU could afford.)

But all this presumes that students of applied courses will avoid the danger inherent in the "demonstrate useful applications first" requirement. This danger seems to cause less concern than it deserves. The danger of the applications–only approach, of course, is that students who take only one or two applied–focus courses will not have acquired, from those courses, repertoires—in the principles, methods, and skills of the science—sufficiently advanced to meet the challenges that they will likely face.

Advanced repertoires are necessary for the long–term effective application of the science. Students lacking these repertoires are likely to encounter complexities and problems that they cannot adequately analyze or solve. They should trace these difficulties to their inadequate preparation in the repertoires of the discipline. But that same lack of preparation may mislead them to suspect, instead, that the discipline itself is inadequate and so not worthy of further study. That conclusion, shared generally, could substantially reduce the chance for behaviorology to receive the attention that would generate full training programs capable of leading to comprehensive contributions.

Establishing behaviorology training programs in the near future in China that initially cover the full range of disciplinary breadth and depth may be unrealistic. Without demonstrating its applications first, behaviorology has little chance of recognition there (although the multitude of published applied research studies may be demonstration enough). A first step may be (a) to teach only the basic skills of various applications along with the basic principles that inform those skills *at that level only,* while (b) at the same time continually pointing out, especially by examples from the applied literature, how more sophisticated skills can be learned and effectively applied when the more advanced principles and methods of the science are studied. Students taught this way may indeed blame their minimal training when they face problems that they cannot solve. They may then seek further training and thereby create the demand for more comprehensive training programs. (See Ledoux, 1997c, for a discussion of behaviorology curricula.)

Resistance from Outmoded Opinion

Another aspect of China's higher education that affects China's development of behaviorology is partly a function of the seniority–autoclitics relation described earlier.

This aspect concerns the amount of the science that is already known and the outmoded opinions about that knowledge that senior personnel may hold.

Repeatedly, Chinese colleagues pointed out that Skinner's work was followed through the 1940s and taught through the 1950s. But in the thirty years since then, little (including new advances) was available or taught. (Many disciplines faced this type of problem as a result of the derailing of the positive aspects of the Cultural Revolution by the Gang of Four.) Today, the behavior science being taught is mostly the knowledge available in the 1950s.

Chinese professionals' opinions of the "Skinnerian behaviorism" *that they know from the 1950s* too often hold that the principles of the science seem inadequate to account for the complexities of human behavior. The advances in the years since then, however, provide justification to change that opinion. This behavior science has proven as capable as, if not more so than, other disciplines in accounting for the complexities of human behavior. *Due to the lack of access to these advances,* however, many of China's behavior scientists have thought the science had stalled. Consequently, the low opinion of it went unchallenged. In a similar way, much of the credence Chinese colleagues have given to psychoanalysis and the cognitive/mentalistic mainstream may stem from the same factor. They have simply not had access to a suitable, more applicable, scientific, parsimonious, effective, and comprehensive alternative to those approaches. They are now appreciating that such an alternative is available.

Contributory Action

As a citizen of this planet, every human being has a stake in the successful outcome of efforts to bring the benefits of the natural science of behavior, behaviorology, to all the world's peoples, including the people of so populous a country as China. People who wish to contribute to such efforts are unlikely to have their contributions refused.

Western behavior scientists can make valuable contributions. Reestablishing contact with Chinese colleagues and engaging in personnel exchanges and conferences between countries are good examples. These are similar to the procedures already in use for updating and maintaining contact. But they must now occur to support the efforts of China's scholars to develop *behaviorological* science. (See Latham, 1997, for an important, explicit, practical, and justified suggestion along these lines.)

Other types of contributions by Western behavior scientists may be especially valuable in supporting these efforts. For starters, transfers of resources (e.g., behavioral textbooks and sets of behavioral journals) to departments providing behavior science training would help improve training contexts immensely, with all the subsequent benefits to the quantity and quality of behavioral research and applications.

Conclusion

The vast majority of Western psychologists lay claim to the level of behavior science available in the 1950s. They also often insist that behavior science is "dead" (Wyatt, *et al.*, 1986). Due to the advances outside psychology since the 1950s, the former is irrelevant. The latter is correct, but only *within* psychology; again, advances have been made and reported mostly outside psychology, in the natural science discipline that has come to be called behaviorology.

The advances in behaviorological science since the 1960s show its principles accounting for complex human behavior, and further advances are to be expected (for example, see Ledoux, 1997d). If behaviorology in China is to become a part of, and inform, the cultural–practice repertoire of the fifth of the world's population living in that country, then the resources of the whole discipline (with the advances since the 1960s, including the paradigm and other developments leading to separate disciplines) must be more thoroughly introduced to the professionals concerned with behavior in China for extension within that cultural context. For that introduction to be successful (with behaviorology being added to university curricula, leading to higher degrees and China's own laboratories and research in the science), the outdated opinions about behaviorological science must be modernized, and the "applications first" dilemma must be addressed and resolved. Expansion of training opportunities will follow, along with improvements in the behavior– and cultural practice–related services for the people of China and beyond. Material and intellectual contributions are appropriate actions in support of our Chinese colleagues in their efforts to meet these challenges.

Endnotes

Parts of this paper first appeared in the spring 1991 issue of the *TIBA Newsletter* (*3* [1], 4–5). Early versions were presented at the fourth annual convention of The International Behaviorology Association in New Orleans, LA, January 1992, and at the eighteenth annual convention of the Association for Behavior Analysis in San Francisco, CA, May 1992. The paper was fully revised for publication in *Behaviorological Commentaries, Serial No. 4*, pp. 24–36. Before receiving further minor revisions for inclusion in *Origins and Components of Behaviorology* (Ledoux, S.F. [1997]. Canton, NY: ABCs.), it received minor revisions for inclusion in the 1992 edition of this book of readings.

The author thanks those Chinese and Western colleagues who provided many helpful comments on various drafts of this material. Address correspondence regarding this paper to:

Stephen F. Ledoux, Ph.D.
SUNY–CTC
Canton NY 13617–1096
USA

References

Beach, S. (1991). Behaviorology and space settlement. *CONTACT Newsletter, 2* (2), 2–3.

Cautela, J.R. (1994). General level of reinforcement II: Further elaborations. *Behaviorology, 2* (1), 1–16.

Cautela, J.R. & Ishaq, W. (Eds.). (1996). *Contemporary Issues in Behavior Therapy: Improving the Human Condition.* New York: Plenum.

Chiesa, M. (1994). *Radical Behaviorism: The Philosophy and the Science.* Boston, MA: Authors cooperative.

Christophersen, E.R. (1988). *Little People (Third Edition)*. Kansas City, MO: Westport Publishers.
Clark, L. (1996). *SOS! Help for Parents (Second Edition)*. Bowling Green, KY: Parents Press. (Also available in Chinese.)
Cooper, J.O., Heron, T.E., & Heward, W.I. (1987). *Applied Behavior Analysis*. New York: Macmillan.
Epstein, R. (1981). Of pigeons and people: A preliminary look at the Columban simulation project. *The Behavior Analyst, 4*, 43–55.
Fraley, L.E. (Contributing Editor). (1980). *Behavioral Analyses of Issues in Higher Education*. Reedsville, WV: Society for the Behavioral Analysis of Culture.
Fraley, L.E. (1988). Covert mini–courts within judicial and law enforcement operations. *Behavior Analysis and Social Action, 6* (2), 2–14.
Fraley, L.E. (1996). *General Behaviorology* (fall edition). Morgantown, WV: Lawrence E. Fraley (609–C Allen Hall, WVU, Morgantown, WV 26506–6122 USA).
Fraley, L.E. & Ledoux, S.F. (1997). Origins, status, and mission of behaviorology. In S.F. Ledoux. *Origins and Components of Behaviorology*. Canton, NY: ABCs.
Johnson, K.R. & Layng, T.V.J. (1992). Breaking the structuralist barrier: Literacy and numeracy with fluency. *American Psychologist, 47* (11), 1475–1490.
Krapfl, J.E. & Vargas, E.A. (Eds.). (1977). *Behaviorism and Ethics*. Kalamazoo, MI: Behaviordelia.
Latham, G.I. (1994). *The Power of Positive Parenting: A Wonderful Way to Raise Children*. Logan, UT: P and T.
Latham, G.I. (1997). China through the eyes of a behaviorologist. In S.F. Ledoux. *Origins and Components of Behaviorology*. Canton, NY: ABCs.
Ledoux, S.F. (1982). *Control of Simultaneously Reinforceable Concurrent Human Operants by a Multiple Reinforcer–Source Procedure*. Doctoral dissertation, Western Michigan University, Kalamazoo. Reprinted, with extensive revisions, as "Multiple selectors in the control of simultaneously emittable responses" in (1997) S.F. Ledoux. *Origins and Components of Behaviorology*. Canton, NY: ABCs.
Ledoux, S.F. (1997a). An introduction to the origins, status, and mission of behaviorology: An established science with developed applications and a new name. In S.F. Ledoux. *Origins and Components of Behaviorology*. Canton, NY: ABCs. Reprinted with revisions from (1992) *Behaviorological Commentaries, Serial No. 3*, 11–31.
Ledoux, S.F. (1997b). An introduction to the philosophy called radical behaviorism. In S.F. Ledoux. *Origins and Components of Behaviorology*. Canton, NY: ABCs. Reprinted with revisions from (1992) *Behaviorological Commentaries, Serial No. 4*, 3–10.
Ledoux, S.F. (1997c). Behaviorology curricula in higher education. In S.F. Ledoux. *Origins and Components of Behaviorology*. Canton, NY: ABCs. Reprinted with revisions from (in press) *The International Behaviorologist, 1*.
Ledoux, S.F. (1997d). Increasing tact control and student comprehension through such new postcedent terms as added and subtracted reinforcers and punishers. In S.F. Ledoux. *Origins and Components of Behaviorology*. Canton, NY: ABCs. Reprinted with revisions from (in press) *The International Behaviorologist, 2*.
Michael, J.L. (1982). Distinguishing between discriminative and motivational functions of stimuli. *Journal of the Experimental Analysis of Behavior, 37*, 149–155.
Schlinger, H. & Blakely, E. (1987). Function–altering effects of contingency–specifying stimuli. *The Behavior Analyst, 10*, 41–45.

Sidman, M. (1960). *Tactics of Scientific Research.* New York: Basic Books. Reprinted, 1988, Boston, MA: Authors Cooperative.

Sidman, M. (1986a). Functional analysis of emergent verbal classes. In T. Thompson & M. Zeiler (Eds.). *Analysis and Integration of Behavioral Units* (pp. 213–245). Hillsdale, NJ: Erlbaum.

Sidman, M. (1986b). The measurement of behavioral development. In N.A. Krasnegor, D.B. Gray, & T. Thompson (Eds.). *Developmental Behavioral Pharmacology* (pp. 43–52). Hillsdale, NJ: Erlbaum.

Sidman, M. (1989). *Coercion and its Fallout.* Boston, MA: Authors Cooperative.

Sidman, M. (1994). *Equivalence Relations and Behavior: A Research Story.* Boston, MA: Authors Cooperative.

Sidman, M., Wynne, C.K., Maguire, R.W., & Barnes, T. (1989). Functional classes and equivalence relations. *Journal of the Experimental Analysis of Behavior, 52,* 261–274.

Skinner, B.F. (1957). *Verbal Behavior.* New York: Appleton–Century–Crofts. Reprinted, 1992, Cambridge, MA: The B.F. Skinner Foundation.

Skinner, B.F. (1989, May). A world of our own. Major address presented at the fifteenth annual convention of the Association for Behavior Analysis, Milwaukee, WI.

Skinner, B.F. (1993). A world of our own. *Behaviorology, 1* (1), 3–5.

Ulman, J.D. (1991). Toward a synthesis of Marx and Skinner. *Behavior and Social Issues, 1* (1), 57–70.

Vargas, E.A. (1991). Behaviorology: Its paradigm. In W. Ishaq (Ed.). *Human Behavior in Today's World* (pp. 139–147). New York: Praeger.

Vargas, E.A. (1996). A university for the twenty–first century. In J.R. Cautela & W. Ishaq (Eds.). *Contemporary Issues in Behavior Therapy: Improving the Human Condition* (pp. 159–188). New York: Plenum.

Vargas, E.A. & Fraley, L.E. (1976). Progress and structure: Reorganizing the university for instructional technology. *Instructional Science, 5,* 303–324.

Vargas, J.S. (1988). *Behaviorology for Teachers.* Morgantown, WV: L.E. Fraley.

West, R.P. & Hamerlynck, L.A. (Eds.). (1992). *Designs for Excellence in Education: The Legacy of B.F. Skinner (Limited Edition).* Longmont, CO: Sopris West.

Whaley, D.L. & Malott, R.W. (1971). *Elementary Principles of Behavior.* Englewood Cliffs, NJ: Prentice–Hall.

Wyatt, W.J., Hawkins, R.P., & Davis, P. (1986). Behaviorism: Are reports of its death exaggerated? *The Behavior Analyst, 9,* 101–105.

Increasing Tact Control and Student Comprehension through such New Postcedent Terms as Added and Subtracted Reinforcers and Punishers

Stephen F. Ledoux

The verbal behavior of scientists plays a crucial role in their continuing to operate effectively with respect to the principles and practices of their science. As behaviorology changes through advances in research and technology, the terms used to describe the parts and processes of the science may also change. If newer terms enable more accurate tacting of those parts and processes than the older terms, if newer terms enhance effectiveness and reduce confusion, then the newer terms may become widely adopted.

The concern with terminology is also often felt in circumstances where behaviorological scientists need to describe research variables, experimental findings, and the resulting implications and technological applications to persons not yet familiar with even the fundamental laws discovered by their science (e.g., students). If confusion is not avoided at this early point, it becomes even harder to deal with later when more complex issues receive scrutiny.

Over the last two decades, this author has considered the suggestions of various authors (e.g., Comunidad Los Horcones, 1987; Vargas, 1984, 1985) regarding the terms to use when describing the variables involved in behaviorological processes, especially in the fundamental selective processes of reinforcement and punishment. This author has also tried a variety of terms in the classroom. These efforts to improve terminology have been focused on terms which concern events in the position of the third term of the three–term contingency, the events that follow the occurrence of some type of behavior. In the last couple of years, a particular set of systematically related terms—some old and some new—has evolved from these efforts. This set of terms has been used successfully in the author's classroom. These terms evoke less confusion than other terms evoke; they seem easier to learn and use.

This paper presents that systematic set of terms. To start, it considers the problems addressed by these terms. Then it considers solutions provided both by particular terms and by the organization of this set of terms. This set also respects, and in a small way extends—through the use of the term "selector," the evolutionary perspective shared by the different levels of life–science disciplines (see Glenn & Madden, 1995).

The material in this paper evolved as the author regularly presented it to his classes starting in 1988. The material achieved its present form in early 1992. Four additional years of use with students showed little need for further revision at this stage.

Problems

Different terms have different histories. Some terms have had a long and useful history, such as reinforcers and punishers which denote the stimuli whose post–behavior energy change at receptor cells ultimately selects physical changes that appear later as changes in the frequency of behavior. Other terms, such as positive and negative that have been used to describe certain types of reinforcers and punishers, have a history of causing confusion. This long–standing problem needs a solution.

The confusion occurs because the terms positive and negative have connotations in non–technical language that compete with their technical usage. In everyday usage positive connotes good or pleasant while negative connotes bad or unpleasant. As a result people have some difficulty with the concept of a *negative* reinforcer strengthening behavior. They have even greater difficulty with the concept of *positive* punishment; they have trouble imagining much that is positive about punishment.

Another question is more of an issue than a problem. This question concerns how to integrate the various proposed terms that have arisen from the expansion of the science, and especially its conceptualization of causality, into a systematic set of terms.

Solutions

A solution to the problem of the terms positive and negative is to replace them with terms having the same technical connotation but not having other, competing connotations. The terms that the author has found to work the best with his students are the terms *added* to replace positive and *subtracted* to replace negative. These terms lack the complicating connotations of positive and negative. Yet at the same time they are consistent with the signs (i.e., + and -) used in the symbols for the several types of reinforcing and punishing stimuli. Furthermore, by using the terms added and subtracted, the replaced terms of positive and negative are still available to be used in their non–technical sense without confusion. That usage would no longer cause confusion with their technical usage because they would no longer have a technical usage. For example, using the common, non–technical connotations of the terms, one could speak non–technically of rewards and punishments as positive and negative consequences respectively without fear of automatic confusion with technical terms.

Alternative solutions to the problems of the terms positive and negative are available. The author has also tried replacing positive and negative with *plused* and *minused*, and with *additive* and *subtractive*. But each of these pairs had its own difficulties, and neither worked as well with students the way added and subtracted worked. Another suggestion, for which this author cannot claim originality, is simply to drop the terms positive and negative. But this alternative seemed to cause even more confusion for students, not less.

An answer to the question of how to integrate various proposed terms into a systematic whole comes from the hierarchical nature of the different questions about events that different terms can address. The focus narrows onto more and more specific characteristics of the events as these questions are asked: Does the event precede or follow the behavior? Does the event affect subsequent responding? Is the event produced by responding? Is the effect of the event to increase or decrease the frequency of the type of behavior the event followed? Does the effect occur when the event occurs as a presentation of a stimulus or as the reduction of a stimulus? (Each possible answer, of course, requires the next question to be asked more than once, with a corresponding increase in the number of terms properly applicable to a particular event.)

Different terms can be used to differentiate all the different types of events implied by the possible answers to those questions; the definitions of the terms also derive from the answers to those questions. The terms so used here are postcedents, selectors, consequences, accidental selectors, and the opposites of these (plus added and subtracted reinforcers and punishers as already described).

Postcedents (following Vargas, 1984, 1985) are events that follow responding regardless of whether or not they are produced by responding *and* regardless of whether or not they affect subsequent responding. The opposite of postcedents is antecedents (which will be discussed elsewhere).

Selectors are postcedents that affect subsequent responding regardless of whether or not they are produced by responding. The opposite of selectors is non–selectors; non–selectors are postcedents that do not affect subsequent responding regardless of whether or not they are produced by responding.

Consequences are selectors (affecting subsequent responding) that are produced by responding. The opposite of consequences is non–selecting consequences; non–selecting consequences are non–selectors (not affecting subsequent responding) that are produced by responding.

Accidental selectors are selectors (affecting subsequent responding) that are not produced by responding. The opposite of accidental selectors is accidental non–selectors; accidental non–selectors are non–selectors (not affecting subsequent responding) that are not produced by responding.

Figure 1 provides a diagram of these systematically related old and new terms for various postcedent events, in increasing specificity. Figure 2 provides even further specific details concerning consequences and accidental selectors.

The hierarchy of the terms can also be seen in the breakdown of the sixteen varieties of the selector type of postcedents. Of these sixteen, eight are produced by responding (called consequences) and eight are not produced by responding (called accidental selectors). Of each of these eight, four are types of reinforcers and four are types of punishers. Of the four types of either reinforcers or punishers (regardless of whether they are consequences or accidental selectors), two have their reinforcing or punishing effect when they are added to the situation while the other two have their reinforcing or punishing effect when they are subtracted from the situation. Of each two types of added or subtracted reinforcers or punishers, one is unconditioned (primary) and the other is conditioned (secondary).

A more general perspective is achieved by returning to antecedents, the opposite of postcedents. Antecedents occupy the first position in the three–term contingency as events that precede the occurrence of some type of behavior. Antecedents can be one of two types. (1) Antecedents can be events that both precede a behavior and affect that behavior; in this case they can be called setting events. Leigland, 1984, argued that the nature of the term *setting events* was rather general. He pointed out:

> The functional relations that *are* subsumed by the term include what may be complex or conditional discriminative stimuli, deprivation/satiation variables, and perhaps others left unspecified. (p. 42)

Yet this general nature is what makes the term usable here (also, see Vargas, 1985). Or (2) antecedents can be events that precede a behavior but do not affect that behavior;

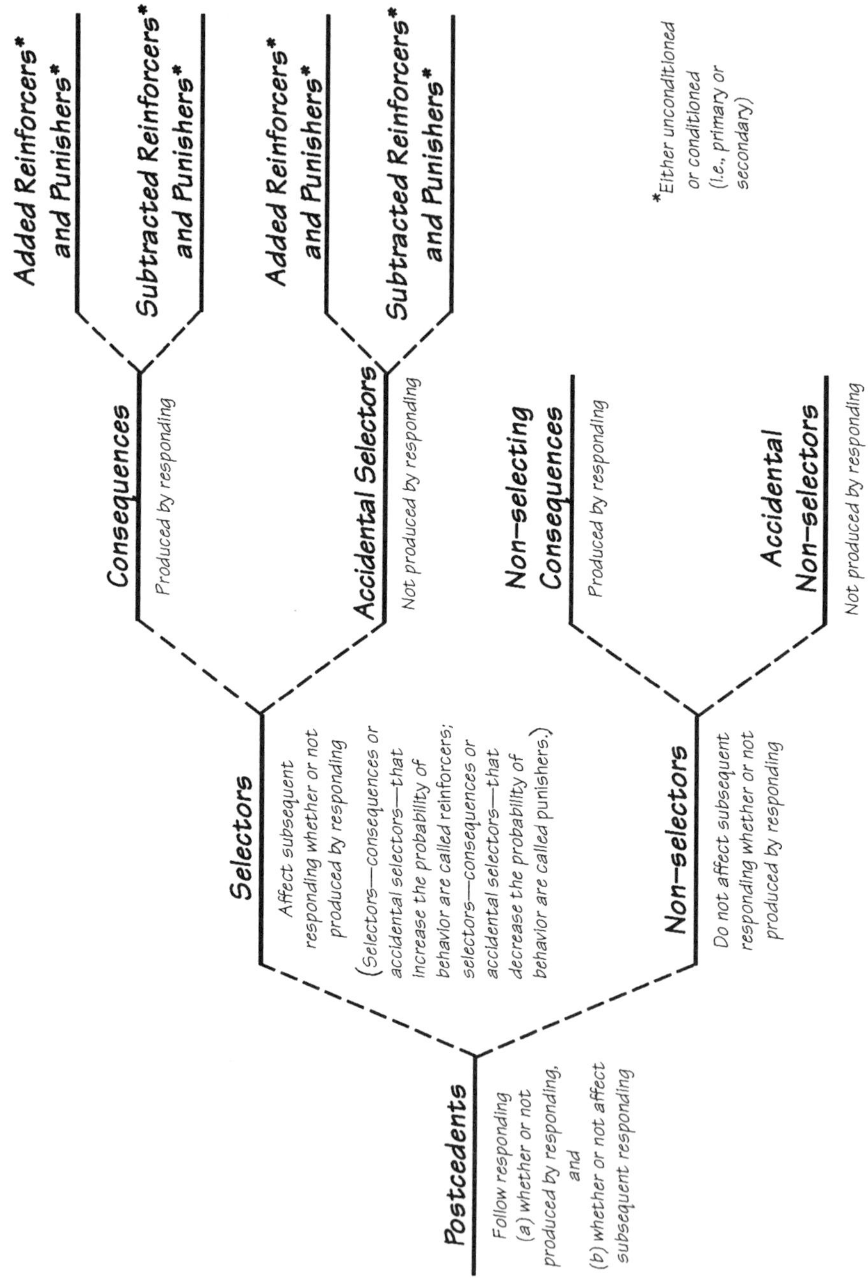

Figure 1. Diagram of the interrelated terms for various postcedent events in increasing specificity.

in this case they may be called *non–setting events.* Antecedents that are setting events can be of several types, including discriminative stimuli, establishing operations (Michael, 1982), abolishing operations (Leigland, 1984), etc. While this pattern addresses questions similar to those raised in the discussion of postcedents, further elaboration of antecedents goes beyond the scope of this paper.

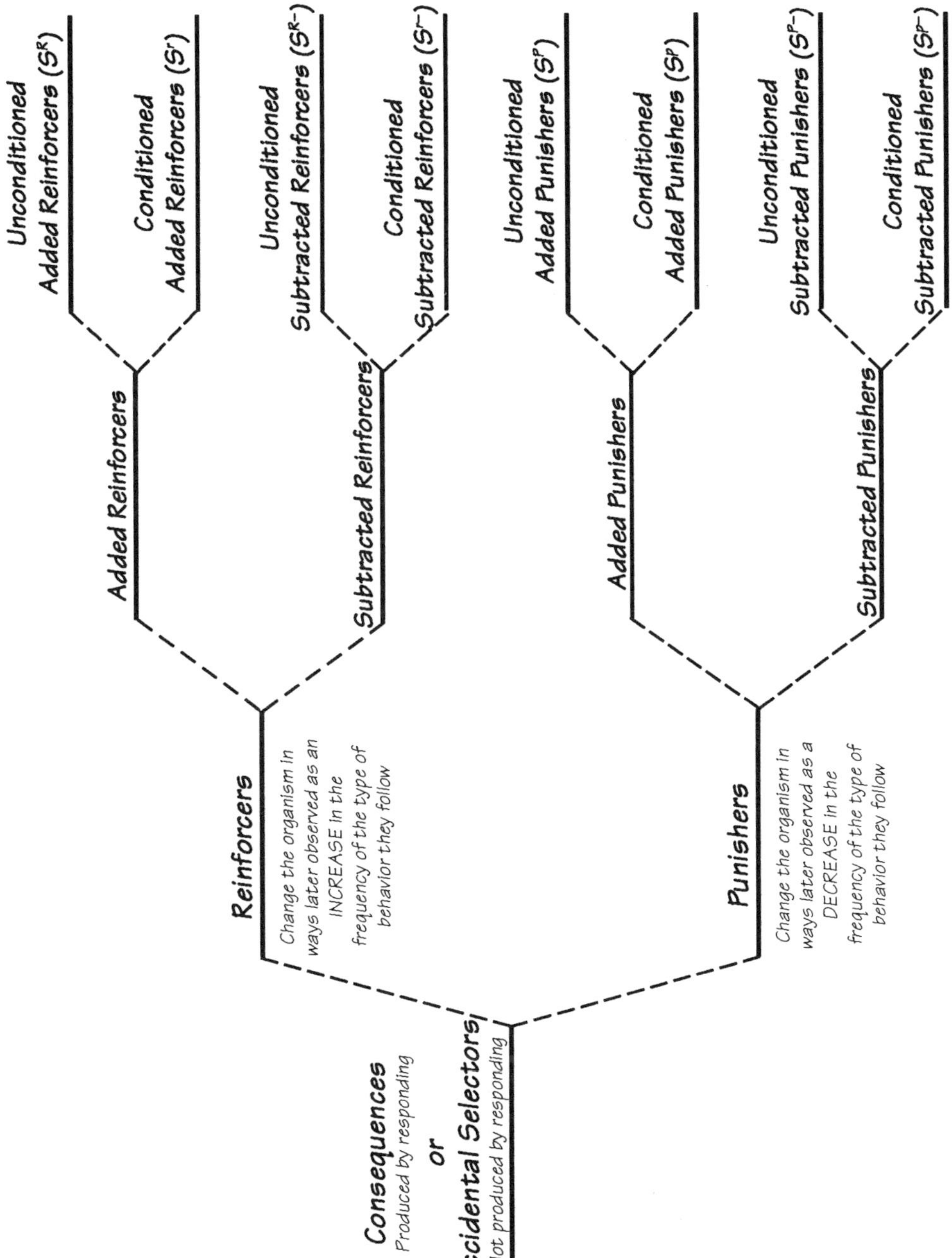

Figure 2. Details concerning consequences and accidental selectors.

Summary

In summary, the following conventions are offered as an adjusted elaboration of those provided by Vargas (1985, p. 132):

For the placement of events in time, use: antecedent—current event—postcedent.

For the general three–term contingency, state: setting events—behaviors—selectors.

For more specific three–term contingencies, indicate: one or more setting events—an overt or covert action, response (etc.)—a consequence or accidental selector.

For an explicit three–term contingency, specify (for example): a discriminative stimulus—a response class—an added reinforcing stimulus.

The author has found that the set of terms used in those conventions reduces the confusion about terminology that students in the past experienced on their initial contact with behaviorological science. Others who teach the science may find this set to be of similar value. Perhaps researchers in the science will also find their tacting to be more accurate, and hence their effectiveness enhanced, through use of this set of terms.

Endnotes

The author sent this paper to *The International Behaviorologist* on 11 February 1994. It has been in press ever since that journal reviewed and accepted it by early May 1994. That journal's publication schedule had fallen behind (see Fraley & Ledoux, 1997, Ch. 4), so the paper received further minor revisions both for presentation at the ninth annual convention of The International Behaviorology Association in Plymouth, MA, March 1997, as well as for inclusion in *Origins and Components of Behaviorology* (Ledoux, S.F. [1997]. Canton, NY: ABCs.).

Address correspondence regarding this paper to the author at SUNY–CTC, Canton NY 13617–1096 USA.

References

Cominidad Los Horcones. (1987). The concept of consequences in the analysis of behavior. *The Behavior Analyst, 10,* 291–294.

Fraley, L.E. & Ledoux, S.F. (1997). Origins, status, and mission of behaviorology. In S.F. Ledoux. *Origins and Components of Behaviorology.* Canton, NY: ABCs.

Glenn, S.S. & Madden, G.J. (1995). Units of interaction, evolution, and replication: Organic and behavioral parallels. *The Behavior Analyst, 18,* 237–251.

Leigland, S. (1984). On "setting events" and related concepts. *The Behavior Analyst, 7,* 41–45.

Michael, J.L. (1982). Distinguishing between discriminative and motivational functions of stimuli. *Journal of the Experimental Analysis of Behavior, 37,* 149–155.

Vargas, E.A. (1984). A new term and some old advice. *The Behavior Analyst, 7,* 67–69.

Vargas, E.A. (1985). The ABP noncontingency: A reply to "The ABP contingency." *The Behavior Analyst, 8,* 131–132.

Multiple Selectors in the Control of Simultaneously Emittable Responses

Stephen F. Ledoux

§

...There is no denying the importance of the methods and equipment which have been devised for long–sustained research, but there is also much to be said for an experiment that lasts half an hour—and for a quick and comprehensive look at the fine grain of the behavior in the cumulative record. (B.F. Skinner, 1976. "Farewell my LOVELY!")

§

This paper improves and broadens the author's report of a past behaviorological research study (Ledoux, 1982a). In its present form this paper discusses (a) the question of complex behaviors, especially multiple operants, and (b) an experiment on such operants using a method involving multiple reinforcer sources which the author developed in 1982 to help study these operants. In addition the paper discusses (c) how this method makes possible a research project that replicates basic research on fundamental operant processes while extending that replication to more complex, multiple operants, and (d) how such a research project can be a systematic and purely inductive investigation and cataloging of what happens when various basic contingencies include complex behaviors of the multiple operant type.

This paper refers to many research studies related to simultaneously selectable or simultaneously emittable operants. These studies appeared in the literature of "behavior analysis" when that was the preferred name for behaviorological science. That was near the end of the time period during which this natural science temporarily shared a history with the social science of psychology (see Ledoux, 1997a). The perspective of this paper respects that history as well as the evolutionary perspective shared by the different levels of life–science disciplines (see Glenn & Madden, 1995; also see Fraley & Ledoux, 1997, Ch. 6). As a practical result, this paper uses some terms that, while of more recent origin than the reported study, are still consistent with that history and perspective (e.g., "postcedents" and "selectors"; see Ledoux, 1997b; Vargas, 1985).

This paper extensively revises the author's report of an older research study to highlight the impact further research based on this study can have on the natural science understanding of complex human behavior.

The simultaneous occurrence of operant responses is an aspect of the behavior of animals, especially humans. Operants regularly, although not always, operate on the environment in ways that provide the selectors that act upon these operants as their own selecting consequences. Since selectors affect any operant whose occurrence precedes them, an operant that occurs simultaneously, or even nearly so, with one or more other operants may be affected by the occurrence of any selectors following any of these operants. In addition, the operant that is producing a particular selecting consequence is sometimes discriminable, and at other times it may not be; this may also affect the selection processes. The effective understanding of why people do what they do, and what can be done about it, requires investigation of these phenomena.

In the dozen years since the research reported here on simultaneously selectable and simultaneously emittable multiple operants was done, the study of complex human behavior has little pursued work on such operants. Instead researchers have focused on other valuable research lines (e.g., on stimulus equivalence; see Sidman, 1994). Some possibly important discoveries must await research into the effects of simultaneous selectors on simultaneously emittable multiple operants.

Introduction

Sometimes complex behavior appears not to be "sensitive" to observed contingencies (i.e., it does not change in ways that observers of those contingencies would predict). Many reasons for this are possible. For instance, some possibly competing contingencies may not be visible to observers. The reasons in particular cases are often unknown. Research should focus on discovering and controlling for these reasons. But research should also do more.

Behaviorological research should develop and promote the use of procedures that improve the sensitivity of behavior to the contingencies in effect because the veracity of data–based conclusions relies on behavior being sensitive to those contingencies. This especially holds in studies of concurrent operants where interactions often occur that might confound the data. Thus, the search for procedures producing greater independent sensitivity of each operant in a multiple operant study is a continuing one. Research on parameters such as the length of change–over delays (CODs) exemplify this search (Allison & Lloyd, 1971; Fantino, Squires, Delbruck, & Peterson, 1972; Pliskoff, 1971; Stubbs & Pliskoff, 1969).

Efforts to enlarge the *range of behaviors* affected by sensitivity enhancing procedures should also increase. Unfortunately, this does not appear to have been the case with previous concurrent operant research where the application of sensitivity enhancing procedures has been limited to behaviors for which these procedures can establish response independence (from confounding schedule effects) *through response succession.*

The discussion in the next three sections reviews that situation, offers a possible explanation of why it occurred, and suggests a line of research using a new procedure to improve "sensitivity" (i.e., functional response independence) and reduce concurrent superstition, all without requiring response succession. This research line also seeks to expand the range of behaviors that show enough sensitivity to make studying them productive. One type of behavior that can be included in the expanded range is simultaneously reinforceable concurrent human operants. ("Simultaneously reinforceable" means that a response on one manipulandum can be selected at the same time that a response on another manipulandum is selected; this implies that the manipulanda are simultaneously available, and that the responses are simultaneously emittable.)

The pivot point for discussing the historical context, present status, and future behaviorological research possibilities with respect to simultaneously reinforceable concurrent operants is Charles Catania's book chapter "Concurrent Operants" (Catania, 1966). At the time the research reported in this paper occurred, this chapter was the seminal treatment of issues affecting research in concurrent operants, including formal aspects of programming, classification of concurrent operants, schedule effects, local interactions, quantitative relations, and various preferences. This book chapter set the pace for nearly all subsequent concurrent operant research. But that turned out to be, in some ways, a hindrance as well as a help.

Historical Background

One difficulty is that Catania's book chapter did not attempt to deal with *simultaneously reinforceable* concurrent operants. In addition, his discussions of procedures, subjects, and future lines of research were such as to reduce researchers' further interest in this type of concurrent operants. This section, after dealing with the issue of definitions, will review studies that *are* relevant to simultaneously reinforceable concurrent operants, and thereby expand on Catania's coverage.

Definitions. In *Schedules of Reinforcement,* Ferster and Skinner (1957) defined concurrent operants as:

> Two or more responses, of different topography at least with respect to locus, capable of being executed with little mutual interference *at the same time* or in rapid alteration, under the control of separate programming devices (e.g., responses to two keys present at the same time under separate schedules). (p. 724, emphasis added)

Catania quotes this definition on his first page, but he proceeds to say "In the case of concurrent operants, the organism's alternatives are...to emit one or another of the available operants" (p. 213). But for his definition to agree with the Ferster/Skinner definition, it would have to read "...to emit one or another *or both* of the available operants." This difference is significant; Catania's definition led, as will be seen, to constraints on the directions subsequent researchers were inclined to take.

The basis of this definitional omission, which pertains to the question of whether response succession is required or not for response independence, and why, will be detailed later. For now, successive responses, in Catania's view, *are* required as they make the occurrence of concurrent superstitions avoidable (Catania and Cutts, 1961, defined concurrent superstition as the accidental correlation of one operant with the reinforcement produced by a different operant; compare this with simple superstition which is a correlation of a response with accidental, non–contingent reinforcement). Catania (1966) further suggests that the use of a COD is the most reasonable way to obtain successive responses. But CODs may not be necessary because obtaining successive responses is only one way to generate independence of schedule effects.

Related research. Ferster (1957, 1959) follows the definition of concurrent operants that he published with Skinner. In his 1957 study, the responses were simultaneously emittable and simultaneously reinforceable. Chimpanzees pressed two keys, one with each hand. The schedule for the two keys was concurrent (CONC) variable interval (VI)

4′ fixed ratio (FR) 120 (i.e., CONC VI 4′ FR 120). These schedules were selected because, when presented singly, they generate quite different yet stable response patterns; so when presented concurrently, the researcher might more quickly notice changes in the response pattern under either schedule. Results showed only minor changes in schedule patterns from those typical of single schedules, and it would be difficult to attribute these changes solely, even mainly, to superstitious effects from simultaneous reinforcement of both responses by one or the other schedule. One interesting observation was that the subjects continued to operate the VI key, at the same rate as before, while eating food from the magazine with the FR hand.

Ferster (1957) preferred to use simultaneously reinforceable operants because "the time spent changing back and forth between the keys would interfere with the characteristic performance under the single schedule of reinforcement" (p. 1090). Ferster also points out the relevance of studying simultaneously reinforceable operants to such human behaviors as piano playing where sometimes each hand must deal with a different rhythm, as well as different notes. And he mentions an additional benefit from studying these operants. The rate from one key can be used to measure any emotional side effects from changes in the schedule on the other key.

Ferster's 1957 study was expanded in his 1959 study. This time the chimps were exposed to a variety of concurrent schedules, including fixed interval (FI) components in complex schedules that involved both concurrent and multiple (MULT) schedules like CONC VI 10′ MULT FR 475–FI 10′. While the data showed fairly consistent independence of schedule effects for each key, some observations were especially interesting. Virtually no scallops appeared during FIs; less responding occurred, from more pausing, on the VI key during FR runs; extinction on the VI key correlated with a small decrement in FI responding; and chimps do not usually sustain high FRs (e.g., FR 475), but these chimps did, perhaps due to minimal superstitious effects of occasional VI reinforcers, especially those occurring during an FR run. (Such an effect is worthy of research in its own right as a possible additional behavior maintenance procedure, or resistance to extinction procedure, in the technology of behavior control.)

Between the appearance of Ferster's two studies, Sidman (1958) published a study using simultaneously reinforceable concurrent operants *and more than one source of reinforcement.* (This was one of two such studies; the other was Hearst, 1961.) Actually, in Sidman's study, the use of dual reinforcer sources was forced by the nature of the schedules. Sidman investigated the effects of a superimposed pre–shock stimulus on concurrent schedules of avoidance and food reinforcement. He initially trained monkeys on CONC VI 4′, avoidance schedules, and included, in some phases, a "free" shock with a pre–shock stimulus. He then tested for any effects, on relative rates of lever pressing, from the superimposition of the free shock/pre–shock stimulus on the CONC VI, avoidance schedule. Even after making various parameter changes on the VI, avoidance schedule, his results consistently showed VI responding being highly controlled by the avoidance contingency. This superstition occurred regardless of whether the response topographies were the same (2 levers) or different (a lever and a chain). So Sidman then changed the VI components to FR components. From repeating the basic procedure with conc FR, avoidance schedules, his results indicated separation of each response class. Thus, Sidman's study exemplifies what will be seen to be a common problem. When results of using VIs as concurrent schedule components are compared with results from using components involving other schedules, the VI results are associated with a greater degree of concurrent superstition.

Five other studies (in the order discussed here: Segal, 1961; Lane, 1961; Hearst, 1961; Bruner & Revusky, 1961; Catania & Cutts, 1963) are relevant to the question of dealing with concurrent superstition, particularly in simultaneously reinforceable concurrent operants. Each will be described in turn, while the various reasons for their relevance will be summarized at the end of this section.

Segal (1961) was interested in demonstrating experimental control over DRL (differential reinforcement of low rate) timing behavior by setting up another response as the timing behavior itself, but on an independent schedule. She did this by training rats to press two levers on CONC VI 1′ DRL 18″. (The responses were not simultaneously reinforceable unless the rats could span the five inches that separated the levers.) Then, extinction (EXT) replaced one schedule component or the other (sometimes CONC EXT DRL; other times CONC VI EXT). Additional component combinations were also tested. The data showed that each concurrent component affected the other, at least initially when it was introduced. For instance, after being replaced by extinction, when the DRL component was re–introduced, the VI response pattern was temporarily disrupted, recovering within a few sessions. Thus, in this study, the occurrence of concurrent superstition, even with time–based schedules, was not a lasting effect.

Lane (1961) investigated the effects of various CONC FR FR schedules on the chirping and pecking of chicks (responses which, in his view, were not incompatible in topography). While the responses were thus simultaneously reinforceable, he found that they were seldom emitted simultaneously. More importantly, he observed some superstitious relations between the two operants and their respective schedules. The rate of chirping changed in the same direction as the rate of pecking, when the pecking schedule was altered. Thus, in this study, while the responses seldom occurred simultaneously, concurrent superstition was still observed with ratio–based schedules; Lane suggested four possible reasons, but these are relevant to the present paper only as reminders that the sources of superstitious effects are many.

Hearst (1961) was interested in whether d–amphetamine would suppress operant response rates as it does consummatory responses. He found that it did so, in a dose–related manner, by exposing rats to different drug doses after they had been trained to press two levers concurrently (CONC VI 2′ VI 2′). The relevance of this study to the present topic is mainly procedural, for while the levers were too far apart for responses to be simultaneously emittable, this study is the only other study besides Sidman (1958) to use two different reinforcer sources. As with Sidman's study, the use of two sources was forced by an aspect of the study; in this case it was forced because one reinforcer was food and the other reinforcer was water.

Bruner and Revusky (1961) wanted to make overt, and record, the "collateral" behavior occurring in the interval prior to the availability of a response–produced reinforcer on a DRL schedule. They did this by having humans press four telegraph keys on a CONC EXT EXT DRL EXT schedule. (The DRL was >8.2″ but <10.25″.) The keys were simultaneously available but the responses were not officially simultaneously emittable (and therefore not simultaneously reinforceable) as instructions were used to generate response succession; the subjects had been instructed to press only one key at a time. The data clearly showed each subject emitting a respectively different but stereotyped pattern of superstitious behavior. Thus, this study also shows superstition with human subjects on time–based schedules, with responses that were successive rather than simultaneously reinforceable.

Catania and Cutts (1963), from an interest in controlling concurrent superstition, attempted to gain experimental control over button–press responses of human subjects on a CONC VI 30″ EXT schedule. In their procedure, some subjects experienced no COD; others had a full session with a COD; for still others, a COD began sometime in the session. Data showed that a COD decreased the amount of superstitious responding.

The work of Catania and Cutts (1963) represents a watershed for research bearing on the present topic prior to the appearance of Catania's 1966 book chapter. This study lays the foundation for saying that concurrent superstition must be avoided—and response independence generated—*through a procedure that separates responses in time* (i.e., generates response succession) such as a COD. Still, the authors go on to point out a number of characteristics about humans that may make even CODs inadequate for this purpose. Furthermore, the subjects had been instructed to press only one button at a time, so even the responses of those subjects experiencing no CODs were not officially simultaneously emittable. Other observations of Catania and Cutts (1963) are also worth noting. There was much variability in superstition across subjects who experienced no COD. On the other hand even subjects with CODs for their full session showed various superstitions. These facts provide some good reasons to seek alternative procedures to CODs for avoiding concurrent superstitions, especially with human subjects (and these reasons are in addition to the incompatibility of CODs with simultaneously emittable, simultaneously reinforceable operants).

Historically, Catania's 1966 book chapter appeared before the last two studies to be discussed. But since its impact is felt mainly in the next section of this paper, it will be sufficient here to note that in the end, Catania advised researchers studying concurrent operants to avoid concurrent superstitions by generating response independence through the use of CODs, making responses successive. With few exceptions, researchers have abided by Catania's advice. Two exceptions will be discussed (Striefel, 1972; then Harrison, 1979).

In Striefel's (1972) study, human subjects operated separate levers under different concurrent FR pairs. Ten different FR pairs were tested per subject. For all subjects the initial preference was always for the shorter of the pair of FR components. Then, a time–out period was introduced at the completion of each preferred component. This period was increased in one–second increments until the subject switched from the preferred but punished component of the pair to the previously non–preferred and unpunished component. After the number of completed "non–preferred" ratios had reached a criterion, a new concurrent FR pair was introduced. Data showed that as the difference between the components of the FR pairs increased, the time–out duration which generated switching also increased. Procedurally, while the levers were simultaneously available, the responses were not officially simultaneously emittable as the subjects were instructed to operate only one lever at a time. The study is pertinent to the present topic for this reason, as well as for not using any COD.

In Harrison's (1979) study, the responses were only potentially simultaneously reinforceable due to the trial–by–trial nature of the procedure (where the first response made ended the trial). Harrison trained rats to press one lever in the presence of sound from one speaker, and another lever in the presence of sound from another speaker. The discriminative stimulus (S^D) was the position of the sounding speaker. For some subjects, responding on the lever adjacent to the speaker that sounded was reinforced; for other subjects, non–adjacent responding was reinforced. Data showed that rats that were reinforced for adjacent responding learned the discrimination quickly and with very little non–adjacent responding. However, rats that were reinforced for non–adjacent responding learned much more slowly. Also, the latter rats started out responding on the non–reinforced lever (the lever adjacent to the sounding speaker) at a high rate which increased before extinguishing (though never completely) as responding on the reinforced lever (the non–adjacent lever) gained strength. Further experiments controlled for novelty and respondent conditioning explanations of this effect, which seems less reminiscent of concurrent superstition than of the type of behaviors observed in autoshaping studies (discussed by Staddon & Simmelhag, 1971).

Historical background summary. A review of some characteristics of the studies that have been considered here will help summarize their contents and highlight their relevant aspects. These characteristics fall into three categories: the species of the subject, the status of the particular operants involved regarding simultaneous reinforcement, and the presence and nature of any superstition.

The subjects in these studies fit four classifications: birds (Lane, 1961, with chicks); rodents (Harrison, 1979; Hearst, 1961; and Segal, 1961; all with rats); non–human primates (Ferster, 1957, 1959, with chimps; Sidman, 1958, with monkeys); and humans (Bruner & Revusky, 1961; Catania & Cutts, 1963; and Striefel, 1972).

Regarding the second category of characteristics, each study can be classified (a) as using actually simultaneously reinforceable concurrent operants, (b) as using concurrent operants whose status as being actually simultaneously reinforceable is ambiguous and in need of qualification, or (c) as using only potentially simultaneously reinforceable concurrent operants. While none of these studies used non–simultaneously reinforceable operants, qualifications to the status of the operants in most of these studies should be noted. (Non–simultaneously reinforceable operants are "biologically successive" operants such as pigeons make when faced with two keys to peck which they are genetically incapable of pecking simultaneously for they have but one head. Catania [1966] refers to these as incompatible operants.)

Three studies used actually simultaneously reinforceable operants. These are the studies by Ferster (1957, 1959) and by Sidman (1958).

For three other studies (Harrison, 1979; Lane, 1961; and Segal, 1961) the possible use of actually simultaneously reinforceable operants requires qualification. Segal's rats had to be able to span the five inches separating the two levers if their responses were to be simultaneously reinforceable, and Segal did not comment on whether or not the rats could or did accomplish this unlikely reach. Lane's chicks seldom emitted their responses simultaneously, and Lane offered no special comments about this phenomenon. And Harrison's trial–by–trial procedure made it difficult to say more about the responses he studied other than that they were procedurally simultaneously emittable.

The other four studies used potentially simultaneously reinforceable operants. They can be classified according to the manner in which their simultaneous reinforcement status came to be only potential rather than actual. One method to do this is to completely separate the responses through the structure of the apparatus; these responses might then be called "structurally successive" (as when Hearst, 1961, spaced the levers so far apart that they could not be pressed simultaneously). Another method that detracts from the simultaneity of the responses is the practice of instructing human subjects not to emit more than one response at a time; this makes the responses "instructionally successive" (as with Bruner & Revusky, 1961; Catania & Cutts, 1963; and Striefel, 1972). A third method involves the use of a COD contingency; this makes the responses "contingently successive" (as with Catania & Cutts, 1963).

The third category of characteristics shared by these studies concerns the presence and nature of superstitious effects, or their absence (i.e., response independence). Each study deserves separate comment on this matter as the particular schedules involved differ from one study to the next.

- Ferster (1957) found little or no superstition with CONC VI 4′ FR 120.
- Sidman (1958) found consistent concurrent superstition with CONC VI, avoidance schedules, but obtained separation of response classes with CONC FR, avoidance schedules.
- Ferster (1959) found fairly consistent independence of schedule effects with complex schedules like CONC VI 10′ MULT FR 475–FI 10′, though his chimps' sustaining of high FRs may be due to an adventitious schedule interaction.
- Segal (1961) observed initial but temporary superstitious effects when extinction replaced either component of a CONC VI DRL schedule.
- Lane (1961), using various FR FR schedules, found that chirping always changed in the same manner that pecking changed when only the schedule component for pecking was altered.
- Hearst (1961) saw little or no superstition with a CONC VI 2′ VI 2′ schedule and structurally successive responses. (For these VI components, using widely separated manipulanda—rather than CODs—generated response independence.)
- Bruner and Revusky (1961) obtained "elegant" (in the engineering sense) superstitious effects with a CONC EXT EXT DRL EXT schedule and responses made successive, but not independent, by instructions (and again, no CODs).
- Catania and Cutts (1963), using CONC VI 30″ EXT, and responses made successive by instructions, found superstition even with the use of a COD, though more was observed in the absence of a COD.
- Striefel (1972) did not report any superstition from using CONC FR pairs with an incrementing time–out period (to generate preference matching), and with responses made successive by instructions.
- Harrison (1979) observed superstitious effects with his trial–by–trial procedure, but these were not seen as appropriately tacted as "concurrent superstition."

Of all of these studies, only the last two were undertaken after the publication of Catania's influential 1966 book chapter. This phenomenon is significant for the next two sections which discuss why it happened and what might be done next.

Tentative Explanation

Between the appearance of Catania's 1966 book chapter and 1982 (when the present study was conducted) the literature offered no other studies that came any closer than Striefel (1972) and Harrison (1979) to dealing with the topic of simultaneously reinforceable concurrent operants. There are reasons for this paucity of research. What can be done about that will be addressed in the next section.

Catania (1966) himself provided some of the reasons for the paucity in research on simultaneously reinforceable concurrent operants. Catania was concerned with the possibility of concurrent superstition, which he defined in his book chapter as "the accidental strengthening or maintenance of one operant by reinforcement programmed for another" (p. 215). Researchers need to eliminate the possibility of such events occurring. But methods to do this that retained full response simultaneity were little examined. Instead, the most common methods used to try to avoid concurrent superstition involved trying to make responses independent by *not allowing them to occur simultaneously,* which makes the responses successive. However, making responses successive is not a guarantee that the responses will be independent.

Various procedures are successful at making concurrent responses successive (not simultaneously emittable/reinforceable), as has been seen with the studies already discussed. The two types of responses that these procedures encompass are those that are successive because they are incompatible (e.g., a pigeon's pecking responses to two separate, even if close together, keys), and responses that are compatible but also successive by virtue of some research technique. These techniques include (a) separating the response manipulanda physically so that the subject cannot operate them at the same time, (b) using instructions that allow the operation of but one manipulandum at a time, (c) using CODs, (d) using various combinations of these techniques, and (e) additional techniques not directly relevant to the present study such as the "Findley" procedure (Findley, 1958). Catania (1966) dealt briefly with most of these methods, but concentrated his efforts on the COD.

With good reason Catania prefers CODs as the technique of choice. Both before and after his 1966 book chapter, so much of the research on concurrent operants was using pigeons as subjects. Since their key peck responses, being biologically successive, cannot be simultaneous, there is no reason for researchers using pigeons to try to control concurrent superstition with a technique that allows response simultaneity. Yet these biologically successive responses necessarily involve switching from one key to the other, and the switching response itself can become a separate, superstitiously controlled operant. In this situation CODs are valuable because they lessen the chance of switching being adventitiously reinforced.

Also, CODs dovetail with the solution to another procedural problem that can arise with subjects whose responses are biologically successive. When the procedure involves concurrent ratio schedules, responding can be limited to the more favorable schedule; the subject does not contact the other schedule. The solution is to use interval schedules; each schedule requires but one response for reinforcement after the interval ends. Responses can be (and are) made on the less favorable key during the favorable interval, and some of these responses get reinforced. Thus, the nature of interval schedules (with researchers seeming to prefer VI schedules) brings the subject into contact with all the contingencies. However, responding on both alternatives with biologically successive responses under VIs necessarily involves switching, with its own problem (i.e., concurrent superstition, as already described, which is more likely with VIs as the discussion of Sidman's 1958 study noted) and its own solution (CODs).

Overall, then, when studying contingencies using biologically successive responses (like pigeons and key pecks), VIs and CODs work especially well together, as Catania suggests. The VIs generate responding on both alternative manipulanda while the CODs lessen the chance of adventitious reinforcement of switching. Thus, satisfactory independence of schedule effects (i.e., response independence) can be achieved.

However, those solutions are not helpful when studying contingencies involving simultaneously emittable/reinforceable responses. For instance, when Sidman (1958) could not get schedule effect independence using VIs, he achieved independence of schedule effects using FRs (rather than CODs, which would have eliminated the simultaneous reinforcement status of the responses). Unfortunately, the possibilities suggested by Sidman's findings received minimal treatment in Catania's book chapter. The findings of other relevant studies (already discussed) shared the same fate. Catania's treatment of the literature showed and encouraged a preference among researchers to avoid concurrent superstition by using incompatible operants (if possible) and then forcing further response succession—and hopefully independence—by using CODs.

Catania never said that incompatible responses and CODs were the only options for avoiding concurrent superstition. However, since the most common responses, in studies involving concurrent schedules, were pigeons' biologically successive key pecks, to which these options apply, it is not that surprising that so little work has been done with simultaneously reinforceable responses, to which these options do not apply.

Tentative explanation summary. There are several reasons to seek alternative procedures to CODs to avoid concurrent superstition, especially with human subjects. The research studies that have been reviewed here were discussed because few dealt with CODs or incompatible responses. Yet none of them could be properly described as being overwhelmed by superstition. Some of them even showed how CODs sometimes are not effective. Ferster (1957) stated a clear preference for simultaneously reinforceable responses, and he pointed out the relevance of these to human behavior. Catania and Cutts (1963) drew attention to some characteristics of humans that argue against the use of CODs with human subjects. And CODs simply do not allow study of more complex behavior in the form of simultaneously emittable and reinforceable responses because they force response succession. Other techniques that generate response succession, along with CODs , simply cannot be used with responses that reflect the complexity of behavior, especially human behavior; they are not adequate analogs of "real life" behavior patterns.

So, especially if human behavior is the behavior of concern, and/or if CODs and other response–succession techniques are inappropriate because simultaneously reinforceable responses are the object of study, then how can concurrent superstition be avoided? Fortunately, other techniques besides those leading to response succession seem to be available to generate sensitivity to contingencies.

Possible Resolution

One important characteristic of the studies already discussed has not yet received much attention. That characteristic is the number of reinforcer sources used in the research. All but two studies (Sidman, 1958; Hearst, 1961) used one reinforcer source, such as a single food magazine or hopper, *located between* the two manipulanda. Sidman, as well as Hearst used two sources because their respective procedures forced them to do so; the use of two sources was not the point of the research. Yet the orderliness of their data suggests that the use of multiple reinforcer sources is worthy of being studied for its own sake.

"Multiple sources" refers to the reinforcer or other selector sources in a situation in which each manipulandum has its own physically associated selector source (e.g., a separate food magazine or point counter or hand slapper located near each lever or chain or key). Multiple sources should be studied because the problem of concurrent superstition may actually be a problem of some ambiguity in the contingencies that results from having only one shared selector source (i.e., some concurrent superstition may be an artifact of the experimental apparatus). Multiple sources may prove to be more discriminable than one source with respect to which response produces any particular selector. If the contingencies used to compare single and multiple sources involve reinforcement for every response (continuous reinforcement frequency, or CRF) and extinction (EXT), then the potential for definitive results is increased; since these contingencies are maximally different, a single source of reinforcement has the most opportunity to control responding without superstitious effects. If greater superstitious effects are observed with single sources than with multiple sources, under these contingencies, then the multi–selector source procedure gains support. A whole area of behavior, complex behavior, particularly human behavior, may be exposed to more thorough investigation: the area of simultaneously selectable operants.

Possible resolution summary. What is desired is sensitivity to the contingencies. Successive responses may not be required to achieve this, and in any case are incongruent with simultaneously selectable operants. These operants comprise an inadequately studied, and potentially significant area in behaviorological science. Only more research will resolve the question of whether or not the use of multiple selector sources will be able to achieve the independence of schedule effects that would indicate experimental control over sensitivity to the contingencies.

The present study addressed that question by comparing the effectiveness of a single reinforcer source (a source that was shared by responses on two manipulanda) with the effectiveness of dual reinforcer sources (sources that were each physically associated with a different response manipulandum). This study assessed the relative effects of the single reinforcer source versus dual reinforcer sources for simultaneously emittable and simultaneously reinforceable responses using concurrent schedules involving CRF and EXT contingencies with human subjects.

Method

Subjects

From the many college students (in an introductory social science course) who volunteered to serve as subjects, the seven who participated were selected on the basis that their schedule matched the experimenter's laboratory schedule. Two subjects were right–handed males, aged 18 and 19, and five subjects were females, with ages between 18 and 25 (mean of 20.4). Of these five, one was left–handed.

All subjects were taking, as non–majors, their first college behavior–related course. They were all naive about the natural science of behaviorology in general and about this experiment in particular. The subjects knew that they would receive a small number of bonus points from their class professor for participating. They were also told, prior to volunteering, that it was possible for participants to earn a maximum of one dollar (US$1.00) from each of their four to eight experimental sessions, and that each session would be about 30 to 60 minutes long. Furthermore, they were asked not to discuss the experiment with other subjects or anyone else. (All subjects reported at the end of the study that they had complied with this request.)

All subjects experienced all levels of the independent variable, with a within–subjects design involving both within–session and between–session comparisons. However, two subjects did not complete all parts of the experiment. One of these (subject ES; subjects are referred to by code letters) became ill and was unable to return, after the within–session comparison, to participate in the between–session comparison. The other (subject FS) was a victim of a scheduling error, and so participated only in the between–session comparison. All five remaining subjects participated in both the within–session and between–session comparisons. All subjects were free to withdraw from the study at any time without penalty, and were so informed.

At the end of the study, all subjects were given the full amount of one dollar for each session that they completed, regardless of how many points–for–money they earned during each session (they had not been informed that this would occur). They were also fully briefed at this time about the purposes, procedures, results, and possible conclusions of the study.)

Apparatus

A room approximately 3.5 m long by 2.5 m wide by 3.5 m high served as the human operant chamber. The wall was painted navy gray, while the ceiling was black. The brick floor was unpainted and uncovered. A light fixture, with eight 48–inch–long florescent tubes, hung from the ceiling. A single door provided access. A two–way mirror, 60 cm wide by 110 cm high, was blocked off from the outside except for a 10 cm square section in a lower corner which could be used for observation during a session. A non–oscillating air–circulation fan was used to mask possible noises from adjacent rooms. A comfortable chair for the subject and a small table for the subject's stimulus/response/consequence panel were the only furnishings in the room. Figure 1 shows the typical arrangement of subject, chair, table, and panel during a session.

The subject's panel was made by putting a wooden, black face plate at a 45° angle (leaning away from the subject) onto a wooden, yellow box shell measuring 21 cm deep at the base, 22 cm high at the rear, and 48 cm across the front. The face plate measured 23 cm deep and 48 cm across. Two standard Acme telegraph keys extended out from the box, beneath the face plate. The center of each key was placed 7 cm from the side edge of the box. A force of 1.15±0.05 N (115±5 g) would displace either key through the 1±0.2 mm distance required to close its circuit.

The face plate contained various stimuli. Directly above each key, 6 cm from the bottom edge of the face plate, was a pair of lights. In the center of the face plate was another pair of lights on the same level as the two side pairs of lights. Each pair of lights was associated with a counter. The left light of each pair was one of three white lights used together as pacing lights. The right light of each pair was yellow and flashed when its associated counter was incremented as part of the occurrence of reinforcement. Above each pair of lights was its associated Veeder–Root, six–digit counter, model B–120506. When incremented, these counters would sound an audible click. No counter could be returned to zero except by the experimenter, for the reset knobs were removed during experimental sessions. A red light was placed 10 cm above each side counter. If this light was off, no consequence of any sort was programmed for the key on the corresponding side, as if the key was disconnected from the programming equipment. These are called "key–connected" lights. In the center, on the same level as the key–connected lights, was a green light used as a house light. A session was in progress so long as this light remained on. Below the house light was a circular switch. This was to be used as a panic switch with which a subject could end the session prematurely. (Its use, however, was not without consequences.)

The subject's panel was connected by cable to a computer, an interface, and two cumulative recorders (one for the responses made by each hand) located in another room across the hall. A Digital Equipment Corporation PDP 8A/620 computer controlled the programming of the sequence of events in each session automatically. Programming was supplied through SuperSKED software (Snapper & Inglis, 1979) operated through a SKED interface (provided by State Systems, Inc. of Kalamazoo, MI). By this arrangement data collection, including the operation of the cumulative recorders, was also automatic. Two G3100 Gerbrands cumulative recorders (Model C3) were used. Paper drive gears with a 2:1 ratio (commonly called "pigeon gears") were used to obtain a paper movement rate of 60 cm per hour.

Figure 2 shows (a) the arrangement of response manipulanda and stimuli on the subject's panel, and (b) the two cumulative recorders used for primary data collection.

Photo by Stephen F. Ledoux

Figure 1. Typical arrangement of subject, chair, table, and panel.

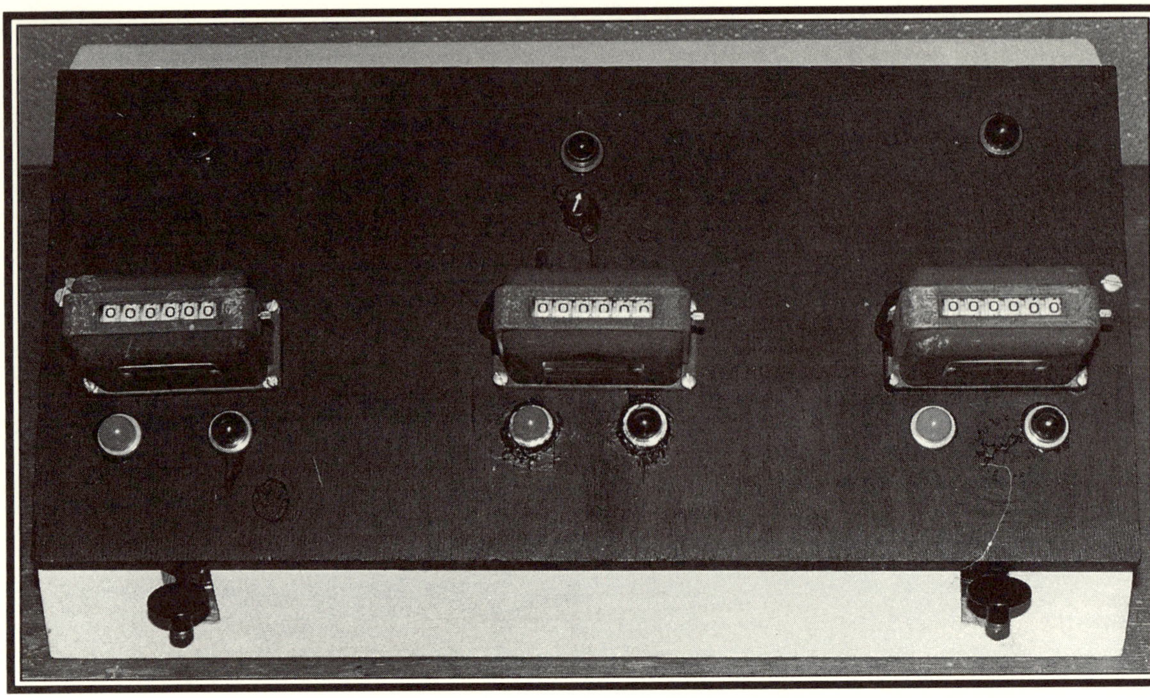

Photo by Stephen F. Ledoux

A. Arrangement of the subject's panel.

Photo by Stephen F. Ledoux

B. Arrangement of the cumulative recorders.

Figure 2. Arrangement of (a) response manipulanda and stimuli on the subject's panel, and (b) the two cumulative recorders.

Procedures

The basic experimental question was whether one source of reinforcement, or two sources of reinforcement, would be more effective—with less superstitious responding—in controlling simultaneously reinforceable concurrent human operants. In addressing this question, certain procedures were used.

General procedures. Instructions to the subjects concerned the operation of the panel, and their task. Regarding the operation of the panel, instructions included these:

- The session begins when the green light goes on, and ends when the green light goes off.
- In the first session only one red light will come on at a time; work only on the key beneath the red light that is on. If the white lights [the pacing lights] flash, press the operating key at a speed such that the yellow light will flash whenever the white light flashes. After the first session, no white lights are ever used.
- In all subsequent sessions both red lights will either be on or be off together. When they are on, both keys are operating. This does not mean that both keys will necessarily be equally effective in producing points. With both red lights on, you may work on one or the other or both keys. When the red lights are off, it is a rest period and neither key will be operating. [No subject was observed to use a key whose associated red light was out.]
- Use the left hand with the left key and the right hand with the right key. [No subject was observed to do otherwise.]
- Sometimes key pressing produces points that are added up on a counter. Each point is accompanied by a flash of the yellow light below the counter. [Points and flashes were the anticipated and observed conditioned added reinforcers for key pressing responses.]
- Sometimes both the points produced by the left key and the points produced by the right key appear on the center counter only. At other times the points produced by left key pressing appear only on the left counter, and the points produced by right key pressing appear only on the right counter. Points never appear on all three counters at the same time.
- If, for any reason, you want to end the session before the green light goes off, you can do so by turning the knob located below the green light. However, if you do this, you forfeit 50% of your earned points for that session. [No subject ever used this panic switch.]

Regarding the subject's task, instructions included these:

- Points equal money! The more points you generate, the more money you earn. Since a fixed amount of money is available for each session ($1.00), while the number of points available for each session varies, the amount of money you receive will be that percent of the money available that equals the percent you earned of the possible points.
- Your task is to generate as many points as possible, working on one or the other or both keys. While working on both keys, press both

keys at the same time. [Responses were simultaneously emittable and, without bringing any other special contingencies to bear, it was preferred that they be emitted simultaneously.]

The daily routine for each subject began with her or his arrival at the laboratory. Each was asked for his or her watch as watches were not allowed in the experimental room. The instructions were then reviewed and the session began. When the session was over, the subject was given a receipt which stated that she or he had earned up to one dollar for that session, and that all earnings would be paid at the end of the study.

The four sessions planned for each subject included (a) a training session, (b) a session of one versus two reinforcer sources as a within–session comparison, (c) a session with only one reinforcer source throughout as the first part of a between–session comparison, and (d) a session with two reinforcer sources throughout as the second and last part of the between–session comparison. Table 1 depicts the sequence of sessions received by each subject. Several abbreviations, which are used in the table as well as in later text, are introduced here: Subjects are designated by letters (AS through GS). The two different types of training sessions are represented by T1 and T2. The within–session comparison session is represented by W. The two sessions of the between–session comparison are represented by B1 (using one reinforcer source) and B2 (using two reinforcer sources). Subjects AS and BS also experienced two other sessions, represented by

Subject	Session Sequence					
	1	2	3	4	5	6
AS	T1*	W**	A1***	A2	B1	B2
BS	T1	W	A1	A2	B1	B2
CS	T1	W	B1	B2		
DS	T2	W	B1	B2		
ES	T2	W				
FS	T2	B1	B2			
GS	T2	B1	W	B2		

* Different types of training sessions are represented by T1 and T2.

** The within–session comparison session is represented by W.

*** The between–session comparison sessions are represented by A1 and A2, and by B1 and B2. (A1 and A2 are parts of another study; see text.)

Table 1. Sequence of sessions received by each subject.

A1 and A2, that were part of another study that assessed one versus two reinforcer sources on variable ratio (VR) schedules (reported in Ledoux, 1982b). These sessions occurred after the T1 and W sessions, but before the B1 and B2 sessions.

Each session lasted about 40 minutes. Each subject was to participate in each of the four planned sessions on the basis of one session per day. However, due to scheduling concerns, two of the seven subjects had two of their sessions on the same day. Subject CS had the last two sessions (B1 and B2) on the same day, some hours apart, while subject GS had the first two sessions (T2 and B1) on the same day, back to back.

In addition to the separate cumulative records for each hand, data collection included recording the number of responses and reinforcements for each hand during each component pair, as well as the duration of each component pair. From these, response and reinforcement rates could be calculated for each hand under each component pair. (A component pair is a pair of schedules, one for each hand, in effect concurrently, that comprises one of six components in each session.)

Training sessions. The T1 training session had been originally designed for both an earlier study (Ledoux, 1982b) as well as for the present study, even though two VR schedules were among its component pairs. However, the initial response rates of early subjects showed too much variability, perhaps partly due to early fatigue for some subjects who were observed to press the keys at a high rate initially. The use of some of the panel lights as "pacing lights," along with the instructions regarding their use, in the training session was predicted to help decrease the variability of subjects' initial response rates. So the T2 training session was designed and successfully used with the pacing lights, and also, for the rest of the present study, without the VR schedules.

In T1 the single, central counter served as the reinforcer source throughout the session. The subject operated each hand alone, alternating with the other hand, with a 15 second time–out between schedules. At first each hand was under CRF for 1000 reinforcements, then each hand was under VR 5 for 200 reinforcements, and finally each hand was under VR 20 for 50 reinforcements.

In T2 the subject also operated each hand alone, alternating with the other hand after a 15 second time–out every 500 reinforcements. The illumination of one or the other key–connected light indicated which key—and thus which hand—to use. At first each hand worked while the pacing lights flashed every 0.4 of a second, with reinforcements accruing on the center counter. Then each hand worked without the pacing lights operating, and with the reinforcements still accruing on the center counter. Next each hand worked with the pacing lights again operating, but reinforcements accrued on the side counter associated with the key in use. Finally each hand again worked without the pacing lights operating, and with reinforcements still accruing on the side counter associated with the key in use.

Experimental sessions. Each of the three experimental sessions involved both hands being able to operate their respective keys at the same time throughout a sequence of six component pairs where one hand was on CRF while the other hand was on either CRF or EXT. The component pairs were separated by a rest period (time–out) of 15 seconds duration. For all experimental sessions the rest period, and thus the change from one pair of schedules to the next, occurred as soon as one or the other hand had produced 1000 reinforcements. Table 2 depicts the number of reinforcement sources, and the sequence of component pairs, used in the three experimental sessions.

During the W session (the within–session comparison session) the first three component pairs used the single reinforcer source (i.e., the center counter). The remaining three component pairs were sequenced exactly as the first three but used the dual reinforcer sources (i.e., the side counters).

The B1 and B2 sessions (the between–session comparison sessions) followed a course similar to the course of the W session. During the B1 session (the first of the two sessions comprising the between–session comparison) the single reinforcer source of the center counter was used throughout the series of six concurrent component pairs. During the B2 session (the second of the two sessions comprising the between–session

Session Type	Component Pair Sequence*		# of Reinforcer Sources per component pair
	Left Hand	Right Hand	
W Session (within–session comparison)	CRF	CRF	1**
	CRF	EXT	1
	EXT	CRF	1
	CRF	CRF	2***
	CRF	EXT	2
	EXT	CRF	2
B1 Session (first part of the between–session comparison)	CRF	CRF	1 (one source used throughout)**
	CRF	EXT	
	EXT	CRF	
	CRF	CRF	
	EXT	CRF	
	CRF	EXT	
B2 Session (last part of the between–session comparison)	All component pairs repeat B1 sequence.		2 (two sources used throughout)***

* Read down for sequence of pairs.

** "One source" always refers to the center counter/light.

*** "Two sources" always refers to the side counters/lights.

Table 2. Number of conditioned reinforcer sources, and sequences of component pairs, for within–session and between–session comparisons.

comparison) the dual reinforcer sources of the side counters were used throughout a repetition of the series of six concurrent component pairs used in the BI session.

Results

The basic dependent variable in this study was the rate of response for each hand during each component pair. In general, while the response rate was high for the hand on CRF irrespective of the number of reinforcer sources, the rate was low for the hand on EXT under two separate sources but high for the hand on EXT under one source.

Figures 3, 4, 5, 6, and 7 show the left and right hand cumulative records for some subjects from each of the three experimental sessions. These examples are typical of the data of all the subjects. In these records, the cumulative recorder pens are not used the same way under both single–source and dual–source conditions. The pens are used in the usual manner under the two–source condition; the hatch marks of the response pen indicate reinforcements (making a thick black line, due to the CRF schedule) along the slope of the response line, while changes from one component pair to the next are noted by the offset or reset of the event pen across the bottom of each record. However, under the single–source condition, pen use is reversed with respect to reinforcer hatch marks and component–change marks; reinforcements are shown as hatch marks (again making a thick black line, due to the CRF schedule) but along the flat of the event pen line, while changes from one component pair to the next are noted by the offset or reset of the response pen on the slope of the response line.

A further reason for using the recorder pens in those ways is that, by doing so, the records could graphically depict whether or not reinforcements appeared on a source associated with the hand/key that produced those reinforcements. Under two sources the record shows each reinforcer hatch mark right on the pen step for the response that produced that reinforcer. However, under one source, while the reinforcer hatch marks still appear on the record of the hand that produced them (along the event pen line of that record) they do not appear with the actual responses that produced them. This is a way of showing that under one source the reinforcements appeared on a counter not physically associated with either key (the center counter), while under two sources each reinforcement does appear on a counter physically associated with one or the other key (the counter on the same side as the key that produced the reinforcement).

Figure 3 shows the left hand and right hand cumulative records for subjects BS and GS during the W session. The response rates are high and steady for each hand of both of these subjects under the single–source condition regardless of whether the contingency involves a CRF schedule or EXT. Under the dual–source condition, their response rates remain high and steady under CRF, and decrease to zero under EXT. The extinction curve of the right hand of BS under the dual–source condition, as aesthetic as it might be, is not typical of most other subjects. The right hand, dual–source extinction "curve" of GS is more typical of other subjects' "curves" under the first occurrence of a dual–source EXT contingency.

Figure 4 shows the left hand and right hand cumulative records for subjects ES and DS during the W session. For ES, rates under all CRF contingencies are high and steady. However, the initial single–source EXT contingency was effective in eliminating right hand responding. Yet in the next component, the EXT contingency on the left hand was

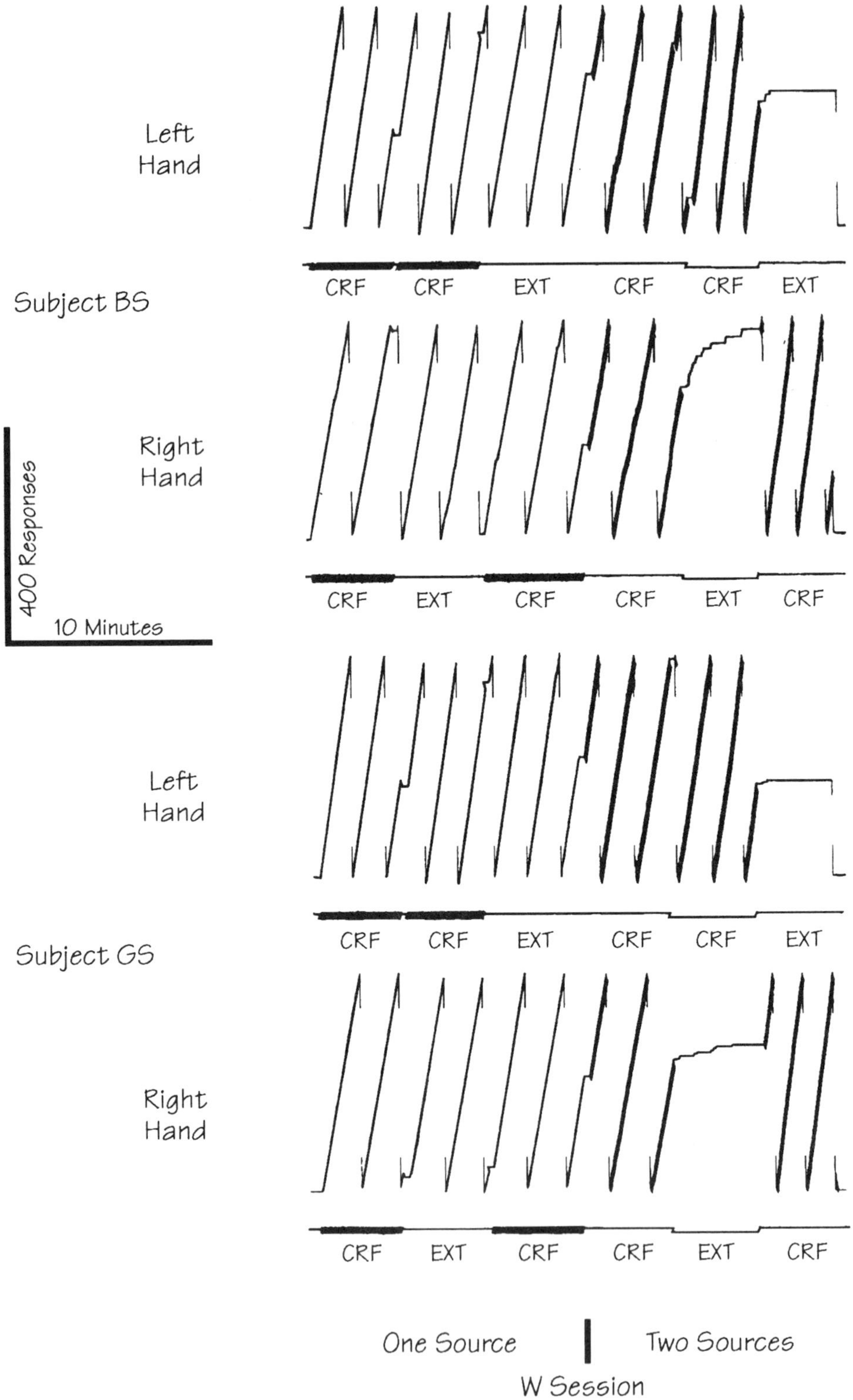

Figure 3. Cumulative records of left and right hand responding for subjects BS and GS during the within-session comparison session (W).

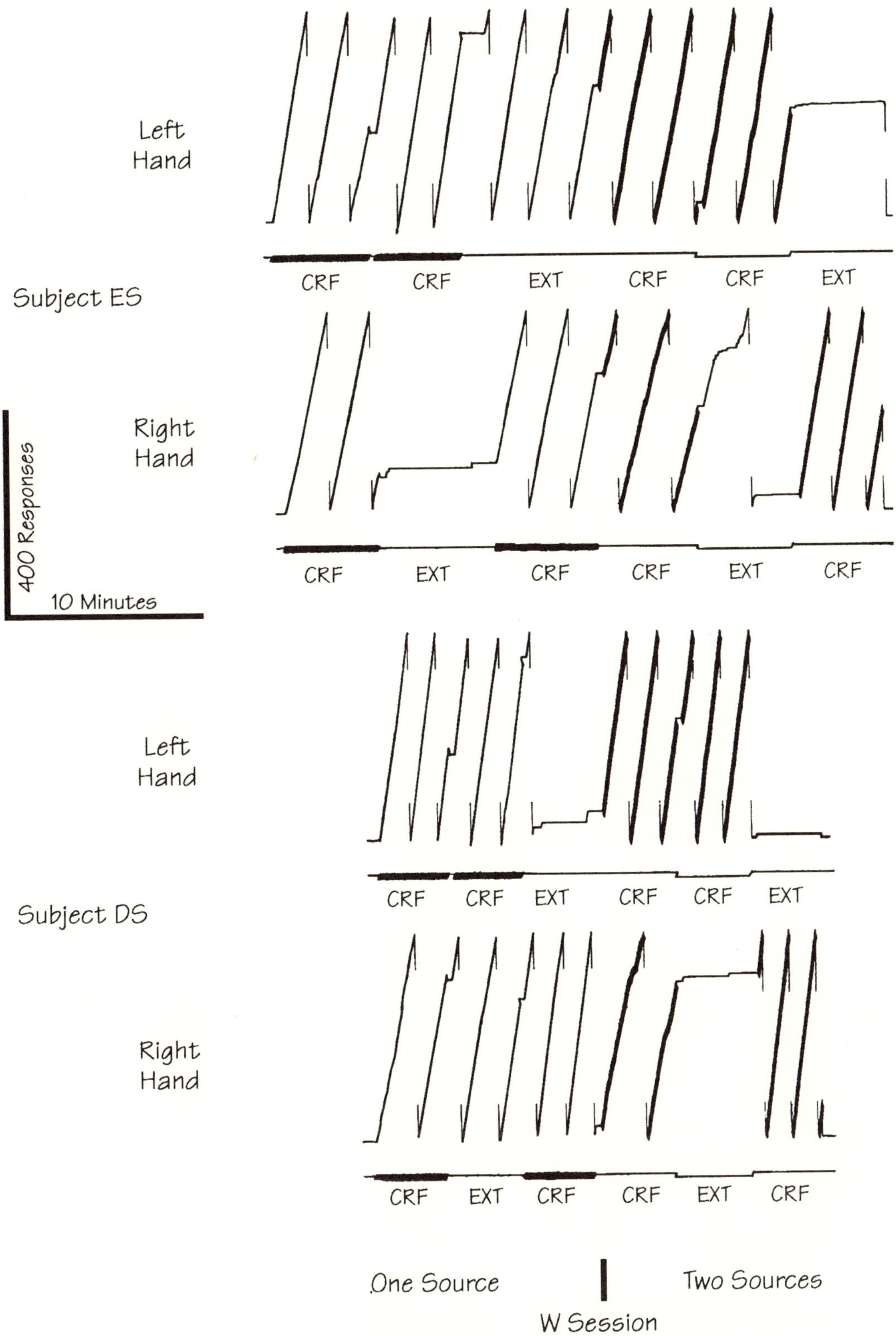

Figure 4. Cumulative records of left and right hand responding for subjects ES and DS during the within-session comparison session (W).

ineffective, as shown by the persistence of a high and steady rate. Subject ES reported that responding did not begin in this component until after an extra minute or so of "rest" had been taken. Subject ES was the only subject who, after being affected by an EXT contingency under the single–source condition, was unaffected by that same contingency in the subsequent single–source CRF/EXT component in the same session. For subject DS the record shows a high and steady response rate under all CRF contingencies, as well as under the initial, single–source EXT contingency (on the right hand). However, under the remaining EXT contingencies, including the second single–source EXT contingency, responding is eliminated.

Figure 5 and Figure 6 show the left hand and right hand cumulative records for subjects GS and BS, respectively, during the B1 and B2 sessions. The response rates are high and steady for each hand of both of these subjects during the single–source B1 session irrespective of whether the contingency involves CRF or EXT. During the dual–source B2 session, their response rates remain high and steady under CRF, and decrease to zero under EXT. Although Figure 5 is too reduced to show it well, throughout all dual–source EXT contingencies, subject GS made a single testing–like response on the EXT key after each 100 points earned on the CRF key. No other subject displayed this type of pattern (a professor, examining this pattern, expressed the hope that this reality–testing student would apply for graduate school).

Figure 7 shows the left hand and right hand cumulative records for subject DS during the B1 and B2 sessions. Regardless of whether the condition in effect is single–source or dual–sources, the response rates for both hands are high and steady under CRF. However, with the exception of one single–source EXT contingency, whenever a hand is under EXT, the response rate drops to zero. The one exception is the first single–source EXT contingency, on the right hand, where the response rate remains high and steady throughout. Also, more responding can be seen as having occurred at the beginning of the other EXT contingencies under the single–source condition before abruptly ceasing, than under the dual–source condition.

The data for subject DS is particularly relevant as it shows that some subjects do come under some control of EXT contingencies even in the single–reinforcer source condition. Yet for *all* subjects responding is eventually if not immediately eliminated by any EXT contingency under the dual–reinforcer source condition. This comparative result between the single–source condition and the dual–source condition is the most reliable, salient and significant result of the study.

An elaboration of the number of responses made in extinction, both during the W session and during the B1 and B2 sessions, allows further comparison between the single–source condition and the dual–source condition. Tables 3 and 4 list the actual number, for all subjects, of responses on keys that were programmed with an EXT contingency.

Table 3 depicts the number of responses in extinction for each subject during the W session. In this table, the reference to the conditions (single–source or dual–source) is a column heading.

Table 4 depicts the number of responses in extinction for each subject during the B1 and B2 sessions. However, in this table, the reference to the conditions (single–source or dual–source) is a row heading.

Comparisons between the single–source condition and the dual–source condition yield two basic observations. In most cases, *the number of responses made on the* EXT *key*

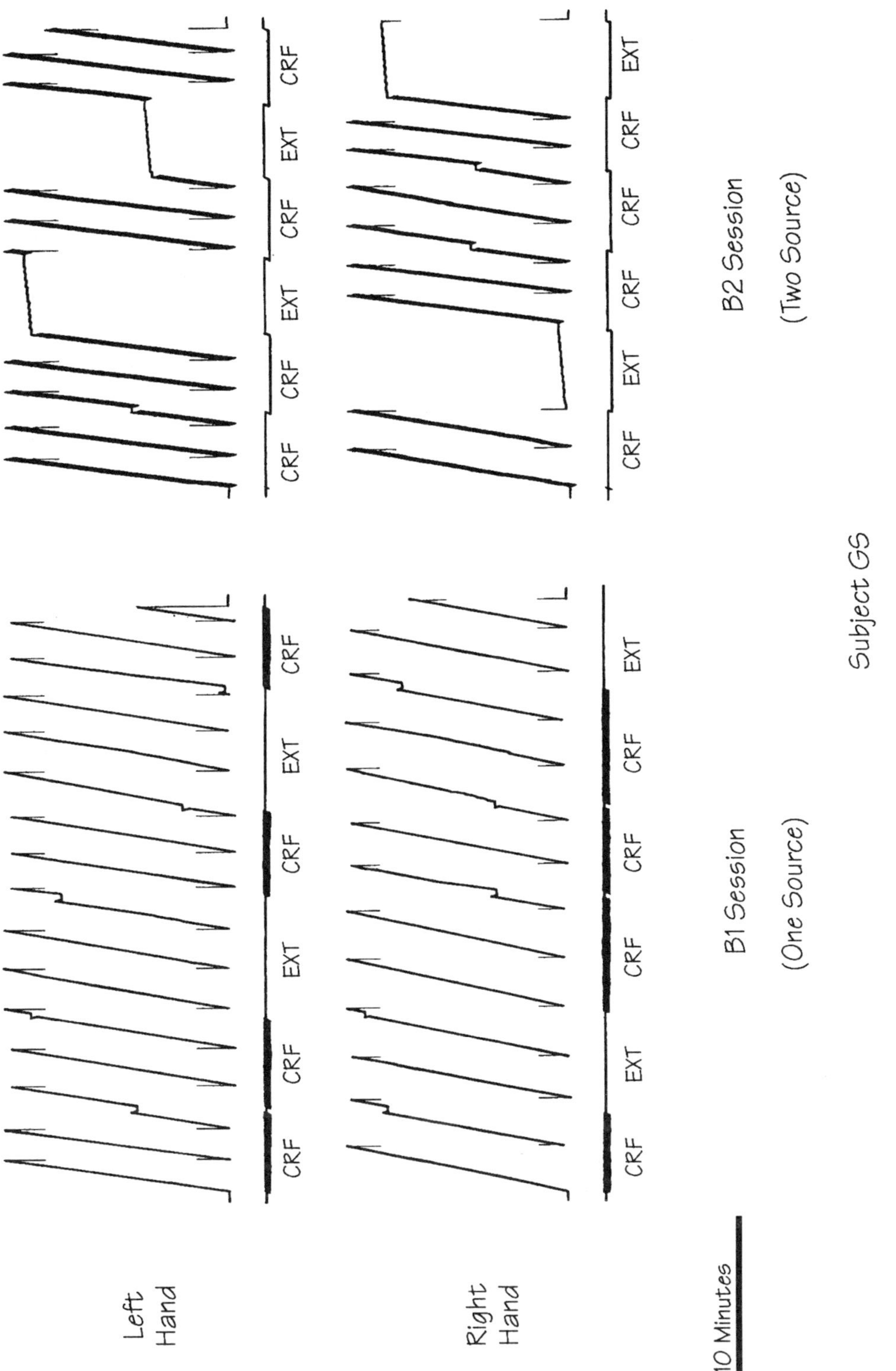

Figure 5. Cumulative records of left and right hand responding for subject GS during the between-session comparison sessions (B1 and B2).

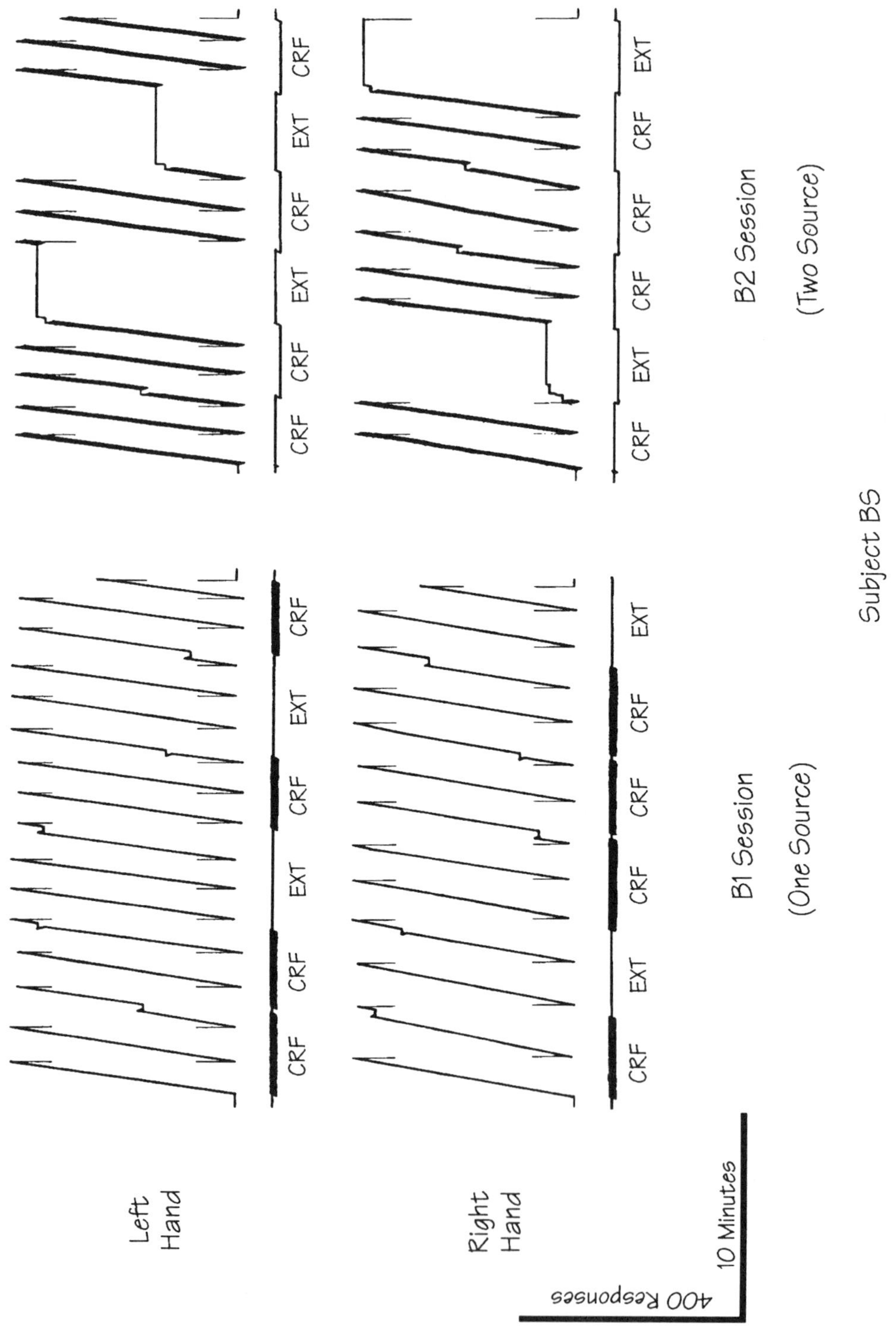

Figure 6. Cumulative records of left and right hand responding for subject BS during the between-session comparison sessions (B1 and B2).

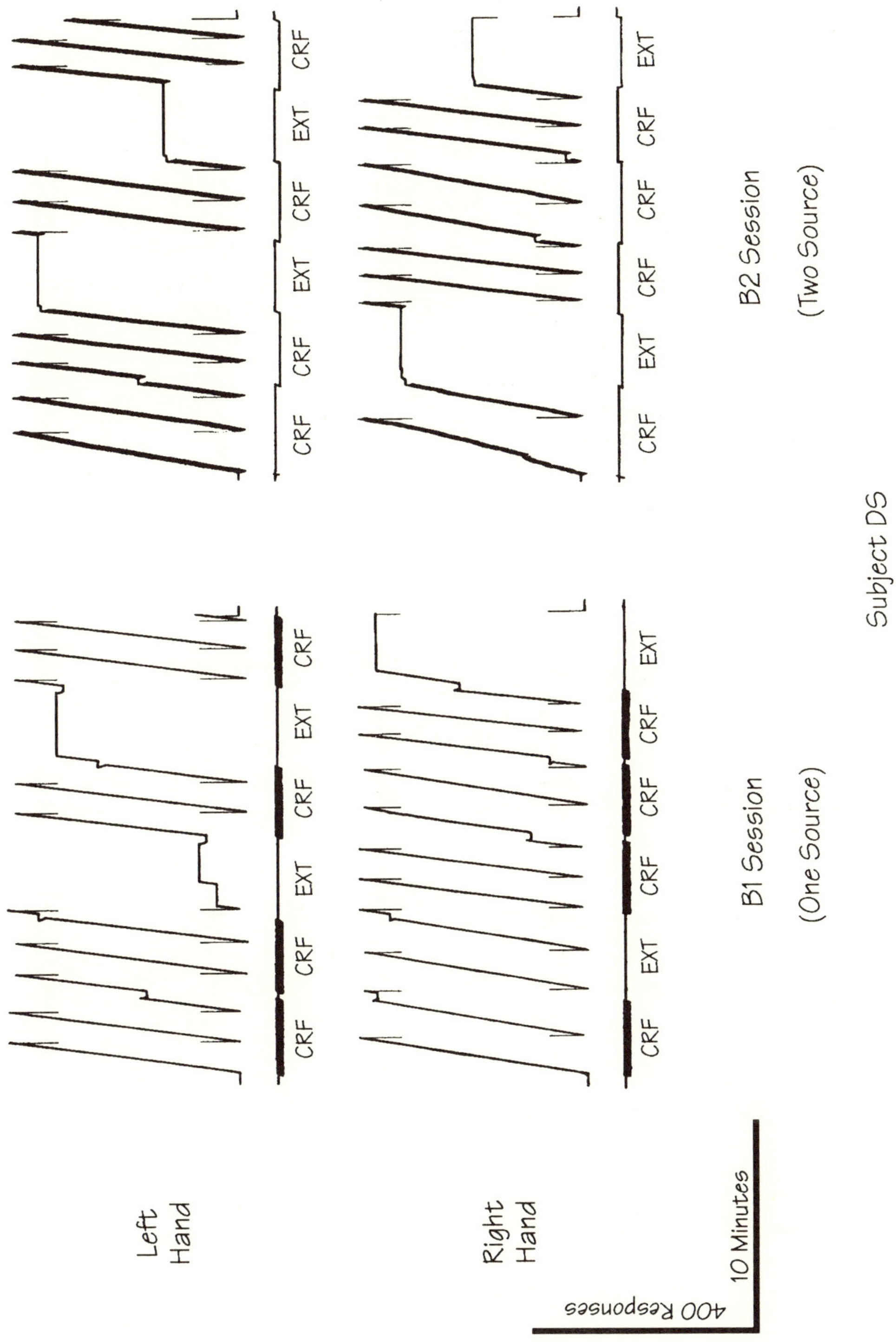

Figure 7. Cumulative records of left and right hand responding for subject DS during the between-session comparison sessions (B1 and B2).

under the single–source condition is of the same magnitude as the number of responses made on the CRF *key,* which had to be pressed 1000 times before the components would change. Where this is not the case, a glance at the single–source components of the cumulative record (or Tables 3 or 4) would reveal an example in which responding on the EXT key had ceased sometime during the single–source component. The W session data show only two cases out of 12 possible cases where responding under a single source was sensitive to EXT. The B1 session data show only seven cases out of 24 possible cases that fit this description. All of these cases are marked with an asterisk in Tables 3 and 4. Contrast this information with the fact that *the number of responses made on the* EXT *key under the dual–source condition is always less than one–third of the 1000 responses required of the hand operating the* CRF *key to change components.* The cumulative records show responding on the EXT key under the dual–source condition to have always ceased during the component. In summary, under the single–source condition, subjects were sensitive to EXT in 9 of 36 cases; under the dual–source condition, they were sensitive in 36 of 36 cases (i.e., under the single source 27 of 36 cases were *in*sensitive to EXT, while under dual sources none of 36 cases were *in*sensitive to EXT).

Rate of response data corroborates number of response data. Table 5 presents rate of response data for each hand of each subject in each component of the W session. Table 6 presents rate of response data for each hand of each subject in each component of the B1 and B2 sessions. (For both tables, minutes were rounded to whole numbers.)

Subject	Sequence of extinction contingencies in the W session*			
	Single reinforcer source		Dual reinforcer sources	
	1st EXT	2nd EXT	3rd EXT	4th EXT
AS	973	1061	332	21
BS	843	1155	111	19
CS	918	978	10	6
DS	778	107**	14	3
ES	18**	1266	232	10
GS	842	1094	28	6

* Each row presents the data for one session.

** See text.

Table 3. Number of responses in extinction for all subjects during the within–session comparison session.

Discussion

This research addressed the question of how to obtain sensitivity to contingencies with multiple operant behaviors that are simultaneously emittable and simultaneously reinforceable. In this study the effectiveness of a single reinforcer source (a source that is shared by responses on two manipulanda) was compared with the effectiveness of dual reinforcer sources (sources that are each physically associated with a different response manipulandum). Multiple operants that simultaneously produced reinforcers from multiple sources, each physically associated with a different response manipulandum, showed no responding that could reasonably be labeled superstitious, while multiple operants that produced reinforcers from single, shared sources showed considerable su-

Subject	# of Sources	Session*	Sequence of extinction contingencies in the B1 and B2 sessions			
			1st EXT	2nd EXT	3rd EXT	4th EXT
AS	1	B1	839	1187	1215	814
AS	2	B2	71	80	67	61
BS	1	B1	768	1239	1204	848
BS	2	B2	31	14	17	12
CS	1	B1	841	985	861	933
CS	2	B2	7	9	8	2
DS	1	B1	786	139**	77**	151**
DS	2	B2	8	6	7	2
FS	1	B1	61**	17**	22**	8**
FS	2	B2	144	59	29	51
GS	1	B1	855	1448	1408	834
GS	2	B2	16	13	12	10

* Each row presents the data for *one* session (B1 or B2).

** See text.

Table 4. Number of responses in extinction for all subjects during the between-session comparison sessions.

Subject	Component pairs in the W session											
	Single–source condition						Dual–source condition					
	CRF-LH	CRF-RH	CRF-LH	EXT-RH	EXT-LH	CRF-RH	CRF-LH	CRF-RH	CRF-LH	EXT-RH	EXT-LH	CRF-RH
AS	219	181	207	201	225	212	239	238	226	75	6	266
BS	269	217	274	231	250	217	236	218	379	36	6	316
CS	267	266	275	252	283	289	285	233	287	3	2	314
DS	295	217	299	232	32	296	276	192	305	4	1	322
ES	216	194	238	4	226	178	217	162	235	55	2	235
GS	267	229	278	234	272	248	259	223	279	8	2	315

Table 5. Each hand's number of responses per minute in each component of the W session for each subject.

Subject / # of Sources / Session			Component pairs in the B1 and B2 sessions											
			CRF-LH	CRF-RH	CRF-LH	EXT-RH	EXT-LH	CRF-RH	CRF-LH	CRF-RH	EXT-LH	CRF-RH	CRF-LH	EXT-RH
AS	1	B1	220	167	235	197	251	212	143	247	222	183	241	196
AS	2	B2	282	234	274	19	23	288	264	225	20	302	280	17
BS	1	B1	269	211	285	219	297	239	305	261	293	243	301	255
BS	2	B2	316	272	323	10	4	318	287	232	5	298	320	4
CS	1	B1	310	239	311	262	269	273	304	245	254	295	284	265
CS	2	B2	273	241	274	2	3	296	282	181	2	300	294	1
DS	1	B1	287	267	301	237	44	314	317	246	25	321	310	47
DS	2	B2	244	178	316	3	2	327	293	224	2	319	343	1
FS	1	B1	273	245	231	20	6	344	312	267	8	373	331	3
FS	2	B2	257	221	317	46	20	341	314	288	10	329	324	17
GS	1	B1	268	201	245	209	282	195	251	204	274	194	268	224
GS	2	B2	282	235	294	5	4	306	286	234	4	310	307	3

Table 6. Each hand's number of responses per minute in each component of the B1 and B2 sessions for each subject.

perstitious responding. This was the case even though the single–source condition in this study had the greatest possible chance to control responding without superstitious effects due to the concurrent use of two schedules, CRF and EXT, that are maximally different in terms of the availability of reinforcement under each.

The data indicate that when human subjects' simultaneously emittable responses (here, key pressing) are simultaneously reinforceable under CRF and EXT contingencies, the operant under EXT is seldom sensitive to that contingency when the setting involves a single source of reinforcement not physically associated with any of the manipulanda. On the other hand, these subjects were always sensitive to the EXT contingency when the setting involved two sources of reinforcement, each physically associated with a different manipulandum. These results suggest, in comparison with the usual single source of reinforcement, that, for multiple operants, multiple sources of reinforcement are (a) more discriminable with respect to which response produced any particular reinforcer, and (b) more effective in generating sensitivity to the contingencies.

Facing Extinction–Contingency Sensitivity

However, the responding of three of the subjects in this study was sensitive to an EXT contingency under the single–source condition in one or more of the CRF/EXT components in one or both of the sessions that involved single–sources. One subject (ES—see Figure 4) was sensitive to the EXT contingency in the first of the two CRF/EXT components in the first half of the W session. Another subject (DS—see Figures 4 and 7) was both (a) sensitive to the EXT contingency in the second of the two CRF/EXT components in the first half of the W session, and (b) sensitive to the EXT contingency in the second, third, and fourth (of four) CRF/EXT components in the BI session. The third subject (FS—see Table 4) was sensitive to the EXT contingency in all four of the CRF/EXT components in the BI session. In suggesting explanations for these occurrences, a number of factors can be considered; any of these may have operated singly or in combinations in any particular instance of EXT sensitivity.

One possible explanation of some of the instances of single–source effectiveness of an EXT contingency is the change in reinforcement density from one component pair to the next. When a CRF/CRF component is followed by a CRF/EXT component, a 50% reduction in reinforcement density for simultaneous responding occurs (as will be seen, this reduction may be irrelevant if responding is alternating rather than simultaneous). Although, under the single–source condition, all reinforcements accrue on the shared, center counter, this reduction may still have made the density in the CRF/EXT component discriminable (in the usual functional sense, not in any "agency" sense; see Baum, 1995) from the greater density of the preceding CRF/CRF component, ultimately resulting in the EXT contingency effectively controlling EXT key responding (eliminating that responding) for some subjects. The responding of subject ES (Figure 4) in the first single–source component of the W session, and subject DS (Figure 7) in the third single–source component of the BI session, and subject FS (Table 4) in the first and third single–source component of the BI session, provides examples of the possible effects of the reinforcement–density change.

The second single–source CRF/EXT component of the W session for subject ES, however, also needs explaining. In this component, the only remaining single–source CRF/EXT component in the W session, the already reduced reinforcement density remained the same, and EXT did not eliminate responding on the EXT key. (Even though such insensitivity is basically unsurprising, its occurrence after an EXT–sensitive CRF/EXT component is a curiosity demanding attention.) This component and the preceding component were identical *except for the reversal of the hand producing reinforcement.* Perhaps in this case the lack of sensitivity to extinction occurred due to a sequence effect. The reinforcement density on each key would have reversed, with one hand changing from every response being reinforced to none being reinforced, while the other hand changed from no responses being reinforced to every response being reinforced. However, all reinforcers continued to accrue only on the center, single source. The key on which responding in extinction occurred in this second CRF/EXT component was actually the key for the hand on which *the opposite contingency had produced all of the reinforcers*—but on the center, single source—in the preceding component. The relevance of this possibility needs further research, and the matter is not considered to have been given an adequate account here.

Subject DS (Figures 4 and 7) and subject FS (Table 4) often differed from subject ES. The responding of both subject DS (in the second single–source CRF/EXT component of the W session and the second and fourth single–source CRF/EXT components of the BI session), and subject FS (in the second and fourth single–source CRF/EXT components of the BI session), provides examples in which a single–source EXT contingency *was* effective in a CRF/EXT component that was preceded by a CRF/EXT component, regardless of whether or not the EXT contingency had been effective in that preceding component. The explanation of these subjects' responding being sensitive to the EXT contingency under most single–source CRF/EXT components is incomplete. It may involve yet another possible explanation of single–source effectiveness of an EXT contingency. This explanation concerns some subjective observations. Those subjects who were sensitive to single–source EXT contingencies (e.g., subject FS) were often observed to emit pressing responses on the two keys in a noticeably alternating pattern—first one hand, then the other hand, then the one hand, and so on—that made their responses sequential and successive rather than simultaneous (potential reasons offered by subjects for this pattern included keeping time with hummed music and avoiding fatigue). However, those subjects who were *not* sensitive to single–source EXT contingencies (e.g., subjects BS and GS) were observed to emit pressing responses in a simultaneous pattern, each hand pressing its key essentially at the same time as the other hand, rather than sequentially. Is this an observation of a functional relationship? This question needs to be researched, although generating response succession (e.g., through CODs) is a standard practice for reducing concurrent superstition even though it eliminates response simultaneity.

In studying that question the effect of equipment functioning on response patterns needs to be considered. Due to the constraints of computer functioning and logic, no two responses could be *measured* as simultaneous. They could, however, still be considered functionally simultaneous; for instance, they could occur during the same clock tick (on the order of one to five nanoseconds). Yet even if they actually occurred simultaneously, the computer necessarily dealt with them in a sequential manner, according to state table priority rules. In essence, any pair of actually or functionally simultaneous responses had an artifactual, enforced delay (a sort of minimal COD).

That delay did not seem to play any noticeable part in the contingencies. Subjects who were observed to respond "simultaneously" (i.e., whose responding approximated the artifactual delay) were not sensitive to single–source EXT contingencies. On the other hand subjects who were observed to respond "sequentially" (i.e., whose responding contained delays, between the alternating responses in any pair of responses, that were considerably longer than the artifactual delay, possibly on the order of 0.1 to 0.5 seconds) were sensitive to single–source EXT contingencies. A parametric study to assess the effects of very short CODs (0.001 to 1.0 seconds) may determine a minimal COD duration at which one reinforcer source *can* be effective in generating sensitivity to contingencies with simultaneously reinforceable responses. The important point for the present study, however, is that the two–source procedure was *always* effective in controlling responding, regardless of whether the subjects emitted sequential or simultaneous responses. While previously no procedure seemed adequate to the task, the two–source procedure enables the further study of simultaneous operants.

One additional curiosity should be mentioned. While the EXT key responding of subject DS was superstitious in the first single–source CRF/EXT component in the W session, it did extinguish under the EXT contingency in the second and only remaining single–source CRF/EXT component in this session. At the later B1 session, responding on the EXT key again occurred in the first single–source CRF/EXT component (although in all other CRF/EXT components in this session, EXT key responding extinguished). This *reappearance* of responding under EXT in the first single–source CRF/EXT component in the later B1 session is an example reminiscent of spontaneous recovery. This possibility also needs further research.

Under the single–source condition, no surprise occurs when EXT key responding is insensitive to the EXT contingency, though some related circumstances can arouse further curiosity. The potential explanations for EXT key responding being sensitive to an EXT contingency under the single–source condition can be summarized. (a) When a CRF/CRF component was followed by a CRF/EXT component in which EXT–key responding was sensitive to EXT, one possibly responsible factor may have been the reduction in reinforcement density. (b) When a CRF/EXT component, in which EXT–key responding was sensitive to EXT, was followed by another CRF/EXT component in which EXT–key responding was not sensitive to EXT, one possibly responsible factor (though such insensitivity is basically unsurprising) may have been a sequence effect. And (c) when a CRF/EXT component, regardless of whether EXT–key responding was sensitive to EXT or not, was followed by another CRF/EXT component in which EXT–key responding was sensitive to EXT, one possibly responsible factor may have involved responses being emitted in a distinctly alternating, sequential manner rather than simultaneously. These and other factors, such as the possible occurrence of some sort of spontaneous recovery, deserve further investigation.

Other Considerations and Improvements

During the study a number of other factors had the potential to affect the results. These factors included (a) the subjects' age, sex, and handedness, (b) the two different types of training sessions, (c) the occurrence of the extra sessions involving VR schedules for another study, (d) the occurrence, for some subjects, of two sessions on the same day, and (e) the occurrence, for one subject, of the W session between the B1 and B2 sessions. While these factors were not explicitly assessed for their effects, no aspect of the data seemed to be systematically related to any of them.

Overall, the dual reinforcer source procedure used here makes the study of simultaneously reinforceable operants viable by generating adequate schedule–effect independence—and thereby limiting the concurrent superstition commonly present when only one reinforcer source is used—without, by definition, requiring response succession. Consequently, a whole category of complex behavior, the category of simultaneously emittable, simultaneously selectable operants, is opened to more effective study.

Some improvements that would facilitate further research must be mentioned. Two of these concern the manipulanda and the point counters used in the present study. Manipulanda that are more controllable than telegraph keys would be preferred. The resulting capability of precisely adjusting the response requirement, in terms of both force and duration, would enhance the resolution of both the experimenter's control of the variables and the analysis of the results. Similar advantages would accrue from the use of digital, or computer generated and displayed, counters whose speed and accuracy are greater than the electro–mechanical counters used in this study.

The problem with the use of electro–mechanical counters was that they required an electrical impulse a full tenth of a second in duration to guarantee their consistent operation. This was quite slow and raised the possibility of some reinforcers being skipped during high rate response bursts. The state table avoided this by counting reinforceable responses in a variable and decrementing that variable for each delivered reinforcer. This was cumbersome for two reasons. First, delays became possible between a response and the occurrence of the reinforcer it produced; while these were extremely short, they were nonetheless longer than the virtually instantaneous changes normally expected from computer–controlled equipment. Secondly, the necessity of this state–table technique (caused by using the available but old electro–mechanical counters) put constraints on the types of parametric manipulations that could be made, especially with regard to reinforcement parameters (e.g., reinforcer magnitude). Fortunately, the primary concerns of this study were molar in nature and so showed no problematic effects from these equipment limitations. More molecular and necessary experimental analyses will not likely be as fortunate, and so should be undertaken only with more appropriate equipment.

Another class of independent variables, relevant to both the present study and future studies, concerns subjects. Humans typically bring to experiments verbal repertoires and differential histories with respect to both instructions and "self–instructions" (rules and rule–governed, or verbally–mediated, behavior). The latter may be especially relevant to the present study to the extent that it bears on functional relations. A subject might behave differently depending on his or her history regarding verbal rules and self–instructions particularly with respect to experience with the workings of equipment such as might comprise experimental apparatus. For instance, a history that results in a subject stating to herself or himself that "equipment either works or doesn't work" could predispose that subject to continue pressing both keys under one reinforcer source in spite of a change from CRF on *both* keys to EXT on one key. The present study held instructions consistent across conditions; it did not apply any other control procedure with respect to any aspect of subject history.

Instructions and history variables would also be likely to generate behavior that differs from the behavior other animals might emit under the same contingencies. One aspect of the data, while not relevant to the overall conclusions of the present study, implies that those variables may indeed have been operating. Different subjects showed different response patterns in extinction. Only one subject showed an extinction curve similar to those typically generated by other animal subjects; this was subject BS (see the right hand record in Figure 3). Another subject made simple testing–like responses on the EXT key after each 100 points, or so, was earned on the CRF key; this was subject GS (see the B2 session records in Figure 5). After a burst of responses under the EXT contingency, the other subjects were more likely simply to stop EXT key responding completely, with virtually no "curve" at all (although each pattern is slightly different). On a speculative level, it may be possible that these different types of extinction curves are due to the different and unanalyzed verbal repertoires and histories that the subjects brought to the study.

Due to those possibilities caution would be appropriate in considering the extension of the multiple reinforcer source procedure to non–human subjects. The extent to which the present data are a function of the verbal repertoires and instructional and rule–stating/following histories of human subjects rather than a function of more basic processes has yet to be determined.

The consistency of results between the within–session and the between–session comparisons suggests that the use of both may be unnecessarily redundant. However, retaining both types of sessions for each subject provides a source and crosscheck for clues to understanding whatever is discovered in the data. Additional sessions with each subject, either under the same controlling variables, or under different ones (providing data on history effects), can only benefit the fine–tuning and further use of the multi–reinforcer source procedure in the study of complex, especially human, behavior.

Later data may show that the results reported here are typical of performances only early in the subject's exposure to the contingencies. Given more time, stable, *sensitive* responding might occur even under the single–source condition (though one would still have to ask: Why then and not earlier?). The relevant questions, though, are still these: Which generates more sensitivity to contingencies, the single–source condition or the multiple source condition? And which of these conditions is more analogous to the contingencies experienced in everyday reality? Only more research will tell.

Conclusion

Complex human behavior involves both simultaneous and sequential/alternating response patterns, and both need attention from researchers. Even though simultaneous responses may be more resistant to analysis, they may also more accurately characterize reality. The multiple reinforcer source procedure reported here may make possible a research project that replicates basic research on fundamental operant processes by extending the study of these processes to more complex, multiple operants. Such a research project can be a systematic and purely inductive investigation and cataloging of what happens when various basic contingencies include complex behaviors.

Before developing that kind of project, replication of the present study is needed. This replication should include both variations in the number of selector sources, and other factors (e.g., different rest periods—or none—between the component pairs in a session, other types of selectors, additional sessions that run dual/multiple sources first instead of single sources first, variations in instructions, and variations in contingencies—since sensitivity to the maximally different contingencies of CRF and EXT is no guarantee that sensitivity will hold under contingencies that are more similar). If that replication shows the multiple reinforcer source procedure to be reliable, then this procedure might evolve into a more general *multiple selector source procedure,* and additional variables can be investigated, singly or in combination. The investigation of some of these variables will benefit from the continued comparison of single and multiple selector sources; other variables may be addressed adequately with only multiple sources. Many antecedent and postcedent variables are worthy of study including (a) establishing operations, (b) stimulus discrimination, (c) generalization, (d) reinforcement schedules, (e) punishment control, (f) schedule–induced effects, (g) competing selectors (e.g., reinforcers and/or punishers of different magnitudes), and (h) multiple or varying selectors (sometimes the same type and sometimes different) for each separate, simultaneously emittable operant.

Most of those additional variables would be worthy of study both with and without the presence of discriminative stimuli in the contingencies. With some of those additional variables various selector parameters can also be researched. Such parameters could include added and subtracted (see Ledoux, 1997b) reinforcers and punishers, and primary and secondary reinforcers and punishers, as well as the latency, duration, and magnitude (a) of one or more reinforcers and punishers, and (b) of one or more response topographies. And any or all additional variables can be studied, for instance, (a) with and without instructions or variations in instructions, (b) with three or more, rather than two, simultaneously emittable responses, (c) with response–independent selectors (e.g., playing back non–contingently what the subject just produced contingently), and/or (d) with and without known or provided or (with younger subjects) short histories.

To answer those questions could take several decades (probably more) of work by many researchers. Additional, more complex or more detailed questions, worthy of attention from candidates or holders of M.A. and Ph.D. degrees, will undoubtedly arise from the data of the basic studies, as they have even from the present study.

A research project of this type can also provide a level of research effort that is especially suited to the training of behaviorological scientists by involving undergraduate as well as more advanced students and experienced researchers. The conceptual and technological levels of the basic research program are well within the reach of undergraduate students who are training in behaviorological science. Undergraduates in particular can benefit from participation in this research. They could experience early in their training (a) the requirements of study, patience, and careful planning, (b) the thrill of discovery when their efforts answer research questions, (c) the satisfaction of making an original contribution to a growing body of knowledge about complex, especially human, behaviors, and (d) the further satisfaction when they find ways to apply those answers to concerns in the world at large.

At this point, one cannot predict what important discoveries await research expansion into the effects of simultaneous selectors on simultaneously emittable multiple operants. One can reasonably predict, based on the beneficial results that have come from previous basic behaviorological research efforts, that beneficial results will also accrue from the research proposed here.

Endnotes

Parts of this work were presented at the eighth annual convention of the Association for Behavior Analysis in Milwaukee, WI, May 1982, and at the ninth annual convention of the Association for Behavior Analysis in Milwaukee, WI, May 1983, and at the fifth annual convention of The International behaviorology Association in Little Compton, RI, March 1993. The paper was then revised for inclusion in *Origins and Components of Behaviorology* (Ledoux, S.F. [1997]. Canton, NY: ABCs.).

The author thanks Chris Cherpas, Jack Michael, Alan Poling, Arthur Snapper, and Ken Stephens for collegial assistance with the research here reported. The author also thanks the poster–session attendants at TIBA–5 (especially Beatrice Barrett and Julie Vargas), and Lawrence Fraley, all of whom provided many helpful comments on various versions of this material. Address correspondence regarding this paper to the author at SUNY–CTC, Canton NY 13617–1096 USA.

References

Allison, T.S. & Lloyd, K.E. (1971). Concurrent schedules of reinforcement: Effects of gradual and abrupt increases in changeover delay. *Journal of the Experimental Analysis of Behavior, 16,* 67–74.

Baum, W.M. (1995). Radical behaviorism and the concept of agency. *Behaviorology, 3* (1), 93–106.

Bruner, A. & Revusky, S.H. (1961). Collateral behavior in humans. *Journal of the Experimental Analysis of Behavior, 4,* 349–350.

Catania, A.C. (1966). Concurrent operants. In W.K. Honig (Ed.). *Operant Behavior* (pp. 213–269). New York: Appleton–Century–Crofts.

Catania, A.C. & Cutts, D. (1963). Experimental control of superstitious responding in humans. *Journal of the Experimental Analysis of Behavior, 6,* 203–208.

Fantino, E., Squires, N., Delbruck, N., & Peterson, C. (1972). Choice behavior and the accessibility of the reinforcer. *Journal of the Experimental Analysis of Behavior, 18,* 35–44.

Ferster, C.B. (1957). Concurrent schedules of reinforcement in the Chimpanzee. *Science, 125,* 1090–1091.

Ferster, C.B. (1959). A complex concurrent schedule of reinforcement. *Journal of the Experimental Analysis of Behavior, 2,* 65–80.

Ferster, C.B. & Skinner, B.F. (1957). *Schedules of Reinforcement.* New York: Appleton–Century–Crofts.

Findley, J.D. (1958). Preference and switching under concurrent scheduling. *Journal of the Experimental Analysis of Behavior, 1,* 123–144.

Fraley, L.E. & Ledoux, S.F. (1997). Origins, status, and mission of behaviorology. In S.F. Ledoux. *Origins and Components of Behaviorology.* Canton, NY: ABCs.

Harrison, J.M. (1979). The control of responding by sounds: Unusual effect of reinforcement. *Journal of the Experimental Analysis of Behavior, 32,* 167–181.

Hearst, E. (1961). Effects of d–amphetamine on behavior reinforced by food and water. *Psychological Reports, 8,* 301–309.

Glenn, S.S. & Madden, G.J. (1995). Units of interaction, evolution, and replication: Organic and behavioral parallels. *The Behavior Analyst, 18,* 237–251.

Lane, H. (1961). Operant control of vocalizing in the chicken. *Journal of the Experimental Analysis of Behavior, 4,* 171–177.

Ledoux, S.F. (1982a). *Control of Simultaneously Reinforceable Concurrent Human Operants by a Multiple Reinforcer–Source Procedure.* Doctoral dissertation, Western Michigan University, Kalamazoo. Reprinted, with extensive revisions, as "Multiple selectors in the control of simultaneously emittable responses" in S.F. Ledoux. (1997). *Origins and Components of Behaviorology.* Canton, NY: ABCs.

Ledoux, S.F. (1982b, May). A procedure to control simultaneous concurrent human operants. Report presented at the eighth annual convention of the Association for Behavior Analysis, Milwaukee, WI.

Ledoux, S.F. (1997a). An introduction to the origins, status, and mission of behaviorology: An established science with developed applications and a new name. In S.F. Ledoux. *Origins and Components of Behaviorology.* Canton, NY: ABCs. Reprinted with revisions from (1992) *Behaviorological Commentaries, Serial No. 3,* 11–31.

Ledoux, S.F. (1997b). Increasing tact control and student comprehension through such new postcedent terms as added and subtracted reinforcers and punishers. In S.F. Ledoux. *Origins and Components of Behaviorology.* Canton, NY: ABCs. Reprinted with revisions from (in press) *The International Behaviorologist, 2.*

Pliskoff, S.S. (1971). Effects of symmetrical and asymmetrical changeover delays on concurrent performances. *Journal of the Experimental Analysis of Behavior, 16,* 249–256.

Segal, E.F. (1961). Behavioral interactions under concurrent spaced–responding, variable–interval schedules of reinforcement. *Journal of the Experimental Analysis of Behavior, 4,* 263–266.

Sidman, M. (1958). By–products of aversive control. *Journal of the Experimental Analysis of Behavior, 1,* 265–280.

Sidman, M. (1994). *Equivalence Relations and Behavior: A Research Story.* Boston, MA: Authors Cooperative.

Skinner, B.F. (1976). Farewell, my LOVELY! *Journal of the Experimental Analysis of Behavior, 25,* 218.

Snapper, A.G. & Inglis, G.B. (1978). *The SKED Software System: SUPERSKED.* Kalamazoo, MI: The SKED Users Group.

Staddon, J.F.R. & Simmelhag, B. (1971). The superstition experiment: A re–examination of its implications for the principles of adaptive behavior. *Psychological Review, 78,* 3–43.

Striefel, S. (1972). Timeout and concurrent fixed–ratio schedules with human subjects. *Journal of the Experimental Analysis of Behavior, 17,* 213–219.

Stubbs, D.A. & Pliskoff, S.S. (1969). Concurrent responding with fixed relative rate of reinforcement. *Journal of the Experimental Analysis of Behavior, 12,* 887–895.

Vargas, E.A. (1985). The ABP noncontingency: A reply to "The ABP contingency." *The Behavior Analyst, 8,* 131–132.

Quoted*

§

§

* The original *TIBA stationary header*, as designed by Stephen F. Ledoux and Scott Beach, featured the actual name of this natural science—or the most probable approximations of the name—in the five languages of people showing interest in the behaviorology movement soon after TIBA was founded.

Successful Smoking Control as an Example of a Comprehensive Behaviorological Therapy

Stephen F. Ledoux

Different therapies and interventions address different concerns. Those based on behaviorological science aim at analyzing and directly controlling the variables that are in explicit functional relations with the presenting problems. But other therapies try to deal with their concerns while ignoring the analysis and direct control of such variables. Instead these therapies focus on other variables that may relate, if at all, only indirectly to the relevant functional variables (although sometimes with a measure of adventitious success; see Fraley & Ledoux, 1997, Ch. 3). The benefits of the behaviorological approach include a greater likelihood of clinical success. Through a detailed examination of the reasons for the success of a particular therapy example, this paper suggests how success can be improved in other areas. The successful therapy used to exemplify these benefits is an early therapy that took a behaviorological approach in addressing the problem of smoking cigarettes.

A Comprehensive Therapy

Professionals engaging in therapies that address cigarette–smoking problems can be sorted according to a particular criterion: They essentially guess what steps to have their clients take to try to stop smoking while also *adding new variables to control smoking behavior* (which usually takes the form of adding "The Record" of time since the last cigarette). Or they emphasize analyzing the variables explicitly responsible for the smoking behavior and take steps to counter–control those variables directly. At the April 1973 convention of the Western Psychological Association, Joseph Morrow, Susan Gmiender, Lewis Sachs, and Helene Burgess (Morrow *et al.*, 1973) reported their design and evaluation of a therapy (a) that addressed (i.e., counter–controlled) the variables that explicitly generated and maintained smoking behavior, and (b) that showed a far higher success rate than other smoking–control therapies available at that time. They continued to use this therapy successfully in what amounts to an on–going replication. These authors attributed this success to several factors including, implicitly, what today would be called the general approach of behaviorologically analyzing and address-

---

Based on the research of others and the author, this paper originated as lecture and discussion material (a) detailing how therapies can and should focus *comprehensively* on the problems, such as smoking, presented for therapeutic intervention, and (b) describing how explicitly *analyzing and addressing* the variables directly responsible for those problems appears to be substantially responsible for the success of some therapies.

ing variables with explicit functional control over the behaviors to be increased or decreased. For smoking control this involved designing, implementing, and evaluating techniques that directly counter variables that contribute to smoking behavior.

With that attention to the details of functionally relevant variables, therapies that take this behaviorological approach tend to address their target behaviors more comprehensively than therapies lacking this approach, and also tend to succeed. Hence this paper focuses (a) on the Morrow *et al.* therapy as an example of this successful kind of comprehensive therapy, and (b) on how the general behaviorological approach can benefit clients—in this example by reducing smoking behaviors. Through extension, this same approach will likely benefit people with other kinds of concerns, large or small.

Today, over twenty years later, therapists using more recently developed smoking–control therapies often incorporate one or more of the techniques that Morrow *et al.* used directly to address functionally controlling variables (which amounts to another type of replication of the techniques Morrow *et al.* used). However, some therapists do so not because a natural science (e.g., behaviorological science), informing their practices, has led them to do so, but because they have heard or recognized how effective these techniques are. These therapies are seldom founded on a scientific approach from which practitioners can derive effective techniques. The original Morrow *et al.* therapy—as old as it may be—is featured here because it was the earliest *comprehensive* smoking intervention that was founded on a scientific approach, the approach of behaviorological science, from which practitioners can and do derive effective techniques.

Other more recent "behavior analytic" smoking interventions also use the techniques that directly address functionally controlling variables because they share the behaviorological science that gave rise to these techniques. Over the years these interventions have had a substantial impact on US health policy (see Henningfield & Higgins, 1989, for the impact of these interventions on the Surgeon General's report on some health consequences of smoking). However, the development of these interventions goes beyond the scope of this paper; the point of this paper is not to encourage a particular approach to controlling smoking as much as it is to examine the substantial success rate of one early smoking control therapy to learn something that seems to be fundamental about what might be done in general to enhance the success of most efforts to improve the human condition.

The therapy described by Morrow *et al.* differs from most non–behavioral smoking–control therapies by treating smoking "as a learned behavior, not as a pathological symptom" (p. 7 [stand–alone page numbers in this paper are from Morrow *et al.*, 1973]). Morrow *et al.* instructed clients:

> to look for environmental or situational "cues" for their urges to smoke, and, by recognizing these stimuli, manipulate their environment to ease "desires to smoke." (p. 7)

The therapy by Morrow *et al.* also differs in three other fundamental ways from most smoking–control therapies, both behavioral and non–behavioral, with which it co–existed. Each such difference will receive attention: (a) This therapy demonstrates a higher clinical success rate than those therapies. (b) This therapy provides an extension in time, with a concomitant reduction in intensity, for formal therapeutic intervention. And (c) this therapy focuses on counter–controlling the explicitly analyzed functional variables of smoking while avoiding use of the added variable of the client's "record" of time off cigarettes (on which many other smoking therapies tend ultimately to rely to control smoking). Some of these differences are also present with one or another more recent non–behavioral smoking therapy.

The overall strategy of Morrow *et al.* was to weaken the contingencies that produce smoking, while a more common overall strategy in other therapies has been to "add another variable" to treat smoking. The usual implementation of the latter strategy is to arrange a supplementary contingency to counter smoking such as a marked calendar that increasingly functions as a sort of reinforcer for the behaviors that are connoted by phrases like "not smoking" or "avoiding/resisting smoking."

(a) Therapy Success Rate

Perusal of the smoking–control literature reveals that the phrase "smoking–control therapy" covers many different interventions. All attempt to help clients stop smoking through a variety of separate or intermingled strategies.

Most of these therapies invoke aversive techniques, singly or in some combination, as the main method to bring the client's cigarette smoking down to a low daily rate, even to zero. Such aversive techniques, which directly address only one or two of the variables functionally related to smoking, include using nausea–inducing drugs, electric shocks, horror stories and discussions of the diseases to which smokers are more susceptible than non–smokers, frightening films of surgeries needed because of smoking, gory slide–show or *in vivo* comparisons of tissues from smokers with tissues from non–smokers (e.g., healthy and diseased lung tissues in jars), depressing pictures depicting negative social stereotypes of smokers, ash trays shaped like open lungs, or emotional appeals about children wanting to imitate smoking parents and about children and others suffering from inhaling secondary smoke.

These therapies typically schedule the aversive techniques for the first week or two, or several weeks at most (which may be the full extent of the therapy). During this intervention period some therapists interact with their clients individually while others do so in groups. Some therapists meet with their client or clients once each day during this period while others meet only once or twice each week.

Regardless of all that variety, nearly all of these therapies are initially successful. By the scheduled end of the aversive technique period, nearly all clients have dropped their daily smoking rate to zero or nearly zero.

At the end of the scheduled therapy intervention, after the initial success, clients are on their own. But too many of them are inadequately prepared for developments still to come, even though they know what to expect. Morrow *et al.* described the problem:

> All [subjects] reported that they had previously stopped smoking for some period of time, but began smoking again after allowing themselves what they believed to be "just one cigarette." Apparently, this first cigarette, in response to strong [discriminative stimuli] in a particular environment, has a potent reinforcement effect which results in the [subject] returning to his previous smoking level in a relatively short period of time. (Morrow *et al.*, 1973, Appendix A, item viii)

To prepare clients to stay off cigarettes after their initial success, most therapies leave clients with only one fundamental controlling variable. This variable, which does *not directly* address the majority of variables functionally related to smoking, takes the form of their "Record" of how long they have gone without smoking a cigarette. But a single post–quitting cigarette breaks the record, and the smoking problem resumes.

Some therapists thus see the record of smoke–free days as a powerful but fragile variable. "How long have I gone without smoking? Six days!" Later: "Six weeks!" Later still (maybe): "Six months!" And even later (rarely): "Six years!" The longer one goes without smoking, the more power the variable seems to exert. The problem with this variable is its fragility. Sooner or later, for most clients, too many stressors pile up on a particular day (e.g., a spouse gets upset over undone household chores, and the boss threatens to terminate and increases the work, and a broken pipe floods the basement, or the family's teenager crashes the car). The result is that the otherwise successful quitter smokes a single cigarette. And then, usually, more cigarettes. "How long since my last cigarette? Just six minutes? My record [of weeks or months or years] is wrecked. I might as well have another cigarette!" The unbroken record, so powerful while unbroken, is erased.

After engaging in therapies that leave control over smoking to that record, clients end up acting as though they can never, indeed must never, have another cigarette. This is not true. In terms of health, any single cigarette probably causes less damage than taking a long walk on a summer afternoon in a smog–polluted city. A single cigarette after—perhaps long after—quitting, may be a powerful inducement to return to smoking, but that return *is* avoidable (see Morrow *et al.*, 1973). The erasing of the record, however, which a single post–quitting cigarette accomplishes, can be a powerful inducement to return to smoking. Since that cigarette is nearly inevitable whether or not a client is relying on such a record, its very use as a controlling variable may be seen as undercutting continued success.

As a result of the fragility of the record variable, nearly all therapies that rely on it show a low, long–term clinical success rate:

> Within a few weeks the majority of quitters are back at original rate and within a year there is scant evidence that the few remaining abstainers differ in number from "spontaneous" quitters. (p. 1)

That low success rate produces adverse effects. Clients' self–esteem aside, not only have they returned to smoking but also their efforts to quit have ultimately gone unrewarded making quitting yet again even more difficult to attempt. The joke that "it's easy to quit smoking; I've done it hundreds of times" is not funny to smokers who have tried, and failed, to quit.

In contrast, the behaviorological smoking–control therapy featured in the Morrow *et al.* study shows a high, long term clinical success rate. Their study involved 55 clients, 25 women and 30 men. Ages ranged from 28 to 65 years. Initial smoking age ranged from 13 to 28 years. The number of years that these clients had smoked ranged from 9 to 45 years. The daily rate of cigarette smoking at the start of the study ranged from 15 to 60 (three–quarters of a pack per day to three packs per day). As with clients in other smoking–control therapies, these clients all ceased smoking, as scheduled, by the end of the initial week of therapy. Overall, of the 55 clients starting the program, 34 (or 62%) were not smoking one year later. However, the therapy consisted of two sequential components, one individual–based (that first week) and the other group–based (three months of weekly meetings). So Morrow *et al.* tracked long–term success rates separately (a) for those who did not complete both components and (b) for those who did complete both components. Their results show that 35 clients (64% of the 55 starting clients) completed only the first therapy component; of these, only 16 clients (46%) were still not smoking one year later (a recidivism rate of 54%). Their results also show that 20 clients (36% of the 55 starting clients) completed *both* therapy components; of these, 18 clients *(90%)* were still not smoking one year later (a recidivism rate of only 10%).

That is a clinical success rate which therapies seldom achieve (regardless of the presenting problems they face). To what might the success rate of this therapy be due? As the choice of names for the techniques they used will show, Morrow *et al.* implicitly suggested, and this paper explicitly suggests, that the success is due to the comprehensive, designed connection, based on a behaviorological analysis, between the therapy techniques and the variables functionally related to smoking. This paper makes that connection through an elaboration of the analysis by detailing the behaviorological process and procedures of this therapy, including how to get more clients to complete both therapy components and so increase their chances for long–term success.

(b) Therapy Process

The process of this therapy contains two sequential components. The first involves daily individual sessions and the second involves weekly (and later, monthly) group sessions. (Descriptions of all the self–control techniques, which are mentioned only by name in this section, are included in the "Therapy Procedures" section. Some techniques, such as satiation smoking, may at first seem like they would make smoking cravings worse, but on closer inspection they would not, and do not, have this effect.)

Individual daily sessions. In the therapy Morrow *et al.* describe, the first component is individual based. The client and therapist meet Monday through Friday for five daily sessions, each one hour long. These sessions have some activities in common, including these which occur each day: (a) The therapist collects the record of the number of cigarettes the client smoked in the previous 24 hours and praises drops in smoking rate (a part of valuable rapport establishment; in several different ways, more successful clients reported good rapport with their therapist—see Morrow *et al.*, 1973). (b) The therapist supervises while the client engages in the technique called *satiation smoking* (a maximum of three "satiation cigarettes" per session). (c) The therapist and client discuss the previously introduced techniques and any difficulties the client may have experienced using them. (d) The therapist teaches the client any self–control techniques that are scheduled for introduction and together they work out and record the details of the client's application of the techniques, taking the client's particular circumstances into account. (e) The therapist provides any instructions relevant to the client's efforts between then and the next session (e.g., any restrictions on smoking between sessions, and the need to continue to keep an accurate record of how many cigarettes get smoked between sessions). And (f) to a client's doubts about his or her ability to succeed in quitting, the therapist responds with empathy for the difficulty the client is experiencing, expresses confidence, draws comparisons with similar clients who have quit smoking, and engages in other helpful verbal exchanges.

Each of the five individual daily sessions has some different activities also. These focus especially on the introduction of additional self–control techniques. (For details of therapist/client interactions regarding the common and different activities listed in this paper, see the "Therapist Manual" that accompanies Morrow *et al.*, 1973).

On Monday the therapist first stresses the importance of client cooperation if the client is to reach zero smoking by the end of the first week; the therapist's role is to aid the client in reducing smoking so that non–smoking is possible between the Thursday and Friday sessions. Then the therapist teaches the client the technique called *satiation smoking.* The client smokes three satiation cigarettes during the session, using the client's normal brand of cigarettes. The client intersperses these satiation cigarettes with learning the three self–control techniques called *pure activity, anti–social chair,* and *difficult to obtain.* The therapist also explains the purpose of these and later–introduced techniques in ultimately eliminating smoking. Clients may smoke normally as much as they wish between the Monday and Tuesday sessions, provided that they engage in all relevant self–control techniques which their therapist has introduced.

On Tuesday the client again smokes three satiation cigarettes, the first two of the client's normal brand. The third is an unfiltered Camel provided by the therapist (if the client normally smokes Camels, the therapist provides an even stronger tasting brand imported from Asia). Between these satiation cigarettes, the therapist reviews previously introduced techniques, and introduces more self–control techniques. These include the techniques called *alternative behaviors, review emotional responses,* the filter–related part of *change cigarettes* (a two–step technique; the therapist will introduce the second step, the brand–related part, at the next session), and *damage cigarettes.* Between the Tuesday and Wednesday sessions, clients may again smoke normally as much as desired provided that they engage in all relevant, introduced self–control techniques.

On Wednesday the client again smokes three satiation cigarettes. Only one is of the client's normal brand; the other two are unfiltered Camels. Between these, the therapist reviews previously introduced self–control techniques, and introduces several more. The first two are for immediate use. These include the technique called *rehearsal of difficult times,* and the second, brand–related part of the two–step *change cigarettes* technique. The therapist also introduces the technique called the *quitter's procedure* for later use. The therapist stresses the importance of getting the smoking rate down to the lowest possible level between this session and the next so that the client can more easily reach the zero rate between the Thursday and Friday sessions. To help reduce the rate to the lowest possible level, the client is to postpone smoking as long as possible. When the client does smoke, he or she is to engage all introduced self–control techniques while smoking that cigarette as a satiation cigarette (inhaling every six seconds using the seconds indicator on his or her clock or watch). Finally, the client is to destroy or give away all of his or her cigarettes just before the Thursday session.

On Thursday the client smokes only two satiation cigarettes, both Camels. For most of this session, the therapist emphasizes to the client the importance of going without cigarettes for the next 24 hours, and again reviews all the self–control techniques. As part of that review, the therapist advises the client on managing any problems experienced in the application of those techniques. As an aid to abstaining, the client can look forward to smoking only one satiation cigarette at the Friday session. And from now on the client is to use the technique called the *quitter's procedure* for any cigarette he or she smokes.

On Friday, the last individual session, the therapist allows the client to smoke one satiation cigarette (a Camel). Having abstained for 24 hours already, most clients experience great discomfort over this cigarette; should they so chose, they need not complete it. The client and therapist review what the client has been through and discuss what the client might experience in the adjustment to non–smoking. In the rest of this session, the therapist describes to the client the scheduling, purposes, and benefits of the upcoming weekly (and later, monthly) group sessions.

Virtually all clients achieve zero smoking between the Thursday and Friday individual sessions. Something akin to a shaping process usually occurs as they extend this one–day success to three days by abstaining from the Friday individual session to the first group session scheduled for the following Monday, and then from this first group session to the next one a week later, and so on.

Group sessions. The second therapy component is group based. The therapy Morrow *et al.* describe continues with eleven weekly group meetings spread over three months. Each group meeting is of two hours duration, and is usually held on Monday evenings. The group is comprised of clients who have completed the individual–therapy sessions. At any particular meeting some clients may be attending for the first time, others for the last time, and most somewhere between these points.

At each group meeting similar activities take place. In an informal atmosphere of healthy beverages and snacks (No smoking!) clients introduce themselves, state how long ago they quit smoking, and describe any problems they are encountering or what topics they would like to see the group discuss. Together they discuss events in their lives related to smoking, the difficult situations they described facing, and how to handle these. Thus each client can benefit from the experience of the others. When they exhaust smoking–related subjects, they are free to discuss any other topics of mutual interest. In these ways they bond together into a mutual support group of non–smoking friends (the first and often the only such friends some clients have) who have had similar quit–smoking experiences. For some clients these friendships and social contacts endure on their own after the end of formally scheduled meetings (a variable whose contribution to client success is difficult to assess).

The therapist keeps the group focused and provides verbal reinforcement when applicable. Should a client need additional help, the therapist works out an appropriate individual program with that client.

(c) Therapy Procedures

The therapy Morrow *et al.* describe employs a particular set of procedures for the client to use. Most of these are self–control techniques that can be found, in general and specific ways, in the literature (e.g., Skinner, 1953; Stuart & Davis, 1972). The differentiation among these techniques derives in part from the relation between each technique and a particular variable functionally related to smoking, and in part from the convenience thereby afforded in simplifying the presentation of the techniques to clients. Also, based on the author's work with clients, this paper further subdivides the techniques, so some names differ from those used by Morrow *et al.*

Morrow *et al.* specifically designed each technique to counter one or another of the variables, or variable components, explicitly controlling smoking. These variables fall under four headings, each of which will receive attention: (a) *antecedent stimulus variables* involving respondent aversive and other emotional considerations as well as discriminative stimulus considerations, (b) *response considerations,* (c) *postcedent stimulus variables* involving conditioned and unconditioned reinforcement, and (d) *the combination of variables* when clients are "on their own" during and after the second, group–based component of the therapy.

Antecedent stimulus variables. Four techniques address antecedent stimulus variables. One addresses aversive respondent variables. One addresses other emotional respondent variables. And two address two different types of discriminative stimuli.

The therapy technique called *satiation smoking* is the aversive respondent technique in this therapy. In this technique, the client inhales on a cigarette every six seconds. As the rate of smoking outside the sessions decreases, satiation smoking becomes increasingly uncomfortable. While the aversive effects are temporary, clients may extinguish a satiation cigarette if they find it too uncomfortable.

The therapy technique called *review emotional responses* addresses respondent emotional variables. In this technique clients list (on a card that they carry with them) all their reasons for quitting smoking and for not smoking. As time passes clients remove from the list any reason that fails to elicit the appropriate, strong emotional reaction. Examples could be feeling pleasure elicited by a positive reason for ending smoking (e.g., pleasure at being able to smell flowers again) or feeling fear elicited by a negative reason for ending smoking (e.g., fear that the client's toddler might play with the cigarette lighter). Clients also add to the list reasons newly discovered to elicit appropriate emotional reactions. They attempt to increase the anti–smoking effects of the reasons on the list by reading the list before engaging in reinforcing activities such as eating a meal. Therapists instruct their clients to review the list several times each day during the week of individual sessions. In reviewing the list they should focus on each reason until it elicits the relevant emotion. They also review the list as part of the quitter's procedure. This technique is needed to replace old emotional ties operating to support smoking with new emotional ties operating to support non–smoking.

Two other therapy techniques address discriminative stimuli. Even though both decrease in relevance as clients progress past the initial cessation of smoking, both play valuable roles in bringing about that initial cessation.

One discriminative–stimulus focused technique is called *difficult to obtain.* In this technique clients put their cigarettes and matches in places that are separated in space as much as reasonably possible. The locations should necessitate additional response effort, such as bending over, to retrieve an item. This makes satisfying an urge to smoke more difficult (see Ledoux, 1973, for research support of the response status of urges to smoke). For example, at home the cigarettes might be kept in a chest in an upstairs bedroom (with the TV located in the downstairs living room) while the matches might be kept on a high shelf in the basement. Should an urge to smoke occur during a TV program, the increase in time and effort required to obtain the needed items is likely to preclude the actual occurrence of smoking at that time. The inconvenience is often simply too great to bother with; clients report saying to themselves such things as "Do I really want to bother going and getting those things [cigarettes and matches] right now? No. If I must smoke, I'll just smoke later." The difficult–to–obtain technique is needed because the normal proximity of cigarettes and matches, to the client as well as to each other, affords these items a detrimental level of evocative power, as discriminative stimuli, over smoking. Little, if any, more is needed to get a smoker to light up a cigarette. A smoker reaching into a shirt pocket for paper and pen to write down a telephone number advertised by a commercial on TV would, upon finding a pack of cigarettes also in that pocket, likely light up.

The other discriminative–stimulus focused technique is called *rehearsal of difficult times.* In this technique the client makes special arrangements with everyone from whom he or she might receive cigarettes. For one day (the day immediately after this technique is introduced) all these people are to offer cigarettes unexpectedly to the client. The client is never to accept an offered cigarette but instead is to practice saying "no" to the offers. Clients who experience an excessive urge to smoke are to get their own cigarettes under already introduced techniques. Morrow *et al.* sometimes made quite specific not only their analysis of the relation between a technique and a smoking–controlling variable but also the occasions for the use of the technique. Rehearsal of difficult times allows:

> ...the discriminative stimuli... to occur in certain situations, which previously had always resulted in the response, without allowing the response to occur. In the present study, this procedure was recommended to all subjects who had a spouse who smoked and from whom they had often accepted cigarettes, or who frequently had "bummed" cigarettes from others in the past. (Morrow *et al.*, 1973, Appendix A, item vii)

The rehearsal of difficult times technique is needed because most smokers find saying "no" when someone offers a cigarette to be very difficult, especially given the price of cigarettes. Some report *never* having said "no" under such circumstances. Under conditions of deprivation during and after stop–smoking therapy, saying "no" is likely to be all the more difficult. The rehearsal of difficult times techniques enables the client, under contrived but also controlled conditions, to practice saying "no." Having said "no" at least in the past under relevant stimulus circumstances, clients find saying "no" easier when they are later faced with a real need to say "no."

Response considerations. The therapy technique called *alternative behaviors* addresses the problems associated with the response status of smoking. In this technique the therapist helps the client construct a list of alternative behaviors in which the client is increasingly to engage as smoking decreases. For this list many clients emphasize past activities, such as hobbies or skills, in which they no longer engage but to which they would like to return. (The cessation of smoking may even make some preferred activities affordable.) Morrow *et al.* provided these details:

> They are asked to include at least three activities in each of three categories: physical activities (such as jogging, bike riding, gardening, walking, etc.); quiet activities (i.e., crossword or jigsaw puzzles, sewing, arts and crafts, carpentry, reading, etc.); and oral activities (such as sucking, chewing or biting on lemon drops, life–savers, gum, celery, fruits, various non–toxic objects, etc.). (Morrow *et al.*, 1973, Appendix A, item iv)

The alternative behaviors technique is needed because behavior does not occur in a vacuum; it occurs in time. For smokers, smoking behavior fills part of each day. As smoking drops through therapy, more of each day becomes behaviorally empty. If no plans are made to fill this time by design with beneficial activities, then troublesome activities may fill it by accident. Extra eating is a common, undesirable replacement. Many people who have quit smoking have reported an increase in eating, and consequently weight. The origin of such problems may reside in the normal behavioral process of response generalization, in this case from one consumption response class to another. The alternative behaviors technique fills this time by design.

Postcedent stimulus variables. Four therapy techniques address the reinforcing capacity of cigarettes and smoking. All work to weaken that capacity. The first two focus on counter–controlling *conditioned* reinforcing capacity. The other two focus on counter–controlling *unconditioned* reinforcing capacity. These four techniques are needed to help counter any continued generation and maintenance of smoking due to its reinforcement value, for this value probably constitutes the most powerful of the variables responsible for the behavior of smoking. (The unconditioned reinforcing capacity of nicotine may be more powerful for most smokers than any conditioned reinforcing capacity of cigarettes or smoking. However, since the therapist usually cannot be sure if a client trying to quit is more affected by unconditioned reinforcers or by conditioned reinforcers, both deserve therapeutic attention.)

One of two techniques focused on *conditioned*–reinforcement is called *pure activity*. Normally a smoker engages in other activities while smoking. This pairs the *physical* (and social) stimulus components of these activities with cigarettes and smoking, which establishes some of the conditioned reinforcing capacity of cigarettes and smoking. The pure activity technique counter–controls much of this normal, automatic pairing of physical reinforcers with smoking, for a pure activity is one that lacks connection with any previously associated physical reinforcers. In this technique, when clients smoke, that is *all* that they do; they engage in no other activities while they smoke. That means, for instance, no television viewing, no stereo listening, no drinking, no eating, no window gazing, no reading, no driving, no studying, no dancing, and no socializing. This technique thus reduces some of the conditioned reinforcement value of smoking, because it stops the pairing of smoking and most other physical reinforcers.

The other technique focused on conditioned–reinforcement is called *anti–social chair* (sometimes called "smoking spot"). Engaging simultaneously in smoking and social activities, a common occurrence, also pairs the *social* stimulus components of those activities with smoking. This again increases and maintains some of the conditioned reinforcement value of smoking. The anti–social chair technique extends the pure activity technique by counter–controlling much of this normal, automatic pairing of social reinforcers with smoking. In this technique the therapist and client discuss locations, suitably isolated from the normal social environments, that the client can use as smoking spots where he or she will be *alone* when smoking. Consistent with the pure activity technique, these are locations where the client can keep a chair to be used exclusively for smoking. (The overlap of the pure activity technique and anti–social chair techniques is not an issue.) The client selects one spot for use at home and one spot for use at work. The client is not to smoke anywhere else; when away from these places, a public toilet is a suitable, anti–social smoking spot. Spots that some clients have chosen include spare rooms, bathrooms, stairwells, basements, attics, and garages. This technique thus further reduces the conditioned reinforcement value of smoking because it stops the pairing of smoking and most social reinforcers.

Morrow *et al.* kept the two techniques that are focused on the *unconditioned* reinforcement value together. They referred to the combination as *reduction of reinforcement value* because both shared in reducing this reinforcement value. Here these two techniques are described separately.

One of the two techniques focused on reducing unconditioned–reinforcement is called *change cigarettes.* In this technique clients change their cigarettes in two steps. The first step is filter–related. At the scheduled session, clients who smoke filtered cigarettes remove the filters, making the cigarettes aversive (or "distasteful," as clients describe them). Clients who smoke unfiltered cigarettes change to a filtered brand. The second step is brand–related. At the next session all clients change to a strong unfiltered brand, making the cigarettes even more distasteful. Thus the clients' actions changing the cigarettes offset some of the unconditioned reinforcement value of smoking by making smoking increasingly aversive.

The other technique focused on reducing unconditioned–reinforcement is called *damage cigarettes.* In this technique clients damage their cigarettes by poking pin holes in them (a minimum of five pin holes) or by waterlogging them, or both. Damaging the cigarettes in any of these ways before smoking them makes them distasteful. Thus the clients' action of damaging the cigarettes also offsets some of the unconditioned reinforcement value of smoking by also increasing the aversiveness of smoking.

(Used alone, these techniques might condition clients to tolerate stronger cigarettes. But clients, working on many smoking–control techniques concurrently, are observed by therapists to reduce smoking, not to tolerate smoking stronger cigarettes.)

The combination of variables. The therapy technique called the *quitter's procedure* addresses the combination of variables *after* the client has completed the one–week, individual–based therapy component. During this period some previously introduced techniques stand alone (e.g., the alternative behaviors technique that continues whether or not other techniques are in use) while others are no longer relevant to the client's efforts (e.g., the difficult–to–obtain technique since the client no longer owns cigarettes). The quitter's procedure combines all remaining, relevant techniques in a way that avoids clients having to rely on an "it's been x amount of time since the last cigarette" record that verbally implies falsely to them that they can never again have another cigarette. Instead the quitter's procedure allows future cigarettes but only under specific, rate–reducing controls.

Morrow *et al.* designed the quitter's procedure so that successful clients need not fear falling for the temptation to have a post–quitting cigarette.

> This technique was developed in response to the expressed fear of (subjects) that they would again return to smoking if and when they ever had a cigarette after they quit, and their expressed inability to stop smoking if that meant they never, under any circumstances, could have another cigarette. (Subjects) were told that they could have a cigarette, after a period of zero smoking, which would satisfy their urge to smoke while at the same time making the smoking response so aversive that the probability of emitting the smoking response would not be increased... (Morrow *et al.*, 1973, Appendix A, item viii)

Therapists describe the quitter's procedure to clients, in lay language, as a series of steps. These become successively more difficult so as to counter increasingly strong urges to smoke. In the quitter's procedure, when an urge to smoke occurs, clients face a series of what may conveniently be called choice, or decision, points.

Prompted by an urge to smoke, the first decision point occurs after clients initially observe and report to themselves (as a "public of one"; see Ledoux, 1973) their own momentary high probability of smoking. (For the level of discourse in this paper and with clients, this can be more simply, though less accurately, described by saying that clients verbally decide whether or not to smoke a cigarette.) Throughout therapy clients come to understand the fact that smoking has causes. After experiencing an urge to smoke, verbal responses regarding both the recollection of this fact and the realization that one or another cause is currently operating to make the client smoke are often adequate to prompt the further verbal, self–instructional response, and compliance behavior, of a decision not to smoke.

If the decision is to smoke, then the second decision point occurs after clients leave the immediate situation in which they decided to smoke. One stimulus or another has exerted enough control while they were in that environment to evoke the decision to smoke; the first step in weakening that control is to move away from that environment. Once in another setting they are to consider again whether or not to smoke. Simply changing environments is often adequate to prompt compliance with the verbal self–instruction not to smoke.

If the decision still is to smoke, then clients are to review their emotional responses list. The third decision point occurs after this is done when they again consider whether or not to smoke. Reviewing this list is often adequate to prompt compliance with the verbal self–instruction not to smoke.

If the decision to smoke continues, then other decision points occur both before and after clients walk, if possible, to a store where they might *buy* a pack of cigarettes, since they do not own or "bum" any. But before walking or buying, they review the final sequence of the quitter's procedure; they review what they must do *if* they let stand the decision to smoke: (a) They must buy an expensive pack of specified, strong tasting, unfiltered cigarettes. (b) They must trash 19 of the cigarettes from the pack right then at the store (because they had an urge to smoke only one cigarette, and keeping the other 19 would only provide them with 19 more temptations). And (c) they must take the remaining cigarette to an agreed upon smoking spot where they must put pin holes into the cigarette and/or waterlog it before smoking that cigarette as a satiation cigarette! Having reviewed what they must do in the final sequence of the quitter's procedure, they again consider whether or not to smoke. Reviewing this final sequence, experiencing the aversive emotional reaction to it, is often adequate to prompt compliance with the further verbal self–instruction not to smoke.

If the decision to smoke stands, then the client buys a pack of the specified brand of cigarettes and continues through that final quitter's procedure sequence (why clients follow these rules is discussed later). By completing the quitter's procedure, the client has satisfied the urge to smoke but has not reinforced smoking. (See Morrow *et al.*, 1973, for more detail and the rationale on the parts of the quitter's procedure.)

One other factor bears on the continued successful application of the quitter's procedure. As part of the discussions on this procedure, therapists also repeatedly remind clients that smoking a post–quitting cigarette in any way other than through the use of this procedure (or using the quitter's procedure too often) carries a high probability of returning to smoking.

The quitter's procedure is needed because virtually everyone who has smoked and quit can expect to experience an occasional urge to smoke. Presumably one or another as yet unaddressed smoking–evoking variable has momentarily raised the probability of smoking. (Some of these variables are essentially unaddressable. For example, only a very rare client would have the authority to ban, say, cigarette vending machines from all of the places he or she ever encounters. Yet such a measure would be required if a person were to minimize the smoking–evoking stimulus control effects of these machines. Nevertheless, such measures are simply beyond normal reach.) Under these circumstances the quitter's procedure seems vital to continued success in non–smoking because it provides the client a way to "satisfy" urges to smoke while minimizing the reinforcers from smoking.

The quitter's procedure also increases the understanding of those who have never smoked regarding the extent of the problems faced by smokers who want to quit. The rigorous rate–reducing controls of the quitter's procedure surprise many of these non–smokers who see such controls as extreme. They ask "How could anyone ever follow that procedure? How could they throw the money tied up in 19 cigarettes away, or take those other steps? Why would they put themselves through all that?" Smokers who quit through using the quitter's procedure provide the answer: They experience, in various ways, that the quitter's procedure works, so they follow it, finding this procedure to be an invaluable aid to successfully quitting smoking. Most smokers find the prospect of never again having another cigarette to be a virtually impassible barrier to successful quitting. Yet those who have used the quitter's procedure to stop smoking have shown, through their compliance with it, that using this procedure is easier than never ever again having another cigarette.

A summary table. Table 1 summarizes the self–control technique information. The name of each technique appears in relation to the type of variables it addresses and the session at which it is introduced.

A Partial, Small Scale Replication and Extension

After using the Morrow *et al.* therapy with a group of clients in Australia in the late 1970s, the author had occasion to work with a small number of American clients (about half a dozen) who hoped to quit smoking in the early 1980s. While the procedures for

Session	Variables		
	Antecedent	Response	Postcedent
Monday	❧ Satiation smoking ❧ Difficult to obtain		❧ Pure activity ❧ Anti–social chair
Tuesday	❧ Review emotional responses	❧ Alternative behaviors	❧ Change cigarettes (filter part) ❧ Damage cigarettes
Wednesday	❧ Rehearsal of difficult times		❧ Change cigarettes (brand part) ❧ Quitter's procedure (only introduced)
Thursday			❧ (Quitter's procedure—begin use)

Table 1. Names of self–control techniques by the type of variables addressed and the session at which introduced.

most of the author's clients were basically identical to those Morrow *et al.* used with their clients, the process differed.

One difference in process concerned the number of meetings after the daily sessions. Interested in reducing the recidivism rate found in their study, Morrow *et al.* recommended that clients continue attendance at group meetings on a monthly basis for nine more months, This schedule would extend therapy duration to a full year, while increasing the interval between meetings through an additional step (daily to weekly *to monthly*). Such a schedule more gradually reduces—compared to the original Morrow *et al.* study—the therapist's part in the contingencies generating and maintaining clients' efforts to quit smoking. This gradual reduction in reliance on the therapist (akin to a fading procedure) seemed to contribute to clients' success when the therapy was completed and they proceeded independently. Based on preliminary evidence of benefits to clients, this practice seemed to contribute to reducing recidivism.

The author implemented this recommendation. But his clients were not numerous enough at any one time to meet as a group. However, they did meet individually with the therapist about 20 more times over a full year. The first eleven meetings occurred once each week over about three months, and the remaining nine meetings occurred once each month. To the extent possible these meetings covered the same ground, and served the same purposes, as the group meetings in the Morrow *et al.* study.

Another difference between the process for the author's clients and the process for clients in the Morrow *et al.* study concerned special fees. These were fees that also related to the recurring concern about recidivism. To reduce recidivism in their smoking–control therapy, Morrow *et al.* suggested another strategy besides extending meetings from weekly to monthly intervals. Based on their preliminary data, they also suggested that recidivism would likely decrease if therapists required each client to pay a special fee that would be refunded if, and only if, the client had attended nearly all therapy meetings regardless of whether or not the client had quit smoking. They suggested that making the refund contingent on attendance rather than on success might reduce the chance of clients quitting therapy; this should increase the likelihood of their quitting smoking. Given the money that quitting smoking saves (even after paying the therapist's regular fees) this special fee strategy was easy to institute. In addition, some clients saw the refund as a nice bonus for their successful efforts. The author implemented this recommendation also.

Compared with the Morrow *et al.* results, do longer therapy duration, or more gradually increasing the interval between meetings, or instituting special fees, work well for individuals or for groups? These are questions for further research as the limited data available at present are insufficient to provide an answer for them.

Only one of the author's clients can serve here as an example, since over the last ten years he has been able to keep in touch with only one of them. Even this has usually been through the accidental and occasional contact (e.g., spotting her in a grocery store about once each year). Even this type of contact was possible only because this client has remained in the "local" rural area, although residing about 20 miles from the author's residence. She has granted permission for her data to be reported here. (Clients had originally been told that their data was being collected solely for therapeutic purposes. No others could be reached regarding permission to use their data. So, except to point out that her success is typical of the other clients, nothing more will be said about their data.)

The one client whose data can be used was one of those who paid a special fee of $50 that she did earn back solely by meeting the therapy contact requirements. She also quit smoking. Her characteristics showed her to be similar to the clients in the Morrow *et al.* study. Smoking just under one pack per day, she began smoking–control therapy at age 41, having begun to smoke 22 years earlier at age 19. She had twice previously tried to quit. After seven years of smoking, she tried "Bantron" for one week (although she is unsure, she recalls that this was a gum for controlling smoking). Five years later she tried special smoke–reducing filters for one month. Another ten years passed before she tried quitting again, this time with the therapy discussed here.

Her data show a pattern similar to that of the successful clients in the Morrow *et al.* study. Due to the 40–mile round trip required to meet with her therapist (and the long winters along New York State's border with Canada where that driving took place) her "daily" sessions had to be spaced two to four days apart. Nevertheless, she achieved zero smoking by the fifth therapy session in early March 1985. Due again to that driving distance, she continued in contact with her therapist by telephone once or twice each week for 15 weeks. In June 1985 the phone contacts became monthly until formal contacts stopped a year later in July 1986. At that time she had not resumed smoking. A formal follow-up in June of 1987, one–year after therapy ended (and over two years after therapy had started) found that she had still not resumed smoking. In early 1990, nearly three years after the formal follow-up and while preparing to be away for a year (teaching abroad), the author checked again and found that no return to smoking had occurred. At this point she had not smoked for over four years.

Two developments in this client's experience may be of interest to therapists and others. One development concerned the client's bowling once each week. From the time she achieved zero smoking to the end of the bowling season that year (in September), she found that the only occasion that was difficult for her to handle was bowling night. The situation presented great pressure to be sociable and to smoke. Sometimes she resisted successfully and other times she required a slightly modified quitter's procedure cigarette: no anti–social chair was available (she had to be present to take her turn). In spite of these difficulties, she did not return to smoking.

The other development that may be of interest concerns the circumstances around which she *did* once return to smoking. In July of 1996, while recomposing lecture materials to form this paper, the author had checked with this client for permission to use her data and found that some problems had occurred, and been resolved, in the years after he left for the year abroad. (As could happen, no contact had occurred in the years between his return and her resolution of the problem).

In mid–1990 the client experienced an overload of stressors. Her mother–in–law suffered a stroke, and died a couple of months later. She began smoking again when the stroke occurred. By the time of the death, she was back to a pack per day. This rate maintained until December 1993 when she became ill with pneumonia. Upon recuperation she found herself reinstituting many of the self–control techniques from her previous experience with the therapy. This action reduced her smoking rate again to zero in a matter of weeks. She has not smoked since then.

These data, from only one client, while enticing for what one might hope they say about the therapy as conducted by the author, are clearly insufficient to answer any questions about the particular changes, from the Morrow *et al.* processes, upon which the data are based. On the other hand these data do not contradict the data reported by Morrow *et al.* In their own limited way, these data provide a small measure of support for the conclusions of both Morrow *et al.* and this author.

Conclusion

The smoking–control therapy used by Morrow *et al.* and the author *provides an example* of a therapy that addresses its concerns comprehensively, is successful, and is theory based in that it derives its practices from established behaviorological principles. Its substantial clinical success rate shows this therapy to be a valuable example of how the general approach of behaviorologically analyzing *and addressing* explicit functionally controlling variables can benefit clients, in this case clients with smoking problems. Extension of these characteristics to many other kinds of concerns, large or small, will likely enable people with those concerns to attain similar success rates.

Endnotes

This paper achieved final form both for presentation at the ninth annual convention of The International Behaviorology Association in Plymouth, MA, March 1997, and for inclusion in *Origins and Components of Behaviorology* (Ledoux, S.F. [1997]. Canton, NY: ABCs.).

The author thanks Grace Baron, Dale Bower, Lawrence Fraley, Richard Malott, and Bruce Thyer for providing many helpful comments on various drafts of this material. Address correspondence regarding this paper to the author at SUNY–CTC, Canton NY 13617–1096 USA.

References

Fraley, L.E. & Ledoux, S.F. (1997). Origins, status, and mission of behaviorology. In S.F. Ledoux. *Origins and Components of Behaviorology.* Canton, NY: ABCs.

Henningfield, J.E. & Higgins, S.T. (1989). The influence of behavior analysis on The Surgeon General's Report, "The health consequences of smoking: Nicotine addiction." *The Behavior Analyst, 12,* 99–101.

Ledoux, S.F. (1973). *The Experimental Analysis of Coverants.* M.A. thesis, California State University, Sacramento.

Morrow, J., Gmiender, S., Sachs, L., & Burgess, H. (1973, April). Elimination of cigarette smoking behavior by stimulus satiation, self–control techniques, and group therapy. Paper presented at the annual convention of the Western Psychological Association. Printed (1976) for private study purposes, Churchill, Victoria, Australia: GIAE. [Contact Stephen Ledoux at the address above to arrange for a copy.]

Skinner, B.F. (1953). *Science and Human Behavior.* New York: Macmillan.

Stuart, R.B. & Davis, B. (1972). *Slim Chance in a Fat World: Behavioral Control of Obesity.* Champaign, IL: Research Press [clinican's edition: ISBN 0-87822-060-7].

Creative Life–style Management Through On–line and Real–time Application of the Behaviorological Education Practices of Precision Teaching

David R. Feeney

Ever since the founding of their science in the 1930s, behaviorological scientists and practitioners have been dedicated to applying their discipline to the many, many behavior–related concerns of people and society (Ledoux, 1997a; Skinner 1953). For instance, concerns about education represent a major area receiving attention since the middle of the twentieth century (e.g., Skinner, 1968; West & Hamerlynck, 1992). One of the most successful educational approaches to come out of behaviorological science is *precision teaching* (Youth Policy Institute, 1988). Another area of concern that has received attention is life–style management (e.g., smoking control; see Ledoux, 1997b).

However, new delivery methods for behaviorological interventions are less common than the interventions themselves. Delivery methods for precision teaching and life–style management interventions have been mostly of the face–to–face variety. With the increasing development of interconnected personal computer technologies, another delivery method, *on–line delivery,* has become available for research and application.

This paper discusses pilot research that combines problems from life–style management with solutions from precision teaching techniques that are delivered on–line, with occasional real–time elements, using personal computer technologies. Precision teaching practices are applied to the management of various life–style concerns through creative computer–based interactions between the client and the educator (often called a therapist). The research reported here involves clients presenting life–style management problems regarding decreases in smoking and weight, and increases in college study skills. A brief overview of precision teaching, including its core principles and various applications, will be followed by a basic description of the methodological elements common to the experimental interventions. Then the experimental interventions with each of the three life–style concerns will be discussed, including the

This paper originated in discussions between its author and the author of *Origins and Components of Behaviorology* (Ledoux, 1997a) concerning a topic suggested for editorial expansion of another paper in this book (Ledoux, 1997b). For reasonable treatment, though, the suggested topic deserved its own space. It is included in this book of readings not only for the value of any particular therapeutic successes it reports, but more for the forward–looking nature of this research into a new, additional, and beneficial delivery medium for helping professions informed by behaviorological science.

instructional procedures employed with each, and a discussion of results. Finally, a general discussion will include a short review of the feasibility of adapting standard daily measures of rates of response as the "independent variable of choice" in on-line educational methodology for effective behavior change.

Precision Teaching: A Copernican Revolution in Instruction

Precision teaching is a method of instruction derived from both the basic laboratory research of B.F. Skinner (1953) and applied operant research of Ogden Lindsley (1956, 1960). Lindsley is known as the founder of precision teaching (Lindsley, 1990). Precision teaching principles have been successfully applied in classroom instruction (Lindsley, 1993; Youth Policy Institute, 1988) as well as in therapy (Johnson, 1972), social work (Green & Morrow, 1972), nursing (Dean, 1973), and medical rehabilitation (Merbitz, King, Cherney, Marqui, Grip, & Markowitz, 1996).

Lindsley (1990) identifies the basic components of precision teaching as:

- daily measurement of behavioral frequency of correct (acceptable) responses and incorrect (unacceptable) responses;
- the use of standard charts to display students' self–recorded frequencies as data; and
- a reliance on individual student performance data to guide instructional decision–making, as summarized in the phrase "the child knows best."

Students in a precision teaching instructional system record their own daily learning, and display charts of learning progress to the teacher and others. Using individual student progress charts, teachers facilitate student practice while guiding students through subsequent instruction. Data from students' daily practice of words read, flashcards said, or other target actions, becomes the foremost guide to the teacher in continuing, abandoning, or revising interactive instructional sequences.

The differences between precision teaching and traditional methods are substantial. While conventional teaching methods stem from the *presentation* model of education, precision teaching procedures arise from the *shaping* model of education (see Vargas, 1996, for details on these models). In a related way, whereas conventional teaching methods have been identified as "teacher–centered to a very high degree" (Ellson, 1986, p. 112), the successful adoption of precision teaching procedures results in increased student–centeredness. The student's progress (or lack of it) takes a central position in the constellation of factors that determine the fitness or utility of classroom instructional sequences. "The student knows best" which instruction is effective because student–charted learning data is the main indicator of instructional fitness. As Carl Binder notes:

> Students assume responsibility for their own learning by measuring and charting the results of their own daily practice, and making decisions with their teachers' advice about when and how to change procedures or curriculum objectives. (1988, p. 13)

Far from their typical portrayal as passive participants in drill and practice, students in precision teaching actively record and chart the data which in turn shows precision teachers the value of their teaching. What is typical of precision teaching is daily practice of *active student responding* with respect to instructional content. Active student responding has been shown to generate more learning, and reduce disruptive, off task behavior (Heward, 1994). From the standpoint of student centeredness, precision teaching strategies also generate high rates of active student responding with respect to the self-evaluation and determination of individual instructional progress, since the role of instructional decision maker is shared between student and teacher. Students can see, along with the teacher, whether instruction is producing progress, and can share, along with the teacher, in the decision about "what to do next."

To borrow a metaphor from the history of science, conventional instruction places the teacher in the center of the instructional solar system, while precision teaching principles have spurred a Copernican revolution in which the student is now the star around which instruction revolves. And this revolution in instruction is as significant as the original Copernican revolution in astronomy.

Precision Teaching: Discovering Effective Instruction

Precision teaching has been called "precision measurement" (Julie S. Vargas, personal communication, 10 March 1994) because precision teaching does not prescribe a particular curriculum or teaching method beyond its core principles of measuring rates of observable student behavior, charting those rates, and using charted progress to guide further instruction. "Advocates of precision teaching do not demand that all teachers teach the same way, but they do demand that teachers monitor what they are doing and change if necessary" (Howell & Lorson-Howell, 1990, p. 20). Precision teachers are not instructional automata, dispensing canned activities from an instructional cookbook—precision teaching does not result in "McTeaching." Instead, precision teaching principles allow classroom teachers to become discoverers of new and potentially more effective teaching practices.

Lindsley has asserted that precision teaching has brought about a kind of reconciliation between applied and basic behavioral research, with data-based learning in the classroom providing an impetus for discovery similar to, though speedier than, the impetus provided by learning observed in the laboratory (Lindsley, 1992a, 1996). Since precision teachers are guided by the actual learning progress of their students when designing and trying new instruction, precision teachers are rewarded not just for increased student learning but also for the discovery of new, more effective instructional practices. Precision teaching offers teachers a new yet integrated role: *discoverer of better teaching.* By adapting the rudiments of repeated measures behavioral research to the everyday classroom, precision teachers teach better; the same process enables them to discover better ways of teaching at the same time.

Using classrooms as research laboratories has led to expanded behavioral curricula. These have, as a major component, daily self-recorded progress data with charting for shared instructional decision making. The *Morningside Model of Generative Instruction* (Johnson & Layng, 1994) incorporates the foundational practices of precision teaching into a comprehensive school-based effective learning system. Implemented at the Morningside Academy in Seattle, WA, as well as at Malcolm X College in Chicago, IL, the Morningside Model is well known for its successes, backed by its money back guarantees of exemplary student achievement, guaranteeing that students will progress "two grade levels per school year or... parents will receive a tuition refund in proportion to the shortfall" (Johnson & Layng, 1994, p. 174).

Common Methodological Elements of Life–style Management Interventions

It was the precision teaching precedent of creative and successful data–based instructional innovations that led to the adaptation of precision teaching techniques to on–line, computer–based instruction for client–centered life–style management. While this paper introduces on–line instructional systems for weight control, smoking control, and study skills, certain methodological elements are common to all three systems:

☙ *Client–countable dependent variables.* The first iterations of the instructional system were explicitly designed for client–countable behaviors. Exercising, smoking and study skills were pinpointed for each client, making a daily count of a rate of response (or response–product) feasible and convenient.

☙ *Daily data reporting, using E–mail.* Clients were asked to report daily data from their self–count regimens in an E–mail document at or near bedtime each evening. Clients mailed the daily self–report to the instructor's E–mail address.

☙ *Client–centered collaborative design of a personalized data collection and reportage regimen based on repeated–measures research designs.* The first weeks of the course focused on achieving reliable, client–customized data collection of the pinpointed behavior or product, as well as reliable daily E–mail reporting. Clients agreed to work with the instructor to construct a personalized data–collection and reporting system during this initial phase of the on–line course, and to defer any systematic attempt to modify the targeted behavior until later phases of the course. This initial "start–up" phase corresponded to a baseline phase in a repeated measures research design, in which clients are measuring their targeted dependent variable(s) but not introducing any condition designed to modify the targeted variable(s).

The baseline phase involved training clients to measure their pinpointed behaviors during the course of their day, resulting in data collection procedures based on client preferences, settings, behavior of concern, and other factors. Once a suitable start–up data collection regimen was designed vía on–line seminar discussions (see chat rooms, below), the client began collecting her/his data and reporting those data each day via E–mail.

Subsequently, the start–up processes of data collection and E–mail reporting tend to shape client participation in the evolving system. This results in a client–centered, instructor–guided measurement and reporting regimen, which was convenient, accurate and reliable. (Certain methodological questions—the extreme of which might be "How do you know your clients are not making it all up, that is, lying?"—were fundamentally addressed, at this early point in the research on this delivery system, in two related ways: [a] No information ever came to light that might indicate that any client might have lied. Also, [b] creating and reporting—and discussing with the instructor—false data that seemed reasonable would seem to require far more effort than observing, reporting, and discussing real data would require. Hence, at this point in this research, parsimony would require the experimenter to presume that clients are honest. Such questions can and will be confronted in additional ways in future research.) Often, clients began the baseline phase with a rudimentary data reporting regimen, only to add more elements based on client curiosity or instructor recommendations. For example, a client may begin the baseline phase by agreeing to write a one–sentence self–count each day, such as "I smoked 28 cigarettes today, 3 January 1995," sending such data via E–mail each day. Then, as daily data continues to be collected and reported by the client in this manner, the client (or instructor) may suggest that "the time at which each cigarette was smoked" could be collected and reported as well. The client can choose to accept such additional tasks, and if so, they are added to the start–up data collection and reporting regimen.

❧ *E–mail reports as small instructor–client discussions of current course procedures.* Clients were asked to note, in a few sentences, any problems, concerns, or issues which arose in the daily process of data collection. As clients described problems or made suggestions as an addendum to the daily E–mail data report, such discussions of the data collection regimen could evolve in the context of the actual incoming data. This was construed as a "daily journal" in which the client reflected on her/his data collection regimen or the emerging data picture.

In this way, daily E–mail served not only as a means to report data, but also as a small writing assignment used to generate client interest and participation in the on–line course. Short daily client feedback (e.g., "I'd rather report my data twice a week instead of every day" or "I'd like to record the time at which I smoke each cigarette") was used to generate "amendments" to the initial data collection regimen. Such ongoing, mutual feedback, suggestions, and amendments served to balance client preferences for convenience versus instructor preferences for accurate, valid transduction of behavioral data, since the instructor's preferences tend to be more task–laden and thus extract more response–cost from the client. The daily E–mail discussion also adds a convenient, conversational forum for praising correct E–mail reportage of data, for celebrating successive days of correct E–mail reportage, or for remediation concerning errors of omission or commission.

❧ *Baseline data reporting regimen mastered before graduating to an intervention phase.* The baseline phase was designed to bring about accurate daily data collection and reporting. To facilitate this, all clients were told that their baseline system needed to be mastered before entering the intervention phase, in which a systematic attempt could be made to modify the behavior of concern. A mastery criterion was established: "14 successive days of E–mail reportage of correct, complete self–counts." After two successive weeks of errorless participation, the client "graduated" and was eligible to begin collaboration on an intervention phase for the on–line course. Since all previous baseline procedures would continue concurrently with any intervention element, it was crucial that the client had mastered the daily data collection and reportage regimen, since incoming data served as evidence of the effect (and utility) of any intervention.

❧ *Chat Rooms used for hour long "on–line seminar" meeting each week to review progress data while discussing instructional amendments.* Clients agreed to schedule an hour long meeting, once per week, in which the client and instructor could "meet" in an on–line chat environment using a commercial on–line service. Such meetings were called on–line seminars.

"Chat" telecommunications involves synchronous, real–time exchanges of text between two or more writers. This is similar to an oral classroom conversation between two people, but with the interchange being textual rather than oral. Writer A composes a text sentence, then "sends" it to the chat room. The speed of the textual transmission is immediate; as soon as a sentence is sent, it is seen in the chat room area by both participants, generally in less than one second. Writer B's response appears underneath

Writer A's initial sentence in the scrolling archives of the chat room. Additional textual responses are composed, sent, and responded to by each writer. The interchange is fluent enough so as to simulate an oral conversation in reading and writing media. Such real–time textual exchanges can be called *conversational writing.* The weight control client used on–line seminars on a weekly basis. The first smoking control client began with weekly seminars which became less frequent. The second smoking control client had seminars as they were needed. The final client, working with college–level study, did not use on–line seminar chat at all, that tool being unavailable in her setting.

❧ *Collaborative, client driven interventions.* Interventions were developed based on client suggestions, remarks, and self–examination of incoming data pictures. As well, interventions were begun at the client's pace (if at all), and could be adopted or abandoned via the on–line seminar discussion. During the collaborative design process for interventions, on–line seminar meetings typically addressed at least three considerations, as listed here: *(a) Program progress from the prior week.* Since both client and instructor were apprised of the client's daily data, part of each on–line seminar hour was spent reviewing the client's progress from the prior week. Discussion of the prior week's data set the stage for clients to remark on their own progress, and to suggest course amendments, new interventions, etc. *(b) Amendments to the course.* Instructor and client discussed how the data–collection system worked, reasons for each procedure, and how the client's current system of recording and reporting data could be made more efficient or effective. After the client had mastered the start–up data reporting system and had chosen to begin an intervention, this portion of the on–line hour focused on collaborative intervention design and planning. *(c) Accepting or rejecting amendments to the course.* The typical attitude during the on–line seminar was one of client–centeredness and brainstorming; the client was urged to generate ideas and suggestions, and to propose amendments to the system based on data–based self–evaluation and personal curiosity. In this sense, the on–line course was an exercise in training a client to conduct "self–research" on the targeted life–style concern.

However, not all amendments were of equal value with respect to maintaining a data–based, research oriented self–management program. To maintain both high–quality data reporting and the client–centered emphasis in instruction, all proposed amendments to the course procedures were discussed in a process of instructional consensus (wherein the instructor added expertise to the client's creativity) and "ratified." That is, both client and instructor had to agree to a course amendment before the suggested procedure could be adopted into the on–line course. When a suggestion was made by the client (such as "I'd like to report data two times per week instead of once per day"), the instructor described advantages and disadvantages to the suggestion, and could accept or "veto" it. Similarly, when the instructor suggested a course amendment (such as "I suggest you start an intervention next week"), the client could evaluate the reasonableness of the suggestion, and could accept or "veto" it. By the end of the hour–long on–line seminar, any proposed changes to the current course procedures were either vetoed (by the client, the instructor, or both), or accepted unanimously. Discussion and unanimous acceptance of a course amendment during the hour–long on–line seminar set the stage for the adoption of the new procedure into the client's course regimen for the coming week.

The "unanimous acceptance" procedure worked in practice. For instance, after mastering the baseline phase, the client could choose when to begin an intervention phase. The instructor explained to the client that she/he could remain at the baseline phase, collecting data and reviewing progress, until she/he saw fit to start the first intervention phase. The client could also end an intervention phase after an on-line seminar, either replacing it with a new intervention or returning to baseline phase procedures. Since each adoption or abandonment of an intervention required unanimous acceptance during the weekly on-line seminar, each intervention lasted for at least seven days, longer in cases where clients did not engage in weekly on-line seminars.

Client-driven collaboration on the design and pace of interventions resulted in personalized course arrangements and innovative research designs. In the case of the first smoking control client, the start-up procedures were in effect for 61 days (almost half of the 18 week course) before the client elected to implement her first intervention phase. In the case of the weight control client, no systematic intervention phase was implemented; the start-up conditions obtained from the outset of the course, serving as a modified treatment-only design (Hawkins & Hursh, 1992).

❧ *Client determines duration of client's participation in on-line course.* Each client was apprised that there was no set date when the on-line course would end; the client was welcome to participate for as long as she/he chose. In the case of the weight control client, the end of the course was determined by the goals set by the client. In all other cases, resignation from the course was left open ended.

❧ *All on-line interactions archived by both client and instructor as electronic files.* Since all client-instructor interactions occurred via writing (either in E-mail or on-line seminar), both participants could easily archive all course materials, data, and seminars as electronic files. The client was urged to review the archives of past on-line seminars in the event that the current weekly baseline or intervention regimen, agreed upon in the previous week, became confusing.

❧ *Course delivered to clients for research purposes at no cost.* All clients reported here participated in on-line courses at no cost. Also, all agreed to have their data and archives used for educational research.

Interventions in Three Life-Style Management Areas

Experimental interventions were undertaken in three different life-style management areas. One area, smoking control, involved helping clients change their environments to bring about decreases in target behaviors while the second and third areas, weight control and college-level study, focused on increasing target behaviors. While various behavioral education procedures were used, the basic principles guiding the design of the on-line educational process were those of precision teaching.

For the purpose of this report, which is to introduce the concept and some early outcomes of on-line interventions, data will be presented for only one client in each of the weight control and college-level studying areas. For the area of smoking control, data for two clients will be presented. The experiments are reported here in the chronological order in which they were developed.

Weight Control

The client whose data will exemplify on-line interventions for weight control was a 33 year old woman living several states away, who was the fiancee of the instructor.

Anne (not her real name) was employed as an office manager, owned a Macintosh computer, and subscribed to a commercial on–line service. Initial meetings and discussions about an on–line course for weight control were conducted via the commercial on–line service and telephone conversations. It was explained to Anne that this on–line course was being conducted partially to fulfill the requirements of a doctoral seminar in behavioral medicine in which the instructor was enrolled. Anne reported an historical baseline of weight maintenance or weight gain in the months preceding the course. Anne began participating on 2 March 1995. All subsequent interactions with respect to this project were conducted via the commercial on–line service.

Weight control client's instructional procedures. Anne expressed strong interest in losing weight *via the acquisition of a daily exercise regimen,* which would begin at low intensity yet increase in intensity at her own pace. The framework which emerged during the start–up phase of the project emphasized client–chosen exercises at client–chosen levels of repetition, duration, and intensity, which were easy enough to be performed for seven successive days with no avoidance or "errors of omission." Once an exercise (such as sit–ups, yoga stretches, straight leg lifts, or crunches) and its corresponding number of repetitions were chosen by Anne, she agreed to perform the exercise(s) to her chosen criteria for one week before adding exercises or reps. She was advised to begin with one exercise at low repetitions, and to aim for "errorless exercise," gradually increasing either the number of exercises or the number of reps per exercise only after errorlessly performing at lower intensity levels. In the spirit of "avoiding avoidance," special emphasis was placed on making the course procedures as personalized and aversion–free as was possible within the framework of data–based life–style management research.

Anne chose a "goal weight" of 25 pounds to be lost. She also chose a "goal date," the date at which the goal weight should be lost. Both Anne and the instructor were interested in a medically reasonable, gradual weight loss (around one pound per week). Therefore, the planned duration of the course was set at 16 weeks. Anne formally ended the course on 14 June 1995.

Anne's preferences were considered in the design of daily data collection, reporting, and instructional feedback. She counted her daily rate of repetitions of exercises, and recorded the rates of each exercise in a client–designed computer database. She used the database to record her self–measurement immediately after exercising, with each rate recorded in a field next to the exercise name in a "journal" format. If no exercise occurred, she recorded a zero. She then attached that day's database to an E–mail document, and sent it each evening to the instructor using the commercial on–line service.

Both Anne and the instructor used the same Macintosh integrated software program. Thus all course materials, client data, subsequent instructor feedback, and other electronic documents could be exchanged, opened, viewed, and edited immediately and directly, with no loss of document quality or data via telecommunication.

While measurable exercise increase was the vehicle of change, weight reduction was the desired result. However, the mechanics of weight measurement and reporting were a source of aversive emotional reactions for Anne. Managing the course procedures to minimize such aversion led to a number of small, practical innovations in weight measurement. Anne expressed a preference not to report her starting weight to the instructor, preferring instead to report how much, if any, weight had been lost. This was adopted as the standard weight measurement strategy; Anne would report only a number of pounds lost, rather than her current weight. She also reported aversive reactions to viewing her starting weight on a scale. In the interest of reducing unneeded aversives, the instructor suggested that the client use masking tape to cover the first two digits of her digital scale. The remaining digit could be reported, and accurate weight change noted, without reference to the aversive preceding digits.

Although data on exercise was reported every day, Anne did not measure and report her weight each day. The instructor advised her to weigh herself approximately once a week, recording any pounds lost in her database journal. However, there was not a requirement to do so, with Anne being urged to weigh herself at her own pace. A review of Anne's database journal shows that, using self–paced weigh–ins, she reported 12 weight measurements across the 16 weeks of the course. On average, Anne weighed in, reporting a weight–change measure in her database journal, every nine days.

In addition to daily exercise and self–paced weight measures, Anne also engaged in a weekly on–line seminar for an hour. These on–line discussions focused on revising her data reporting procedures, discussing the progress in the data, and evaluating suggestions for course changes. For example, Anne suggested adding a food diary to her daily database journal. By adding a second layout to her database, She was quickly able to add fields in which to record her food choices for each day. Such personalized, client–centered changes were easy, as well as accurately recorded, since the beginning of any new procedure is "date–stamped" automatically by the database. A review of the database shows that Anne began her daily food diary on Wednesday, 10 May 1995, the tenth week of the course. Other informal changes could be discussed in on–line seminar meetings, adopted, and subsequently tracked easily and accurately by virtue of using a computer database document to collect, record and report behavioral data.

Anne reported previous difficulty maintaining a daily exercise regimen. At her suggestion, Anne and the instructor collaborated on the design of a contingency contract element, which made a chosen activity contingent on Anne's achieving her goal weight by her goal date. This contingency contract was in effect from the start of the project until 16 April 1995, when the contingency contract element was removed based on performance data, Anne's preference, and the professional judgment of the instructor. The project continued, without the contingency contract element, until its end.

While the instructor had pre–designed an element of graphic feedback for weight loss progress, Anne expressed a preference to track "number of pounds lost" on an add/subtract graph, so that chart movement increased for each pound lost. The instructor created such a progress chart as an electronic file in the Macintosh integrated software application owned by both Anne and the instructor. The resulting progress chart listed the goal weight at the goal date, along with a minimum celeration line, illustrating graphically how much weight needed to be lost to achieve the goal weight by the goal date. This was a modification of the precision teaching procedure of establishing an aimstar (Wolery, Bailey, & Sugai, 1988, p. 132) which the instructor called a "weightstar." As Anne reported her weight measures, the instructor plotted incoming data on the electronic progress chart, with weekly on–line seminars setting the occasion for electronic chart–sharing and discussion between Anne and the instructor. Figure 1 shows Anne's data plotted on the weightstar chart. (Since many of the figures in this paper were also used to provide information to clients, the figures are often presented here as clients would have seen them, at "screen resolution" and with all their parts.)

Weight control client's results and discussion. This study could be considered an informal version of a treatment–only instructional design (Moxley, 1995, 1996), with the treatment conditions present at the start of measurement. During the contingency contract, the client lost an average of 0.175 pounds per day. After the removal of the contingency contract element on 16 April her weight loss slowed to a consistent 0.148 pounds per day on average. The client lost 16 pounds across the 16 weeks of the course.

The steady weight loss was correlated with systematically increasing daily levels of exercises chosen by the client. The client's database journal documents the date, number of exercises, reps for each exercise, and weight loss (if any) for each day. While those data are too extensive for detailed analysis here, a description of the first few weeks of the client's exercise regimen is illustrative. The client began with two exercises, sit–ups (20) and yoga (10 minute episode) on 2 March. On 21 March (by which time the client had lost 3 pounds), the client elected to drop yoga, adding straight leg lifts (50), crunches (50), and aerobic movements (50), as well as increasing sit–ups to 35. These four exercises continued until 4 April, when sit–ups, straight leg lifts, and crunches were dropped, and scoops (20), alternating leg lifts (20), inner leg stretches (100), biceps curls (30), and triceps curls (30), were added; aerobic movements remained.

This pattern of adding new daily exercises with repetition criteria continued throughout the course. The client chose exercises at "doable" levels of intensity, and completed them for at least seven days in succession, often without errors of omission.

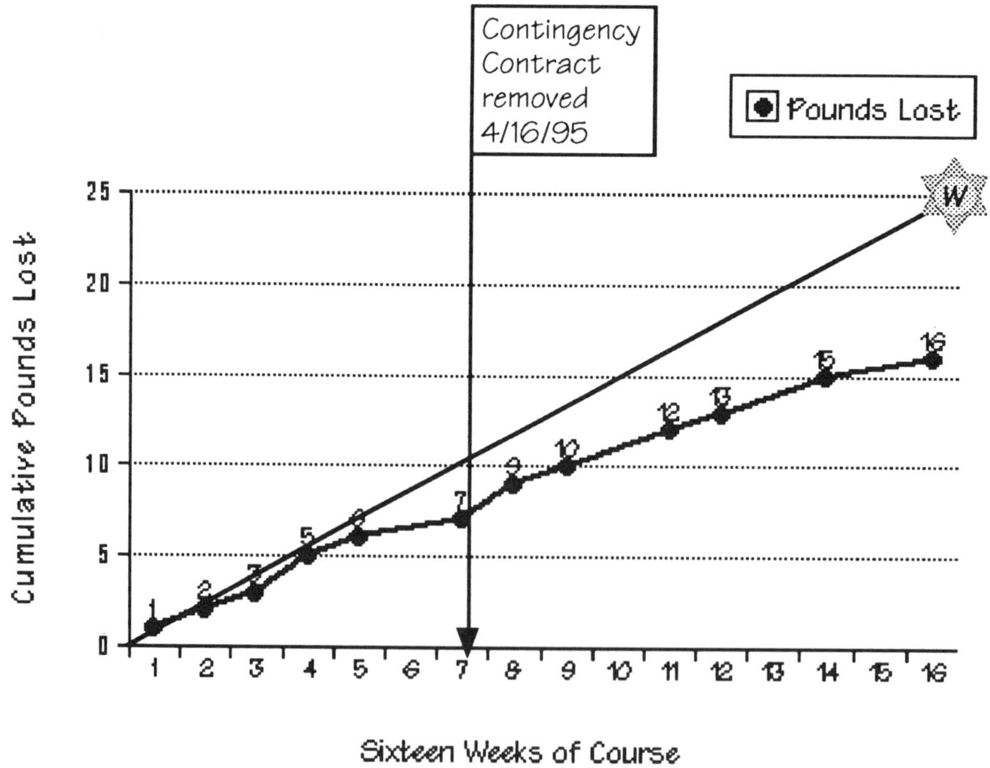

Figure 1. Weightstar chart with results of on–line weight control course.

As the course continued, and more weight loss ensued, the client added more exercises to her daily routine, often at higher reps, and continued to complete them with few errors. At most, the client was performing eleven separate exercises every day, and reporting those data, along with any weight–loss data, every evening.

After the completion of the formal course, the client composed a short essay about her participation in the course. Here are excerpts from that essay:

> I have gained and lost weight many times in my life. Sometimes with a "program," and sometimes on my own. What I have found from these experiences is, when I am trying to do it by myself, I have a hard time with consistently doing the things I know I need to do. I will do well for a week or so, then have a bad day, then have another bad day, and with nothing to check me, just give up. I will tell myself it's not important, and that I will "get back" tomorrow, or next week.
>
> On the other hand, with the other programs, I would be consistent about it, but primarily for fear of humiliation. That never worked for long. I did lose weight, twice through programs, but gained it back as soon as I was no longer being held to a specific diet....
>
> Beginning this plan was entirely my idea, and the development of it has been totally guided by me. I wanted someone to talk to about it, without criticism... and I knew that I needed to report my progress, but on my own terms. We both reasoned that "our program" would help me through the hard times and, most importantly, keep me going.
>
> It has worked remarkably well....

Smoking Control (Client One)

Jane (not her real name) was one of two clients who will exemplify on–line interventions for smoking control. She was a 27 year old female client living in the same city as the instructor. Jane was employed as a free-lance writer, owned a Macintosh computer, and subscribed to a commercial on–line service. She reported being fluent in the tools now used for the course, E–mail and Chat writing.

After an initial, informal face–to–face meeting in early July, 1995, Jane agreed to participate in a multi–week on–line course devoted to measuring and modifying her daily rate of smoking. She indicated in this informal meeting that she wanted to reduce or cease smoking from a current "one pack plus" per day habit. At the initial face–to–face meeting, the rudiments of the on–line research methodology were explained, along with the basics of the on–line course procedures.

Jane entered into the on–line course with the assurance that the course procedures were modifiable on the basis of her performance and preferences. The course would begin with a basic data–collection phase and, once the data collection procedures were mastered, would proceed at the her chosen pace toward intervention phases intended to slowly reduce or eliminate smoking. Once intervention was begun, she would receive customized progress charts at regular intervals showing the emerging data picture from her project. Since Jane and the instructor did not own the same software applications, uploading such progress charts would be problematic; Jane elected to receive laser–printed paper copies of her progress charts via USMAIL.

Smoking client one's instructional procedures. Jane expressed an interest in reducing smoking slowly so that she could be smoking "two cigarettes per week" by January 1996. She was skeptical about her ability to quit "cold turkey," but felt that a slow decrease to just a few cigarettes per week would be feasible. On 6 July 1995, she began the course by counting and recording the number of cigarettes smoked per day, making a written mark on paper after each cigarette during the course of her day, and adding the totals before bed (e.g., "Thursday, 7/16: 30 cigarettes"). Jane would then copy her self–count sentence into E–mail and send the self–count to the instructor before bed, so that subsequent smoking would not tend to occur after that day's E–mail. When late–night smoking did occur after a nightly E–mail, those cigarette counts were noted in the next E–mail data report.

Any day in which an E–mail self–count was not received was treated as an error; data for that day was not applicable to the project. Missing, incomplete, or incorrect data meant that Jane would have to achieve 14 more, errorless days of data reportage to be eligible to begin an intervention. She did have five "errors of omission" days; these were days in which data were not reported. She missed no other days of data reporting during the course.

Jane began on–line, hour–long seminar discussions starting on 10 August 1995. These meetings were conducted weekly until 18 September 1995, at which time she elected to schedule further seminars "on demand," at her own pace. She subsequently scheduled five more on–line seminars before her resignation from the course on 9 November 1995 for a total of 12 on–line seminars across the entire course.

On–line seminar discussions in the presence of her graphed data set the stage for Jane to personalize her data collection regimen during the baseline phase of the course, and to move toward an intervention. Figure 2 shows the progress chart derived from data she provided, to which Jane was responding.

Jane's personalization of data collection expanded her task load. She reported her daily data count of cigarettes smoked from the start of the course until the third on–line seminar on 21 August 1995. During that discussion, she suggested that she would like to collect more data, specifically the time of each cigarette, who (if anyone) was with her during each cigarette, and where each cigarette was smoked. The instructor supported Jane's curiosity, and suggested that Jane supply her "basic" one–sentence report each day, and send in her "expanded" data once per week as a text document. Table 1 provides an example of one of Jane's expanded data reports.

Jane reported summary data in this form weekly, while continuing to send the smaller daily E–mail report each day. This daily/weekly data collection system was adopted on 22 August 1995 and continued until the end of the course. (Methodologically, the increase in the effort of such data reporting is one of the natural constraints against client faking of data. Errors aside, this level of writing and self–measurement tasks would seem to make deliberate faking of data contain a higher level of response cost than the simple count for the ordinary E–mail report. As well, the extent of the subtasks needed, in the more comprehensive data recording process, to arrive at a daily total of cigarettes smoked means that the risk of being discovered as a fake is commensurately higher. The more complex process means more chances for a deliberate faker to be caught. These two, the complexity of tasks and the likelihood of being discovered, would provide some automatic deterrent to data faking.)

Jane implemented the first of several interventions on 6 September 1995. She had been "eligible" to begin an intervention for several weeks, but she elected to continue refining her daily smoking measurement and reporting system until then. During this

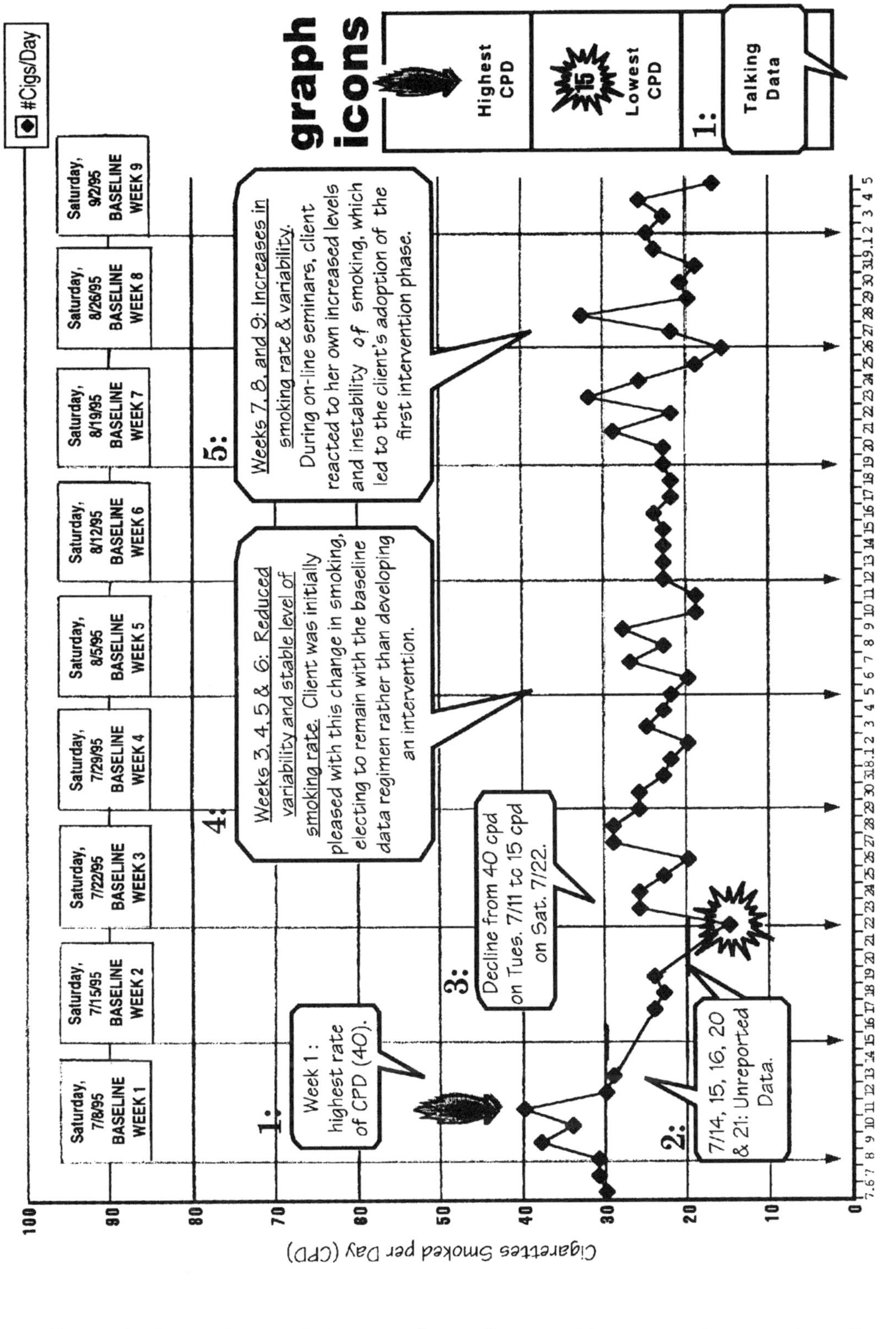

Figure 2. Data chart of client one's on–line smoking control course baseline.

time, the instructor began to format progress charts and send them to Jane via USMAIL approximately every two weeks. Figure 3 shows her data during these interventions.

Jane's first intervention consisted of an agreement to smoke one less cigarette per day ("CPD" in the figures) starting from 23 cigarettes per day (which was her average rate during baseline). This intervention was termed a "daily decrease smoking cap," since each day carried a limit or "cap" on the number of cigarettes to be smoked that day. This intervention continued until 19 September 1995.

During an on–line seminar discussion on 18 September 1995, Jane reported aversive withdrawal symptoms as she approached ten cigarettes per day. She suggested adding a reward system, begun the next day, in which she would earn one point per day for smoking no more than ten cigarettes per day. This intervention was termed "point reward for cap maintenance." When she earned three successive points (for three succes-

Cigarette #	Tuesday 22 August		
	Where	With Whom	Time of Day
1	Home	Alone	10:20 A.M.
2	Home	Alone	10:40
3	Home	Alone	11:00
4	Home	Alone	11:15
5	Home	Alone	11:55
6	Walking street	Alone	1:55 P.M.
7	Walking street	Alone	2:15
8	Coming out of store	Alone	2:55
9	Coming out of store	Alone	3:20
10	Home TV	Alone	3:45
11	Home desk	Alone	3:55
12	Home desk	Alone	4:20
13	Home desk	Alone	5:15
14	Home desk	Alone	5:35
15	Home desk	Alone	5:56
16	Standing in street	Alone	8:02
17	In restaurant 1	Alone	9:00
18	In restaurant 2	Jack	9:10
19	Outside resting	Jack	11:00
20	Home	Joe	11:35
21	Home	Joe	11:50
22	Home	Joe	12:30 A.M.

Table 1. One of client one's expanded data reports.

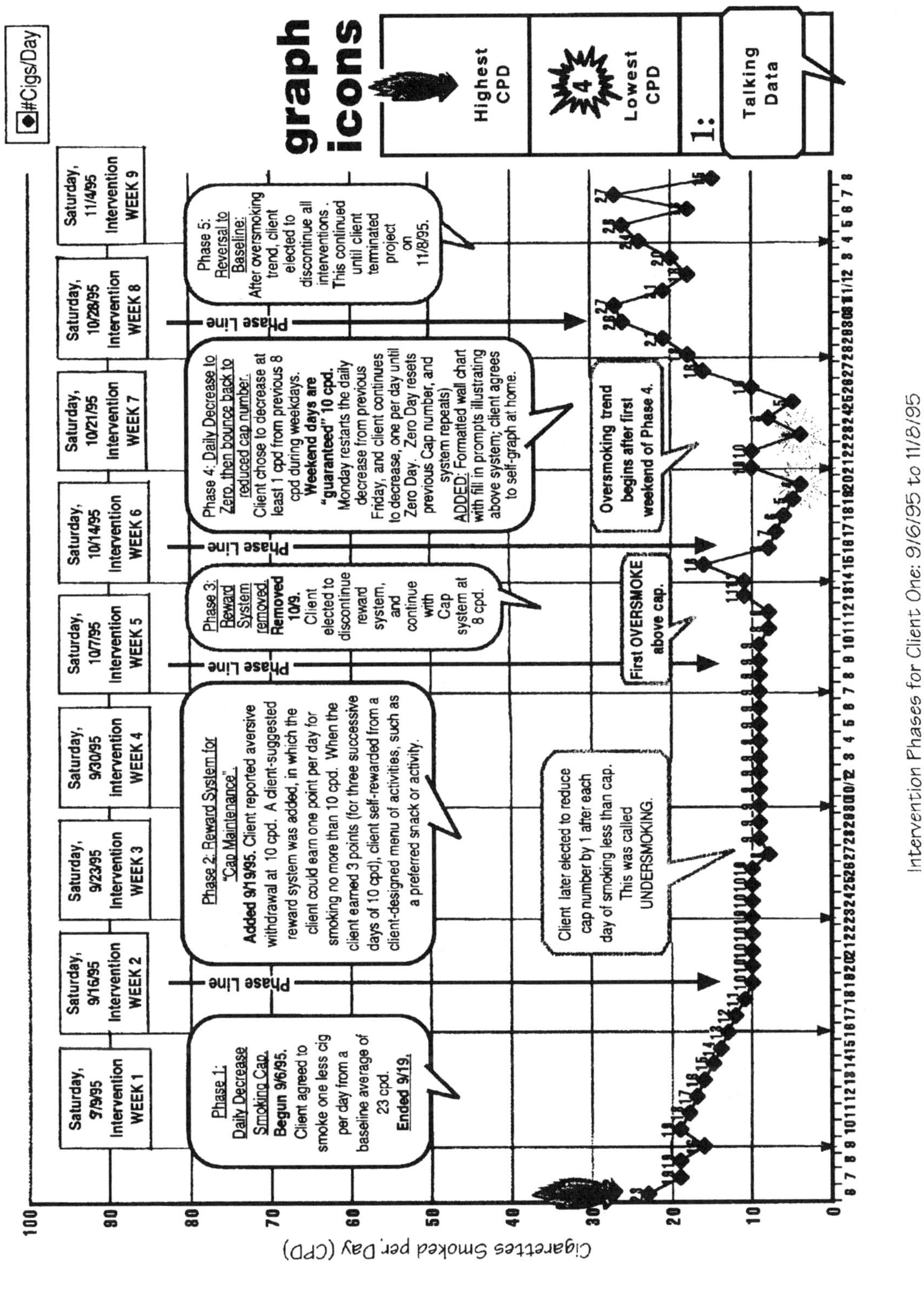

Figure 3. Results of client one's on–line smoking control interventions.

sive days of no more than ten cigarettes per day), she rewarded herself with a preferred snack or activity selected from a menu of rewards she had constructed. Point–tracking was added to Jane's daily and weekly data reports; when a reward was earned, she described what reward she had chosen in that evening's E–mail report.

Nine days into this intervention, Jane managed to smoke less than her daily cap number. So she elected to add a new rule to this intervention. She would reduce her daily cap number by one cigarette per day after each day of smoking less than cap. Smoking less than the daily cap limit was called *undersmoking.* For example, Figure 3 shows that on 27 September 1995 Jane smoked eight cigarettes per day, two below her allotted cap of ten cigarettes. According to her new rule, her daily cap number would drop to nine cigarettes per day, since she had undersmoked on the previous day. Jane expressed confidence that such a rule would allow her to maintain (and acclimate to) her present daily cap of cigarettes per day, while still allowing her to gradually reduce if she found herself able to smoke less.

The third intervention phase involved the removal, on 9 October 1995, of the point system for maintenance. While Jane was successful with the system, never failing to earn her reward for three successive days of cap maintenance, she considered the point system to be too task–intensive, and judged it unnecessary in order for her to maintain control of the rate of her smoking. As further data would address the accuracy of this judgement, the reward system regimen was removed after discussion in an on–line seminar. Jane elected to continue on with a daily cap of eight cigarettes per day.

The fourth intervention phase sprang from an on–line seminar discussion on 16 October 1995 in which Jane expressed an interest in attempting to stop smoking completely. Noting that weekday smoking rates were easier to manage than weekends, she thought that reducing to zero cigarettes per day during a weekday might be possible, if she could summarily return to a higher rate of cigarettes per day during the weekends. With these preferences in mind, the instructor designed the fourth intervention, which was termed "daily decrease to zero, then bounce back to reduced cap number." Jane agreed to decrease at least one cigarettes per day (from her current eight cigarettes per day) during Monday through Friday. Weekend days would allow a "guaranteed" cap of ten cigarettes per day; that is, no matter what cigarettes per day cap resulted on a Friday, Jane could smoke ten cigarettes per day on Saturday and Sunday. On Monday, the decreasing cap would begin again, from the level established on the previous Friday. Jane would continue to decrease during weekdays until she finished one day of no smoking. After her day of zero cigarettes, the cap would "reset" to her previous cap number, minus one, and the cycle would begin again. For example, Jane might progress from eight cigarettes per day on Monday to seven on Tuesday, six on Wednesday, five on Thursday, and four on Friday. On Saturday and Sunday, she could smoke ten cigarettes per day. Come Monday, Jane would "cap" at three cigarettes per day, with two on Tuesday, one on Wednesday, and zero cigarettes per day—no smoking—on Thursday. If Jane completed her zero smoking day, she would reset her cap to "one less cigarette than last time," in this case, seven, and begin another daily decrease to another zero smoking day (with weekends still reserved for ten cigarettes per day).

Since this "precision smoking schedule" was complex, the instructor formatted a programmed data collection booklet with a matching graphic wall chart for Jane to use at home. The booklet was a daily smoking diary which had a page for each day of the intervention, listing the programmed cap number for each day. Jane could use the booklet to record her daily data and be reminded of her cap schedule. The wall chart consisted of a graph with hollow points corresponding to each day's cap number. She could see each dot at it's corresponding cap number (such as "eight cigarettes per day for Monday") and could see the decreasing patterns, weekend increases, approaching zero days, and resets. She agreed to fill in each dot to chart her own progress at home during intervention four.

The fifth and final phase of the course was a reversal to baseline measurement procedures, begun on 31 October 1995, after an on-line seminar the previous day. This phase continued until Jane resigned from the course on 9 November 1995.

Smoking client one's results and discussion. The use of client-driven collaborative design and pacing of baseline and intervention elements results in personalized, unique versions of repeated measures research designs. For this client the changing-criterion design (Wolery, Bailey, & Sugai, 1988, p. 158) would seem to be the closest analogue. While the first intervention reduced the daily smoking criteria by one cigarette per day, the second intervention added a reward system for maintenance of a target level of smoking rate, although the client could bring about a change in the criterion by undersmoking her daily cigarettes per day cap. Intervention three reinstated the changing criterion design of intervention one, while intervention four was a more precise, programmed version of a changing criterion design with supplemental workbook and home graph. The final phase was a reversal to the baseline conditions.

The baseline phase lasted for 61 days. During baseline, the client ranged from 40 cigarettes per day to 15 cigarettes per day with a mean of 23 cigarettes per day. During baseline weeks one and two, the client reduced her smoking rate considerably, reaching the lowest daily rate of the entire baseline, 15 cigarettes per day, on 22 July.

During weeks three, four, five, and six, the client's daily rate of smoking stabilized between the 20–30 cigarettes per day level, with the range between points slowly narrowing through week six. However, this pattern did not persist during the last three weeks of baseline, as shown in Figure 2. It was this "loss of control," as the client described it, that set the stage for the client to collaborate on the design and implementation of her first intervention.

As Figure 3 shows, the first intervention systematically reduced the client's daily rate of smoking from 23 cigarettes per day on 6 September to ten cigarettes per day on 19 September. Variability from the client-chosen changing criteria existed only insofar as the client smoked less than her daily cap, as she did on 7, 8, and 9 September. On every other day of intervention one, the client smoked every cigarette allowed by her cap.

During intervention two, the client either maintained her stable daily smoking cap of ten cigarettes per day, or undersmoked. This intervention involved a reward for maintaining her smoking cap for three successive days; the client earned every possible reward for this intervention. On 27 September the client undersmoked her daily cigarettes per day cap. This resulted in a changed criterion to nine cigarettes per day, which the client maintained up to the end of this intervention on 9 October.

Intervention three was a reversal to the changing criterion of intervention one. The client experienced both new lows of eight cigarettes per day, and her first oversmoking days (consumption of more cigarettes than her daily cap) on the weekend of 13, 14, and 15 October. This bout of oversmoking led the client to request, on 16 October, an on-line session in which intervention four was designed and implemented.

Early in intervention four, the client resumed her downward trajectory according to criteria and continued to her lowest cigarettes per day rates of the entire course. During this week, the programmed criteria of intervention four can be seen in the systematic one–per–day reduction from six cigarettes per day on Monday 16 October to two cigarettes per day on Friday 20 October. As per the programmed criteria, the cigarettes per day for Saturday and Sunday was ten cigarettes per day, which the client met. However, according to the programmed workbook and home graph, the criteria on Monday 23 October was one cigarette per day; the client oversmoked at four cigarettes. While the programmed criteria were scheduled to decrease to zero cigarettes per day on Tuesday 24 October, the client continued to oversmoke her daily criteria. Within a few days, the client's smoking rate had shot up to baseline levels.

In an on–line seminar meeting on 31 October, the client expressed her frustration with the complexity of intervention four, as well as the amount of writing required to submit data both daily and in a weekly summary. After discussion, she elected to continue reporting daily and weekly data, but to abandon all interventions. During this phase, her smoking returned to near–baseline level and variability, with a range from 15 to 27 cigarettes per day and a mean of 21.6 cigarettes per day.

While the client considered the course a success, she was disheartened by her "blowing it" during intervention four, and continued to echo her disappointment with her performance through the end of the course. The client also considered her data collection regimen to be too labor–intensive to result in her preferred levels of smoking by 1 January 1996. For these reasons the client elected to resign from the course on 9 November 1995. (For an hour–long, on–line follow–up interview in April 1996, the client collected smoking data for one day. She had smoked 28 cigarettes.)

Smoking Control (Client Two)

Jim (not his real name) was the second of the two clients involved in on–line interventions for smoking control. He was a 40 year old male living in the same city as the instructor. Jim was employed in marketing, owned a Macintosh computer, and subscribed to a commercial on–line service. He reported being fluent in the tools used for the course, E–mail and Chat writing. Jim also reported fluency in using a commercial spreadsheet software program, which soon became his preferred method for recording and reporting his course data.

After an initial, informal on–line meeting on Sunday 17 March 1996, Jim agreed to participate in a multi–week on–line course devoted to measuring and modifying his daily rate of smoking. He indicated in this informal meeting that he was a "binge" smoker on top of showing a typically very high rate of smoking. He also indicated that he enjoyed smoking very much, but had worries about his health and the impact of smoking on his life–style. Jim expressed skepticism about his ability to modify his smoking rate, but indicated curiosity about the course, specifically the process of counting each cigarette each day.

Jim entered into the on–line course with the assurance that the course procedures were modifiable on the basis of his performance and preferences. The course would begin with a basic data–collection phase and, once the data collection procedures were mastered, would proceed at his chosen pace toward intervention phases intended to slowly reduce smoking.

Once intervention was begun, Jim would receive customized progress charts at regular intervals showing the emerging data picture from his project. Since the instructor and client did not own the same software applications, uploading such progress charts would be problematic; Jim elected to receive laser-printed paper copies of his progress charts via USMAIL. He also expressed an interest in viewing his progress charts using the World Wide Web; so his progress charts were also posted to a web page designed by the instructor, the address of which was given to Jim for his perusal.

Smoking client two's instructional procedures. In the initial on-line seminar, the rudiments of the on-line research methodology were explained, along with the basics of the on-line course procedures. As well, Jim was asked to compose a 1000 word essay in which he described his smoking, his history of smoking, the settings in which he smoked, and his personal goals for the course. Along with the essay, he was asked to turn in a simple smoking count for one day in order to begin to contact the idiosyncrasies of the data-collection process. He understood that he could formally begin the course after he provided the completed essay and data assignment via E-mail. Within 24 hours, Jim had returned not only his first daily data count but also a 998 word essay detailing his smoking history and various concerns and goals for the project. (Methodologically, this procedure of assigning an introductory expressive essay and free-form data count was valuable both in getting information from clients, about themselves, and as a method of screening out—at this stage of the research—those potential clients who were unlikely to complete the extensive writing and self-count tasks which the evolving on-line methodology required. Clients who expressed an early interest in an on-line course, yet were unable to accept or complete such an introductory assignment would self-select themselves out of consideration for participation in the course. This reduces "false starts" and course dropouts as well as helping clients to acclimate to expressive, criterion-based writing tasks. How to help those so screened out is on the agenda for future research.)

In his introductory essay assignment, and in later discussions, Jim expressed an interest in reducing smoking, but considered the prospect very difficult due to his self-described "binge" smoking patterns. He also expressed some aversion to the process of reducing smoking because he felt he would experience strong withdrawal and eventual failure. Nevertheless, Jim expressed his willingness to participate, saying "I'm giving this my best shot."

On Monday 18 March 1996, Jim began the course by counting and recording the number of cigarettes smoked per day, and reporting that number in his essay assignment. Based on subsequent on-line seminar discussions, he constructed a spreadsheet document which allowed him to track the number of cigarettes per day. The document used columns of his daily weekday and weekend activities to record how many cigarettes were smoked during these routine activities. He listed subtotals during weekday activities, with weekday totals. The same procedures were applied to typical weekend activities. Table 2 shows the information from a typical week under this procedure.

Jim mailed an updated version of his data spreadsheet every evening via E-mail. Any day in which an E-mail self-count was not received would be treated as an error and that data would not applicable to the project. Jim had no such errors during the 15 weeks of the course.

While Jim began the course with two on-line seminars during week one, he expressed his inability to schedule on-line seminars on any regular basis, because he was

	A	B	C	D	E	F	G	H	I	J
1	WEEK 5	Mon 4/15	Tue 4/16	Wed 4/17	Thu 4/18	Fri 4/19	WEEKEND	Sat 4/20	WEEKEND	Sun 4/21
2	am Home	6	4	4	3	4	am Home	5	am Home	8
3	2 Sub	1	1	1	1	1			Afternoon	13
4	2 Off	1	2	1	1	1	Errands	1	Late Afternoon	7
5	Mid am	3	3	2	2	2	Mid am	5	Evening	20
6	Pre Lunch	3	4	6	4	2	2 Subway	1	Late Night	16
7	Post Lunch	3	3	3	3	4	2 Class (1:30)	1		
8	Mid Day	2	0	0	0	2	Walking	7		
9	Late Afternoon	0	4	4	4	2	Back Home	8		
10	2 Sub	1	3	1	3	3	Evening	16		
11	2 Class (6:45)	0	0	1	0	0	2 Sub	1		
12	2 Sub	0	0	1	0	0	2 Bar	1		
13	2 Store	0	0	0	0	0	At Bar	10		
14	2 Home	0	0	0	0	0	pm (am) Home	7		
15	pm Home	30	26	22	23	22				
16	Total Day	50	50	46	44	43	Total Day	63	Total Day	64
17	$ Spent	$5.09	$5.09	$4.68	$4.48	$4.38	$ Spent	$6.41	$ Spent	$6.51

Table 2. Smoking data from week five of client two's data spreadsheet.

enrolled in night classes several evenings each week. For this reason, the majority of interactions between him and the instructor occurred via E–mail, with on–line sessions occurring infrequently. Jim scheduled and completed only six on–line seminars during the 15 weeks of his participation. This resulted in fewer opportunities for adoptions/abandonments of intervention phases.

As was the case with other clients, on–line seminar discussions set the stage for Jim to collaborate on interventions as well as daily self–measurement. During the third on–line seminar on Tuesday 9 April 1996, Jim was told that he was eligible to begin collaborating on an intervention. During this particular discussion, Jim articulated several ideas about self–control strategies (such as "substitution," "denial," and "delay") as being possible, but difficult. He expressed reservations about interventions being "the hard part." An excerpt from the transcript of on–line seminar three illustrates directly the collaborative writing process of this type of intervention design. (On–line sessions involve active but occasionally incorrect conversational writing. For this excerpt grammar, punctuation and spelling have been partially corrected, and sentence format and writer labels have been added.) Here is the transcript excerpt:

> Instructor: First of all... congrats! You have graduated to "Interventionhood." Hurrah!
>
> Instructor: Your data taking consistency, and formatting, are really coming on line, so to speak.
>
> Client Two: Yea! I think.
>
> Instructor: Why "I think?" Are you reticent about continuing?
>
> Client Two: No. It's just that it sounds like the hard part is about to begin.
>
> Instructor: Well, perhaps. Perhaps not. We need not begin anything, if you'd rather. In fact, a few more weeks of detailed data collection is fine with me!
>
> Instructor: However, you have graduated. What that means is... when you're ready, you're ready!
>
> Client Two: Intervene away!
>
> Instructor: Well, we have more to discuss before any intervention is tried. But, we can start talking about interventions—and you can start writing about them! Fun!
>
> Client Two: OK.
>
> Instructor: Any rate, I planned to talk about your data collection "ways," but we can skip that, since that is what that optional writing assignment covered. Make sense?
>
> Client Two: YES!
>
> Client Two: Didn't mean to shout.
>
> Instructor: Do you have anything else you'd like to say before I continue? Please feel free to talk at any time.
>
> Client Two: I'm with you. Keep going.
>
> Instructor: All right...
>
> Instructor: When you feel like doing some intervening, we need to think about intervention type procedures. We can continue refining data taking, but we need to shift toward the "control" aspect of smoking control. Questions?
>
> Client Two: The self control aspect?
>
> Instructor: Yes. Discovering how you can control your daily rate of cigarette smoking.

Client Two: Since there is no one to physically intervene, do you mean "substitution?"

Instructor: This will be a discovery process... you need to understand that. When you try some intervention, you don't "fail"... you just keep looking for another way.

Client Two: OK.

Instructor: What do you mean when you say "substitution?" Explain your usage, and I will try to cast an intervention in those terms…

Client Two: Substitute an action or prop for a particular urge for a smoke.

Instructor: Pragmatically, the intervention can be anything you feel might work. If by substitution you mean "competing activities" for cigarette smoking...

Client Two: Sounds like what I was thinking.

Instructor: Well, hmmm. When YOU think of things that may result in less smoking, does substitution seem like a good workable procedure you can deal with?

Client Two: Yes.

Client Two: And there is always "denial" or "delay."

Instructor: I am looking to you, Jim, to actively conceptualize your own intervention. Don't copy what you think I may want to hear... Express what you think you want to try, in practical terms.

Client Two: OK, we've got substitution, denial, and delay.

Instructor: Now you're talking. What else?

Client Two: I really can't think of anything else at the moment. All of the above are pretty challenging.

Jim expressed an interest in beginning an intervention as soon as possible, so he was given the option of either developing an original intervention over the course of subsequent weekly on–line discussions, or choosing from a list of pre–designed intervention plans from an "intervention menu" and beginning immediately. During subsequent discussion in the same on–line seminar, Jim elected to begin an intervention with two strategic elements.

Jim began his first intervention phase on Wednesday 10 April 1996 with the first strategy of adding calculation cells to his data spreadsheet. The total dollar cost for smoking would now be displayed for each day, as would the total dollar cost per week (see Table 2). Other cells located elsewhere calculated Jim's *average* dollar cost per week. The contingencies of adding new subtotals of smoking per day were such that, for each cigarette Jim entered, his daily, weekly and average weekly cost per cigarette was updated immediately and automatically! This literally demonstrated the dollar cost to Jim after each cigarette number entry. Table 2 shows that Jim generally entered smoking rate subtotals from five to fourteen times per day, with each increment in rate being consequated with a precisely incrementing dollar cost measurement of 10.17 cents per cigarette. While the cost calculation element was not begun until week three, Jim calculated his cost per cigarette data retroactively to the start of the course as part of intervention one. Jim's data spreadsheet, including updated cost per cigarette data, continued to be attached to an E–mail document and submitted daily.

The second strategy of intervention one was the use of bimonthly customized progress charts which were begun at the same time as the first strategy. The client agreed that a new, updated chart would be mailed contingent on two weeks of errorless data reportage. The instructor's continuing work with digital data processing, customized graphing, and client–driven instruction led to the development of an experimental "dual–scale" progress chart, using an interval scale to present Jim's first few weeks of course data, and a semi–logarithmic scale to present later weeks of his baseline data, on the same page. The semi–log graph aspect was the closest convenient approximation of Lindsley's Standard Behavior Chart, usually called the Standard Celeration Chart (Pennypacker, Koenig, & Lindsley, 1972). In recent research, the Standard Celeration Chart has been integrated into data–based smoking control training programs for adult smokers (Abba & McLaughlin, 1995). Figure 4 shows this dual–scale data for the early weeks of Jim's course. (Since the first few days were an incomplete week, the chart starts with "week zero.")

The dual–scale progress chart was designed to convey both conventional and semi–log data pictures. Jim could easily discriminate between the two charting styles, and could then choose the style that helped him the most. As well, the use of the add/subtract scale for the first few weeks of the course emphasized each incremental change in smoking with a larger chart movement. It was reasoned that Jim (or any smoking reduction client) would profit most at the beginning of the course by seeing small incremental changes in smoking rate as large chart movements; decreases would look larger, as would increases. Later weeks rendered in the semi log style showed less incremental chart movement for each increment of change in rate; the lines were more flat. This was designed to demonstrate that the client needed to reduce his smoking rate by a larger increment if he wanted to "see as much chart movement" as in earlier weeks.

Intervention one obtained from the start of week four until the start of week 13. This was due both to Jim's inability to schedule on–line seminar discussions and to his satisfaction with his weekly smoking progress during intervention one. However, by week 12, Jim was eager to begin a new intervention which he felt might enhance his weekly smoking control; the new intervention being discussed was a changing–criterion system with programmed graphing worksheets to be used at home. As he stated during on–line seminar five on 4 June 1996,

> A month ago my goal was to become comfortable as a pack–a–day smoker. I'm nearly there. I'm a comfortable pack–and–a–quarter–a–day smoker. I'm hoping that the home graphing tools will help get below the pack–a–day threshold."

The second intervention phase, a "daily decrease by minus one cigarette" rule with programmed graphing worksheets, was implemented after on–line session six on Tuesday, 11 June 1996. Jim and the instructor discussed a starting rate from which to decrease, and settled on 35 cigarettes per day; a number which was purposefully higher than the Jim's average daily smoking rate during intervention one. This was based on his expressed apprehension that he could not keep his daily rate under 30 cigarettes per day for an entire week. Jim chose to begin "ratcheting down" from the retroactive date of Monday, 10 June 1996.

By starting with a "cap" of 35 cigarettes per day on 10 June 1996 and decreasing by at least one cigarette per day, Jim would be limited to 30 cigarettes per day by 15 June, 25 cigarettes per day by 20 June, and 20 cigarettes per day by 25 June. Because of their procedural and graphic acquaintance with Jim's daily smoking data, both Jim and the instructor realized that such a "ratcheting down" of his smoking would be, by 27 June, a real challenge. To smoke 20 cigarettes per day consistently for an entire week would

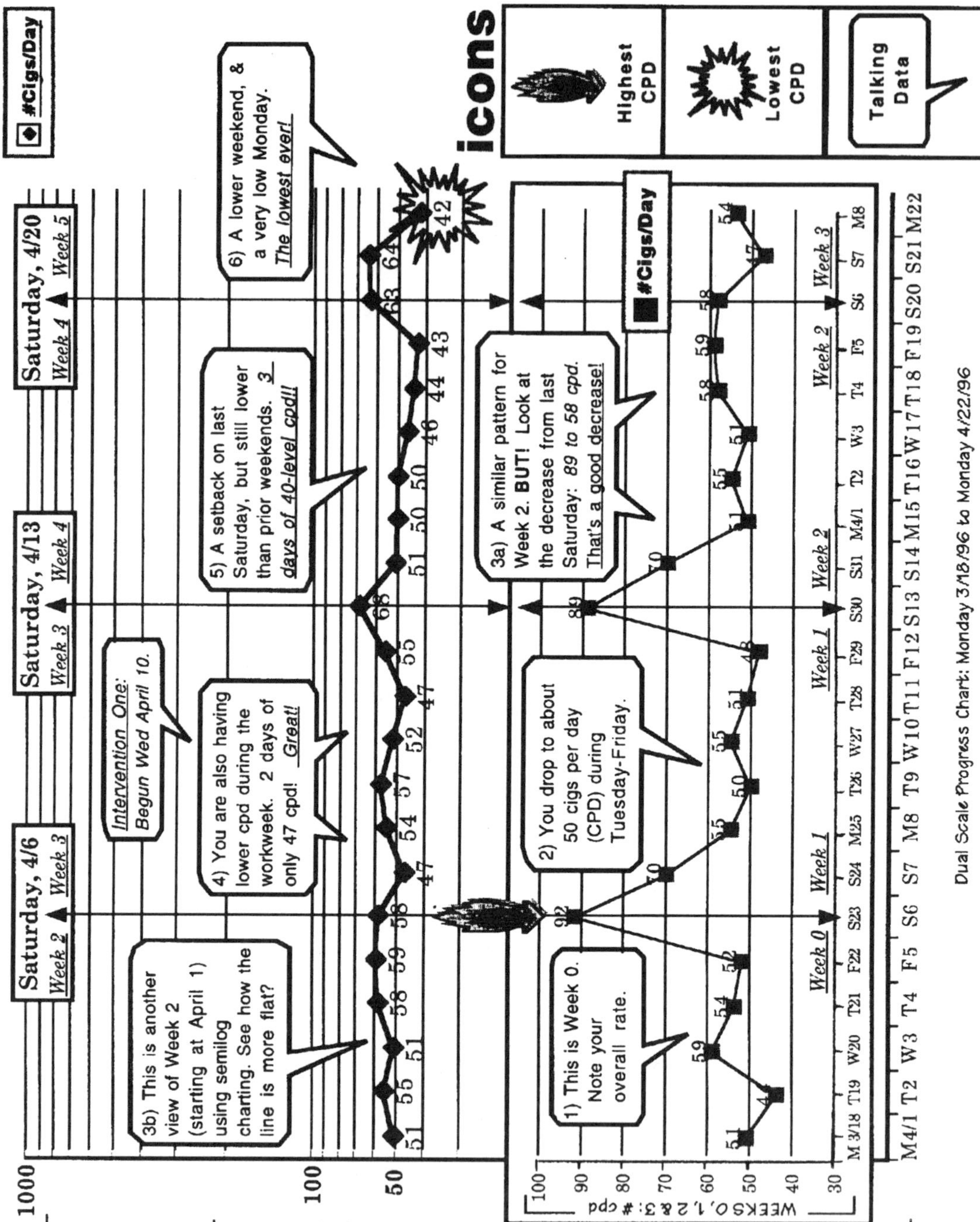

Figure 4. "Dual-scale" progress chart with data from weeks 1–5 of client two's on-line smoking control course.

be an additional challenge, especially during the weekend. Jim agreed to maintain his cap at 20 cigarettes per day if possible.

The second element of intervention two was to involve programmed worksheets. On these Jim could pencil in his daily rates, daily costs, weekly average, and cost for each week in a small formatted table.

Jim was provided with worksheets formatted for use through week 18, and he agreed to fill in the home graphing materials and turn them in to the instructor via USMAIL when completed. Intervention two lasted from 12 June 1996 until the end of the course, which occurred 19 days later.

Jim resigned from the course on 1 July 1996 after a job change during week 15 which decreased his available time to complete tasks for the course. Also, he found the home graphing worksheets difficult to complete; while he said he completed the first worksheet, he never turned any in. He considered the course a success, but reflected that perhaps he had decreased his smoking as much as was possible.

Smoking client two's results and discussion. Like client one, work with this client involved a personalized changing–criterion element, but in an A–B–C sequence of (a) baseline, (b) cost analysis with graphic progress charts, and (c) a changing criterion rule with home charting worksheets. Figure 5 shows client two's data (daily smoking level) and dates throughout the project.

The baseline phase lasted 23 days. The client smoked a mean of 57.83 cigarettes per day, with a range between 92 and 44 cigarettes per day. The client smoked a total of 1,330 cigarettes during baseline, for which he paid $135.26, making a mean of $5.88 spent per day for cigarettes.

During weeks one through three, the client showed high peaks on an otherwise fairly level smoking rate, with the peaks in smoking occurring on weekends. This pattern of large incremental increases during weekends would recur. The overall level of weekday smoking remained in the high 40s to 60 cigarettes per day range throughout the baseline phase. What is most notable is the large reduction in weekend smoking rate during week three. Based on discussions of incoming data, both client and instructor soon began to talk about, then explicitly plan for, "weekend rates" as opposed to just weekday smoking rates.

During intervention one, which began on Wednesday 10 April, the client experienced gradual reductions in the level of his weekday smoking rate, with weekend rates remaining higher than weekday rates but decreasing in comparison with prior weekends. Intervention one lasted 77 days, in which the client smoked a mean of 30.6 cigarettes per day. The range of smoking was from 15 TO 68 cigarettes per day, with the client smoking a total of 2,361 cigarettes at a cost of $240.11. The client spent a mean of $3.12 per day on cigarettes during intervention one. This was a decrease of $2.76 per day from the baseline level mean.

During on–line seminars, the client expressed his satisfaction with his smoking performance during intervention one. He noted in an on–line seminar that he had saved $212.52 during intervention one alone, by reducing his daily consumption of cigarettes. He felt that the cost analysis was particularly effective at reducing his smoking rate by directly equating each cigarette with a visibly increasing cost measurement. He also felt that the progress charts were useful, since he was able to see previously numerical data in the form of levels, trends, and "weekend" jumps. He expressed no difficulty in understanding the progress charts, the dual–scale format, or the progression of weekly

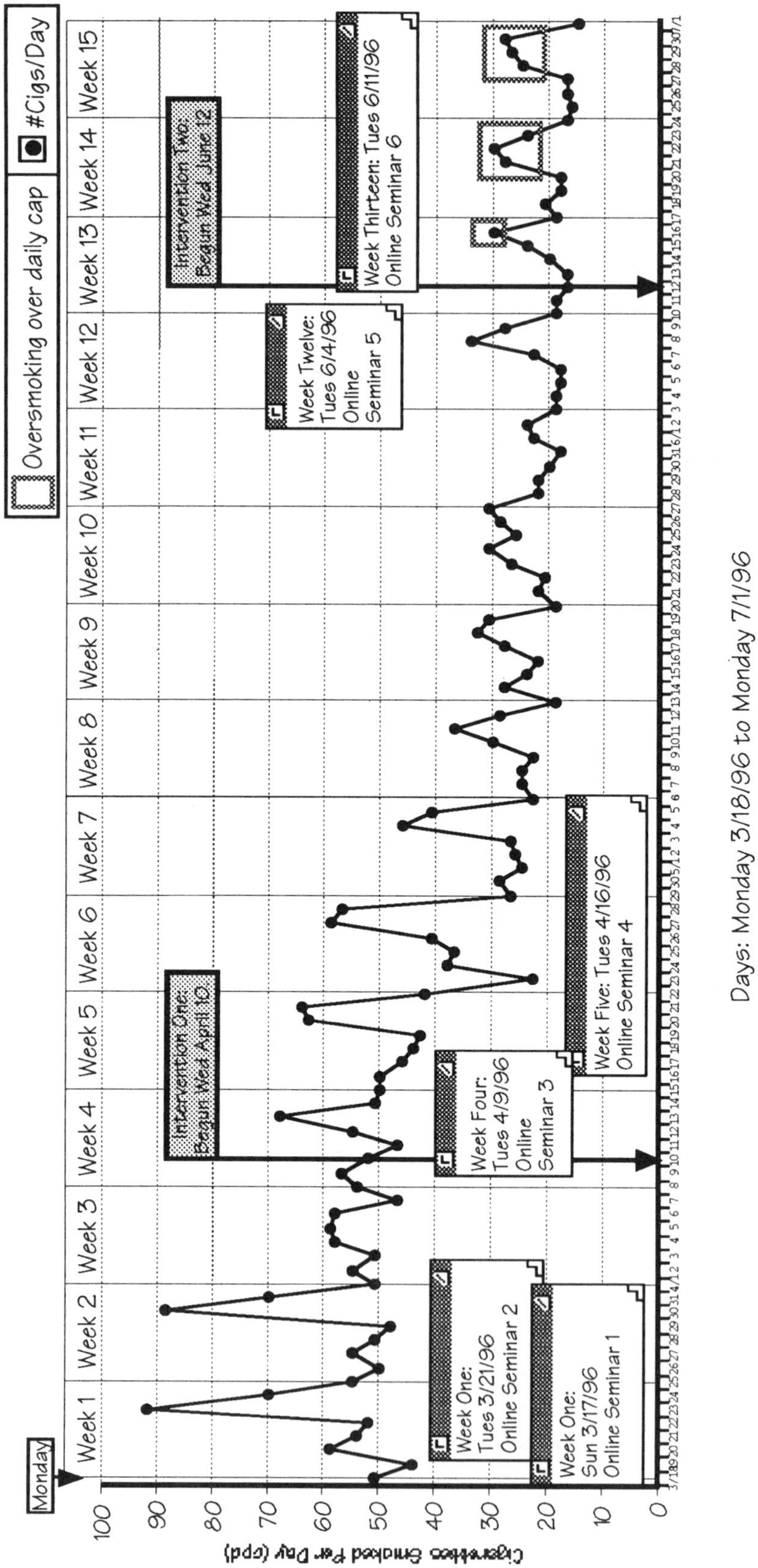

Figure 5. Client two's project data, intervention dates, and on-line seminar dates.

data. And he explicitly mentioned the "talking data" speech balloons as adding motivating, easy-to-understand information (e.g., see Figure 4).

However, by week eleven, the client seemed to reach, with respect to the then-current contingencies, a "smoking floor," both for weekday rates (from 17 to 23 cigarettes per day) as well as weekend rates (from 25 to 30 cigarettes per day). During week 12, the last week of intervention one, the client had experienced his first serious "uptick" in smoking rates, with a visible increase in weekend smoking. As was the case with client one, the onset of incremental and highly variable smoking rates after periods of consistent decrease ("loss of control") was a motivating factor in client two's pursuit of an intervention to enhance his downward smoking trajectory; it led him to discuss and adopt intervention two.

Intervention two, a daily decrease smoking cap with home charting worksheet, continued for only three weeks before the client resigned from the course. During the 20 days of intervention two, the client smoked a total of 428 cigarettes for an average of 21.4 cigarettes per day. The total cost for cigarettes was $43.53, with a mean cost per day of $2.18. This constitutes a further decrease in costs—and hence an increase in savings—compared to the level of costs and savings in intervention one, which itself was better than the level in baseline.

While the client continued to make progress during intervention two, in terms of reducing his daily smoking rate from previous weeks, he was not successful in matching his daily rate to the stated decreasing cap number. As Figure 5 shows, his weekend smoking rates for weeks 13, 14, and 15 exceeded the given cap numbers, resulting in oversmoking. He oversmoked for six of the 20 days of intervention two, with each day of oversmoking being either a Friday, Saturday, or Sunday. He seemed to take this oversmoking as proof of his assertion that the increased task load of home graphing was not worthwhile; he felt he had reached the personal bottom of his smoking rate.

The results from this client illustrate that high rates of "binge" smoking can be systematically and sizably reduced via the use of on-line life-style intervention methodology. While the end of the course resulted in some disappointment, the client considered the course very successful overall.

Also of interest is the relative infrequency of on-line seminars for client two in relation to the effects obtained. Further research is needed to determine to what degree on-line chat seminars are essential ingredients in the on-line intervention process, especially in light of client two's dramatic reduction in smoking rate over several successive weeks without on-line seminar contact.

During the practical stewardship of the course, the applicability of cost measurements of daily smoking rates as an intervention became apparent. Cost measurements seem to provide especially powerful behavior changing stimuli when arranged in the manner of intervention one. Cost measurements may transfer to each cigarette an additional, verbally mediated response-cost. In one on-line seminar, the client remarked that "I thought about how much I was spending when I smoked... I thought about how much I was saving when I smoked less." Such verbal descriptions of costs per cigarette (and savings per decrement) can be effectively delivered to (and echoed by) the client in an on-line seminar, as well as by the mechanics of daily data reporting, and thus contribute to reducing the smoking rate.

Cost per cigarette measurements were also easily projected into future savings based on current rate reductions. For example, were this client to smoke for one year at his baseline rate of consumption, he would spend $2,146.20 per year on cigarettes. In contrast, if he continued to smoke at the reduced rate demonstrated during intervention two, he would spend $795.70 per year on cigarettes, a savings of $1,350.50, compounded yearly. It remains for future research to ascertain if such cost per cigarette calculations, linking dollar savings to each decrement in smoking, may be generally effective; the practical results of this study support more investigation.

College Study Skills

An on–line course to enhance college study skills extends the range of on–line applications of behavioral methodology. Peg (not her real name) was a 19 year old female enrolled as a third–semester sophomore at the State University of New York (SUNY) campus in Oswego. She was a full–time college student who had access to E–mail via a computer and modem installed in her dorm room by the University. She reported being fluent in using E–mail, which was the sole tool available for use in the course; chat tools were not available at her terminal. Since Peg was not fluent in other software or computer applications, all instruction was delivered via the university PINE E–mail system. It should be noted that she was the niece of the instructor, and had asked for "study help" in a phone conversation.

After an initial E–mail correspondence on 17 September 1996, Peg agreed to participate in a study skills course based on E–mail. She related that her freshman year grade point average was 3.0, and that she had never attained an A level grade on any college exam or for any college course. Peg was enrolled in four college courses, plus she worked as a work–study student. She indicated at the start of the course that she desired help with studying and time management, as well as with test anxiety.

Study skill client's instructional procedures. Since she was a psychology major, Peg elected to apply her work for the on–line course to studying for a 300–level course in abnormal psychology. Her class met every Tuesday and Thursday morning for an hour and a half. She wrote out her schedule of classes in an E–mail essay, along with her abnormal psych course exam schedule. Her first exam was scheduled for 3 October 1996. Because Peg's first exam was rapidly approaching, her previous lack of A grades was accepted as a documentable baseline, and the first intervention arrangements were implemented at the start of the course on 17 September 1996.

The first intervention arrangements were for Peg to review her notes from class by typing a short synopsis of her class notes, questions, etc., into an E–mail document. Along with her synopsis, she volunteered to locate the "key terms" listed at the end of each chapter covered in exam one, and to write the key terms and their definitions into the same E–mail. She was also asked to concentrate on writing out her questions and comments about the material while writing her daily E–mail "study journal." Peg was asked to schedule 15–30 minutes per day for these activities, sending one E–mail per day to the on–line instructor's E–mail address. She was also advised to ask her college professor the questions she generated when she next went to class.

Peg did well at these tasks, generating class synopses, lists of key terms, and questions on a daily (or twice daily) basis. However, by 25 September 1996, she needed almost an hour per evening to complete these tasks. Both client and instructor felt that, while allowing for extensive writing coverage of the material, the initial intervention was too task–intensive. This gave it too much potential to become aversive, which could lead to quitting. In her E–mail of concern, sent on 26 September 1996 (and partially reformatted, etc.) Peg said,

> I got a review sheet today for the exam next Thursday. We have some multiple choice, matching, and three short answers. She gave us questions to look over and she will ask five, of which we can choose three to answer.

Fifteen questions followed, after which she added,

> I feel very frustrated seeing these questions because I feel like I don't know what the answers are already. I read and study and will get to the test and do badly. I should know these answers after all this work but I feel like I don't.—Peg

As a result, the instructor sent E–mail to Peg detailing a change to another "study style," which would be intervention two. This style would be a SAFMEDS ("Say All Fast [one] Minute Each Day Shuffled") flashcard fluency–building procedure (Lindsley, 1995). The SAFMEDS element was a conspicuous attempt to focus Peg's writing work into making flashcards, then changing from daily E–mail writing to daily flashcard practice. (The instructor also provided Peg with a short exercise in "imagery," a concept in which she had evinced considerable interest, to help her with her test anxiety.)

Peg began intervention two on 27 September 1996. Instead of writing key terms from the chapter into an E–mail document, she located the answers for the 15 questions from her review sheet for exam one and copied each question, with its corresponding answer, in flashcard format, into an E–mail document. Concurrently, she made actual 3x5 flashcards of the same material. Once the flashcards had been copied textually into E–mail, she sent the E–mail to the instructor. The instructor then explained how to practice with the flashcards. Peg agreed to practice with the flashcards in the SAFMEDS procedure, and to report her fluency data with the cards (rate per minute of corrects/incorrects in a card practice session) via E–mail.

The instructions for how to work with the flashcards included several steps: Peg was to assemble all the cards with the question–side up and read the question side of the first card, preferably out loud. Then she would attempt to answer the question, as speedily as possible (in the typical one–minute SAFMEDS manner), after which she would turn the card over, read the correct answer, and evaluate whether or not her answer had been right. If she could not answer (or answered incorrectly), she placed that card in a pile of incorrect cards which were called "not–yets." If she answered the question correctly, the card went into a "correct" pile. After working through all cards, Peg would have generated a number of corrects and a number of not–yets. She would then record her rates of corrects and incorrects (not–yets) for each iteration of the cards, and report her practice data via E–mail. Before each practice, she would shuffle the cards.

Peg completed her 15 flashcards, as well as her E–mail version of the flashcard material on 29 September 1996. On 3 October 1996, in the morning before her first exam, Peg reported the data from her subsequent flashcard practice. She took her first abnormal psychology exam after her morning flashcard practice session.

The typical one–minute timing procedure used with SAFMEDS was quickly becoming aversive to Peg. Based on her preferences and performance data, the SAFMEDS procedure was modified into intervention three. Now she recorded not a rate per minute of corrects/incorrects, but a number of corrects/incorrects over the total time for each iteration of the cards.

Peg was also urged to reduce the amount of text on each flashcard, so that each card would take less time to answer. In the case of questions which had multiple answers, she was urged to make two or three cards covering that question. These changes in procedure, which constituted intervention three, were implemented on 4 October 1996 in preparation for Peg's second exam on 23 October 1996.

Between 4 October and 17 October 1996, Peg constructed 46 flashcards based on the key terms of the chapters covered on her second exam. From 17 October to 23 October 1996, she practiced with the flashcards but did not regularly report flashcard data via E–mail. She took her second exam on 23 October 1996.

Peg made 50 new flashcards based on the new content for her third exam, which was scheduled for 14 November 1996. She sent the flashcard content to the instructor via E–mail. However, she continued to experience a low correct rate using the flashcards, and continued to practice less than once per day, while she also continued to study the cards in a non–SAFMEDS manner. As well, Peg continued to E–mail her frustration with the evolving flashcard system.

The instructor advised Peg to practice each set of cards at least five times, so that she could see her rate of corrects go up, and her rate of "not yets" go down. Peg was also urged to practice at least once per day, sending in her flashcard data after the practice.

Peg practiced with her cards and reported her data more frequently, missing only one day of practice between 31 October and 14 November 1996, the day of her third abnormal psych exam. While her rate of flashcard practice and reporting had increased to a daily basis, she was still voicing, a few days before that exam, considerable frustration about her consistently high number of incorrects during each practice. Peg worried that her consistently high rate of incorrects was slowing her progress through the material, as well as making her more anxious about being tested over the material that she was not answering correctly. She considered her inability to reduce her rate of incorrects to be a "mind block," and felt that the flashcard program was becoming aversive. Still, she agreed to continue with her current system for those few days that remained before her third exam.

Meanwhile, in those few days and the few days after that exam, intervention four was discussed and designed. Intervention four was a further modification of the SAFMEDS flashcard procedures. Via E–mail the instructor explained the concepts of "behavior chains" and "task analysis." Peg was then asked to describe her typical process of calling the cards, making a rudimentary task analysis of her flashcard procedure into a short E–mail essay, which she completed and returned on 13 November 1996.

In the evening of 15 November 1996, Peg began making new flashcards for the new content of her fourth exam. Based on her task analysis essay and flashcard data, four changes were made to Peg's flashcard routine:

- Peg would discontinue timing her flashcard routine. She was urged to pay no attention to how long any flashcard iteration took.
- It was revealed in her task analysis that she had been initially practicing with all the cards in a set, but subsequently practicing with only the cards in the "not yet" pile, leaving the "correct" cards out of subsequent practices. She was instructed to repractice her typical way but with *all* the cards.
- She was also instructed to not bother shuffling the cards. She could now practice until she completed all the cards in a set, and keep the cards in the same order for each practice.

- And she was urged to practice with her new cards using the new system at least twice per day.

By 21 November 1996, Peg had completed 21 new flashcards. The new changes of intervention four were sent to her in written form via E–mail, and repeated to her in a follow–up phone conversation over Thanksgiving break. However, she did not practice with her new flashcard routine until returning to her campus on 2 December 1996. In her E–mail that evening, (partially reformatted, etc.) she wrote:

> Hi. I have been practicing and I feel a lot better about everything already. I made a bunch of cards over break, and I have been through half of them today, three times.
>
> These are my results: The first time I went through them I got four out of 21. The second time I had eight out of 21. And the third time I had 15 out of 21. Sounds better, huh?!

From 2 December 1996 until the end of her on–line course (for this term) after her final exam, Peg consistently practiced with her new flashcard system, E–mailing her data daily or every two days. Importantly to Peg, her rates of correct completion of the cards started increasing with every practice. During intervention four, Peg constructed 57 new flashcards; her highest rate, as of 9 December 1996, was 42 correct of 57. She reported being much more satisfied with her current flashcard procedures than any previous system, and she continued to work in the intervention four manner. Her fourth exam was on 12 December 1996, and her final exam was on 17 December 1996.

Study skill client's results and discussion. The on–line course procedures resulted in 85 E–mail documents exchanged between the client and the instructor from 17 September to 9 December, a period of 84 days. A text document archiving the contents of all the client–instructor E–mail messages amounted to 31,814 words, though this is not a highly accurate gauge of words written.

The system initially increased the client's daily amount of writing with respect to the content of her abnormal psych course. Having her write about the content of the class and restate the key terms of each chapter into regular E–mail documents were the basic elements of intervention one, with which the course started.

During intervention two, which began on 27 September before the client's first exam, the E–mail based writing was used to make and practice with flashcards in a SAFMEDS system. The client found and copied key chapter terms into E–mail, and onto 3x5 cards which were used in the typical one–minute SAFMEDS manner. This process further increased the client's exposure to the text material by virtue of the writing involved in making the flashcards. Also, practice with the cards introduced a fluency training element over the text content of the chapters. This was the intervention which obtained up to the client's first exam on 3 October.

Figure 6 shows all the client's abnormal psych exam scores for the semester. (All scores are percentage scores.) That initial exam score was a solid A, the very first A she had earned in her college career.

Intervention three was begun on 4 October, the day after the client's first exam. (For each exam, several days usually passed before she learned what score she had earned). Intervention three modified the SAFMEDS flashcard fluency procedure by removing the one–minute time constraint; the client was asked only to record her total time to finish her routine. This intervention obtained until 15 November, the day after exam three. As Figure 6 shows, intervention three was correlated with two successive reductions in exam score. While exam two was an A level grade, exam three was several points below A level.

Intervention four, begun on 15 November, was a further refinement of the SAFMEDS fluency training procedure as a result of the client's task analysis of the steps she had actually been taking. This intervention extended through both exam four and the client's final exam. The client received a score of 89 on exam four, an increase to just one point away from A level. She received a score of 96 on her final exam! During intervention four not only did the client's rate of flashcard practice increase but her rate of corrects increased as well.

The client accomplished a mean score of 90.4 for the five exams of her abnormal psych course. However, she reported that under her professor's policy, the lowest score from the first four exams would be dropped; so her 84 was dropped. This results in a mean score of 92 for the remaining four exams (three regular exams and the final exam). As a consequence, she received an A for her final grade. These A scores and grade were the first such marks she had ever earned in her college career. She plans to continue these study practices in the next semester.

During the break between the fall and spring semesters, the instructor had occasion to meet with the client and her family. After an impromptu discussion, the client offered the instructor original copies of each exam along with her original flashcards. The presentation of these materials, before a request could be made for them, provides some validation both for the *in vivo* participation of on–line clients and for the reasonableness of the presumption of honesty on the part of clients.

As the weight and smoking control courses seemed to contribute to those clients' successes, this on–line course seemed to make a contribution to this client's success. More importantly, however, this study was valuable in delineating the idiosyncratic

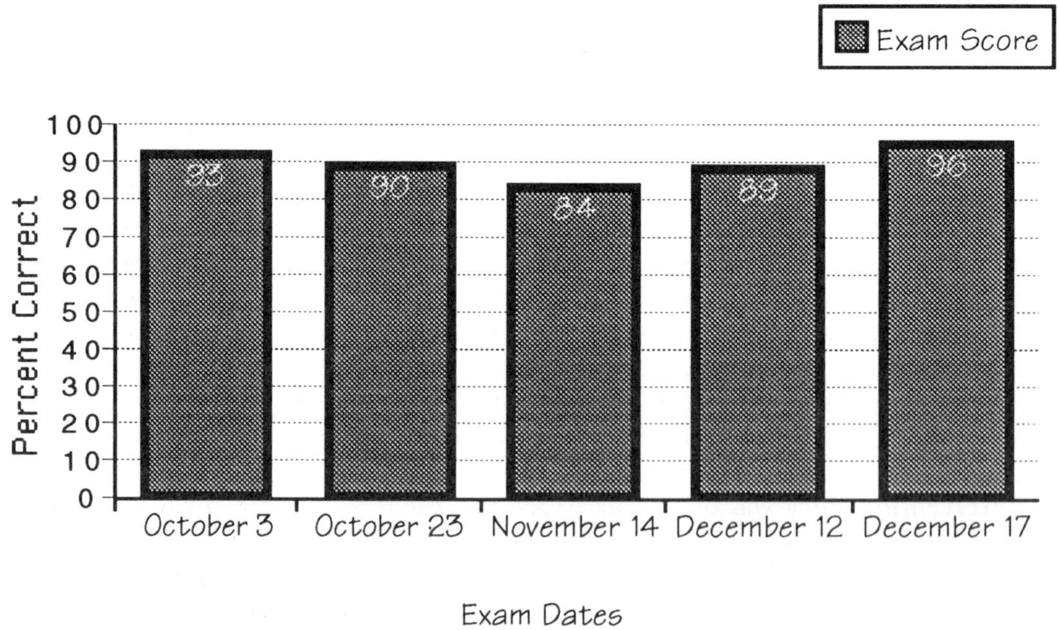

Figure 6. Exam scores for study skill client's abnormal psychology course.

contingencies involved in applying on–line educational methodology to (a) the skills which encompass studying such as reading, writing, and fluency practice, (b) a sole reliance on E–mail as the vehicle of communication, instruction, and data–based feedback, with (c) a college student contemporaneously studying for a full roster of college courses. It points to the value of using on–line resources not only to deliver new educational materials, but also to arrange more successful contingencies for reading, writing, and practicing with conventional college course materials.

General Discussion

In his paper "Why aren't effective teaching tools widely adopted?" Ogden Lindsley (1992b) posed this significant "what if" question:

> Think over the following "what if?" Suppose Sesame Street had been developed by effective educators, from Montessori, through Dewey, Skinner, Keller, to Engelmann... Sesame Street would sell a $199.95 Sesame Street Learning–Remote that plugs into the wall and the TV, and a modem that plugs into the telephone during program transmission. Now Sesame Street would collect learning results from its viewers across the country. With these results, more effective learning programs could have been experimentally designed. The interactive excitement and dollars now squandered on Nintendo® might have been invested in academic learning. (p. 24)

In essence, Sesame Street would have been on–line, and measuring behavior daily to improve itself. The pilot studies reported here support the feasibility and value of adapting daily, repeated measures of behavior to learning activities conducted via on–line communication. While other aspects of behaviorological research and practice were implemented with these clients (e.g., behavioral contracts, changing criteria, token economy, even covert conditioning), the fundamental rudiment of daily, repeated measures of rates of behavior must be considered the most valuable, most salient component in the emergence of measurably effective on–line behavior–change technology.

Like many experiments, these studies raise profitable questions for further research. These questions include:

- What may be the value of either synchronous, real time conversational writing (chat) or asynchronous E–mail exchange? Is one or the other unnecessary?
- What are the advantages (if any) of "live" instructor–client verbal exchanges via E–mail or chat tools, versus the preprogrammed, "canned" machine–client interactions typical of distributed learning software?
- What are the advantages (if any) of each instructor–client verbalization occurring in a written medium? Does the fact that each verbalization is archived as a durable text file lead to a "behavioral contractualization" of the entire interaction?

The various methodological, professional, and cultural issues raised by adapting single–subject behaviorological methods to an on–line learning environment might remain esoteric, were it not for the current "gold rush" on the part of educational and therapy practitioners toward using novel on–line communications tools for distance education and on–line therapy and psychotherapy endeavors. Dozens of universities and colleges have begun to offer college credit courses via on–line learning; Florida's Walden University, along with Thomas Edison State College in New Jersey, are famous for offering master and doctoral level degrees attainable virtually on–line. Other schools such as Boise State University, Brown University, California State University System, Indiana University School of Continuing Education Studies, Kansas State University, New School for Social Research in New York City, State University of New York Empire State College, Union Institute of Cincinnati, University of California at Berkeley Extension, University of California at Los Angeles Extension, and the University of Chicago all offer undergraduate and graduate credit courses via on–line interactions (Newman, 1996). Distance education has moved rapidly toward professionalization, with specialized teacher training programs, guidelines, journals, and E–mail listservers devoted to remote learning practices, a subset of which is on–line education.

On–line psychotherapy, while less professionalized than distance education, is a rapidly developing, pre–professional endeavor which has garnered serious notice from internet print journalists (e.g., see Zgodzinski, 1996) as well as licensing bodies such as the American Psychological Association (APA). According to Sleek (1995, on–line) the APA Board of Directors asked several APA committees to consider "the issue of online psychotherapy services. In fact, APA's Board of Professional Affairs (BPA) will be exploring a wide range of issues concerning the increased use of technology by psychologists."

The APA's ethical concerns about psychologists providing services via the internet may be of significant importance to psychologists. This author finds such concerns interesting in their own right. However, the work described in this paper does not involve psychotherapy. The noted psychologist Dr. Leonard Holmes (personal communication, 1 February 1997) addressed this fact concisely; after reviewing this author's web site, which espouses on–line behavior change, he E–mailed back:

> ...bhavior.com [now, "onlearn.com"] is interesting! The approach of "on–line writing courses in behavioral self–management of smoking, weight control, or study skills" is a novel one which avoids many of the issues involved in "on–line therapy."

In any case, the procedures reported in this paper are applications of the independent *natural* science of behavior which some, including this author, call behaviorology (and which others call behavior analysis); these procedures are not applications of the *social* science of behavior which is known as psychology. As such, only fully and properly trained behaviorological scientists and practitioners should use these procedures, which are subject to the ethical controls laid down by their own discipline rather than the ethical control laid down by psychologists.

A recent search conducted by this author (available upon request) found more than 50 on–line therapy and psychotherapy practitioners on the World Wide Web. Credentials ranged from masters–level counseling psychologists and social workers through MD psychiatrists. Fees ranged from free to $50 dollars per E–mail question, with different fee structures for on–line chat interactions, even per–minute charges for off–line reading of E–mailed client questions.

On–line learning practices, either for education or therapy, will continue to be developed within their respective marketplaces. On–line learning practices which make client or student learning more measurable, accountable, or effective would seem to have generic importance to either distance education or "distance therapy," since the value of any educational or therapeutic intervention is the changed behavior of the student or client. However, this author could not find any other on–line educator, therapist, or psychotherapist who featured daily, repeated measures of student or client behavior. Furthermore, no other educator, therapist, or psychotherapist displayed any data related to the effectiveness of her/his practices. The basic reliance on daily repeated measures of student or client behavior, as rudimentary as these are in the studies reported in this paper, may be unprecedented. This should not come as a surprise. On–line educators and therapists practice primarily from within the aforementioned *presentation model* identified by Vargas. However, behaviorological scientists and practitioners generally eschew that model in favor of the *shaping model* (Vargas, 1996).

These pilot studies inaugurate the application of the shaping model to on–line therapeutic education. The first iterations of this application delineate basic methodological priorities, such as the daily measurement of client–counted rates of a target behavior or response product. Other priorities, such as use of chat room technology, collaborative self–pacing, electronic sharing of chart data, etc., may or may not have been necessary to the success shown by each client. These studies do demonstrate that effective education techniques based on behaviorological science can be adapted to on–line communication, and that elements of the techniques, together or separately, correlated with movement toward each client's explicit goals: weight was lost, smoking was reduced, grades were improved.

A gold rush does not imply gold. Internet education and therapy practitioners may ignore shaping–model practices and still produce behavior change, prestige, and profit (though the behavior change may be adventitious; see the first appendix in Ledoux, 1997c). On–line consumers of behavior–change practices in education and therapy may not yet be in a position to demand measurably more effective on–line learning, even if such practices were more widely disseminated. And, on the other hand, financial interests may deter current distance therapists from adopting *daily* repeated measures of behavior; their current prices per E–mail would be exorbitantly expensive for a client interested in the effective behavior change that would come through the daily interactions required by a repeated measures process of on–line therapy. At their current prices, one would be justified in demanding and receiving evidence of therapeutic effectiveness before paying anything. Is this financial concern among any reasons why some practitioners are against on–line intervention?

The concept of "measurably more effective" on–line education or therapy will hopefully catch on. Without reliable, daily measurement of behavior, claims of effectiveness for on–line education or therapy will continue to rest on mere credentials and personal testimonials—ranging from the gee–whiz exhortations of technophiles to the current anti–on–line stance of some psychologists (reference available from author); on–line interventions without repeated measures methodology will continue to produce more hyperbole than behavior change.

Endnotes

Parts of this work were presented at meetings of various behaviorological science groups in the New York City area during 1994–1996, including Walden Fellowship, at Columbia University, and Young Adult Institute, Inc., in Manhattan. The work was then revised for presentation both at the ninth annual convention of The International Behaviorology Association in Plymouth, MA, March 1997, and at the twenty–third annual convention of the Association for Behavior Analysis in Chicago, IL, May 1997, as well as for inclusion in *Origins and Components of Behaviorology* (Ledoux, 1997a).

The author thanks Stephen Ledoux for providing many helpful comments in review of this work, and Beth Diveney, Lawrence Fraley, Dick Malott, Mark Mattaini, Jerome Ulman, and Dennis Wahlgren for their encouraging remarks about earlier versions of this material. Address correspondence regarding this paper to the author at drfeeney@onlearn.com (E–mail), or at "Onlearn" Co., 183 Pinehurst Avenue Suite 54, New York NY 10033 USA.

References

Abba, S. & McLaughlin, T.F. (1995). Use of daily measurement, standard celeration charting, and a Nicotrol patch to reduce cigarette smoking with a female college student: A case study. *Journal of Precision Teaching and Celeration, 13* (1), 57–63.

Binder, C. (1988). Precision teaching: Measuring and attaining exemplary academic achievement. *Youth Policy, 10* (7), 12–15.

Dean, D.H. (1973). An analysis of the effects of using direct measures in a competency–based professional education program: An example in nursing. *Dissertation Abstracts International, 1973, 34, 5577a,* 41–50. (University Microfilms No. 74–6820).

Ellson, D. (1986). Improving productivity in teaching. *Phi Delta Kappan, 67* (2), 111–124.

Green, J.K. & Morrow, W.R. (1972). Precision social work: General model and illustrative student projects with clients. *Education for Social Work.* Washington, DC: Council on Social Work Education.

Hawkins, R.P. & Hursh, D.E. (1992). Levels of research for clinical practice: It isn't as hard as you think. *The West Virginia Journal of Psychological Research and Practice, 1,* 61–71.

Heward, W.L. (1994). Three "low–tech" strategies for increasing the frequency of active student response during group instruction. In R. Gardner, D. Sainato, J.O. Cooper, T.E. Heron, W.L. Heward, & J.W. Eshleman (Eds.). *Behavior Analysis in Education: Focus on Measurably Superior Instruction* (pp. 283–320). Pacific Grove, CA: Brooks/Cole.

Howell, K.W. & Lorson–Howell, K.A. (1990). Fluency in the classroom. *Teaching Exceptional Children, 22* (3), 20–23.

Johnson, K.R. & Layng, T.V. (1994). The morningside model of generative instruction. In R. Gardner, D. Sainato, J.O. Cooper, T.E. Heron, W.L. Heward, & J.W. Eshleman (Eds.). *Behavior Analysis in Education: Focus on Measurably Superior Instruction* (pp. 173–197). Pacific Grove, CA: Brooks/Cole.

Johnson, T.S. (1972). Precision therapy is the way to go. In J.B. Borden & L.S. Robbins (Eds.). *Let's Try Doing Something Else Kind of Thing* (pp. 41–50). Arlington, VA: Council for Exceptional Children.

Ledoux, S.F. (1997a). *Origins and Components of Behaviorology.* Canton, NY: ABCs.

Ledoux, S.F. (1997b). Successful smoking control as an example of a comprehensive behaviorological therapy. In S.F. Ledoux. *Origins and Components of Behaviorology.* Canton, NY: ABCs.

Ledoux, S.F. (1997c). Appendices. In S.F. Ledoux. *Origins and Components of Behaviorology.* Canton, NY: ABCs.

Lindsley, O.R. (1956). Operant conditioning methods applied to research in chronic schizophrenia. *Psychiatric Research Reports, 5* (3), 118–139.

Lindsley, O.R. (1960). Characteristics of the behavior of chronic psychotics as revealed by free operant conditioning methods. *Diseases of the Nervous System, Monograph, Supplement, 21,* 66–78.

Lindsley, O.R. (1990). Precision teaching: By teachers for children. *Teaching Exceptional Children, 22* (3), 10–15.

Lindsley, O.R. (1992a). Precision teaching: Discoveries and effects. *Journal of Applied Behavior Analysis, 25,* 51–57.

Lindsley, O.R. (1992b). Why aren't effective teaching tools widely adopted? *Journal of Applied Behavior Analysis, 25,* 21–26.

Lindsley, O.R. (1993). Our discoveries over 28 years. *Journal of Precision Teaching, 10* (2), 14–15.

Lindsley, O.R. (1995). Ten products of fluency. *Journal of Precision Teaching and Celeration, 13* (1), 2–11.

Lindsley, O.R. (1996). Is fluency free–operant response–response chaining? *The Behavior Analyst, 19,* 211–224.

Merbitz, C.T., King, R.B., Cherney, L.R., Marqui, H., Grip, J.C., & Markowitz, T.J. (1996). Computerized behavioral data collection and analysis for improved clinical outcomes in rehabilitation. *Journal of Precision Teaching and Celeration, 13* (2), 57–63.

Moxley, R. (1995, March). Treatment only designs. Paper presented at the eighth annual convention of The International Behaviorology Association, Gainesville, FL.

Moxley, R. (1996). Treatment only designs for the classroom. Unpublished manuscript.

Newman, M. (1996). College courses at your convenience on the internet. *The New York Times.* Cyber Times, 6 November. See also: http://search.nytimes.com/web/docsroot/library/cyber/week/1103online.html

Pennypacker, H.S., Koenig, C., & Lindsley, O.R. (1972). *Handbook of the Standard Behavior Chart.* Kansas City, MO: Precision Media.

Skinner, B.F. (1953). *Science and Human Behavior.* New York: Macmillan.

Skinner, B.F. (1968). *The Technology of Teaching.* New York: Appleton–Century–Crofts.

Sleek, S. (1995, November). Online therapy services raise ethical questions. *The APA Monitor,* (on–line at: http://www.apa.org/monitor/nov95/online.html).

Vargas, E.A. (1996). A university for the twenty–first century. In J.R. Cautela & W. Ishaq (Eds.). *Contemporary Issues in Behavior Therapy: Improving the Human Condition* (pp. 159–188). New York: Plenum.

West, R.P. & Hamerlynck, L.A. (Eds.). (1992). *Designs for Excellence in Education: The Legacy of B.F. Skinner (Limited Edition).* Longmont, CO: Sopris West.

Wolery, M., Bailey, D.B., & Sugai, G.M. (1988). *Effective Teaching: Principles and Procedures of Applied Behavior Analysis with Exceptional Students.* Boston, MA: Allyn & Bacon.

Youth Policy Institute. (1988, July/August). *Youth Policy, 10* (7).

Zgodzinski, D. (1996). Cyber therapy. *Internet World, 7* (2), 50–52. See also: http://www.iw.com/1996/02/therapy.html

*Quoted**

§

Better living through better science: Behaviorology... (p. 1)

§

*From the title of an article: Ledoux, S.F. (1990). *TIBA Newsletter*, *2* (1), 1–2.

*Quoted**

§

...[The next paper, Glenn Latham's paper on his visit to China] nicely rounds out this collection of components of behaviorology by providing readers with a continuously timely reminder that the continuation of any science owes as much to reaching out to others, through dissemination, as to conceptualization, experimentation, application, and organization. (p. xxii)

§

*From the 1997 preface to *Origins and Components of Behaviorology* (Ledoux, S.F. Canton, NY: ABCs).

China Through the Eyes of a Behaviorologist

Glenn I. Latham

China is a country with a huge population. It is altogether safe to say that at any given moment there is more behavior going on in China than anywhere else on earth. And, as is the case with people throughout the world, antecedents get behavior going and consequences determine what happens to it after that.

Since I was in China discussing matters of education and parenting, I was not surprised to find that among the people of China, there are two compelling concerns. The "one child policy" has created a sociological dilemma for China that has come to be known in many quarters as the "Little Emperor Syndrome." It is a problem created by members of two and three generations of a family living together in very cramped quarters in high rise apartment buildings with little to no facilities for children to play and romp about outside. In most instances both parents are working and a child is left at home to be tended by two or three sets of grandparents. Before long the child is ruling the roost and chaos reigns.

As these children enter school, they bring with them a repertoire of behaviors that is unlike anything that modern–day school teachers in China have ever experienced; hence, the concern of parents for the schooling of their children—a concern, I hasten to add, that is expressed quietly.

None of the problems created by these perplexing circumstances are the least bit adequately addressed by the reigning political ideology of China. The top down centralized system of government that has ruled and reigned in China for the last 50 years doesn't seem to impress little children at home or students in school. Political and edu-

---

With his wife Louise, Utah State University (Logan) Emeritus Professor of Education Dr. Glenn Latham spent three weeks—29 August through 20 September, 1996—in China (PRC). They were guests of the West China University for Medical Sciences, in Chengdu, Sichuan. Written in November 1996, this is the report of that visit, the author's second professional visit to China.

For several years, the authors of this paper and of *Origins and Components of Behaviorology* (Ledoux, 1997a) have shared an interest in helping encourage the development of the independent natural science of behavior, behaviorology, among the quarter of the world's population residing in China. Due to this shared interest, Latham sent Ledoux a courtesy copy of this paper. Ledoux found that it provided a well founded "call to action" for behaviorological professionals to help develop behaviorology in China. Indeed, this call to action could be timely for a long period as it could also extend to other countries in due time and as resources allow. So, to enlarge the potential audience for this paper, Ledoux invited Latham to include his paper in the same book of readings (Ledoux, 1997a) that contained Ledoux's earlier paper on behaviorology in China (Ledoux, 1997b), a paper to which Latham had already referred his readers.

cational leaders, as well as parents, know they have a mammoth problem and they know they have no solutions.

Subsequent to the two talks I gave at West China University for Medical Sciences in Chengdu, Sichuan, people swarmed about me wanting to know how the science of human behavior could be adapted to the solution of China's parenting and educational problems. The talks I gave were entitled "Major Reform Issues in American Education" and "Strengthening Families." In both talks I stressed the importance of what has been learned scientifically, through the study of human behavior, about the solution of difficult educational and family/parenting problems. (For some detailed information on this science and its application to these areas, see, Binder, 1988; Christophersen, 1988; Clark, 1996; Heward, 1994; Johnson & Layng, 1994; Latham, 1994, 1997; Lindsley, 1990, 1992, 1993; Skinner, 1953, 1968; Vargas, 1996; West & Hamerlynck, 1992; and Youth Policy Institute, 1988.)

In my talk "Major Reform Issues in American Education," I emphasized the importance of addressing educational reform with science rather than intuition, and the importance of focusing on teacher and student behavior in school rather than overarching policies and grand organizational schemes (which, over the centuries, have assured the status quo!). During the question and answer period following my talk, one member of the university faculty made the following observation:

> I think there are two reasons why education never changes. First, in medicine there is more money to be earned if one is up to date in his treatment of patients. Second, there is more immediacy in treating sickness and injury. There is less room for error. A patient could die if the doctor didn't know exactly what to do.

I thought it amusing that this would come from a faculty member in Communist China who didn't know Capitalism but did understand logic. She had grasped with ease something America's educators just can't seem to get!

There is a prevailing feeling across the earth that the margin of error in the education of children is so broad, and the sense of immediacy is so weak, that there is no reason to be concerned; that, as one teacher I interviewed put it, "They (meaning students) will finally get it somewhere along the way." The problem, of course, is that too many don't "finally get it"; hence, the mess we are in, in education.

I was also asked by a faculty member about "systematic methods of instruction for preschool children." He noted, "Surely there must be systematic methods of instruction that are based in science, and are known to work!" In all of my hundreds of school, classroom, and teacher/principal visits, I have never, ever, been asked by an American educator about "systematic methods of instruction" for children at any level. During further discussions with this same faculty member, he was equally interested in "systematic methods of instruction" for older students, "even into college." I told him I would send him information about precision teaching, direct instruction, mastery learning, and Keller's Personalized System of Instruction. As I spoke of these methods to the faculty member and others gathered about me, they were in awe that such systems of instruction actually existed and assumed that they must be in widespread use in America, in fact in universal use. When I told them that the educational establishment of America, generally, had rejected these scientifically sound, data–based approaches to instruction, in favor of intuitive, individualistic, "artsy" methods, they were dumbfounded. One faculty member said to me, "Where can I learn about this wonderful science of human behavior?" (Arrangements are presently being made to bring this faculty member to America to learn about the science of human behavior and how to apply that science to a broad range of educational problems. It appears as though she, and a faculty member from the West China University for Medical Sciences, will be living with Louise and me while they go to school in America to learn about this "wonderful science.")

Everywhere we went in China, whenever it became known that my field of scholarship was the study and treatment of human behavior, great interest became immediately generated. The guides that had been arranged to escort Louise and me would ask questions, specific questions, about their children's behavior. I see China as a nation ready for the science of human behavior. It has such huge needs, and those needs are immediately demanding attention. I would hope that something could be done to arouse the American community of behaviorists and behaviorologists to an interest in getting the science of behavior into that mammoth population of people. I believe it would be well received and I believe that evidences of impact would be felt early on.

Although China is a totalitarian nation that is governed by powerful centralized leadership—a system I don't agree with—there are advantages that could come from it. For example, television is state controlled, as are other forms of media. If video–taped training and awareness programs could be developed that were acceptable by the government for presentation to the masses, it would be possible to get the message of behaviorology into millions and millions of homes rapidly and thoroughly. Such "media campaigns" (Biglan, 1995, p. 486) are already in place relative to health care and other topics of broad concern. Extending such campaigns to include aspects of "behavioral hygiene" (Ledoux, 1997c) such as parenting skills would not be unreasonable. When we were in China, there was interest generated by officials at the West China University for Medical Sciences to do that very thing. I believe it is worth looking into. We behaviorologists might do for the society of China what W. Edwards Deming did for Japanese business. I don't believe that is a farfetched notion.

I'm not prepared at this moment to make many specific recommendations. But I am looking into the matter carefully and intend to have several specific recommendations in the not too distant future.

Regardless of what those next steps might be, this much I know: they will have to be taken at some expense to the Americans involved in working with the Chinese. The Chinese are in a position to help cover local expenses like food and lodging, and some forms of ground transportation, but extensive travel arrangements, consulting fees, and expensive technology will have to be borne by the Americans who take the initiative in getting this ball rolling. China is a terribly, terribly poor nation. Although some things are cheap for the Chinese, like food and lodging, their wages, nevertheless, barely allow them to make ends meet. For example, the average worker's salary in China is $25 a month. The president of West China University for Medical Sciences earns $100 a month as president of the university, and an additional $100 a month for his work as a surgeon. He is a fairly well known surgeon in China, and is active in his profession, even though as president of a university he has heavy administrative responsibilities.

The university is also poor. When visiting with the president and members of his administration, we were told of how they struggle to keep their buildings heated in the winter, and how they can barely afford to make major repairs to keep their facilities functional. But in the long run, I still believe that we in America who have this great science should make every effort we can to get it into China. A relatively inexpensive way of doing that would be to host Chinese scholars in America. They would be able to get to America at their own expense, and their universities would continue to pay their wages which would be anywhere from $50 to $100 a month. But if they were hosted by American faculty members, that is, invited to live in our homes and eat at our tables as our extended guests, they could do quite well, acquire the skills and knowledge they need, and take those skills back to China where they would get the word out amongst their colleagues and the people generally.

One of the nice things about China is that there isn't a philosophical disposition which has biased or prejudiced the academic community against the behavioral approach. Though many Chinese scholars, educators, and university leaders were educated in Russia, and are aware of the psychodynamic approach to treating behavior problems, psychodynamicism is not a compelling force in China. Also, there is nothing about communist ideology that would stand in the way. Communism is virtually meaningless to the masses in China. They could care less. Communism is a stepping stone to moving up in the system. For example, one could never be a university president or a college dean without being a member of the communist party. But beyond that, communism has little or no meaning to the people, and would certainly not be a deterrent to the work I am proposing.

In a word, the Chinese aren't already committed to the "isms" that are plaguing America. That is certainly a big plus. Their cup is relatively empty and waiting to be filled. I think we should start filling it.

To some American scholars and academes, the thought of sharing their knowledge and expertise with a government that would order the massacre of untold numbers of students is offensive—even repulsive. I have a friend who is on the faculty of a large Midwestern university. For years he was active in providing services and training to university personnel in China. He was in China on the night of the Tiananmen Square massacre—in fact, he watched it happen and vowed never again to lift a finger on behalf of such a government. That is understandable. One must deal with his/her own conscience on such matters. As for me, I have concluded that things will never get better for the Chinese if there are no healthy influences from the outside.

I believe strongly that we need to get bright, young as well as seasoned, assertive Chinese scholars to America, where they can be educated and trained, and who can then go back to China and be our contacts for additional work there related to promoting the science. I believe that if we could get a network of behaviorists/behaviorologists located throughout China, that network could become a dynamic force in building the science in that country, and in making it available to the people as a tool in the solution of compelling educational and parenting problems. That is certainly what my wife and I are committed to doing. Within the next few months, we expect to have two of those scholars living with us in our home, taking classes at Utah State University, being mentored by selected faculty members, and given a broad base of hands–on experience so that they will know how to apply this science to the problems facing their country. It is an enriching experience. For what it is worth, my wife and I have already hosted a visiting scholar from China in our home. He was with us for about six months and was a wonderful house guest, a delight to be with, and the fruits of that are already being realized by the influence he is having in China.

For additional insights into this matter, I suggest you read "Behaviorology in China: A Status Report" by Dr. Stephen F. Ledoux. His article (Ledoux, 1997b) was written after Professor Ledoux had spent a year teaching in China. (Also see Case & Ledoux, 1997, for a chronicle of the experiences of Ledoux and his family during that year; it will help you be prepared to appreciate your own visit to China—or provide you with an adventurous, informative, and culturally expanding visit to China from the comfort of your own home.) ᔓ

Endnotes

Hoping that it might enlist the informed assistance of its readers in the worthy endeavor of developing behaviorology in China, the author initially prepared this work as a report of the his experience in that country. The paper received minor revisions for inclusion in *Origins and Components of Behaviorology* (Ledoux, 1997a).

The author thanks his Chinese hosts both for their efforts to make his visit to China possible and for their efforts to increase the availability of the independent natural science of behavior in their country. Address correspondence regarding this paper to the author at Mountain Plains Regional Resource Center, 1780 N. Research Parkway Suite 112, Logan UT 84341 USA.

References

Biglan, A. (1995). Translating what we know about the context of antisocial behavior into a lower prevalence of such behavior. *Journal of Applied Behavior Analysis, 28,* 479–492.

Binder, C. (1988). Precision teaching: Measuring and attaining exemplary academic achievement. *Youth Policy, 10* (7), 12–15.

Case, N.M. & Ledoux, S.F. (1997). *The Panda and Monkey King Christmas—A Family's Year in China.* Canton, NY: ABCs.

Christophersen, E.R. (1988). *Little People (Third Edition).* Kansas City, MO: Westport Publishers.

Clark, L. (1996). *SOS! Help for Parents (Second Edition).* Bowling Green, KY: Parents Press. (Also available in Chinese.)

Heward, W.L. (1994). Three "low-tech" strategies for increasing the frequency of active student response during group instruction. In R. Gardner, D. Sainato, J.O. Cooper, T.E. Heron, W.L. Heward, & J.W. Eshleman (Eds.). *Behavior Analysis in Education: Focus on Measurably Superior Instruction* (pp. 283–320). Pacific Grove, CA: Brooks/Cole.

Johnson, K.R., & Layng, T.V. (1994). The morningside model of generative instruction. In R. Gardner, D. Sainato, J.O. Cooper, T.E. Heron, W.L. Heward, & J.W. Eshleman (Eds.). *Behavior Analysis in Education: Focus on Measurably Superior Instruction* (pp. 173–197). Pacific Grove, CA: Brooks/Cole.

Latham, G.I. (1994). *The Power of Positive Parenting: A Wonderful Way to Raise Children.* Logan, UT: P and T.

Latham, G.I. (1997). *Behind the Schoolhouse Door: Eight Skills Every Teacher Should Have.* Logan, UT: Mountain Plains Regional Resource Center.

Ledoux, S.F. (1997a). *Origins and Components of Behaviorology.* Canton, NY: ABCs.

Ledoux, S.F. (1997b). Behaviorology in China: A status report. In S.F. Ledoux. *Origins and Components of Behaviorology.* Canton, NY: ABCs. Reprinted with revisions from (1992) *Behaviorological Commentaries, Serial No. 4,* 24–36.

Ledoux, S.F. (1997c). An introduction to the origins, status, and mission of behaviorology: An established science with developed applications and a new name. In S.F. Ledoux. *Origins and Components of Behaviorology.* Canton, NY: ABCs. Reprinted with revisions from (1992) *Behaviorological Commentaries, Serial No. 3,* 11–31.

Lindsley, O.R. (1990). Precision teaching: By teachers for children. *Teaching Exceptional Children, 22* (3), 10–15.

Lindsley, O.R. (1992). Precision teaching: Discoveries and effects. *Journal of Applied Behavior Analysis, 25,* 51–57.

Lindsley, O.R. (1993). Our discoveries over 28 years. *Journal of Precision Teaching, 10* (2), 14–15.

Skinner, B.F. (1953). *Science and Human Behavior.* New York: Macmillan.

Skinner, B.F. (1968). *The Technology of Teaching.* New York: Appleton–Century–Crofts.

Vargas, E.A. (1996). A university for the twenty–first century. In J.R. Cautela & W. Ishaq (Eds.). *Contemporary Issues in Behavior Therapy: Improving the Human Condition* (pp. 159–188). New York: Plenum.

West, R.P. & Hamerlynck, L.A. (Eds.). (1992). *Designs for Excellence in Education: The Legacy of B.F. Skinner (Limited Edition).* Longmont, CO: Sopris West.

Youth Policy Institute. (1988, July/August). *Youth Policy, 10* (7).

Appendices

Stephen F. Ledoux

Appendix 1: Excerpt on *"Adventitious Control"*

In helping clients solve problems under actual practical contingencies, non–behaviorological practitioners, including psychologists, sometimes *do* attain control. But that success is adventitious if it occurs merely as a result of the practical contingencies. Those practitioners then make invalid claims of credit for that success on behalf of their preferred theories, which are usually of a cognitive or mentalistic nature. But little if any of that control becomes possible *because* of the supplementary verbal antecedents of their theories. Instead it seems to occur in spite of those theories. Mentalistic analysis hinders control of behavior by misdirecting attention to specious constructs. Physiological analysis hinders control by fixating on a locus where control of behavior is usually not technically feasible. As a result mentalistic and cognitive practitioners can attain behavioral control only by coming under natural contingencies to emit successful technological behaviors that are beyond the reach of their conceptual analyses.

Natural contingencies are those in which verbal supplementary stimuli play no significant role. Under such contingencies those non–behaviorological practitioners, like other professionals, might respond in ways that prove effective. They then lay disciplinary claim to that naturally evoked technique for attaining some control, all in spite of its non–relation to their approach. For example, a cognitive practitioner might be faced with a student's earning poor math grades. He or she may then decide, from his or her particular variety of theory, that this is due, say, to a "minimal brain dysfunction" (MBD), or to what laymen might call a "mental block" within the student. (Why "minimal" brain dysfunction? Because the practitioner cannot find any real, physical dysfunction of the student's brain. But the behavior *is* a problem so the brain surely must be dysfunctional; if the dysfunction cannot be found, then it simply must be "minimal." The problem is that the presumption of a brain dysfunction is both invalid and

---

The first appendix originated in some of the author's interactions with students over the years. These interactions were the regular attempts to disabuse students new to behavior science of their culturally ingrained, automatic acceptance of inner causes (i.e., explanatory fictions) as being somehow adequate as scientific explanations of behavior. The first and second appendices contain modified excerpts from the historically unique 1992 version of the first paper on the origins of behaviorology (Fraley & Ledoux, 1997). Such excerpts, historically valuable as indicators of the verbal milieu at the time of behaviorology's emergence as an *organized* independent discipline, were not included—partly because they added an excess level of detail—in the separately published 1993 version of that paper which formed the basis of the 1997 version. The other appendices provide information supplemental either to one of the papers in *Origins and Components of Behaviorology* (Ledoux, 1997a) or to the general behaviorology movement.

unwarranted in the first place. An initial assumption warranted by the situation, and worth exploring and fixing—as a behaviorologist would do—is that something about the person's environment is "dysfunctional.")

The cognitive practitioner, however, has no intervention technologies, congruent with the natural laws governing behavior, that stem from cognitive/mentalistic analysis while also being appropriate for directly dealing with either MBDs or mental blocks (or perhaps even with ineffective math–focused behaviors). This holds regardless of whether these involve real physiological events or are entirely fictitious.

Real physiological events are sometimes directly investigated (appropriately, if by physiologists). But this still has little bearing on the emergence of a behavior–change technology as opposed to a more medical technology such as some form of drug therapy. More often these putative physiological events are only supposed, hypothesized, invented, or theorized—a well–criticized pattern of non–explanation known as gratuitous physiologizing (e.g., see Skinner, 1953, 1974).

As for fictitious events (explanatory fictions), the chief objection to them is *not* that they do not exist (although that is often a problem as well) but that they are irrelevant to the prediction and control of the behavior they are said to explain. They do not have manipulable, independent variable status. They are not a member of any class of terminal variables. They cannot be changed to bring about a change in the behavior they supposedly cause. One can claim that changing something else, such as an environmental variable, changes the fictitious variable which then changes behavior in the sense of A causing B, and B causing C. But then the relation is similar to relations in mathematics: A causes C, and the middle term is at least unnecessary.

The middle term also has other problems. The major (and often only) source of knowledge or information about these "inner causes" (Skinner, 1953) turns out to be the very behavior they are supposed to explain. These "causes" are *inferred* from that behavior, and then they are used to account for that same behavior. Such a sequence is circular. A more detailed example clarifies the inferential circularity:

"Why does the child do poorly in math?"

"Because he has a mental block [or MBD, or…]."

"How can you tell [or, How do you know] that he has a mental block?"

"Because he does poorly in math."

"But, why does he do poorly in math?"

"Because he has a mental block ."… [and so on…]

The cause is being circularly inferred from the very behavior to be explained (Chiesa, 1994, Ch. 7; Michael, 1989, Ch. 6; Skinner, 1953, Chs. 1–3). From a natural science perspective, laboratory methodologies are wasted to investigate what is not really there, while legions of students are trained to replace the professionals expended on the crusade. (An enlightening exposition appears in Chapter 1 of *Beyond Freedom and Dignity* [Skinner, 1971]. Also, some authors prefer more precise descriptors, as appropriate, such as nominal fallacy, teleology, or reification; see Gould, 1981, and Poling, Schlinger, Starin, & Blakely, 1990.)

Another problem for fictitious variables, perhaps the worst problem, is that they leave the analyzers comfortable; the analyzers seem to have found the sought–after cause. But in reality they have added nothing new to the analysis. Yet the search for the cause stops because one seems to have been found. The result is that accessible causal variables that might be changed to improve (control) the behavior in question remain unanalyzed. These are seldom even looked for when a pat answer is available unless separate, practical contingencies for doing so are in force. The search essentially stops because the mentalistic or cognitive analysis provides no compelling reasons to continue. The *analytical* approach ends without attaining the capacity for control.

The dangers of inner causes may be less important when the behavior being explained presents no problems, such as excelling in math being explained by "intelligence" (inherited or not). But those dangers can be crippling in the opposite case.

Yet a type of control may still be achieved. For example, the job specification of the above–mentioned practitioner (with the student client who is doing poorly in math) may supply the practical contingencies that require effective behavior–controlling technologies. The specification may require him or her to help that student. If he or she finds that student parked in front of a television set for five hours each day to the exclusion of study on school assignments, he or she may change the student's environment by pulling the plug on the set. If the ultimate result of that action is that grades improve, then that *functional* control results from the environmental change. That functional control does not result from the practitioner's cognitively focused, verbal analytical repertoire, but in spite of it. And that fact is not altered by that practitioner trying to tie the beneficial outcome to his or her paradigm by insisting that eliminating access to television must have diminished mental blocks or MBDs.

Mentalists sometimes conveniently disavow control as their goal since their approach will not support analyses that back–track through functionally related variables to the environment. (Radical behaviorists define environment as that milieu, part of which can be inside the skin, in which independent variables can be manipulated in behavior–controlling relations.) Mentalists' analysis precludes control so they argue against it. Instead of stressing control, mentalists emphasize understanding and dwell on predicting behavior. Their practical work is often confined to predicting behavior from other behavior—as when behavior on a specific occasion is predicted from a putative trait inferred from behavior on previous occasions. For example, educational psychology courses in the measurement of behavior typically ignore direct measurements of the properties of behavior (as delineated, for example, by Johnston and Pennypacker [1980, Ch. 7]) and instead feature textbooks devoted to identifying and measuring the intensity of what are assumed to be behavior causing traits.

On the other hand, a complete behaviorological analysis of behavior cannot satisfactorily stop without pursuing the functional sequence further back. Behaviorologists pursue the sequence of antecedent events to a point at which either (a) intervention becomes possible or (b) a behavior is interpretable in the sense of being described in terms of relations of the same kind which on other occasions have permitted control under more technologically feasible circumstances.

The quest to gain control of behavior is sometimes regarded as an allegiance to superficiality. However, failure to include control as at least a planned final step condemns a discipline to scientific immaturity (see Skinner, 1953, Ch. 2). Those who strive for control in their subject matter develop effective behavioral technologies based on the manipulation of real independent variables. They become behavioral engineers discovering largely untapped markets for those skills in all facets of the culture. Those who would not strive for control in their subject matter can only *interpret* life in various ways. But the point *is to change it,* a point made by Marx and echoed by Gould (1987, p. 154) and most important scientists.

An additional thread running throughout these components of adventitious control is the generally unparsimonious nature of the mentioned, non–behaviorological accounts. Here, parsimony refers to reliance on the simplest *yet adequate* explanation for an event until experimental analysis with that explanation demonstrates some inadequacy. Most natural science disciplines developed their subject matter in incremental steps over the last several centuries as they faced more complex questions *arising from their work.* In this process they came to take parsimony for granted; not doing so would be difficult for them.

Disciplines (mostly social sciences) concerned with behavior, however, have had to face the whole range of their subject matter from the beginning. An ancient question of our species, perhaps arising as soon as we could talk, was "Why do people do what they do?" Inventing explanations for behavior has been common ever since (e.g., primitive animism). But the continued invoking of such explanations (e.g., the mind) violates parsimony. The non–critical, cultural–linguistic familiarity with parsimony violations seems to make violating parsimony easy and, conversely, adherence to parsimonious explanations difficult, for some disciplines such as psychology. Psychological explanations continue to involve unnecessary and untestable complexity. This itself reduces sensitivity to the value of parsimony, for one can be easily enamored by the apparent profundity that commonly characterizes psychological discourse.

Together with natural scientists everywhere, however, behaviorologists prefer the most parsimonious principles and practices. With parsimony respected, newer or important points stand out more clearly. Inadequacies are recognized and acted upon more quickly. Confusion, misunderstandings, and untestable interpretations exert less reign. These are substantial benefits for *any* discipline.

As a general example of these questions of control and parsimony, recall what speakers from various disciplines say about the ubiquitous crises in education, and reflect: Are their explanations parsimonious? Do they provide much opportunity for taking effective action? The work of disciplines for which affirmative answers to these questions are justifiable portends greater benefits for the world–wide human culture, as developments in independent natural sciences like behaviorology have shown.

Appendix 2: Other Excerpts

These excerpts, being separated from much—though not all—of their original context, take the form of "notes." Pointers to the original context in the Fraley and Ledoux paper in *Origins and Components of Behaviorology* (Ledoux, 1997a) are provided by the side–heading chapter indicators, the paragraph sub–heads, and some of the text itself.

From Chapter 2

...Behaviorology is the independent natural science of behavior relations (see Ledoux, 1997b, for a comprehensive definition). Natural sciences respect the continuity and interrelatedness of events in space and time that accumulate in, and present as, a pattern often called a natural history. Natural sciences *disallow* the inclusion of metaphysical events in their explanatory accounts because allowing metaphysical events to enter explanatory accounts interrupts and disrespects the interrelatedness and continuity of space–time events. (The use of "continuity" and "interrelatedness," "accumulate in" and "present as," and "pattern" and "history," result from the attempt to undue the bias stemming from the anti–scientific *agency* cryptotype inherent in the English language; see Baum, 1995.) "Scientific" disciplines that *allow* (even if they may not encourage) metaphysical events to enter their explanatory accounts are not natural sciences and are usually referred to as social sciences...

...Behaviorologists study behavior and its contextual relations. They do not explain behavior with "appeals to events taking place somewhere else, at some other level of observation, described in different terms, and measured, if at all, in different dimensions" (Skinner, 1972, p. 69), nor do they study minds, souls, selves, or psyches—some implications of the name "psych"–ology. And they defer to the discipline of physiology to discern information on the physiological bases of behavior in the brain and in the nervous and other bodily systems. (On the other hand they provide physiologists with the information on which to judge which events have bases worth discerning.) While an important qualifying feature of behaviorology is that it addresses behavior contextually, in naming their discipline behaviorologists declined to append additional terms and phrases (e.g., contextualism) to emphasize this fact.

...The concept of "determinism" is used, in the context of behaviorological and other natural sciences, simply in the sense of indicating a starting point with several characteristics. This starting point involves the working presumption that natural events (i.e., events in nature) at least (a) are orderly and lawful, (b) are functionally related to other natural events, and (c) are not related to a–natural, non–natural, un–natural, super–natural, or other metaphysical events.

From Chapter 3

To varying degrees, different classes of contingencies controlled personal commitments to the behaviorology movement. Among the kinds most frequently identified as having been important were those pertaining to (a) the scientific rift (mainly with psychology), (b) behaviorological training, (c) approaches to job markets, (d) improvements in one's capacity to make scientific contributions to the culture, and (e) control over the organizational infrastructure of scientific verbal communities....

Those types of concerns affected people on a continuing basis. In the early 1990s, the small, behavioral division of the American Psychological Association (APA) published the Winter/Spring 1992 issue of its newsletter, *Division 25 Recorder* (*Vol. 27*, No. 1). As was typical of prior and subsequent issues, this one contained a variety of examples of these concerns. Four will be mentioned.

Two examples come from the "For the Record" column. One example regards an APA document on guidelines for school redesign and reform. The columnist (the author was not listed) lamented "that our Division's perspectives, interests, and expertise are underrepresented...[in this document]" (p. 3). (b) In the other example, the columnist took umbrage with the advertising for a new book on cognition. The advertising said:

> Is thought confined within the boundaries of each individual mind? Today, psychologists are pioneering a new alternative to this classic view, claiming that our thinking is shaped by others... (p. 3)

The columnist commented:

> This may be a "breakthrough volume" for APA, but it is hardly startling news to behavior analysts. This "breakthrough" is a central thesis of Skinner's

> (1974) analysis of private events and consciousness—and has been since 1945 (Skinner, 1945). (p. 3)

Two other examples come from another column (Book and Journal Notes) which reprints abstracts. One example concerned an abstract on a study of the extent of misunderstandings about Skinner's work. The abstract said: "Results indicate that subjects at all levels of education hold several myths concerning Skinner's work" (p. 5). In the other example, a report on codes of ethics discussed the resistance among psychologists even to suggestions that they consider tying the use of therapies to evidence of the effectiveness of those therapies. One practitioner "predicted a bloody fight... and complete defeat of the [suggestion]" (p. 10). All this came from a single issue of the *Recorder.*

The scientific rift. ...The scientific rift between the independent natural science of behaviorology and the social sciences focused on behavior, especially psychology, involves a fundamental paradigmatic incompatibility. This paradigmatic incompatibility arises from several related areas ranging from the irrelevance of physiological subject matter to ontological fallacies and quality of science issues.

Physiology is a valid natural science alternative to non–natural mentalism that is not directly relevant to the concerns of behaviorologists engaging in a science of behavior relations. Physiologists shun non–natural assumptions. But some tend not to pursue their analyses of the causes of overt behaviors to more remote but directly manipulable antecedent events. Instead they often turn uncritically to internal cognitions. However, whether those cognitions are real events or not, the independent variables that *are* relevant to practical concerns always remain in the behavior–controlling environment or milieu. Inter–nerve variables can be seen either as playing a mediating roll between independent variables and behavioral manifestations, or as comprising the collateral physiological *basis* of behavior—collateral with respect to the environmental variables of which both are a function. In either case the inter–nerve variables do not lend themselves to feasible intervention even if one could possibly determine, on given occasions, what changes within those nerves might be worthwhile. Thus the capacity for control over behavior cannot accrue through analyses focused on nerve functions.

Some physiologists, apparently influenced by psychology, have accepted mentalistic assumptions. They interpret their work about how bodies mediate behavior as if it sheds some light on an internal genesis of behavioral events without benefit of a natural history. Others uncritically accept concepts such as information processing, relating their physiological findings to this or whichever theories of mind these findings seem to match (Skinner, 1971, p. 195). But as physiologists become apprised of behaviorological principles, they will be in a position to render more useful interpretations about behavior. They can work toward completing the account of what is happening inside an organism when it behaves. They will be able to describe the changes that *are* the internal effects of the environmental variables as these select the behavior that occurs on future occasions. And they could continue to develop a practical behavior–controlling technology at the physiological level to complement that at the behaviorological level.

Skinner (1938) wrote more than fifty years ago:

> ...not only are laws of behavior independent of neurological support, they actually impose certain limiting conditions upon any science which undertakes to study the internal economy of the organism. The contributions that a science of behavior makes to neurology is a rigorous and quantitative statement of the program before it. (p. 432)

Skinner (1966) had summarized scientific–rift issues clearly in his preface to the seventh printing of *Behavior of Organisms.* He first noted that evaluation of that book should consider its historical setting. This setting mainly included Tolman's *Purposive Behavior in Animals and Men,* which had appeared six years before Skinner's book, and Hull's *Principles of Behavior,* which appeared five years after Skinner's book. Skinner later continues:

> Although all three books are ostensibly concerned with explaining observed behavior in terms of observable conditions and events, both Tolman and Hull quickly became preoccupied with internal states and processes. Some such move is inevitable so long as an effort is made to characterize the interchange between organism and environment as input and output. Output can seldom if ever be related to input in any simple way, and internal activities are therefore invented to make adjustments. It is not surprising that modern cognitive psychologists should have been strongly influenced by information theory, where a system is said to convert input into output by acquiring, processing, storing, and retrieving information. Activities of this sort are modern versions of Tolman's substitutes for mental processes. Although Tolman insisted that his behavior–determinants were "to be discovered, in the last analysis, by... experiments" and that "they have to be inferred 'back' from behavior," he nevertheless made them his primary objects of inquiry, and this has set the pattern for cognitive psychology. (p. xiii)

With respect to the current alternative initially presented in his first book, Skinner went on to say:

> As the power of the analysis has grown, more and more complex behavior has been studied, under contingencies that approach the subtlety and complexity of the contingencies to be found in the environment at large. More of what the organism is doing at any given time is analyzed. Multiple stimuli and multiple responses compose complex systems of concurrent and chained operants. Experiments may last for weeks rather than for the standard hour of *The Behavior of Organisms.* Special environments may be maintained from birth. The apparatus required for all this is necessarily much more elaborate: simple relays, timers, and counters have given way to solid state circuitry and computers. ***All these advances were facilitated by a formulation which emphasized behavior rather than supposed precursors of behavior and observable variables rather than inferred causal states or processes.*** (p. xv; emphasis added)

Behaviorologists, in organizing their discipline, were acting on the scientific rift demonstrated by those differences in formulations.

Capacity for contributions to the culture. ...The importance of appearing as a master of frontier thinking in some disciplines fuels eager quests for better concepts, even if these are refinished "rip–offs" of other's well–established concepts which (as one behaviorologist who asked not to be identified puts it) "may be a thing of rags and patches by the time they get through with it." But perhaps behavioral material becomes less palatable to mainstream psychologists when, moved to behaviorology, it becomes more explicitly identified as the intellectual property of another independent discipline.

From Chapter 4

The relevance of contemporary professional organizations. ...As of this writing, the Association for Behavior Analysis (ABA) is playing out a perhaps necessary role. ABA occupies a transition niche in the evolution of behavioral science. Organized behavioral psychology struggles, in ABA as behavior analysis, between leaning toward remaining a facet of psychology or reorganizing as a separate and independent natural science discipline. As such, ABA and behavior analysis sit *between* the evolutionary branches of organized (mainstream) psychology and the organized independent discipline of behaviorology as these two emerge from their shared historical trunk (Ledoux, 1997b).

A journal for TIBA. ...Lawrence Fraley had accepted the assignment from the Executive Board to develop a journal proposal. Throughout 1988, he investigated various options for a journal for TIBA. Members believed that the coalescing verbal community of behaviorology would benefit substantially from the identity and credibility afforded by a quality journal of behaviorology. But such a project would involve breaking some new ground. In keeping with the its organizational approach, TIBA would not permit economic contingencies to degrade the scientific and philosophical integrity of the organization. So Fraley kept plans and estimates non–contingent on economies of scale. Unlike other journals with which TIBA members were familiar, a transition to desktop publishing would enable less expensive computer technologies, at least in part, to replace costly conventional printing services. An early cost estimate for runs of 100 perfect–bound copies, based on a master copy produced on a desktop computer followed by copy center reproduction, was attractive relative to the cost for comparable journals.

Early discussions about a new journal focused on several related difficulties: With so few early members in TIBA and the designed anticipation of slow growth, initially a limited number of potential authors would be available to furnish high quality articles. Questions were raised about the image of a journal that repeatedly offered the works of a small band of contributing authors, and about how much time would pass before the journal attracted more authors. Could the shortfall be overcome by high quality articles from persons peripheral to the discipline? The option of publishing almost anything just to get started and hoping for high quality submissions later was rejected as inappropriate for TIBA. Yet, why should authors of note contribute their best works to a journal with an initial circulation of only a few dozen copies. What could be said that would persuade them to do so?

In response, some suggested that since all significant scientific movements begin small, smallness *per se* need not be regarded as an image problem as long as excellence is maintained in the quality of the product. The emerging discipline needed a quality journal, and a relatively small number of dedicated behaviorologists could produce one. It might have to be issued at a low frequency, or even be occasional rather than periodical, since the contingency to meet deadlines at the expense of quality would also not be acceptable within TIBA. The reviewing arrangements being contemplated were among the most rigorous and involved in scientific publication circles. They included substantial assistance to authors in shaping high quality articles. Gradually increasing membership and institutional subscriptions would both widen the audience and encourage more authors.

At its 26 May 1989 meeting, the Executive Board reviewed and reiterated elements of journal policy: The journal would feature a balance of article types and would maintain quality through careful reviewing procedures. As a member of the incipient publications board, Fraley developed an extensive and detailed proposal for publication operations within a large TIBA organization as envisioned for the future. He also drafted an interim proposal suited to *launching* the new journal and forwarded this to publications coordinator Cheney. By the fall of 1989 about a dozen authors had made commitments to submit specific works, the first of which began to arrive in November. Some people indicated that they were prepared to treat this journal as their principal publication vehicle and promised multiple submissions. But some of those early easy promises would prove difficult to fulfill, especially for behavior analysts who were not really committed to the behaviorology *independence* movement. Several of these would soon commit more explicitly to behavioral *psychology* and subsequently renege on earlier agreements to submit articles.

From Chapter 5

Cultural design and space settlements. An early attempt at cultural control involved the Vicos Hacienda project in the 1950s. In that project anthropologists actually did design and implement new cultural practices. They assisted the residents of the hacienda, who had previously been vassals of the land, to funnel the fruits of their labor back into their own society. The project was deemed controversial within the anthropology community. Colleagues criticized project leaders, perhaps unfairly, claiming they had used their scientific powers to impose their own cultural values on the hacienda community.

Such rifts might presage efforts to design the cultural aspects of off–Earth settlements. Space settlements will require cultural practices respecting new kinds of values that will also have to be conditioned by design. In the years since the Vicos Hacienda project, the interest of the scientific and lay communities in the cultural aspects of off–Earth settlements continually increased, and with it more concern over the values question. The interest arose because the differences in both physical and social environments, between current Earth–based cultures and what might be viable off–Earth cultures, must be considered. But by the 1980s only the physical environment concerns had generally received attention while the social environment concerns had been neglected. Proponents of off–Earth settlements began asking scientists of both anthropology and behaviorology to help design cultural practices respecting new kinds of values that would also have to be conditioned by design—in some cases values not shared by the cultures of the designers, nor, sometimes, by the designers themselves. They asked these scientists to help design cultures whose practices would enable people to thrive, not merely survive, under the alien physical and social conditions, the alien values, of a colony in space, on the moon, on the surface of Mars, or wherever (see Beach, 1991a, 1991b).

Adjustment problems of individuals contemplating the separatist movement. ...For some, the discipline of psychology presented a quandary with respect to its apparent and important mission and its non–natural science. For them, resolution of the quandary was complicated because organized academic disciplines expand or fade on a timetable longer than that used to measure the productive lives of the individuals involved. Did psychology exist to study behavior, psyches, or nerve functions? If it existed to study the behavior that yields environmental effects, its cognitive and mentalistic science was inappropriate and inadequate. Behaviorology was organized to pursue that mission with a more effective science. If psychology existed to study psyches, it focused on figments that, from a natural science perspective, existed only in the assumptions of those pursuing the studies. If psychology existed to study the nerve functions that occur with behavior, it intruded on physiology.

...The exposure of psychologists to behaviorological science has often been limited to parts of one or two courses, or perhaps only parts of one or two chapters, which are usually out–of–date, from an introductory psychology text. These amounts have been described, by some psychologists in conversations with the authors, as being adequate behavioral training at the undergraduate level. But these amounts do no justice to even a superficial survey of basic principles and practices. The typical learning chapter barely covers the acquisition of new behavior. It says next to nothing on all the possible changes in behavior after acquisition. The suggestion that this is adequate only indicates further those speakers' lack of comprehension of the extent of a minimal behavior science repertoire. That repertoire can hardly even be surveyed *by itself* in a one–semester course. To develop a minimal yet still meaningful, usable, and fluent level of knowledge and skills takes mastery of several comprehensive and systematic courses. (See Ledoux, 1997c, for some details on possible behaviorology curricula.) If these psychologists construed *their* professional tasks to be those that behaviorologists have defined for themselves, they would face a repertoire deficit that would typically take years of new study to remove.

The *implications* of coming to comprehend behaviorological science would prove costly to mainstream psychologists in other ways as well. Many kinds of immediate and implicit deferred costs threaten professional scholars when they come to understand not only that their training has been inadequate *for their tasks,* but also that to gain adequate training would require substantial relearning of basics. Such costs are usually too great for an established professional person to bear. Rationally, a person might instead resist, in some cases ignoring scientific evidence and eschewing proper academic debate. Often the resistance takes the simple form of resort to available counter–controlling arrangements embodied in the politics of scientific verbal communities (e.g., denying tenure or promotion to behaviorally oriented faculty) or to remedies available through appeal to other cultural agencies (e.g., law) for help and protection.

From Chapter 6

Disciplinary boundaries, and control. ...Both predictive and *controlling* sciences of *group–produced* effects are possible. Although group effects are necessarily produced by the summation of the behavior of individuals, a science of group effects *can* support intervention technologies in which the analytical repertoire of the cultural engineers does *not* penetrate to the level of individuals. For instance, composers and conductors can reliably produce prescribed group effects without knowing the details of how any particular orchestra member plays his or her instrument. That is because the audience–appreciated properties of the group effect are characteristics of the combined products or activities of the behaving performers. The contributing individual producers of that group effect are not each producing a small one–person version of the group effect appreciated by the audience. What an individual contributes is different—often extremely so—from the appreciated group effect.

Still, the level of the behavior of those individual players is the only level at which interventions pertinent to the group effect can be *functionally* effective. Only when intervention attempts, intended to alter the properties of the hearing response of listeners, reach down to affect the behavior of all or some of the individual players can those group level interventions possibly work. And sometimes the interventions to alter the group effect *must* address changes in just *one* individual's behavior which otherwise would radically alter the group–produced effect. Envision a composition that requires string players to pluck their strings for a certain section of the piece. Consider the effect if, during the period when all other string players are appropriately plucking their strings, one player continues to bow his or her strings. The resulting group effect would be altered in such a way as to evoke very different emotional responses from the audience than would occur if all were plucking. In this instance, an intervention strategy to alter that total group effect need only, but must, reach down to alter just the behavior of that individual player. Culturologists would have few options if their understanding of human behavior were limited only to group effects, and if their intervention technologies were limited only to group–level controls. They would have few alternatives if they were unenlightened as to the workings of events at the individual level.

From Chapter 7

Conclusion. …Having demonstrated needed contributions in the vast range of applied behavioral fields from advertising to zoo keeping—including child care, education, work, leisure, art, academic pursuits, even science itself—behaviorological scientists see further contributions as not only probable but likely vital. Assuming behaviorologists turn out to be correct about the vital importance of behaviorology, if they do not prevail in the effort to put behaviorology into wide use, then the culture—and perhaps eventually the whole planetary biosystem—will likely suffer, possibly approaching extinction. Conversely, if they succeed in that effort, then the culture and bio–system will benefit, becoming more able to survive. Cultural survival appeared to be at stake during the emergence of modern biological science and on other occasions in human history. And so again today. However, the technologies capable of destruction that characterize the present era (whether actively, as with nuclear weapons, or passively, as with unchecked population or pollution) are qualitatively greater than those of previous times. This puts not just cultural survival but the survival of life in general on this planet at risk (e.g., from a *nuclear winter*). The early behaviorologists believed, of course, that that was what was at stake, and so they incurred the costs of organizing the behaviorology movement and discipline.

Appendix 3: Experimental and Applied Course Sequences

The paper on behaviorology curricula in higher education (Ledoux, 1997c) left the sequences of courses in the experimental and applied areas to the reader's surmise. These sequences are presented here.

Experimental Course Sequences

The sequences of experimental courses begin after the completion of the requirements for the *Affiliate of Behaviorology Certificate* (ABC). Each possible sequence consists of four courses. The first two of these are the same for each sequence; a pair of "topics" courses comprise the remaining two. Here is the basic sequence pattern (with prerequisites in parentheses):

Beh. 345: Experimental Behaviorology: A Survey (ABC).

Beh. 350/450: Behaviorology Research Lab: General (345).

Beh. 346/446, or 347/447, or…: The Experimental Analysis of [a Selected Topic] (345).

Beh. 351/451, or 352/452, or…: Behaviorology Research Lab on [a Selected Topic] (350/450, and the corresponding 346/446, or 347/447, or…, topic course).

Applied Course Sequences

The sequences of applied courses also begin after the completion of the requirements for the ABC. However, they also require the completion of Beh. 345 to assure that the student has at least a basic repertoire in *what* is being applied. Each possible sequence consists of four courses. The first two of these are the same for each sequence; a pair of "settings" courses comprise the remaining two. Here is the basic sequence pattern (with prerequisites in parentheses):

Beh. 385: Behavior Technology: A Survey (345).

Beh. 390/490: Behavior Technology Fieldwork: General Experience (385).

Beh. 386/486, or 387/487, or…: Behavior Technology in [a Selected Setting] (385).

Beh. 391/491, or 392/492, or…: Behavior Technology Fieldwork in [a Selected Setting] (390/490, and the corresponding 386/486, or 387/487, or…, setting course).

Appendix 4: TIBA Conventions VI through IX

The Hotel Parador San Javier in Guanajuato (Mexico), was the site of TIBA–6 on 18–20 March 1994. Rebeca Garcia coordinated the site while Nyla Lamm organized the program and chaired the sessions. The convention drew about 21 attendants. Victor Arredondo (*Director General De Education Superior* of Mexico) presented "Reflections on Mexico's higher education system" as the B.F. Skinner Memorial Lecture (see Arredondo, 1995). At this convention, TIBA took the perhaps counter–intuitive step of capping membership at 150 (see Vargas, 1994; some dangers inherent in such a policy are discussed in the "Science club versus cultural mission" section of Fraley & Ledoux, 1997, Ch. 5).

The University Centre Hotel in Gainesville, Florida, was the site of TIBA–7 on 10–12 March 1995. Anne Kupfer coordinated the site, organized the program, and chaired the sessions. The convention drew about 20 attendants. William Baum presented "Radical behaviorism and the concept of agency" as the B.F. Skinner Memorial Lecture (see Baum, 1995). After this convention, TIBA decided that the convention would at least overlap B.F. Skinner's birthday and, preferably, the B.F. Skinner Memorial Lecture would be presented on Skinner's birthday.

The University Inn at Utah State University in Logan, Utah, was the site of TIBA–8 on 17–20 March 1996. Carl Cheney coordinated the site, organized the program, and chaired the sessions. The convention drew about 26 attendants. John Falk presented "Schedule induced behavior" as the B.F. Skinner Memorial Lecture. By this convention, TIBA had added a full day of workshops prior to the regular program.

The John Carver Inn in Plymouth, Massachusetts, is the planned site of TIBA–9 on 20–22 March 1997. Julie Vargas is coordinating the site and the program. The program is to include a special address by Murray Sidman, and Gerald Holton is scheduled to present the B.F. Skinner Memorial Lecture. ❧

Appendix 5: Possible Geographically Based Behaviorology Associations

The natural science of behavior needs to be organized formally and independently if it is to emerge fully to take its place at the natural science roundtable and meet the urgent demands of its cultural mission (see Fraley & Ledoux, 1997). So the development of more geographically based behaviorology organizations can be anticipated. This could parallel the rise of, for example, state and regional organizations affiliated with the Association for Behavior Analysis (ABA) that share in ABA's important political (coalition–and–advocacy) mission. For example, several cooperative regional behaviorology disciplinary organizations would be possible, perhaps based in different countries or sorted on the basis of members' native languages. These organizations may be composed of new as well as established behaviorological scientists from basic laboratories and applied fields around the world. Purposes would include furthering the cultural mission, science development and support, and general disciplinary organizing for all facets of the independent natural science of behavior.

Those groups could also serve to anchor the discipline in each group's geographic area, with mutual support worldwide. Their existence, by extending formal organizing of this independent natural science discipline, could be vital to the success of behaviorological science and its cultural contributions. Natural scientists of behavior everywhere are well–served by continuing to work toward more complete and formal disciplinary integrity. While disciplinary groups around the globe could address the task of formal organizing, The International Behaviorology Association (TIBA) is itself addressing a more precise and exclusive emphasis on the important mission of maintaining and developing the quality and productivity of the experimental science component of the behaviorology discipline through the medium of a small scientific society (see Vargas, 1996). (Also, TIBA may be changing its name to reflect this emphasis; see TIBA, 1996).

Still, behaviorological professionals around the world need organizational structures that support the other facets of their formal independent discipline. These structures could carry out programs of support for the world's increasingly numerous behaviorological scientists and practitioners. Organizational support is needed to consolidate the independent, natural science status of their discipline and thus to promote vigorously their professional activities. The consolidation of behaviorology could redirect—to those professional activities—the energy that is currently directed either to dealing with "survival in disciplinary limbo" (as some experience in "behavior analysis" where disciplinary status is compromised by the competing claims to ownership of that label) or to dealing with "survival in contradiction" (as some experience in psychology, a disciplinary entity that accepts non–natural events in its explanatory accounts and so is called a social science). (Why other existing organizations do not fill these needs was comprehensively addressed in Fraley & Ledoux, 1997, Ch. 4.)

The kind of geographically based organizations of behaviorological science professionals mentioned here could well serve those needs. Another chapter in the history of the organizations of and for behaviorologists—as they more formally organize and support the independence of their natural science discipline and so more capably contribute to world behavioral health—is beginning. Behaviorological scientists must have one or more organizations that promote the reality of behaviorological science and scientists worldwide, and that work to establish officially the accouterments of independent disciplinary status including behaviorology's own academic homes and programs. Developments such as these may not make that much difference in the future of behaviorology; the fact of its natural science status may carry enough momentum. Then again, such developments may make all the difference in the world.

Endnotes

These appendices are either new, short information pieces, or they are parts that were originally in one or another of the papers in *Origins and Components of Behaviorology* (Ledoux, 1997a) but which were more appropriately included here. Regardless of their origin, they were prepared for, or revised before, inclusion in this volume.

The author thanks David Feeney, Lawrence Fraley, and Glenn Latham for comments on some of these appendices. Address correspondence regarding these appendices to the author at SUNY–CTC, Canton NY 13617–1096 USA.

References

Arrendondo, V.A. (1995). Behavioral principles in Mexico's higher education public policy. *Behaviorology, 3* (1), 85–91.

Baum, W.M. (1995). Radical behaviorism and the concept of agency. *Behaviorology, 3* (1), 93–106.

Beach, S. (1991a). The Martians are coming. *Behaviorological Commentaries, Serial No. 1*, 25–28.

Beach, S. (1991b). Behaviorology and space settlement. *CONTACT Newsletter, 2* (2), 2–3.

Chiesa, M. (1994). *Radical Behaviorism: The Philosophy and the Science.* Boston, MA: Authors Cooperative.

Fraley, L.E. & Ledoux, S.F. (1997). Origins, status, and mission of behaviorology. In S.F. Ledoux. *Origins and Components of Behaviorology.* Canton, NY: ABCs.

Gould, S.J. (1981). *The Mismeasure of Man.* New York: W.W. Norton.

Gould, S.J. (1987). *An Urchin in the Storm.* New York: W.W. Norton.

Johnston, J.M. & Pennypacker, H.S. (1980). *Strategies and Tactics for Human Behavioral Research.* Hillsdale, NJ: Erlbaum.

Ledoux, S.F. (1997a). *Origins and Components of Behaviorology.* Canton, NY: ABCs.

Ledoux, S.F. (1997b). An introduction to the origins, status, and mission of behaviorology: An established science with developed applications and a new name. In S.F. Ledoux. *Origins and Components of Behaviorology.* Canton, NY: ABCs. Reprinted with revisions from (1992) *Behaviorological Commentaries, Serial No. 3,* 11–31.

Ledoux, S.F. (1997c). Behaviorology curricula in higher education. In S.F. Ledoux. *Origins and Components of Behaviorology.* Canton, NY: ABCs. Reprinted with revisions from (in press) *The International Behaviorologist, 1.*

Michael, J.L. (1989). *Verbal and Nonverbal Behavior: Concepts and Principles.* Kalamazoo, MI: Psychology Department, Western Michigan University.

Poling, A., Schlinger, H., Starin, S., & Blakely, E. (1990). *Psychology: A Behavioral Overview.* New York: Plenum.

Skinner, B.F. (1938). *The Behavior of Organisms.* Englewood Cliffs, NJ: Prentice–Hall. Reprinted, 1991, Cambridge, MA: The B.F. Skinner Foundation.

Skinner, B.F. (1953). *Science and Human Behavior.* New York: Macmillan.

Skinner, B.F. (1966). Preface to the seventh printing. In B.F. Skinner. (1991). *The Behavior of Organisms* (pp. xi–xvi). Cambridge, MA: The B.F. Skinner Foundation.

Skinner, B.F. (1971). *Beyond Freedom and Dignity.* New York: Knopf.

Skinner, B.F. (1972). *Cumulative Record: A Selection of Papers (Third Edition).* New York: Appleton–Century–Crofts.

Skinner, B.F. (1974). *About Behaviorism.* New York: Knopf.

TIBA. (1996 December 28). Executive Board Meeting Minutes. Meeting of 3 November 1996, Cambridge, MA.

Vargas, E.A. (1994). President's Column. *Selections, 6* (3), 3–4.

Vargas, E.A. (1996). President's Column: T–8 and beyond. *Selections, 8* (2), 1–7.

Quoted*

§

...Cultural survival appeared to be at stake during the emergence of modern biological science and on other occasions in human history. And so again today. However, the technologies capable of destruction that characterize the present era (whether actively, as with nuclear weapons, or passively, as with unchecked population or pollution) are qualitatively greater than those of previous times. This puts not just cultural survival but the survival of life in general on this planet at risk (e.g., from a *nuclear winter*). The early behaviorologists believed... that that was what was at stake, and so they incurred the costs of organizing the behaviorology movement and discipline. (p. 313)

§

*From Appendix 2 (Ch. 7 section) of Ledoux, S.F. (1997). Appendices. In S.F. Ledoux. *Origins and Components of Behaviorology*. Canton, NY: ABCs.

Quoted*

§

...Future readers, should their lives have unfolded within the context of a culture pervaded by behaviorology, might have difficulty appreciating a past era of antithesis to behaviorological science. That people would not have readily invested in a repertoire that effective—one that obvious and well demonstrated in its validity and implications, one that elegant in its parsimonious reduction of false complexities—could tax the comprehension of those who live in such a future.... (p. 158)

§

*From Ch. 7 of Fraley, L.E. & Ledoux, S.F. (1997). Origins, status, and mission of behaviorology. In S.F. Ledoux. *Origins and Components of Behaviorology*. Canton, NY: ABCs.

A Little About the Authors

Stephen F. Ledoux, Ph.D.

Dr. Ledoux began his professional activity in 1972. He has taught courses in psychology, English, and behaviorology, the latter at all levels from high school through post–graduate. He earned his B.A. and M.A. degrees at California State University, Sacramento, in 1972 and 1973 respectively. The behavioral research for his M.A. thesis contributed to the accumulating experimental evidence for accepting that people's private events are most effectively construed as covert behaviors under the same laws affecting overt, public behaviors. He earned his Ph.D. degree in behaviorological science from Western Michigan University, Kalamazoo, in 1982.

Prof. Ledoux has held various positions both at home and abroad. He spent four years (1975–1979) in Australia, teaching at the University of Queensland and at the Gippsland Institute of Advanced Education. Prof. Ledoux also taught at Xi'an Jiaotong University in 1979, and at the Xi'an Foreign Languages University in 1990–1991, both in China (PRC). Since 1982 he has been teaching at the State University of New York campus in Canton.

Over the years, Prof. Ledoux has prepared numerous publications and presentations and been involved in many other ways in his interest areas. With colleague Carl Cheney, of Utah State University, Logan, he worked extensively in the early 1980s with the concept of the Aircrib, invented by B.F. Skinner. Since 1985 Prof. Ledoux has been very much involved with the movement behind formal establishment of the independent behaviorology discipline, being one of the founders of that movement. In 1988 his colleagues elected him president of *The International Behaviorology Association* for a term that expired at the end of 1991. He has also served as chair of the International Affairs (standing) Committee of that organization, as well as in other capacities.

Lawrence E. Fraley, Ed.D.

Dr. Fraley began his career as a teacher of high school physics and mathematics. He holds an undergraduate degree in Geology from the University of Colorado. He earned his Ed.D. degree at the University of Southern California in 1969. Dr. Fraley has taught at West Virginia University since 1969 including, since the mid–1980s, graduate–level behaviorology courses such as general behaviorology, behavior measurement, instructional development, and conceptual foundations of behaviorology.

With wide–ranging interests, Prof. Fraley's publications include works in the applied areas of criminal justice, instructional systems, and the formal organization of scientific disciplines. Other important publications feature conceptual analyses in such areas as the measurement of behavior and the analysis of belief.

Prof. Fraley also has been very much involved with the movement behind formal establishment of the behaviorology discipline, being one of the founders of that movement. He has been an elected officer of *The International Behaviorology Association,* and he has served as editor of *Behaviorology,* the chief journal of that organization.

David R. Feeney, M.A.

Mr. Feeney, a TIBA member studying under the behaviorologists (including Prof. Fraley) at West Virginia University (WVU), earned his M.A. degree in the field of education from that university in 1995. Currently based in New York City, he is the managing partner of "Onlearn" company, a company devoted to research and development in behavior management and education interventions delivered through on–line, and sometimes real–time, interaction between client and educator/therapist. He is also an adjunct professor in education at the New York Institute of Technology.

Mr. Feeney also is completing requirements for an Ed.D. degree from WVU. His doctoral dissertation derives from his research in on–line behaviorological engineering.

Glenn I. Latham, Ed.D.

Dr. Latham earned his B.S. and M.S. degrees at the University of Utah, and his Ed.D. degree from Utah State University. After having been a consultant and advisor to schools nationally and internationally over many years, Dr. Latham is now Professor Emeritus of Education at Utah State University. He continues as principal scientific investigator for the Mountain Plains Regional Resource Center, a Federally funded project operating out of Utah State University, Logan. The Center provides technical assistance to schools with "hard–to–teach" students in the states of Colorado, Iowa, Kansas, Missouri, Montana, Nebraska, North Dakota, South Dakota, and Wyoming, as well as for the Bureau of Indian Affairs.

Prof. Latham has contributed to academic life at several universities. In addition to teaching at Utah State University, he has taught at the University of Utah, the University of Oregon, New Mexico State University, and the University of Hawaii, the latter two as a visiting professor. His professional teaching and research interests encompass parent and teacher training to benefit child and adolescent behavior in both the classroom and the home.

Prof. Latham, a TIBA member, is the author of over 200 works on a wide range of school and family related topics. These works include conference and convention presentations, technical papers, journal articles, book chapters, and books. His larger works include (a) *The Power of Positive Parenting: A Wonderful Way to Raise Children,* (b) *Behind the Schoolhouse Door: Eight Skills Every Teacher Should Have,* (c) *Parenting Prescriptions* (positive parenting audio tapes), and (d) *Managing the Classroom Environment to Facilitate Effective Instruction* (a set of video tapes).

A Selected and Occasionally Annotated Bibliography

(Including sources not cited in *Origins and Components of Behaviorology*)

Articles: Primary Issues (for Behaviorology in the 1990s and Beyond)

Fraley, L.E. (1987). The cultural mission of behaviorology. *The Behavior Analyst, 10,* 123–126.

Fraley, L.E. (1988). You're a what? *TIBA Newsletter, 1* (1), 5–7.

Fraley, L.E. (1990). Thrust and parry. *TIBA Newsletter, 2* (2),7–8.

Fraley, L.E. (1991). The behaviorology movement. *Behaviorological Commentaries, Serial No. 1,* 3–13.

Fraley, L.E. (1992). Behavior analysis and behaviorology. *Behaviorological Commentaries, Serial No. 2,* 22.

Fraley, L.E. & Ledoux, S.F. (1997). Origins, status, and mission of behaviorology. In S.F. Ledoux. *Origins and Components of Behaviorology.* Canton, NY: ABCs.

Fraley, L.E. & Vargas, E.A. (1986). Separate disciplines: The study of behavior and the study of the psyche. *The Behavior Analyst, 9,* 47–59.

Ledoux, S.F. (1997). An introduction to the origins, status, and mission of behaviorology: An established science with developed applications and a new name. In S.F. Ledoux. *Origins and Components of Behaviorology.* Canton, NY: ABCs. Also (earlier version), (1992) *Behaviorological Commentaries, Serial No. 3,* 11–31.

Ledoux, S.F. (1997). An introduction to the philosophy called radical behaviorism. In S.F. Ledoux. *Origins and Components of Behaviorology.* Canton, NY: ABCs. Also (earlier version), (1992) *Behaviorological Commentaries, Serial No. 4,* 3–10.

Ledoux, S.F. (1997). Behaviorology curricula in higher education. In S.F. Ledoux. *Origins and Components of Behaviorology.* Canton, NY: ABCs. Also (earlier version), (in press) *The International Behaviorologist, 1.*

Ledoux, S.F. (1997). Behaviorology in China: A status report. In S.F. Ledoux. *Origins and Components of Behaviorology.* Canton, NY: ABCs. Also (earlier version), (1992) *Behaviorological Commentaries, Serial No. 4,* 24–36.

Skinner, B.F. (1987). Whatever happened to psychology as the science of behavior. *American Psychologist, 42,* 780–786.

Skinner, B.F. (1990). Can psychology be a science of mind? *American Psychologist, 45,* 1206–1210.

Skinner, B.F. (1993). A world of our own. *Behaviorology, 1* (1), 3–5. (This is the published version of Skinner's 1989 "declaration of independence" address to the Association for Behavior Analysis [see Ulman, 1993, p. 54].)

Ulman, J.D. (1990). A memo to the Dean regarding behaviorology. *TIBA Newsletter, 2* (3), 1–3.

Ulman, J.D. (1993). The Ulman–Skinner letters. *Behaviorology, 1* (1), 47–54.

Vargas, E.A. (1987). "Separate disciplines" is another name for survival. *The Behavior Analyst, 10,* 119–121.

Vargas, E.A. (1988). Organizing for the future of the discipline. *TIBA Newsletter, 1* (1), 2–5.

Vargas, E.A. (1991). Behaviorology: Its paradigm. In W. Ishaq (Ed.). *Human Behavior in Today's World* (pp. 139–147). New York: Praeger.

Articles: Directly Related Issues...

Baum, W.M. (1995). Radical behaviorism and the concept of agency. *Behaviorology, 3* (1), 93–106.

Barrett, B.H. (1991). The right to effective education. *The Behavior Analyst, 14,* 79–82. (Brief guidelines supported by most behaviorologists and behavior analysts.)

Cautela, J.R. (1994). General level of reinforcement II: Further elaborations. *Behaviorology, 2* (1), 1–16.

Cheney, C.D. (1991). The source and control of behavior. In W. Ishaq (Ed.). *Human Behavior in Today's World* (pp. 73–86). New York: Praeger.

Eshleman, J.W. & Vargas, E.A. (1988). Promoting the behaviorological analysis of verbal behavior. *Analysis of Verbal Behavior, 6,* 23–32.

Feeney, D.R. (1997). Creative life–style management through on–line and real–time application of the behaviorological education practices of precision teaching. In S.F. Ledoux. *Origins and Components of Behaviorology.* Canton, NY: ABCs.

Fraley, L.E. (1981). The spread of behavior analysis to the applied fields. *The Behavior Analyst, 4,* 33–41.

Fraley, L.E. (1988). Introductory comments: Behaviorology and cultural materialism. *The Behavior Analyst, 11,* 159–160.

Glenn, S.S. & Madden, G.J. (1995). Units of interaction, evolution, and replication: Organic and behavioral parallels. *The Behavior Analyst, 18,* 237–251.

Johnson, K.R. & Layng, T.V.J. (1992). Breaking the structuralist barrier: Literacy and numeracy with fluency. *American Psychologist, 47* (11), 1475–1490.

Ledoux, S.F. (1997). Increasing tact control and student comprehension through such new postcedent terms as added and subtracted reinforcers and punishers. In S.F. Ledoux. *Origins and Components of Behaviorology.* Canton, NY: ABCs. Also (earlier version), (in press) *The International Behaviorologist, 2.*

Ledoux, S.F. (1997). Multiple selectors in the control of simultaneously emittable responses. In S.F. Ledoux. *Origins and Components of Behaviorology.* Canton, NY: ABCs.

Logue, A.W. (1988). A behaviorist's biologist: Review of Philip J. Pauly's *Controlling Life: Jacques Loeb and the Engineering Ideal in Biology. The Behavior Analyst, 11,* 205–207.

McDowell, J.J. (1991). Irreconcilable differences and political reality in these dark ages. *The Behavior Analyst, 14,* 29–33.

Skinner, B.F. (1977). Why I am not a cognitive psychologist. *Behaviorism, 5* (2), 1–10.

Skinner, B.F. (1983). Can the experimental analysis of behavior rescue psychology? *The Behavior Analyst, 6,* 9–17.

Skinner, B.F. (1984). The shame of American education. *The American Psychologist, 39,* 947–954.

TIBA By–laws. (See the Winter 1990 *TIBA Newsletter:* Vol. 2, No. 3, pp. 13–16.)

Vargas, E.A. (1975). Rights: A behavioristic analysis. *Behaviorism, 3* (2), 120–128.

Vargas, E.A. (1982). Hume's "ought" and "is" statement: A radical behaviorist's perspective. *Behaviorism, 10* (1), 1–23.

Wyatt, W.J., Hawkins, R.P., & Davis, P. (1986). Behaviorism: Are reports of its death exaggerated? *The Behavior Analyst, 9,* 101–105.

Articles: Other Related Issues...

Beach, S. (1991). Behaviorology and space settlement. *CONTACT Newsletter, 2* (2), 2–3.

Beach, S. (1991). The Martians are coming. *Behaviorological Commentaries, Serial No. 1,* 25–28.

Epstein, R. (1981). Of pigeons and people: A preliminary look at the Columban simulation project. *The Behavior Analyst, 4,* 43–55.

Fraley, L.E. (1983). The behavioral analysis of *Mens Rea* (doctrine of culpable mental states). *Behaviorists for Social Action Journal, 4* (1), 2–7.

Fraley, L.E. (1984). Belief, its inconsistency, and the implications for the teaching faculty. *The Behavior Analyst, 7,* 17–28.

Fraley, L.E. (1988). Covert mini–courts within judicial and law enforcement operations. *Behavior Analysis and Social Action, 6* (2), 2–14.

Holland, J.G. (1960). Teaching machines: An application from the laboratory. *Journal of the Experimental Analysis of Behavior, 3,* 275–287.

Holland, J.G. (1967). A quantitative measure for programmed instruction. *American Educational Research Journal, 4,* 87–101.

Keller, F.S. (1968). "Good–bye teacher..." *Journal of Applied Behavior Analysis, 1,* 79–89.

Keller, F.S. (1986). A fire in Schermerhorn Extension. *The Behavior Analyst, 9,* 139–146.

Keller, F.S. & Schoenfeld, W.N. (1949). The psychology curriculum at Columbia College. *American Psychologist, 4,* 165–172.

Latham, G.I. (1997). China through the eyes of a behaviorologist. In S.F. Ledoux. *Origins and Components of Behaviorology.* Canton, NY: ABCs.

Ledoux, S.F. (1997). Successful smoking control as an example of a comprehensive behaviorological therapy. In S.F. Ledoux. *Origins and Components of Behaviorology.* Canton, NY: ABCs.

Michael, J.L. (1982). Distinguishing between discriminative and motivational functions of stimuli. *Journal of the Experimental Analysis of Behavior, 37,* 149–155.

Moore, J. (1981). On mentalism, methodological behaviorism, and radical behaviorism. *Behaviorism, 9,* 55–57.

Moore, J. (1984). On privacy, causes, and contingencies. *The Behavior Analyst, 7,* 3–16.

Morse, L.A. & Bruns, B.J. (1983). Nurturing behavioral repertoires within a non–supportive environment. *The Behavior Analyst, 6,* 19–25.

Schlinger, H. & Blakely, E. (1987). Function–altering effects of contingency–specifying stimuli. *The Behavior Analyst, 10,* 41–45.

Sidman, M. (1986). Functional analysis of emergent verbal classes. In T. Thompson & M. Zeiler (Eds.). *Analysis and Integration of Behavioral Units* (pp. 213–245). Hillsdale, NJ: Erlbaum.

Sidman, M. (1986). The measurement of behavioral development. In N.A. Krasnegor, D.B. Gray, & T. Thompson (Eds.). *Developmental Behavioral Pharmacology* (pp. 43–52). Hillsdale, NJ: Erlbaum.

Stromer, R. (1991). Stimulus equivalence: Implications for teaching. In W. Ishaq (Ed.). *Human Behavior in Today's World* (pp. 109–122). New York: Praeger.

Thyer, B.A. (1991). The enduring intellectual legacy of B.F. Skinner: A citation count from 1966–1989. *The Behavior Analyst, 14,* 73–75.

Ulman, J.D. (1983). Toward a united front: A class analysis of social and political action. *Behaviorists for Social Action Journal, 4* (1), 17–23.
Ulman, J.D. (1986). Working class strategies for world peace. *Behavior Analysis and Social Action, 5,* 36–43.
Ulman, J.D. (1988). Just say no to commodity fetishism: A reply to Rakos. *Behavior Analysis and Social Action, 6,* 25–31.
Ulman, J.D. (1991). Toward a synthesis of Marx and Skinner. *Behavior and Social Issues, 1* (1), 57–70.
Vargas, E.A. (1985). Cultural contingencies: A review of Marvin Harris's *Cannibals and Kings. Journal of the Experimental Analysis of Behavior, 43,* 419–428.
Vargas, E.A. (1988). Verbally–governed and event–governed behavior. *The Analysis of Verbal Behavior, 6,* 11–22.
Vargas, E.A. (1996). A university for the twenty–first century. In J.R. Cautela & W. Ishaq (Eds.). *Contemporary Issues in Behavior Therapy: Improving the Human Condition* (pp. 159–188). New York: Plenum.
Vargas, E.A. & Fraley, L.E. (1976). Progress and structure: Reorganizing the university for instructional technology. *Instructional Science, 5,* 303–324.
Vargas, J.S. (1989). The road less travelled by. *The Behavior Analyst, 12,* 121–130.
Vargas, J.S. (1990). Cognitive analysis of language and verbal behavior: Two separate fields. In L.J. Hayes & P.N. Chase (Eds.). *Dialogues on Verbal Behavior* (pp. 197–201). Reno, NV: Context Press.
Wood, S.W. (1976). Responsibilities of the college teacher: A behavioral perspective. In L.E. Fraley & E.A. Vargas (Eds.). *Behavior Research and Technology in Higher Education* (pp. 11–20). Reedsville, WV: Society for The Behavioral Analysis of Culture.

Books: Primary Issues...

Chiesa, M. (1994). *Radical Behaviorism: The Philosophy and the Science.* Boston, MA: Authors cooperative.
Fraley, L.E. (1996). *General Behaviorology* (fall edition). Morgantown, WV: Lawrence E. Fraley (609–C Allen Hall, WVU, Morgantown WV 26506–6122 USA). (This is the first behaviorology text to be written as such, and it covers both the fundamental behaviorological principles and some basic practices of behaviorological engineering.)
Holland, J.G. & Skinner, B.F. (1961). *The Analysis of Behavior.* New York: McGraw–Hill. (This is the original comprehensively programmed text; the authors successfully applied to its design and use the very laws of behavior that it teaches.)
Ledoux, S.F. (1997). *Origins and Components of Behaviorology.* Canton, NY: ABCs. (A collection of articles.)
Sidman, M. (1960). *Tactics of Scientific Research.* New York: Basic Books. Reprinted, 1988, Boston, MA: Authors Cooperative.
Skinner, B.F. (1948). *Walden Two.* New York: Macmillan.
Skinner, B.F. (1953). *Science and Human Behavior.* New York: Macmillan. (Paperback edition published by Free Press, 1965.)
Skinner, B.F. (1957). *Verbal Behavior.* New York: Appleton–Century–Crofts. Reprinted, 1992, Cambridge, MA: The B.F. Skinner Foundation.
Skinner, B.F. (1971). *Beyond Freedom and Dignity.* New York: Knopf.
Skinner, B.F. (1974). *About Behaviorism.* New York: Knopf.

Books: Directly Related Issues...

Bjork, D.W. (1993). *B.F. Skinner: A Life.* New York: Basic Books.

Cautela, J.R. & Ishaq, W. (Eds.). (1996). *Contemporary Issues in Behavior Therapy: Improving the Human Condition.* New York: Plenum. (A collection of articles.)

Cooper, J.O., Heron, T.E., & Heward, W.I. (1987). *Applied Behavior Analysis.* New York: Macmillan.

Ferster, C.B. & Skinner, B.F. (1957). *Schedules of Reinforcement.* Englewood Cliffs, NJ: Prentice–Hall.

Fraley, L.E. (Contributing Editor). (1980). *Behavioral Analysis of Issues in Higher Education.* Reedsville, WV: Society for the Behavioral Analysis of Culture. (A collection of articles.)

Fraley, L.E. & Vargas, E.A. (Eds.). (1976). *Behavior Research and Technology in Higher Education.* Reedsville, WV: Society for The Behavioral Analysis of Culture. (A collection of articles.)

Johnston, J.M. & Pennypacker, H.S. (1980). *Strategies and Tactics of Human Behavioral Research.* Hillsdale, NJ: Erlbaum.

Krapfl, J.E. & Vargas, E.A. (Eds.). (1977). *Behaviorism and Ethics.* Kalamazoo, MI: Behaviordelia. (A collection of articles.)

Michael, J.L. (1989). *Verbal and Nonverbal Behavior: Concepts and Principles.* Kalamazoo, MI: Psychology Department, Western Michigan University. (This is a collection of several noteworthy papers. A later book with overlapping contents was titled *Concepts and Principles of Behavior Analysis.*)

Sidman, M. (1994). *Equivalence Relations and Behavior: A Research Story.* Boston, MA: Authors Cooperative.

Skinner, B.F. (1968). *The Technology of Teaching.* New York: Appleton–Century–Crofts. (A collection of articles.)

Skinner, B.F. (1969). *Contingencies of Reinforcement: A Theoretical Analysis.* New York: Appleton–Century–Crofts. (A collection of articles.)

Skinner, B.F. (1972). *Cumulative Record: A Selection of Papers (Third Edition).* New York: Appleton–Century–Crofts. (A collection of articles.)

Skinner, B.F. (1978). *Reflections on Behaviorism and Society.* Englewood Cliffs, NJ: Prentice–Hall. (A collection of articles.)

Skinner, B.F. (1987). *Upon Further Reflection.* Englewood Cliffs, NJ: Prentice–Hall. (A collection of articles.)

Skinner, B.F. (1989). *Recent Issues in the Analysis of Behavior.* Columbus, OH: Merrill. (A collection of articles.)

Vargas, J.S. (1988). *Behaviorology for Teachers.* Morgantown, WV: L.E. Fraley. (A relatively complete update, based on J. Vargas's 1977 book of similar content, on the application of the behaviorology discipline to concerns in the field of education.)

West, R.P. & Hamerlynck, L.A. (Eds.). (1992). *Designs for Excellence in Education: The Legacy of B.F. Skinner (Limited Edition).* Longmont, CO: Sopris West. (A collection of articles.)

Youth Policy Institute. (1988, July/August). *Youth Policy, 10* (7). (A special issue devoted to data–based reports on the successes of the educational applications of behaviorological science.)

Books: Other Related Issues...

Christophersen, E.R. (1988). *Little People (Third Edition).* Kansas City, MO: Westport Publishers. (A prevention–oriented, behaviorologically based child rearing practices book.)

Clark, L. (1996). *SOS! Help for Parents (Second Edition).* Bowling Green, KY: Parents Press. (Behaviorologically based child rearing practices; also available in Chinese.)

Daniels, A.C. (1989). *Performance Management (Third Edition, revised).* Tucker, GA: Performance Management Publications. (The application of behaviorological science in business and industry.)

Gardner, R., Sainato, D., Cooper, J.O., Heron, T.E., Heward, W.L., & Eshleman, J.W. (Eds.). (1994). *Behavior Analysis in Education: Focus on Measurably Superior Instruction.* Pacific Grove, CA: Brooks/Cole. (A collection of articles.)

Gore, A. (1993). *Earth in the Balance.* New York: Plume.

Gould, S.J. (1981). *The Mismeasure of Man.* New York: W.W. Norton.

Harris, M. (1979). *Cultural Materialism: The Struggle for a Science of Culture.* New York: Random House.

Ishaq, W. (Ed.). (1991). *Human Behavior in Today's World.* New York: Praeger. (A collection of articles.)

Keller, F.S. & Schoenfeld, W.N. (1950). *Principles of Psychology.* New York: Appleton–Century–Crofts. Reprinted, 1995, Cambridge, MA: The B.F. Skinner Foundation. (The original behaviorological "intro" text.)

Latham, G.I. (1994). *The Power of Positive Parenting: A Wonderful Way to Raise Children.* Logan, UT: P and T.

Latham, G.I. (1997). *Behind the Schoolhouse Door: Eight Skills Every Teacher Should Have.* Logan, UT: Mountain Plains Regional Resource Center.

Ledoux, S.F. & Cheney, C.D. (1987). *Grandpa Fred's Baby Tender or Why and How We Built Our Aircribs.* Canton, NY: ABCs. (Includes "The first baby tender," a short introductory article provided by B.F. Skinner.)

Lee, V.L. (1988). *Beyond Behaviorism.* Hillsdale, NJ: Erlbaum.

Sagan, C. (1995). *The Demon–Haunted World: Science as a Candle in the Dark.* New York: Random House.

Schoenfeld, W.N. (1993). *Religion and Human Behavior.* Boston, MA: Authors Cooperative.

Sidman, M. (1989). *Coercion and its Fallout.* Boston, MA: Authors Cooperative.

Skinner, B.F. (1938). *The Behavior of Organisms.* Englewood Cliffs, NJ: Prentice–Hall. (Seventh printing, of 1966, with special preface.) Reprinted, 1991, Cambridge, MA: The B.F. Skinner Foundation.

Skinner, B.F. (1979). *The Shaping of a Behaviorist.* New York: Knopf.

Skinner, B.F. (1983). *A Matter of Consequences.* New York: Knopf.

Skinner, B.F. & Vaughan, M.E. (1983). *Enjoy Old Age.* New York: W.W. Norton.

Stewart. B. & Vargas, J. (1990). *Teaching Behavior to Infants and Toddlers. A Manual for Caregivers and Parents.* Springfield, IL: Charles C. Thomas.

Vargas, J.S. (1972). *Writing Worthwhile Behavioral Objectives.* New York: Harper & Row.

Whaley, D.L. & Malott, R.W. (1971). *Elementary Principles of Behavior.* Englewood Cliffs, NJ: Prentice–Hall. (A classic "must read" primer on behaviorological science and applications that students find fun to read. Some of them cannot stop reading it!)

Index

(Also, see "Full–Outline Contents" on pages vii–xvi.)

E

F

G

H

I

J

K

L

M

N

O

P

Q

R

S

Reader's Notes